African American FAMILIES

For Travis and Emma: May you make the
world a better place than the one you inherited.

—Mom

To my collaborator, colleague, and friend, Earl.
Thanks for bringing your intellectual curiosity and
your vast knowledge of social theory, the African American
family, prisons, and so many other areas to bear on this project.
Mostly, thank you for all the times I needed to laugh so that
I wouldn't cry. I never could have done this without you.

—Angela

To my adult sons Daniel
and Edward, may you as well make
the world a better place than the one you inherited.
Please note we did the best we could. Always strive
for the best, because it is there for you. To my coauthor,
colleague, and friend, Angela, thanks. You made this project
and from interview to interview, from airport to airport
(including the almost mandatory plane delays), thank you
for including me in this research. You are an excellent teacher,
scholar, and intellectual.

—Earl

African American FAMILIES

Angela J. Hattery ■ Earl Smith
Wake Forest University

SAGE Publications
Los Angeles • London • New Delhi • Singapore

For information:

Sage Publications, Inc.
2455 Teller Road
Thousand Oaks,
California 91320
E-mail: order@sagepub.com

Sage Publications India Pvt. Ltd.
B 1/I 1 Mohan Cooperative
Industrial Area
Mathura Road, New Delhi 110 044
India

Sage Publications Ltd.
1 Oliver's Yard
55 City Road
London EC1Y 1SP
United Kingdom

Sage Publications Asia-Pacific Pte. Ltd.
33 Pekin Street #02-01
Far East Square
Singapore 048763

Printed in the United States of America

Library of Congress Cataloging-in-Publication Data

Hattery, Angela.
African American families / Angela J. Hattery, Earl Smith.
    p. cm.
Includes bibliographical references and index.
ISBN 978-1-4129-2466-5 (pbk.)
    1. African American families. 2. African Americans—Social conditions—1975-
3. African Americans—Economic conditions. 4. United States—Race relations.
5. United States—Social conditions—1980- 6. Social problems—United States.
I. Smith, Earl, 1946- II. Title.

E185.86.H38 2007
306.85089′96073—dc22

2006031960

Printed on acid-free paper.

07   08   09   10   11   10   9   8   7   6   5   4   3   2   1

Acquiring Editor:	Cheri Dellelo
Editorial Assistant:	Anna Marie Mesick
Production Editor:	Sarah K. Quesenberry
Copy Editor:	Liann Lech
Proofreader:	Theresa Kay
Indexer:	Will Ragsdale
Typesetter:	C&M Digitals (P) Ltd.
Cover Designer:	Candice Harman
Associate Marketing Manager:	Amberlyn M. Erzinger

Brief Table of Contents

Table of Contents

Preface

An overwhelming number of young African American males . . .
are committed to civility and law-abiding behavior. They often
have a hard time convincing others of this, however, because of
the stigma attached to their skin color, age, gender, appearance,
and general style of self-presentation.

—Anderson (1990), p. 163

B ased on the experiences of prior researchers, the lack of contemporary research, and the reviews of our own book manuscript, we can, with confidence, claim that studying the African American family today remains ferociously contentious. Our attempts to engage difficult and controversial topics ranging from intimate partner violence to HIV to teen pregnancy are made more difficult by the fact that open communication about race in the contemporary United States remains taboo.

One of the most remarkable things that emerges when one engages in serious research about African Americans and African American families is the incredible resiliency shown by a people who have faced an unrelenting 400-plus years of systematic, institutionalized oppression. African American families have existed as social institutions despite being illegal (during slavery) and despite the adversity of a peonage/sharecropping plantation economy embedded within Jim Crow segregation. And underneath all of this success were African American men and women who managed to forge intimate connections, keep households together, and raise their children.

Similarly, we have examples of individuals, such as Frederick Douglass, who were self-educated. Douglass became a major resistor to slavery. With the abolition of slavery, we have examples of African Americans such as Booker T. Washington, Ida B. Wells, George Washington Carver, and W.E.B. Du Bois, all of whom earned respect. And several were among the very first to earn advanced degrees, using their education to better the plight of African Americans, their families, and their communities. African Americans such as Booker T. Washington established colleges and universities that educated African American doctors, lawyers, dentists, engineers, and educators. History is full of examples of individual African Americans who have created successful professional and personal lives despite unimaginable barriers that were institutionalized across more than 400 years of second-class citizenship. These successes are to be applauded and celebrated.

In post-civil rights America, as institutions have desegregated, African Americans have made progress in all spheres of life: politics, the military, business, sports, higher education, and professional occupations. For example, there are now six or seven African American CEOs of Fortune 500 companies. There are African Americans serving in the U.S. Congress; more than 1,700 African Americans earn a PhD each year; and the number of African American physicians, dentists, and architects totals more than 200,000 and grows each succeeding year. Yet we are reminded that in each of these institutions, African Americans are grossly underrepresented. For example, whereas African Americans make up approximately 13% of the U.S. population, they are only 4.5% of architects, 1% of the U.S. Senate, and 1.5% of the CEOs of Fortune 500 companies. In contrast, African American men make up 50% of all incarcerated individuals (men and women) in the United States. Forty-seven percent of African Americans receive some sort of welfare, 33% of African American children live in poverty, and more than half of all African Americans have no health insurance. The average life expectancy for African American men is 7.5 years shorter than that for their white male counterparts and some 12 years shorter than that for white women. African American women are now the fastest growing sector of the U.S. population heading to prison and the fastest growing sector of the U.S. population diagnosed with HIV/AIDS.

This book is about hard social facts. The fact that despite the major advances in technology, medicine, and education, despite the growing U.S. economy, African Americans and their families continue to fall behind all other Americans except Native Americans on all of the social, economic, and political indicators we use to measure success and mobility. Not only are African Americans disproportionately likely to be poor, but among those who are professionals and affluent, they consistently fall behind similarly situated whites. For example, although there are six or seven African American CEOs at Fortune 500 companies, none of the companies headed by African Americans is represented in the top Fortune 25 firms. African Americans earning in the top 20% of the income distribution for all Americans have only one third the wealth of their white counterparts. And among African Americans in the U.S. Congress, only one is in the more prestigious Senate.

This last point about the U.S. Senate has not changed since Reconstruction. The purpose of this book is to expose these inequalities that cross over so many different aspects of African American family life.

This book is written from the analytical and theoretical perspective that the strongest predictor of gaps between African Americans and whites, be they gaps in marriage rates, health insurance, incarceration, or employment, are a result of structural impediments that continue to block full access to the opportunity structure (education, housing, employment). Furthermore, we note that African Americans continue to face discrimination, especially in areas such as mortgage lending and home ownership. We further argue that the 400-plus years of denied access has a *cumulative effect* for both whites and African Americans. African Americans cumulate disadvantages whereas whites cumulate advantage. (We will use examples to illustrate this that include the accumulation of wealth and the accumulation of privilege through systems such as legacy).

This book is not an indictment of African Americans, their families, their communities, or their "culture." We do not see African American civil society as being pathological, nor do we simply see all African Americans as "victims." Although we acknowledge that individual African Americans make poor choices (as do individual whites, Asians, Hispanics, Native Americans, and others), the focus of our attention is in explaining the over-representation of African Americans who are in some type of trouble (in poverty, living with violence, incarcerated, living with poor health) and the underrepresentation of African Americans among the elite and affluent in the United States.

We acknowledge the successes of African Americans and the strides individuals have made in the past 30 to 40 years—for example, African American males make up approximately 75% of all National Basketball Association (NBA) players. Yet there is only one NBA team that has a majority African American owner. We attribute most of these successes to individual actions, not the loosening up of social institutions. Thus, our argument focuses on the need for social institutions to open up fully so that they are accessible to all Americans. Our argument focuses on the need for each child in this country to be assured of adequate housing, a nutritious diet, and the kind of education that will enable him or her to seek any profession in adulthood that he or she might be interested in pursuing.

The statistics and stories in this book are not what we would like to see; in fact, many statistics we report are grim. Yet we do not shy away from telling this story of social, economic, and political inequality. And, we will not stop telling this story until all Americans have equal access to the American Dream.

As sociologists, we have become frustrated by what we see as two equally flawed standpoints from which to theorize about the African American family. The first approach interprets everything that is different and unique about the African American family as pathological. The second interprets these same qualities as strengths. Perhaps the most frequently cited example of this is teen pregnancy, but participation in the illegitimate economy is another example. Not every mode of behavior that is associated with white middle-class society, such as completing one's education, getting a job, and raising a family, is negative, even if it has developed out of a system of race and class privilege. We believe we can recognize the strengths of African American families and respect the choices of individuals while still making recommendations for improving the lives of African American men, women, and children without these suggestions being interpreted as racist or motivated out of a desire to "whiten" African Americans. Rather, what we propose is a scientific examination of African American families with the goal of identifying ways in which barriers to the opportunity structure have rendered many African American families living on the margins of society with less human capital; less financial stability; fewer freedoms; and shorter, less healthy lives.

The organization of this book and the objectives that guide it can perhaps be best illustrated with a discussion about how we came to write this book. During 2003 and 2004, we conducted interviews with 40 African American men and women who were living with intimate partner violence. A cursory examination of the table of contents will reveal that we will devote an entire chapter to a discussion of violence in African American families. When we set out to do this research, our focus was on learning more about the process and outcomes of intimate partner violence. How is it, we wondered, that on any given day someone (usually a man) slaps, punches, hits, beats up, or even kills the person (usually a woman) whom he claims to love? This is the process. What are the effects of this kind of abuse on the individuals themselves? On their relationships? On their children? These are the outcomes. These topics will be addressed in great length in Chapter 5.

When we entered into these interviews, we tried to prepare ourselves for what the interviews would expose us to: namely, a high rate of severe violence among people who lived and worked in our home community. And although a researcher can never adequately prepare him- or herself for these types of interviews, and we absolutely heard stories that to this day turn our stomachs, what we had not prepared for at all was the fact that *interviews about intimate partner violence were really interviews about family life.* Embedded and intertwined within the stories of horrific violence (one woman had survived a beating by a professional boxer who had killed an opponent in the ring a few weeks before we interviewed him) were stories about incarceration (mostly of the men, but a few of the women as well), health crises, unemployment, and most notably, poverty. Thus, we learned immediately that one cannot understand intimate partner violence as an isolated event without understanding its relationship to poverty, unemployment, health, and incarceration. This is especially the case in African American families, where these struggles are ever present for far too many. Thus, in preparing to write this book, we broadened our research to include these social issues, and intimate partner violence became the subject of only one chapter in this text, with the other issues also receiving the attention they deserved. By providing the reader with the most up-to-date and accurate research on African American families,[1] we hope to contribute to a broader understanding for others, as well as provide a resource for policymakers who are addressing the issues we describe. Finally, because we are sociologists, we provide a structural framework for this information; it is a framework that recognizes individual choice but situates that choice within a context of patriarchy, class hierarchy, and racial domination.

Note

1. During the initial stages of this project, we, as well as the reviewers, examined texts on the African American family and found that the most recent publications were a decade old.

Acknowledgments

A s authors always note, the writing of a book, although an extremely solitary endeavor, could not be done without the help and advice of many people. We would like to publicly acknowledge those who have helped us with this book. Any and all errors that remain are ours alone.

At Sage Publications, we would like to thank Jim Brace-Thompson for believing in our project when it was only a proposal and accepting our book into the Sage collection. We thank Cheri Dellelo for taking over midstream and helping us to see this project through to the end. Working with Sage has been so seamless, and we are grateful to the many people there who allowed us to write the book we wanted to write.

Many people helped us to arrange the interviews with the men and women whose stories are the basis for this book: Joetta Shepherd and Kevin Sidden and their staff at Family Services of Winston-Salem, North Carolina; Pat Dean-McRay and her staff at the battered women's shelter in Winston-Salem, North Carolina; and Michele Valletta and her staff at Child Protective Services in Olmsted County, Minnesota. Michele carefully coordinated our schedule, thus allowing us to collect interviews with men and women with whom they work. We will always remember the cooperation and warm welcome the staff in Minnesota gave to us, especially our last meeting with them, which included "North Carolina BBQ."

To the highway patrolman in Zumbrota, Minnesota, Highway # 52, who rescued us at 3 a.m. after our rental car hit a raccoon. The 90 minutes we waited for a tow truck in the backseat of his cruiser proved more interesting than either of us could have imagined. Once we warmed up as he blasted the heat for us, he, too, told us story after story of battering in the all-white suburbs wherein judges, lawyers, and "city fathers" were engaging in some of the most brutal, but hidden, interpersonal violence that will never be told in a social behavioral scientist way. It will simply move from one generation to the next.

We are grateful to Melissa Williams, Wake Forest University class of 2005, who took an interest in our project and conducted evaluation research for Family Services in Winston-Salem, North Carolina. That project became, at a later date, the subject for her honors thesis in sociology. Her work greatly informed our understanding of the efficacy of the batterer intervention program known as Time Out in Winston-Salem, North Carolina.

We are grateful to Sarah Hazlegrove, who efficiently and tirelessly transcribed every interview. Despite less than ideal equipment and recording situations (babies were often crying, television sets were on), the work Sarah did for us was impeccable.

We are grateful to Mrs. Linda McIntyre at the Mississippi State Penitentiary at Parchman for providing us with the chance to talk to the inmates there, especially Walter and Calvin, who were willing to share their stories of incarceration and the devastating impact it had on their families.

We are grateful to Mr. Darryl Hunt, who has shared so much of his experience with the most atrocious part of the criminal justice system: the conviction and incarceration of innocent people. Mr. Hunt spent more than 18 years in state prison for a crime he did not commit. He has now dedicated his life to helping others like him—the many innocent men and women who rot inside our prisons. He does all of this work through his foundation, the Darryl Hunt Project for Freedom and Justice.

We are grateful for the funding we received from the Social and Behavioral Sciences Research Fund at Wake Forest University. We thank Provost Mark Welker for this award and for all of his support for our project. We are also grateful to the American Sociological Association's Fund for the Advancement of the Discipline, which provided the funding for a good portion of this project.

We are grateful to the anonymous reviewers who took the time and care to offer critiques of our work. This book is better because they challenged us to get it right.

We thank those who have believed in us all along: Emily Kane, the late Senator Paul Wellstone, Cindy Gendrich, Bob and Diane Hattery, and so many friends and colleagues far too numerous to name here.

Finally, to the men and women who so graciously opened up their lives to us. We are grateful. They shared the deepest, most intimate—and often painful—parts of their stories with us in offices, in their homes, in the hospital, and even from jail cells. Without you, there would be no book. Thanks!

Our names are listed alphabetically. Our contributions to the book have been equal.

Angela Hattery and Earl Smith

Winston-Salem, North Carolina

July 27, 2006

Publisher's Acknowledgments

Sage Publications gratefully acknowledges the contributions of the following reviewers:

Makungu M. Akinyela, PhD
Georgia State University

Pade Badru
University of Louisville

Michael C. Lambert, PhD
University of Missouri-Columbia

Richard Lewis Jr., PhD
University of Texas at San Antonio

Edward Opoku-Dapaah
Winston-Salem State University

Ron Stewart, PhD
Buffalo State College

1

African American Families

A Brief Introduction

The Black population for two-thirds of its history in the United States—248 of 377 years or .6578 of its history, to be exact— was an enslaved group, physically, economically, socially, legally, sexually, morally, and psychologically, subjected not only to the exploitative whim of individual white owners but at the violent mercy of all whites, and, under the encouragement and protection of the predatory dominant whites.

—Patterson (1995), p. 187

Objectives

- Provide the latest empirical data on a variety of aspects of African American families.
- Provide a theoretical framework for understanding African American families by employing the race, class, and gender paradigm.
- Illuminate the ways in which social structures and institutions, such as family form, the educational system, the criminal justice system, and the economy or world of work, influence the lives of African Americans and their families.
- Explore the ways in which the social history of chattel slavery and the system of Jim Crow segregation shaped the contemporary African American family.
- Provide an honest discussion of the issues that face contemporary African American families.

Introduction

Africans were transported to the "New World" aboard slave ships some 400 years ago, and in this book, we refer to their descendants as African Americans.[1] These human beings (remembering that for a long time, whites did not consider African Americans as human) came to North America and lived an existence and life very different from all other Americans, including American Indians. This is not a history book, nor does it include a lengthy history of the development of the African American family.[2] This is a book about contemporary African American families that relies on the most up-to-date empirical data as well as interviews with African American men and women about their experiences with family life. Yet we acknowledge that any investigation of contemporary African American family life must be contextualized within the history of race relations in the United States.

For example, in 2005, one of the worst natural disasters ever experienced in the United States, Hurricane Katrina, hit the city of New Orleans—and other parts of Louisiana, Mississippi, and Texas—and exposed, for all the world to see, the very issues we will discuss in this book. Hurricane Katrina did not create inequality; rather, it exposed a deep layer of inequalities based on race and social class that exists not only in New Orleans, but indeed to varying degrees throughout the United States. It is these inequalities of economics, health, education, and wealth, and their impact on the African American family, that are the substance of this book.

Our book approaches the subject of contemporary African American families by addressing both individual and structural explanations for the conditions they face. This absolves us from picking and choosing rights and wrongs perpetuated against and/or inflicted upon African Americans. This particular tension, between the individual and the structural, will frame our discussion throughout the book.

What We Hope to Accomplish

Our primary objective in writing this book is to examine the state of African American families in the early 21st century. In this book, we tackle the most important issues facing researchers, policymakers, social service providers, and African Americans themselves. These issues, which are central to the academic discussions of family scholars and germane to discussions of any type of family, include family composition, childbearing patterns, health, education, employment, and violence. We also include a chapter on incarceration, which is rarely discussed by family scholars, because it has become a part of life in many African American families (Pettit & Western, 2004; Western, 2006). We take a straightforward approach to these issues, many of which have reached the level of crises of epic proportions in African American families.

Thinking that they are protecting the image of African American families, far too many researchers have sugarcoated some of the most dangerous and damaging issues. We contend, however, that this sugarcoating merely prevents us from acknowledging the severity of these problems and inhibits us from developing serious attacks on and solutions to these problems. Although we will go into deeper details throughout this book, we illustrate our main point here.

Many scholars who write about African American families argue that talking about teen childbearing in negative terms only contributes to the perpetuation of stereotypes about African American sexuality and family composition (Dash, 2003).[3] These scholars seek to underscore the strengths of teen childbearing, such as the fact that it illustrates the great value African Americans place on children. Or, they attempt to provide explanations for this social problem that excuse it, such as the idea that teen childbearing is a reasonable response to the fact that African American women have shorter life expectancies than their white counterparts and thus early childbearing is a way of guaranteeing the presence of a grandmother for subsequent generations. Though perhaps noble in intention, we argue at length, and from an empirical standpoint (in Chapter 4), that teen childbearing has no positive consequences for African American families and it is a key factor in producing the poverty into which more than half of all African American children are born. We do not pass moral judgment on teen mothers; that is not our role, nor do we believe there is anything to be gained by it. This argument is not about teen sexuality or sex education programs in schools. This argument is about the empirical evidence surrounding teen childbearing. Furthermore, we argue that by ignoring this crisis, by sticking our heads in the sand or sugarcoating the issue, we are delaying the development and implementation of programs that would delay childbearing among teens and reduce poverty rates among African American children.

Finally, we note that our approach and perspective throughout the book address the continued neglect and misrepresentation in mainstream family textbooks of all major race/ethnic groups in America and, in this instance, especially the faulty assumptions and accusations of African American families.

In a major review of some 20 best-selling U.S. marriage and family textbooks, Shaw-Taylor and Benokraitis (1995), extending the early work of Bryant and Coleman (1988), underscore the fact that these textbooks devote little attention to minority families: "Overall, 2.1% of the space was devoted to racial-ethnic families, even though people of color constitute 25% of the US population" (p. 122), and when the books do devote attention to them, the families are discussed from a culturally deviant perspective (Shaw-Taylor & Benokraitis, 1995). Throughout, we challenge these perspectives as they have been applied to African American families, and we focus on the structural barriers these families face in their attempts to achieve what most Americans desire: a share of the American Dream.

This book relies on a variety of empirical data, from U.S. census data to qualitative data we generated through interviews conducted with 40 African American men and women in two regions of the country, the South and Midwest. The utilization and incorporation of both large-scale, nationally representative data and rich qualitative data set this book apart from many others that rely exclusively on secondary data sources. The narratives of these African American men and women enrich and thicken the analyses in the subsequent chapters. And these narratives provide the kinds of powerful illustrations that engage students and scholars of the African American family. We are certain that the lives of these men and women as they are laid out here will be remembered as illustrations of larger concepts long after the reader completes the book.

Furthermore, although there are several key theoretical frameworks for understanding African American families and many more that constitute the body of family theory, we chose, for reasons we will explicate in Chapter 2, to rely on the race, class, and gender paradigm to provide the theoretical and analytical framework in which to situate this empirical data. This paradigm, developed primarily by black feminists such as Angela Davis, Maxine Baca Zinn, Bonnie Thornton Dill, Patricia Hill Collins, and Deborah King, has proved to be instrumental in moving forward the theoretical discussions in such areas as gender sociology and the sociology of race and ethnicity. However, this paradigm has received less attention by traditional family scholars. Therefore, our book departs from many of the other texts on the African American family because it is written using the lens provided by the race, class, and gender paradigm.

The Question of Social Class

The field of sociology has had a traditional focus on the problems that face humanity: poverty, inequality, access to health care, education, and poor housing, and of course the social institution of the family. Although there have been a few forays into studying the middle and upper-middle classes, such forays have been based primarily on examinations of records, such as the social register, and the public lives of the affluent (Baltzell, 1964). This is true regardless of the race or ethnicity of those being studied (Pattillo-McCoy, 1999). This book is a discussion of African Americans who are faced with the problems sociologists study: violence, blocked access to health care, unemployment, incarceration, and poverty. We recognize that there is a solid African American middle and upper-middle class, although we note that African Americans are grossly underrepresented in these class locations. Therefore, our focus is on those African Americans who are twice as likely to live in poverty as whites, as well as on those who are underrepresented in the upper echelons of higher education, business, and government. We also note that a text on the white family would be similarly focused. Furthermore, we note that although many of the issues facing African American families are tied to poverty, others, such as intimate partner violence and access to health care, are only partially correlated. Health insurance coverage, for example, is tied more to one's occupation than to one's salary, although the poor are more likely to work in occupations that do not provide health insurance than are the middle class. Finally, we note that African Americans at all social class levels face outright racial discrimination. For example, Tiger Woods, one of the most successful golfers of all time and a multimillionaire, is still prohibited from golfing at certain country clubs that do not allow African Americans as members (Lieber, 2003).

Data Sources

The interviews we conducted with 40 African American men and women who live with violence form the basis of our research. Throughout the book, we will use these interviews (qualitative data) to provide empirical support for our arguments. Using qualitative data means using the voices of the people we interviewed to tell the story. Throughout the book, we will include descriptions of particular people we interviewed, and we will present their stories as direct quotes that are unedited. Qualitative interviews are an important and rich data source. They allow the reader to both see and hear the story, and they provide a kind of illustration for the empirical point that is being made. For sociologists, the quotes that are generated by qualitative interviews complement statistics in much the same way that photographs enhance written descriptions or text. We will use the qualitative interviews to paint pictures of African American families and family life.

However, in order to truly understand the broader implications of the picture, we need to examine statistics. Statistics provide the kind of empirical data needed to make broad, sweeping generalizations about a particular phenomenon. So, for example, reading about what it feels like to be hit on the head with a ball peen hammer provides the illustration of intimate partner violence, but it doesn't tell the researcher anything about how common this experience is. Thus, in each chapter, for each topic, we provide statistical data so that the reader can understand the likelihood of an event occurring within a population. Although we are careful to make citations for the statistical evidence we include (both in the text and in tables), we note here that most of the statistical evidence comes from a few sources: the U.S. Census, conducted in 2000; the Centers for Disease Control and Prevention; the Bureau of Labor Statistics; and the Bureau of Justice Statistics, all of which collect data continuously and produce both monthly and annual reports. All of these data sources are the "official" source and rely on data collected from the entire U.S. population (or appropriate samples based on the U.S. population). Finally, most of the statistics on intimate partner violence at the national level are taken from the Violence and Threats of Violence Against Women Survey, which was based on a nationally representative sample of more than 7,500 respondents.[4] Thus, this book is based on combining the best of both qualitative and quantitative data to help improve our understanding of contemporary African American families.

Organization of the Book

The table of contents makes clear the topics that will be covered in this book. However, we want to expound on the topics because several of them are somewhat different from what is typically found in an African American family text. We begin the book with an overview of African American families. Along with this, we also provide in-depth reviews of the various theoretical frameworks that have been employed in studies of the African American family along with a description of the theory framing our analysis: the race, class, and gender paradigm. This allows the reader to examine for him- or herself the analytical power and shortcomings of the various perspectives.

The third and fourth chapters in our book examine African American family formation. This is one of the key and most controversial issues in discussions of African American families. Specifically, we examine marriage, cohabitation, and childbearing patterns with attention to the factors that shape these patterns and the ways in which these patterns shape social class, work life, interpersonal violence, and so forth. These chapters are built on empirical data as well as theoretical discussions of the African American family. In addition to reviewing relevant and often controversial theories, we also build a case for understanding family form through the lens of the race, class, and gender paradigm.

Each of the remaining chapters, except for the final chapter, which is focused on solutions, is devoted to an issue and/or institution that affects African American families both directly and indirectly: intimate partner violence, health, education, work, poverty, and incarceration. This is, perhaps, where our book departs most from others. As sociologists, we concern ourselves most significantly with the role that institutions play in shaping the lives of individual actors. We believe this strengthens and enhances our discussion of African American families.

Finally, perhaps the most unique feature to this book is the decision to include a discussion of incarceration in the lives of African American families. Again, although criminologists and scholars of race and ethnicity recognize the importance of the role that incarceration plays in the African American community, few scholars discuss the role of this powerful institution in African American families. Data from the Bureau of Justice Statistics demonstrate that between 25% and 33% of African American men will spend some time in jail or prison, with many more under the supervision of other parts of the criminal justice system (parole and probation). Thus, the impact of incarceration is significant in African American families. We devote Chapter 9 to a lengthy discussion of this issue.

In closing this introduction we point to one of the main problems with previous work on African American families. That is, most, if not all, of the single-authored monographs failed to incorporate competing systems of race, class, and gender that shaped, in the first place, the day-to-day lives and final outcomes for African American families.

As we show in this book, the African American family is not an isolated entity; the family and other institutions—from spouses, to cousins, to school, to jobs, to prisons—are an interconnected web of relationships that, in the final analysis, shapes the family unit and how that unit is able to (or not able to) access the American Dream.

What we argue is that there is a continuum, and on that continuum rests a ripple effect that bounces from one set of circumstances to another. Underemployment and unemployment are connected to choices that families make at the supermarket and the types of food purchased to the choices that these families make about housing and day care options. The ripple reverberates and extends through the continuum and checks and rechecks valuable resources, including family and friendship networks, that taken together influence, on a day-to-day basis, how the family survives or not. One dislocation, like an illness that interrupts work or a prison sentence that interrupts both

---

parenting and work, can derail the family for long periods of time—sometimes even a lifetime. For example, it was not uncommon for us to hear in our interviews that a family's entire savings had been depleted, including insurance, to pay for illness or to pay bail and/or legal fees.

Finally, the theoretical framework that we employ to provide the lens for analyzing and interpreting the empirical data on African American families rests on the assumption that systems of oppression (specifically race, class, and gender) intersect to create a web that shapes access to opportunities and experiences that vary depending on the actor's position in the social hierarchy (his or her race, class, and gender). Because the theoretical framework that underlies our discussion is based on an intersectional approach, the organization of our book will reflect this. In other words, in some textbooks, each topic is relegated to the chapter that addresses that issue. Violence is discussed in the violence chapter, work is discussed in the work chapter, divorce is discussed in the divorce chapter, and so on. Because our research demonstrates to us the ways in which these issues are interrelated, and that understanding one *requires* a discussion of several others, the chapters are grouped, out of necessity, by topic, but each topic is discussed in virtually every other chapter. Although this may seem redundant at times, the purpose is to demonstrate clearly the intersectional nature of social phenomena.

We move now to Chapter 2, in which we will do the following: (a) use empirical data to paint a broad picture of African American families, (b) review the various theoretical paradigms used to analyze African American families, and (c) review in some detail the methods we employed to generate the data that provide the content for the various chapters in the book.

Notes

1. We are noting early on that we will not engage in the rhetorical debate over what to call American Blacks. It seems from our reading of the literature that *African American* is the most appropriate term.

2. For such a discussion, we recommend Lerone Bennett's *Before the Mayflower: A History of Black America, 1619–1962*. The Bennett book is a tested and sound chronicle on the introduction of Africans to the Western Hemisphere and eventually their transformation into African Americans in what becomes the United States (Bennett, 1987).

3. The Dash book is critical of this body of work. See Burton (1990) for the "alternative life course" approach to understanding African American teen childbearing.

4. This survey was conducted by Patricia Tjaden and Nancy Thoennes and is available for analysis at the Inter-university Consortium for Political and Social Research at the University of Michigan.

2

African American Civil Society

Issues, Approaches, Demography, and Theory

The popular image for Blacks as a group pressing for change in the area of race relations and economic opportunities often is translated into the image of a radical group in the forefront of social change. Other than being opposed to unfair discrimination against any group favoring liberal social and economic policies, Blacks often hold very traditional, even conservative, attitudes on other social issues—attitudes that place them in the mainstream of American mores and folkways. . . . While these attitudes remain very traditional, the family lifestyles and arrangements of Blacks are definitely unconventional. . . . We explain it as a conflict between [Blacks'] family ideology and structural conditions.

—Staples (1991), p. 29

Objectives

- Define critical concepts and recognize key issues relevant to the study of the African American family.
- Synthesize a profile of the African American family based on the various topics covered in the book.

- Identify the two theoretical paradigms that have been employed in analyses of African American families: social pathology theory and the strength-based approach.
- Explore the race, class, and gender paradigm and the ways in which it can be used to analyze African American families.
- Understand the scientific bases (data and methods) used in the analyses and discussions of African Americans presented in this book.

Introduction

Like any other scientific field of inquiry, when one begins a sociological examination of a phenomenon it is essential to begin with definitions. This is especially important when one is studying everyday phenomena, such as families, because most people believe they know precisely what is being studied. We all have experiences with families—the families in which we grew up, the families we create, and the families we observe on television. However, as a result of our many different individual experiences with families, we all have different ideas about what constitutes a family. Thus, when we talk about families from an analytical and scientific perspective, we need a set of definitions in order to increase precision. Similarly, we all believe we understand what race is. We all have a racial identity. We know people of other racial identities. We talk in the United States about "race." Yet when social scientists use race as an analytical and conceptual category, it is necessary to specify what we mean when we use the term so that we are working from a common definition.

Definitions

Family

Family scholars have developed several different definitions of family, of which we discuss five:

1. Family is a set of people with whom you live and with whom you share biological and/or legal ties.

This definition focuses on what many of us refer to as the "nuclear family." This definition restricts family primarily to parents (who are married) and their biological and/or adopted children. This is the definition of family that is used by the census, and it is the most common definition of family in use by both scholars as well as the "average" American.

2. Family is a set of people with whom you may or may not live but with whom you share biological and/or legal ties.

This definition of family is often referred to as the "extended family." As such it is used to recognize that both in the past and continuing today, many households include extended family members such as grandparents. It also recognizes the continued importance of family once children have moved permanently out of the house.

3. Family is a set of people with whom you live but with whom you may or may not share biological and/or legal ties.

This is a much more contemporary definition of family that is designed to recognize several changes in family life, but specifically the rise of cohabitating couples who are increasingly likely to be raising children together. Specifically with regard to the African American family, this definition recognizes both higher rates of cohabitation but also the practice of sharing childrearing with nonrelatives in response to a variety of forces, such as incarceration.

4. Family is a set of people with whom you share social, physical, and/or financial support.

This definition is very inclusive and was developed primarily to recognize the existence of gay and lesbian households that are still, as of the writing of this book, not legal. Furthermore, this definition is designed to emphasize a key feature of families: the fact that members are interdependent. Families generally provide support of various sorts for their members. The flow and direction of this support may change over time, such as from parent to child during the period of childrearing to one of child to parent during the later years.

5. Family is a set of people whom you love.

The most inclusive of all definitions, this one recognizes that increasingly people create their own "families" that may or may not be based on formal ties (biology or law) and that these important people may or may not live together. The classic example used to illustrate this concept is a popular television program like *Friends*. *Friends* represents a set of young men and women who provided support for each other and loved each other, but did not share *any* biological or legal ties. Some of the "friends" lived together but others did not. Yet they provided for each other most of the very things that historically have been provided by people with formal family ties. Again, with regard to this study of African American families, this definition is of particular importance as we analyze family relations across history. During slavery, African Americans had no legal means of creating family, but this did not mean that they weren't families in every other sense of the word. And today, as noted above, many African American children live in a "family" that is not composed of either biological or legal ties. Finally, we note that family scholars often refer to this form of family as "fictive kin," and this is especially common when referring to African American family relationships. We note that some may find the term *fictive kin* offensive because it assumes that some relationships—those based on biology or law—are real and those not based on biology or law are "fictive" or not real. Thus, we refrain from this kind of distinction.

Our book is not based on one definition of family or another. Furthermore, our use of the term *family* is not technical in the sense of referring to only one type of family. Across the chapters, as we discuss African American families and the forces that shape them, we are in some instances talking about marriage or coupling (this is the focus in Chapter 3), but in other instances we are talking more inclusively. For example, intimate partner violence, incarceration, unemployment, and health crises often affect many members of a family, from parents to children to grandparents and grandchildren and even close friends. Where we are talking about a specific type of family, we will make that clear. In other instances, the reader can assume a more inclusive definition of family: a circle of people who care about each other and either provide or draw some social support from each other.

Race and Ethnicity

One of the central debates within the field of sociology is the definition of race and ethnicity (Omi & Winant, 1986). Many texts distinguish between the two by pointing to biological versus cultural factors. Namely, these texts suggest that race is a biological construct based on physiological characteristics arranged in a particular pattern and associated with a particular group. These types of definitions of race point to skin tone, hair texture, and certain facial features such as breadth of the nose and shape of the eyes. In contrast, many definitions of ethnicity hinge upon the notion of shared culture, namely, language, food, and religion.

Definitions of race and ethnicity are so contentious and so powerful that the U.S. government has changed the way it categorizes people by race and ethnicity nearly every decade when the decennial census is taken. In the most recent census (2000), there were four racial categories: white, black, Asian, and Native American/Pacific Islander. In addition, there was only one category for ethnicity: Hispanic (or not). Finally, there were several categories for nationality or national origin, but only for people from Asia and the South

Pacific. So, for example, people of Japanese origin would select "Asian" for their race, and they could choose to select "Japanese" for their country of origin. In contrast, individuals identifying as white, black, or Native American/Pacific Islander were not able to check a country of national origin. Furthermore, those identifying their ethnicity as "Hispanic" were required to choose a race separately—typically either "white" or "black." Yet this was not the case for any other ethnic group, such as Italians. An examination of census categories, which represent the official set of designations for race and ethnicity, across the past 200-plus years would reveal the same patterns. The categories for race and ethnicity have changed with virtually every census in response to the political climate at the time.

Why is this important? As sociologists, we believe it is important for several key reasons. First, the designations themselves are symbolic of power. During the late 18th century and for much of the 19th century, the only census categories were "white" and "nonwhite." At the time, most laws were written such that privileges and opportunities were available only for whites, so it was necessary only to separate those who were eligible (to vote or buy land, for example) from those who were not. During the late 19th century, when waves of immigrants began arriving from the Far East (mainly from China) and the Mediterranean (mainly from Italy and Greece), officials wanted to be able to identify these individuals and designate them separately, and thus categories that facilitated this were added to the census. (These categories were later removed and replaced with other categories that were deemed relevant.) Thus, as sociologists, we argue that the categories of race and ethnicity are based on the underlying need to separate those who should be awarded privilege and those who should be excluded from it. For many sociologists in the early 21st century, race is defined as a social construct.

Race as a Social Construct

Defining race as a social construct is controversial, especially outside of the sociological community. Therefore, it is worthy of an explanation. Defining race as a social construct does not mean that we do not recognize physical characteristics as being arranged in a pattern. Furthermore, it also means that we do recognize that these important traits (skin color, hair texture, eye shape) are inherited and passed down from one generation to the next. What we mean when we define race as a social construct is that (a) racial variation is significant and (b) the designation of an individual into a certain racial category changes over time and can change across generations.

1. Racial variation. Many social and behavioral scientists (sociologists and anthropologists, for example) as well as many biologists note that there is tremendous variation within each racial category (white vs. black) and that there is more variation within each racial category than across racial categories. To use a very simple example, within the racial categories "white" and "black," there is a significant amount of variation in skin color. Furthermore, there is a great deal of variation across racial boundaries, such that there are "white" people whose skin tone is darker than that of some "black" people, and vice versa.

2. Racial categories change over time. In terms of the census, as a starting point, people of Irish and Italian descent were considered "black" at the turn of the 20th century, and at the close of that same century, they were considered "white." Thus, their "race" was not passed down to their children. Instead, racial identity was assigned based on the current political climate. Second, a phenomenon long recognized in the African American community is that of "passing." African Americans who were of light complexion could often "pass" as whites, particularly passing themselves off as Italian or Greek. Again, this is evidence for the importance of thinking about race as something that can change and that is not tied to biology. In the case of passing, it is something that is chosen by the individual. Both of these illustrations point to the fact that race is not fixed as a category—it is not fixed on an individual (passing) nor on a "people" (the Irish), it is not handed down intergenerationally, and it can change over time.

All of this is important to note, and for our discussions in this book. we use the racial terms *white* and *African American* not because we believe they are fixed but because we believe that they are part of a political construction that is based on power, access to the opportunity structure, and privilege. Therefore, they are important, even if they are not immutable. When we refer to racial categories using the terms *white* and *African American,* we are referring to classes of people with particular histories, particular locations in the status hierarchy, and particular relations to each other, in the same way that Karl Marx writes about the social relations between the proletariat and the bourgeoisie.

Racial categories have meaning only in relation to each other. Furthermore, as with class, the clustering of privilege with one group and the exploitation of the other occurs only when at least two racial categories (composed of individual actors) are in relation to one another. In other words, slavery cannot occur without both the master and the slave. Each actor's status is of equal importance in defining the status of the other. We easily see that the slave would not be enslaved without the master, but we seldom notice that the master would not have his or her status as master without the slave's status as "enslaved." Therefore, we recognize that although, in the abstract, racial categories are simply social constructs used to distinguish one group or class of people from another, in reality, these racial categories, the ways in which they are constructed, and the ways that they fit into a hierarchy are emblematic of a power differential that leaves one group (African Americans) oppressed by another (whites), who gain privilege through the oppression of the former.

African American Families

Finally, thinking about the intersection of definitions of "family" and "race," we note that this book is about African American families. As such, we do not restrict ourselves to a study of families that is limited to social relationships based on birth or law. Similarly, we do not restrict our discussion to families that are made up of only those people who meet some rigid definition of "African American." We recognize that families are not limited by race. Although in Chapter 3 we will discuss at length the issue of inter-racial marriage between African Americans and all others (the rates are *very* low; according to the census, less than 5% of all African Americans marry "out"), in fact, most "African American" families do *not* include people of other races, and even when they do, the children in these families are identi-fied as African American (or black). Thus, based on low rates of intermar-riage and the custom of identifying children born to a black parent as black,[1] we refer to these families as "African American."

Finally, it is important to note that African American families are com-posed of individual actors who create those families, and thus they bring into families their experiences as individual actors. When African Americans are involved in families, regardless of the race or ethnicity of the other members, the family can be considered an African American family by virtue of the fact that the African American individual actor or actors bring to the family all of their experiences as African Americans. So, when we talk about issues such as unemployment or incarceration that affect African Americans differently from whites, and when we argue that these issues affect families, it is not necessary to concern ourselves with ensuring that the families we discuss are composed exclusively of individuals who identify as "African American." Doing so would be nearly impossible anyway because of the issue of passing.

We use the terms *African American families* and *African American com-munity* in order to denote that this book is about people living in the United

States who identify as African American or black. We fully recognize, however, that there is no single African American community nor a single type of African American family, anymore than there is a single white community or gay community. African American families are diverse in size, shape, membership, and social class. They are not monolithic. We recognize and celebrate that, but for ease of language, we use terms such as *family* and *community*.

Structural Versus Individual Explanations

As noted at the beginning of the book, we address both individual and structural explanations for the conditions that plague contemporary African American families. Here, we broaden our discussion of this particular tension between the individual and the structural that will frame our discussion throughout the book. We quote here from Professor Henry Louis Gates (2004), who puts it thus:

> It's important to talk about life chances—about the constricted set of opportunities that poverty brings. But to treat black people as if they're helpless rag dolls swept up and buffeted by vast social trends—as if they had no say in the shaping of their lives—is a supreme act of condescension. Only 50 percent of all black children graduate from high school; an estimated 64 percent of black teenage girls will become pregnant. (Black children raised by female "householders" are five times as likely to live in poverty as those raised by married couples.) Are white racists forcing black teenagers to drop out of school or to have babies? (p. A21)

Gates's comments are focused on the specific issue of nonmarital childbearing among African American teenage girls. This is a good example with which to start our discussion because it is so controversial in both scholarly and public discourses of African American family life. For example, when one talks about the issue of nonmarital childbearing among African American teens, many people label this as a "bad" thing (teens should not be having sexual relations, it is irresponsible behavior, etc.), whereas others note that Americans (read: white America) should not be so critical of these young women who are struggling against racism and sexism and institutions that have discarded them. Later in this chapter, we will give a profile of the African American family. How are African American families doing in terms of measures of well-being? We examine issues such as poverty; wealth; educational attainment; health; and, of course, marriage rates and nonmarital childbearing. These issues are just as difficult to discuss and just as controversial. We note that there are two important and related issues raised here.

First, there is a difference between identifying facts and trends that are troubling and passing judgments. We do not pass judgment on teens who have children or battered women who stay with their abusive partners or men who contract HIV through anonymous sex with other men. What we do is note the ways in which these "facts" have some positive, but mostly negative, consequences for men, women, children, and family life.

Second, we recognize fully that structural factors constrain individual behavior. In short, we acknowledge the fact that African American teens living in low-income households and attending underresourced schools have very little chance to attend college or even look forward to a life of gainful and meaningful employment compared with their middle- and upper middle-income African American or white counterparts (Edin & Kefalas, 2005). Thus, early childbearing, as noted by Linda Burton (1990) and Edin and Kefalas (2005), may not be seen as a negative choice, although it will most likely still result in negative outcomes. This example illustrates the way that structural constraints (in this case, poverty and racism) shape individual choice. Thus, we are challenged by Gates: "Are white racists forcing black teenagers to drop out of school or to have babies?" The answer, we argue, is both "yes" and "no." It is highly unlikely that individual whites, racists or not, are forcing African American teenagers to become single mothers. However, as we will argue in Chapter 4, white, racist institutions contribute to teen childbearing by limiting other paths to adulthood (for example, meaningful employment) as well as restricting access to means of preventing and terminating pregnancies. This framework will be critical to an examination of a variety of issues (health, poverty, violence, education, unemployment, marriage, and childbearing) facing African American families.

African American Families: A Profile

The African American family and community are in trouble (Tilove, 2005). We base this statement not on some moral argument or edict, but rather on empirical facts. Many scholars (McLanahan & Sandefur, 1994) as well as noted journalists (Herbert, 2005b; Kozol, 2001) and even public figures (Cosby, 2004) have noted that the African American family is in trouble.

In the preface of the book, we argued that despite great strides made by individual African Americans over the past 50 years and moderate gains, especially in terms of access—attained by the hard-fought struggles of the civil rights movement—the overall picture for African American men, women, and children is dismal. And on some measures, as we will demonstrate in our discussions of wealth, health, incarceration, and overall access to the American Dream, the situation has actually gotten worse.

As we have noted, there are many different African American families. Our discussion here is designed to paint a picture of the issues facing many African American families as they struggle to find housing, educate their children, stay well, earn a living, and nurture their intimate relationships. Few families find it easy to accomplish all of these goals, and for many African American families, the challenges are great. As Jimmy Carter argued, the measure of any community or political state is the way it responds to its most vulnerable members. With that in mind, we summarize the issues and empirical data that will form the basis for the rest of the book.

Family Structure

Scholars of the family pay a great deal of attention to family structure and the changes in family structure across time. For example, in many agricultural economies, fertility rates are high, family sizes are large, and households include members across generations (extended family). Because of the importance of family structure, and because of the fact that family structure in the African American community has been so contested in public discourse, we devote two chapters (Chapters 3 and 4) to this discussion.

As an introduction to this issue, we note here that there are two key issues in a discussion of family structure in the African American family: marriage and childbearing. We begin with a discussion of marriage. Of all Americans, African Americans are the least likely to marry. Among whites, three fourths of them (75%) marry. However, only slightly more than half of African Americans (58%) ever do. There is no theoretical reason why rates of marriage matter. Furthermore, we compare rates of marriage and childbearing patterns of African Americans to whites simply as a point of reference, not because we believe whites provide the standard. However, we do note that there are several negative outcomes associated with not marrying, and chief among them is poverty. Although African Americans are more likely to be poor than their white counterparts, regardless of family structure or composition, marriage provides some moderate buffer for poverty among African American families (see Table 8.5 in Chapter 8).

Related to the issue of marriage is nonmarital childbearing. Although the fertility rate for African American women (58.5) is similar to that for whites (60.0), because African Americans are significantly less likely to marry, they are significantly more likely to have nonmarital births than are whites. In 2005, 62% of babies born to African American women were nonmarital births, whereas only 25% of babies born to white women were nonmarital births (Dye, 2005).

One of the strongest predictors of poverty for adults, but particularly for children, is the number of adults in the household. For a variety of reasons, children (and adults) living in single-parent households are significantly more likely to live in poverty than are those living in two-parent households (married or cohabiting). Family structure, which is directly linked to poverty, has a serious and detrimental effect on African American children. We will explore these issues more extensively in Chapter 4.

Intimate Partner Violence

Intimate partner violence is a serious problem facing families of all types. Battering is not limited to families of any particular race or ethnic group; it crosses all social class boundaries, it crosses all religious boundaries, and it occurs in all regions of the country. Intimate partner violence occurs in both rural and urban homes, and among both teenagers and senior citizens. Intimate partner violence occurs between people who are married, but it also occurs between people who are dating, living together (cohabiting), even among those who are separated or divorced (Hattery, in press-a; Tjaden & Thoennes, 2000). The only consistent finding in regard to the prevalence of intimate partner violence is that it is a gendered phenomenon: Ninety percent of the violence involves *men* hitting, beating, kicking, choking, and sometimes murdering *women*. We include a discussion of intimate partner violence in our profile of African Americans because it directly affects at least one in four African American women. Intimate partner violence is the single biggest threat to the health and well-being of African American women, far greater than threats that receive more attention, such as HIV/AIDS. It poses a serious threat to their partnerships and marriages as well as to the health and well-being of their children. Campbell, Gary, Campbell, and Lopez (2002) note that intimate partner violence constitutes the greatest threat to the health and well-being of African American women.

Intimate partner violence in the African American community is a troubling phenomenon beyond the fact that women are being subjected to violence (as if that is not bad enough!) because the vast majority of intimate partner violence is intraracial. In other words, the intimate partner violence that African American women experience is at the hands of African American men (Hattery, in press-a).[2] In other words, intimate partner violence constitutes a major problem in African American families, a problem that affects the quality of the relationship itself as well as the health and well-being of each member in the family, including the women who are beaten, the men who are engaging in the violence, and the children who see and hear it.

Although intimate partner violence may seem to be primarily a problem "inside the family," a problem that is explained exclusively by the choices and behavior of individual African American men and women, we will explore (in Chapter 5) the intricacies of intimate partner violence in the African American community with attention to the ways that it, too, is structured by forces of racism, poverty, and gender ideology that leaves African American women more vulnerable than their white counterparts to severe and frequent violence and even homicide.

Health, Well-Being, and Access to Health Care

There are many different measures of health and well-being. Health data indicate race/ethnicity and gender are two of the most significant predictors of health and well-being. These differences exist across the entire life course from birth to death. For example, we know that African American babies are *twice as likely* to die in their first year of life (infant mortality rate = 14.6) than are white babies (infant mortality rate = 7.1). And at the end of life, we know that the average life expectancy for African American men is 12 years less than that of white women. Looking beneath the surface, however, we realize that the *primary* factor that is driving all of these health and well-being disparities is wealth and its converse, poverty.

Although African Americans have higher rates of many diseases, one of the fastest growing health risks to African Americans is HIV/AIDS. Especially among young African American men and women, AIDS is a leading cause of premature death that robs families and communities of productive citizens. African Americans are disproportionately more likely to have AIDS than their white counterparts. Specifically, African Americans make up approximately 13% of the U.S. population, but they make up nearly half of all the AIDS cases in the United States. And African American women comprised 69% of all HIV/AIDS cases in women in the United States (Centers for Disease Control and Prevention [CDC], 2004). Again, although many aspects of health and illness are the product of individual choice (e.g., choosing to smoke), as noted above, health and well-being are heavily structured by forces outside of the individual, such as access to health insurance and access to health care. These topics will be the focus of Chapter 6.

Work and Education

Work is a theme that is interwoven with many of the earlier discussions. Unemployment and underemployment are significantly connected to the likelihood of living in poverty (Wilson, 1996). Without significant work, one negative outcome of being poor is having less access to health care and a healthy lifestyle. Employment is key—perhaps the strongest predictor of both access to financial resources but also to health insurance that is vital to healthy living, reduced infant mortality, longer life expectancy, and overall life chances. And the strongest predictor of employment is educational attainment. Among low-income African Americans, only about half of the young men graduate from high school (Greene & Winters, 2005). Educational attainment is also strongly linked to incarceration: More than half of all African American men who do not graduate from high school will be incarcerated by the time they turn 30 (Western, 2006).

The Bureau of Labor Statistics reports that African American men are more than twice as likely to report being unemployed as their white counterparts (11% compared to 5%). How can we explain higher rates of under- and unemployment among African Americans, and especially among African American men? The literature on employment and work offers several plausible explanations that include different levels of educational attainment and the relationship between incarceration and employment, and we must also recognize the role that racial discrimination in hiring and promotion plays in the work experiences of African Americans. We will examine several key cases that expose this discrimination. In Chapter 7, we will explore in much more depth the experiences of African Americans in the economy and the struggles they and their families face as a consequence of structural factors such as less access to education as well as outright racial discrimination. In addition, we will examine the links between employment and poverty, access to health care, and so on.

Poverty and Wealth

There are many different ways of measuring poverty, and we will not discuss all of them or provide empirical data for each because to do so would be a book in itself. However, we note here that on many measures of poverty and its converse, wealth, African Americans as a "people" and their families fall behind other American citizens, including whites and Asians.

Being poor means living in substandard housing for which one has trouble paying the rent on a regular basis, being behind on one's bills, going without meals each week, and having one's children qualify for free breakfast and lunch programs at school. One of the most fundamental and basic measures of poverty is the "official poverty rate." However, as we will examine in Chapter 8, the official poverty line is so low that in order to talk about people who are poor, we must focus on those who earn 1.5 or 2 times as much as those who fall below the official poverty line. And when we talk about those living below the poverty line, we are talking about the very poorest of Americans whose standard of living is worse than many who live in developing countries.

Although the largest number of poor in the United States are white Americans, African Americans are the *most likely* to live in poverty. Nearly one fourth of all African Americans live in poverty. This is often attributed to family form, based on the assumption that most African American households are single-parent and female headed, but the data indicate that the disproportionately high rates of poverty for African Americans hold regardless of family form. At the other end of the income spectrum, we note that among the affluent, those earning more than $150,000 per year, whites possess 2.5 times more wealth than African Americans in the same income bracket. We will explore other issues related to poverty, and also affluence and wealth, in Chapter 8.

Incarceration

As previously noted, incarceration is a serious and understudied problem in the African American community. The United States incarcerates more citizens than any other industrialized nation in the world. In terms of the total prison population, although African Americans make up only 13% of the U.S. population, African American men make up nearly *half* of all inmates, men *and* women. On any given day, 1 million African American men are in prison, and many more are in jail or under the supervision of the criminal justice system (e.g., parole, probation, electronic monitoring, etc.). On any given day, 250,000 children have a mother in prison and 1.5 million children have a father in prison (Greenfeld & Snell, 1999; Mumola, 2000); thus, literally *millions* of African American families are destroyed forever because of incarceration (see especially the book by Mauer & Chesney-Lind, 2002). The effects of incarceration are devastating to the African American community. We will devote a lengthy discussion to incarceration in Chapter 9, and we note here that incarceration will weave its way through virtually every chapter in this book.

Theoretical Approaches to Studying African American Families

There are several different theoretical approaches to studying the African American family. The two that are the most prominent for sociologists are the social pathology approach and the strength approach. We will review

both of these approaches and then present our own approach for understanding African American families.

Social Pathology

The social pathology approach to studying the African American family is
rooted in the belief that there is something different and wrong with African
Americans and their families. The social pathology approach identifies the
origins of these deficiencies as the "savage" and "uncivilized" manner in
which Africans were said to be living before they were captured and stolen
and brought to the New World. When Africans were brought to the New
World, their family lives (of whatever form these took) were abolished, and
for more than 300 years, the lives of newly transplanted Africans were never
ensconced within what we call "families" (Du Bois, 1908). Furthermore, the
social pathology approach assumes that African slaves brought with them
low morals and uncivilized behavior that have remained part of the constitution of African American individuals as well as their family formations and
culture to this day (Rodman, 1968).

Critics of this assumption that African slaves were immoral or even
amoral and had no regard for the importance of the "Christian" family
argue that regardless of the family patterns African slaves brought with them
to the New World, it was the system of the slave plantation that prohibited
the development of any form of family life (Friedmann, 1980). In brief, during slavery, there was no legal definition of a marriage contract for African
Americans. Yet blacks did have relationships across the long years of
enslavement, and many of these relationships were what we would describe
as loving relations between a man, his "wife," and their children. The late
John Blassingame of Yale magnificently described these relationships in
his book *The Slave Community* (Blassingame, 1979). Gutman (1976) also
argues that upon the first instances of freedom, slaves were literally running
all over the South to find their lost husbands, wives, and children who had,
over the years, been separated from them—a widespread practice of southern slave owners especially after children were born (Blassingame, 1979;
Gutman, 1976). This is clear evidence that slaves formed long-term, stable,
intimate relationships regardless of the fact that slave owners did not allow
slaves to codify these relationships legally and despite the practice of selling
and trading individual slaves with the specific intent of breaking up slave
families (West, 1999).

That said, we are well aware that legally these unions did not exist.
Hence, theorists working within the social pathology model argued from
within an already established framework that took into consideration the

nonexistence of the slave family and interpreted this as pathological and deviant. Furthermore, theorists of social pathology suggested that because African slaves and their descendants were never able to form *legal* family units, African Americans living in the 20th century would lack the desire to establish legal families as well. They argue that this explains the lower rate of marriage and higher rate of nonmarital childbearing patterns that we see in contemporary African American families. Critics of the social pathology approach argue that this perspective ignores or underestimates the impact of societal forces such as unemployment and discrimination on the shape that African American families take. Finally, this approach also tends to portray African Americans as victims rather than as individuals imbued with agency.

The study of African American families has been strongly influenced by the perspective of social pathology.[3] In its most thought-out form, we find this perspective embedded in most of the work of sociologist E. Franklin Frazier, a graduate of the University of Chicago. Frazier set in place the model for research on African American families, having learned this approach from his mentors at the University of Chicago, namely Ernest Burgess and Robert Park, who were pioneers in studying newly arriving immigrant groups in the Midwest (Platt, 1991). Aside from the work of William Edward Burghardt Du Bois (Du Bois, 1909), who himself is somewhat critical of the postslavery "black family" but not fatalistic about the African American family, Frazier took this research agenda to another level, systematically, and laid the groundwork for almost all research on African American families following his own research in 1932 (master's thesis) and again in 1939 (doctoral dissertation) up through the massive study by historian Herbert Gutman that was published in 1976 (Gutman, 1976).

Frazier's work on the study of African American families was highly influential in not only developing but also reinforcing the social pathology perspective that was used to frame the research on African American families. According to the body of work by Frazier,[4] the African American family is deeply pathological. Social disorganization is central to his analysis encompassing individual behaviors of, but not limited to, high rates of unemployment, crime, and infidelity. This theme, systematically started by Frazier (1932, 1939, 1957), was subsequently taken up by the social psychologist Kenneth Clark. In his book *Dark Ghetto* (Clark, 1965/1989), he summarizes the assumptions of the social pathology paradigm: "The symptoms of lower class society affect the dark ghettos of America—low aspirations, poor education, family instability, illegitimacy, unemployment, crime, drug addiction, and alcoholism, frequent illness and early death" (p. 24).

Although other scholars had written from this approach (Rodman, 1968), it enters the mainstream of popular discourse with the work of Daniel

Patrick Moynihan, then a Washington bureaucrat and later a Harvard professor and four-term U.S. senator from New York. He wrote a paper while working for the Department of Labor titled "The Negro Family: The Case for National Action" (Moynihan, 1965), in which he argued that despite the social uplift efforts within the President Lyndon B. Johnson administration, these progressive forms of legislation did not and would not bring about social equality for blacks. Instead, argued Moynihan, the disintegration of black families had reached a point of "social pathology." He put it this way:

> The principal challenge of the next phase of the Negro revolution is to make certain that equality of results will now follow. If we do not, there will be no social peace in the United States for generations. To stem the tide of isolation, poverty, joblessness, crime, and other social ills plaguing the black community in America beginning with the three hundred years of injustice has culminated in a "tangle of pathology" which can only be broken by a national effort to support and empower the black family. (Moynihan, 1965, p. 2)

To ground his argument in empirical facts, Moynihan cited high levels of African American unemployment, especially for men. He also cited decades of welfare dependency and high rates of nonmarital births that signaled to American society the moral decline and instability of African American families. He cited female single-headed households as the *predominant problem* facing African Americans in the late 1960s and located its origins, as framed by social pathology theory, in slavery. The public critique that Moynihan suffered caused him to abandon this course of inquiry and strongly influenced others to stay away from this topic.

In the 1970s and 1980s, the social pathology approach also takes root in Oscar Lewis's "culture of poverty" perspective (Valentine, 1968). Lewis doesn't adopt a trait or inherent argument, but does argue that African American culture socializes individuals to be lazy, to lack the ability to defer gratification (which is a trait necessary for pursuing higher education), and to be unable to make a commitment to work or to intimate relationships.

In summary, the main theoretical assumption of the social pathology approach is that African Americans or their "culture" have inherent traits that predispose them to pathological behavior. Examples include the following:

- High rates of unemployment, poverty, and welfare dependency are a result of the inherent laziness in African Americans.
- High rates of nonmarital births and infidelity are the result of an inherent hypersexualization of African American men and the loose social/sexual morals of African American women.

- High rates of incarceration of African American men are a result of a lack of proper socialization and an inherent inclination toward deviance.
- Low rates of marriage among African American men and women are a result of a lack of proper socialization (dating back to slavery), loose morals, and a lack of the influence of Christianity.

This approach to the study of African American families became standard in North American sociology up through the 1970s, wherein we begin to see an alternative approach couched under the heading of "strengths."

The Strength Approach

In direct response to the social pathology approach and the critiques it inspired, Robert Hill and others (Carol Stack, Betty Lou and Charles Valentine, etc.) flipped this approach on its head and made heroes out of the victims. Whereas the social pathology paradigm interpreted alternative family forms such as low marriage rates and high rates of teen pregnancy as deviance and evidence for the inherent inferiority of African Americans, the strength approach interpreted these same behaviors and patterns as evidence for the inherent strength of African Americans, especially women. For example, single-parent, female-headed households were no longer defined as "deviant" or "pathological" and instead were used to illustrate the strengths of African American women who raised their children and kept their families together during slavery through Jim Crow and into the contemporary era. Furthermore, theorists using this framework argued, for example, that the high rate of single mothers leading African American families also indicated a resistance, if only symbolic, to the oppressive conditions of both racism and patriarchy. Essentially, the strength approach interpreted distinct patterns in African American family formation as both inherent (African Americans are strong) and a reaction to past (slavery, Jim Crow) and current conditions (resisting systems such as patriarchy).

Perhaps the most influential research in this vein was that of Robert Hill (1972). Hill, a nonacademic, unleashed an ideological diatribe against the social pathology school of thought that no scholar could or did take seriously. In his early work, Hill proposed five such strengths that had been culturally transmitted through African ancestry to contemporary African American families. The strengths that foster resilient families and members were identified as a strong kinship bond, a strong work orientation, a strong achievement orientation, flexible family roles, and a strong religious orientation (Hill, 1972). More recently, Hill (1999) defines family strengths as those "traits that facilitate the ability of the family to meet the needs of its members and the demands made upon it by the system outside the family unit" (p. 42).

Several years later, arguing in the same vein, Professor Bette Dickerson edited a volume on single mothers arguing against traditional paradigms, claiming that they further endorsed the social stereotype of the African American family. The editor and contributors, taking an Afrocentric perspective, made it clear that the dominant scholarship of the sociological profession had not captured the social reality of African American family life (Dickerson, 1995).

Critiques of the social pathology approach continue to be developed (Massey & Denton, 1993), and there have been several important contributions to African American family theory made by scholars who write from this strength approach, most notably the recognition of diversity in the experiences of family members and family units (Doherty, Boss, LaRossa, Schumm, & Steinmetz, 1993). Embedded in this perspective, and perhaps the greatest contribution of it, is the challenge to a monolithic definition of family. For example, many of the contributors to Dickerson's 1995 volume challenged the basic assumption that a family necessarily be composed of a heterosexual couple and their biological or adopted children. This challenge to the theoretical and empirical study of families forced a discussion that expanded the definition to one that many scholars following this approach adopted. Recall that in our previous discussion of definitions of family, we noted that several definitions that are in use by family scholars depart significantly from the traditional and exclusionary argument that the nuclear family represents the only viable family form. Therefore, our own work has benefited from the development of more inclusive definitions of family.

Finally, we note that the strengths approach for studying African American families is a direct reaction to E. Franklin Frazier, Kenneth Clark, and others. This is important because in some cases, scholars working from this perspective were so intent on refuting the social pathology perspective that they defined almost any alternative family form as "strength." Although we believe it is valuable to look for strengths in any place one can find them, we believe that this approach has had negative consequences for the continued development of theory as well as policy designed to examine the issues facing African American families. Why? Because scholars who write from this perspective have a tendency to view any critique of African American families as an assault. This makes it difficult to provide honest, empirically based analyses that can be used to develop policies that respond to crises in African American families and improve the opportunities and life chances of all, but especially those who are living on the margins. Wilson argues the same, noting that in the post-1965 period, after the assault on the Moynihan report (1965), social conditions for African American families actually declined at the same time that scholars were reluctant to call attention to these declining conditions because they feared being labeled as "racists."

The danger that arises from this tendency of the strength approach to interpret all responses (single parenting, teen childbearing, etc.) in terms of their strengths is the tendency to ignore or avoid the empirical data (as opposed to ideologies) that demonstrate the embedded nature of these big social problems. For example, we would never condemn any family form that does not conform to the stereotypical heterosexual nuclear family. Yet good statistical research shows that in our society, it is clearly evident that single women who have children at an early age and who have little to no education or access to wealth or other means of support will live in poverty and raise their children in poverty (Dickerson, 1995; Rodman, 1968).

Another major problem in the strength approach has been that although it identified some very positive aspects of African American families and African American civil society, such as racial pride, uplift, diversity in experiences, and alternative family structures, scholars writing from this approach simultaneously falsely identified the acquisition of power through such entities as government-funded federal poverty programs and community development. Theorist Robert K. Merton underscores this tendency for subordinate groups to overvalue their strengths:

> When a once powerless collectivity acquires a socially validated sense of growing power, its members experience an intensified need for self-affirmation. Under such conditions, collective self-glorification, found in some measure among all groups, becomes a predictable and intensified counter response to longstanding belittlement from without. (1972, pp. 18–19)

Finally, we note that the neo-Marxist theorist Erik O. Wright, whose work we will examine in much greater detail throughout the book, identifies the modern welfare system as a system that effectively cordons off classes of people who are then denied access to the mainstream opportunity structure (Hughes, 1945; Royster, 2003).[5] In other words, although welfare systems are important in providing a safety net for citizens, they are not a system from which a group can derive any real power. In fact, long-term reliance on these systems effectively keeps citizens who would have access to real power in the mainstream economy from gaining this access and thus this power.

We concur with those writing from the strength approach that these traits and patterns have allowed African American families to survive in the face of severe challenges (Hill, 1999), yet it is difficult to argue, with the exception of a small percentage of African American families, that these traits and patterns have resulted in a *thriving* African American family.

In summary, the main theoretical assumption of the strength approach is that all variations in family formation and patterns of family life in the African American community can be interpreted as positive responses to stressful life circumstances.

- Teen childbearing is a positive choice because it allows for the involvement of multiple generations (mothers, grandmothers, great-grandmothers) of women in the raising of the child (Burton, 1990).
- Nonmarital childbearing is a positive choice because it separates marriage from childbearing, thus disentangling the role of mother from the oppressive role of wife (Burton, 1990; Edin & Kefalas, 2005).
- Matrifocal households among African Americans re-create family life and its positive aspects in the African villages from which slaves were stolen.
- Single-mother households provide strong evidence for the strength and survival skills that African American women have developed in response to 400 years of racial oppression designed with the explicit purpose of breaking up African American families.

The neglect of African American families in the sociological literature can be summed up as being of the nature wherein by the late 1960s, caution and avoidance were the key ingredients instead of good, systematic research, informed by empirical studies and a variety of methodologies, about these families. Much of this had to do with the reality of researchers arriving at conclusions that did not sit well with the politics of the time. Hence, "cultural" conclusions reached by mainly white researchers (but also African American scholars like Orlando Patterson) became suspect. The authors were labeled racists (Rainwater & Yancey, 1967).

William J. Wilson, former president of the American Sociological Association and a leading scholar of poverty, notes in his 1990 presidential address that this type of research is usually abandoned for reasons that are far from the frontiers of the research site itself. The point that he makes is that the "contentious and acrimonious" debates surrounding research on contentious issues forced well-meaning and competent scholars to look elsewhere for the issues to which they devote their research time. The result is that critical issues are abandoned and neglected, and then all of a sudden, the research community is surprised that there are immense problems among African American families staring us quite frankly in the face (Wilson, 1991).

We value this dialogue between the social pathology approach and the strength approach because it helps us to situate our thesis. For example, we argue herein that, like Lenski (1984), we see the need for synthesis in our analysis. The synthesis allows us to systematically pull together the concerns we have about the pathological/social disorganization approach as well as concerns we have about the strength approach.

However, we argue that both the social pathology approach and the strength approach suffer from a similar flaw: For the most part, they focus singularly on either the strengths or the deficits of African American families. Furthermore, both theoretical approaches have become tied to political agendas (either racist or Afrocentric). This fact makes them difficult to use in research.

Second, both approaches are inadequate in that they were developed with the singular intent of explaining variation in the family patterns, especially family formations, of African American families. Neither of these approaches can be applied to other racial/ethnic families, including whites or other minorities. Nor can these approaches be applied to other parts of family life, such as intimate partner violence, that are studied by family scholars. Thus, our research relies on a broader theoretical model, the race, class, and gender paradigm, to provide the analytical framework for analyzing empirical data on African American families. The strength of this paradigm is that it is sensitive to the diversity and variation in families of different race/ethnicity, but it also allows one to see similarities that may exist because of other structural forces, such as social class.

Race, Class, and Gender Paradigm

We examine the issues facing African American families through the lens of the race, class, and gender (RCG) paradigm. We argue that the most effective way to analyze and explain the situation facing African American families is through the lens that focuses our attention on the context of a web of intersecting systems of oppression: primarily, the systems of racial domination, class oppression, and patriarchy. We must also explore ways in which these systems are created, maintained, and mutually reinforcing.

Every system of domination has a countersystem of privilege. In other words, oppression is a system of both costs and benefits. For example, we know that African American men die prematurely and 7 or 8 years earlier than their white counterparts. Generally, a discussion of this gap in life expectancy focuses on the reasons why African American men die early, including hard work, poverty, lack of access to health care, discrimination, and the stresses associated with being an African American man. Yet a race, class, and gender framework forces us to ask the opposing question: Why is it that white men live so much longer? When we pose the question this way, we realize that the gap is also created by the fact that white men tend to have more access to white-collar employment and the best quality health care, and their affluence affords them the ability to pay for the "dirty" work in their lives, such as cooking and cleaning both at work and at home, to be taken care of by others, mostly African American men and women (Hill-Collins 1994; Padavic & Reskin, 2002; Romero, 1992). Thus, the intersection of race and social class creates both a disadvantage for African American men and simultaneously an advantage for white men. Furthermore, when we dig deeper into this question of life expectancy, we see that there are both race and social class differences. Affluent African American men have better life expectancy than poor men, be they African American or white. Yet African American men are also more likely to suffer from certain health issues and diseases than white men, regardless of their social class. Therefore, the relationship between race, social class, and health is very complex. Our understanding of racial disparities in health and illness are improved when we layer these explanations with attention to social class. (At this point, we will not flesh out the role of gender in this discussion, but a cursory examination of the life expectancy table—Table 6.7—demonstrates clearly that gender oppression and privilege are also critical in understanding issues such as health and life expectancy in the lives of African Americans and whites.)

The race, class, and gender approach can be described as one that recognizes various systems of oppression and privilege as existing in a matrix that results in various intersections of each system. At the individual level, this means that the experiences of black women in the labor force are unique and may be similar to those of black men and white women, but they are not completely consistent with either. Deborah King refers to this as "double jeopardy" and argues that the interweaving of these systems is not additive (race effects plus gender effects) but rather multiplicative (King, 1988). From an analytical perspective, the race, class, and gender approach underscores the importance of conducting both quantitative and qualitative analyses with attention to this framework. In other words, when we examine the impact of educational attainment on earnings, we must examine the impact and outcome with regard to all of the possible race, class, and gender configurations: affluent African American women, poor white men, and so on.

Maxine Baca Zinn and Bonnie Thornton Dill (Zinn & Dill, 2005) refer to this as the matrix of domination. At the structural level, the race, class, and gender framework illuminates the ways in which different systems of domination are mutually reinforcing: Patriarchy is woven with racism (or race supremacy), both of which are woven with capitalism. The focus at the structural level is on the systems of domination themselves and how they interact. For our work, then, the race, class, and gender perspective provides a framework for understanding, for example, the role that racism in the criminal justice system plays in sentencing decisions. Second, we can layer this analysis by examining the role that social class plays and how it inter-acts with race. For example, how can we explain the fact that African American men serve sentences that are disproportionately longer than those served by white men who commit the same crimes, while at the same time, affluent African American sports heroes may see the criminal justice system adjust for them in ways that it never would for similarly affluent white men? We illustrate with an example from the Kobe Bryant hearings in Eagle, Colorado. In the Bryant case, the judge adjusted the court schedule around the Los Angeles Lakers game schedule. Yet there is no evidence that Ken Lay, former CEO of Enron, found the court similarly sympathetic.[6]

A Comparison of Race, Class, and Gender Theory With Critical Race Theory

Two of the most important advances in social theory in the past 25 years are the development of race, class, and gender (RCG) theory and critical race theory (CRT). The latter is most often associated with the research of legal scholars and the former with sociologists who research issues related to women and members of racial/ethnic minority groups (Crenshaw, 1995; Delgado & Stefancic, 2001).

What differentiates RCG theory from CRT is the relative role of race in understanding social phenomena. As the name suggests, CRT implies that the system of racial domination is the central system of oppression operat-ing in the contemporary United States. Although critical race theorists acknowledge the role of other systems of oppression, the theory holds that in our world, how individual actors perceive events is shaped, more than any other variable, by one's racial background. The RCG framework is different from CRT and is unique in two key ways.

First, it allows for a shifting of the core form of oppression. Some phe-nomena, for example, may be shaped primarily by gender oppression and privilege, but reinforced by race and social class. For example, we argued in response to the Duke lacrosse alleged gang rape that at its core, this was an expression of sexism. Rape, after all, is a gendered crime. However, we noted that in this instance, the class and race dynamics of the individuals involved (affluent white men and a low-income African American woman) shaped this incident differently from how it would have been shaped had they been absent (Brady, 2006).

Second, the RCG framework allows for the assumption that there are phenomena best explained by thinking about the various systems of oppres-sion as being of equal importance (King, 1988; Zinn & Dill, 2005). In other words, in some cases, the pattern we observe may not be attributable to one key form of oppression (e.g., social class) and reinforced by the other systems (patriarchy and racism). It may not be possible to disentangle and attribute centrality to one system; rather, the data are best analyzed by a model in which all three systems of oppression are of equal importance and working in a constantly mutually reinforcing fashion. For these reasons, we find that the RCG framework has the greatest utility in analyzing the data on African American families.

Data and Methods

This book will explore the realities of African American families in the contemporary United States based on the analyses of empirical data that come from a variety of sources, including the U.S. Census, the Bureau of Labor Statistics, the Bureau of Justice Statistics, and the Centers for Disease Control and Prevention. In each chapter, we will provide a review of the related literature as well as a detailed examination, based on these empirical analyses, of a particular issue or a set of related issues. Finally, when relevant, we will include illustrations for a phenomenon drawn from the rich qualitative data generated through the interviews we did with African American men and women.

Qualitative Interviews

During the spring, summer, and fall of 2004, we interviewed 40 African American men and women—20 men and 20 women—in the Midwest and the South[7] about their experiences with family life. Specifically, we conducted interviews in two states: North Carolina and Minnesota. Because our research initially focused on intimate partner violence (IPV), our subjects were all selected because they had experienced at least one incident of IPV that had come to the attention of either the criminal justice system or social services. However, the interviews were broadly focused on the respondents' experiences growing up (family of orientation) and their adult intimate relationships (family of destination). We essentially collected life histories focused on family life, relationships, dating, work, and so forth. (A lengthier description of the methods and sampling as well as a list of the subjects, identified by pseudonym, can be found in Appendix A.)

For a variety of reasons, we felt it was important to collect data in more than one part of the United States. The South has such a particular (and peculiar) sociopolitical economy, and thus, collecting data in the

Midwest allowed for a more diverse overall sample. The Midwest is predominately white, for example and the African American population in Minnesota is very small (in this particular county, African Americans make up only 2.5% of the residents). Furthermore, most of the African Americans in this county have migrated there in the past generation. Because we chose the Midwest specifically to create diversity in the sample, we did not want to interview African Americans in the Midwest who had been reared in the South, where the racial politics are decidedly less progressive. Thus, we restricted our sample in Minnesota to African Americans who had *not ever* lived in the South. In this way, we would ensure a Midwestern sample that had not lived, for example, under the vestiges of Jim Crow–style segregation. They would not have grown up in the heat of the school desegregation battles of the early 1970s, nor would they have attended racially segregated schools or witnessed the Ku Klux Klan presence we still see today.

The Midwest provides diversity in many other ways as well. States in the upper Midwest—namely, Minnesota, Wisconsin, and, to a lesser degree, Michigan—have a history of progressive politics on issues such as race, social class, and gender. For example, states like Minnesota were at the forefront of progressive laws regarding violence against women (rape and battering). In Minnesota, domestic violence is defined in a *feminist framework* that makes room for including women who batter men and same-sex battering. In North Carolina, however, domestic violence is defined in a gendered way: The only conceivable pattern is men beating up women. Thus, the legal charge retains the vestiges of patriarchy: "assault on a female." Some of these differences in state law influence family form. For example, in Minnesota, families experiencing an incident of violence may continue to live together as long as their safety is monitored by a social worker, whereas in North Carolina, the parents must physically separate. This shaped our sample such that most of the women we interviewed in the Minnesota sample were still living with their partners whereas none of the women we interviewed in North Carolina were.[8]

In terms of class politics, it is important to note that the most important political party in these upper Midwestern states is the Democratic Farm Labor party, a party with strong ties to rural labor organizing and labor organizing among miners in the Iron Range.[9] In contrast, the South historically has been the most resistant to labor organizing. As a result, both class relations and attitudes toward class politics are more progressive in the Midwest than in the South, thus creating differences in the workplace that may affect employment, the availability of health insurance, and so forth.

Triangulation of Method

One of the strengths of this study and one of the things that makes it unique is the weaving of quantitative and qualitative methods and data. The large-scale national and government data sets provide the most up-to-date prevalence estimates available for analysis. These data allow us to say, for example, what percent of African Americans are living below the poverty line, what percent graduate from high school, what percent marry, and what percent are incarcerated. Furthermore, because these data have been collected in the same form over many decades, they allow us to look at trends in disease, teen childbearing, labor force participation, and so forth.

However, quantitative data contained in these large data sets tell us very little about what it means to be poor: what kind of food the poor eat, what their housing looks like, how they are treated when they seek medical care. This is where the qualitative data shine. The interviews with African American men and women allow us to learn in rich detail about the fight that led up to the episode of violence, or the discrimination they faced trying to find a job, or the reasons they dropped out of high school.

When we triangulate methods—when we combine the strength of estimation provided by the quantitative data with the rich detail of the qualitative data—we are far more accurate in painting a picture of African American family life in the early part of the 21st century.

The African American men and women we interviewed are in many ways reflective of the profile of African Americans we presented earlier in this chapter. In terms of social class, the majority of these men and women come from the lower end of the socioeconomic spectrum; most are working class, although some of them are college educated and hold professional jobs. Compared to the North Carolina sample, the sample in Minnesota is equally diverse by race/ethnicity and equally limited by socioeconomics. Many of the men were employed, but most of the unmarried women were either currently on welfare or had received it in the past. About half of the men and women we interviewed were married, and the rest were cohabiting. All had children, and the majority had begun their childbearing during their teenage years. The men and women we interviewed ranged in age from 20 to 55, although the majority were in their 20s and 30s. As a result of such a young sample, most had not yet experienced age-related diseases such as diabetes, heart disease, stroke, and so forth. However, consistent with the national data on race and health, our sample included young men and women with serious health problems ranging from sickle cell anemia to diabetes to HIV. All were experiencing intimate partner violence (that is how they were selected for an interview). The vast majority of men (90%) had been incarcerated, for periods ranging from several months to more than a decade, for convictions ranging from drug offenses to attempted murder. In most ways, then, the sample of men and women whose narratives we will use to illustrate the topics covered in this book are reflective of the general African American population.

These interviews were conducted using an interview schedule that had been pretested and verified for reliability and validity (see Hattery, in press-a). Interviews were designed to follow a semi-structured set of questions. The men and women we interviewed were asked to begin by talking about the families in which they grew up, what the relationships were like between their parents, among their siblings, with grandparents, and so on. Then they were asked to talk about their experiences with dating and marriage or cohabitation. The focus was on both their "healthy" or violence-free relationships as well as the relationships that involved IPV. Thus, the interviews were essentially mini life histories, each taking between 1½ and 2 hours to complete. In these interviews, we learned about the subjects' experiences with poverty; employment; health and illness (i.e., sickle cell anemia, diabetes, and HIV/AIDS); intimate partner violence; sexual abuse; and incarceration. These interviews provide the data that we share in this book. In each chapter, we will use the qualitative data generated from the interviews to provide the case study for the chapter. (For a lengthy discussion of analytical techniques, see Appendix A.)

Notes

1. Dating back to the 1600s, the "one drop rule" for assigning racial identity was both law and custom. A child with one black ancestor was identified as black. Furthermore, we note that we live in a society where a white woman can give birth to a black baby, but a black woman cannot give birth to a white child. Thus, African American families with a white (or Hispanic or Asian) parent are still African American.

2. We do not argue that the violence perpetrated by African American men against African American women is not influenced by the system of racism and racial superiority that dominates race relations in the contemporary United States, but we do argue that intimate partner violence in any community is primarily a vestige of patriarchy.

3. For our purposes, social pathology is defined as a condition wherein the cumulative effects of racial oppression, poverty, ill health, crime, and poor housing combine to account for how individuals, groups, and families encounter on a daily basis their social lives and institutional interaction. The pathology, then, becomes a daily obstacle course to be navigated for survival.

4. Frazier completed his graduate work at the University of Chicago, and in his postgraduate work, one will find several books on the African American family.

5. Royster (2003), in her book on blue-collar trades and the cordoning off of African American males who have similar training as their white counterparts, makes a good case for continued segregation in the labor market. Almost 60 years before the Royster study, sociologist Everette C. Hughes (1945) published in the *American Journal of Sociology* a paper on "status inconsistencies" wherein he shows that African Americans who achieve physician status find that this status creates a dilemma for "average whites." The dilemma has to do with the small number of African American men who, in Hughes's time, achieve physician status and whites' inability to see beyond their race. This is exactly what Royster and others find when their research shows that even today, whites cannot handle the fact that African Americans can obtain skills on their merit and abilities, and want to ascribe African American achievements to policies such as affirmative action.

6. Angela Davis's (1983) work on lynching also provides an excellent illustration of this approach.

7. Half the men and half the women were interviewed in each region. We also selected individuals for interview who were "native" to that region in order to reduce the conflation that might occur between region and experience if we interviewed individuals who had moved from one region to another.

8. All of these sorts of variation in the sample will be addressed when appropriate. We would argue, however, that rather than making the sample less consistent, these variations contribute to a sample that better represents the experiences of women in the United States who are living with IPV. Thus, we think the sample is one of the strengths of the study.

9. Minnesota Senator Paul Wellstone was a member of the Democratic Farm Labor Party and organized farmers throughout southern Minnesota and miners in the northern Iron Range region.

3

Family Formation, Marriage Rates, and Cohabitation

Mass media images of Black masculinity and Black femininity can have an especially pernicious effect on how Black men and women perceive one another. African American men who see Black women as being physically unattractive, domineering, and promiscuous and African American women who see Black men as being criminally inclined, promiscuous, and dangerous evaluate the worth of potential sex partners and love interests through distorted lenses.

—Hill-Collins (2004), p. 255

Objectives

- Use empirical data to examine the patterns of marriage and cohabitation among African Americans.
- Analyze differences in patterns of marriage and cohabitation between African Americans and whites using a theoretical framework, specifically the race, class, and gender paradigm.
- Understand how ideologies and norms affect relationships in African American marriages.
- Examine the outcomes, both positive and negative, of low rates of marriage on African American families.
- Develop solutions to the negative outcomes associated with low rates of marriage.

Introduction

Marriage rates in the African American community are one of the most contentious issues both inside and outside the African American community. White Americans often discuss the issue from a morality perspective, arguing that it is somehow not "normal" for adults not to marry and remain in monogamous relationships throughout adulthood. As sociologists, we find this such an interesting phenomenon as well as an interesting argument because, of course, although marriage rates are higher among white Americans, the likelihood of staying married is quite another issue. Many of the very people who are accusing African Americans of living immoral lives because they don't marry are in fact divorced themselves![1] In contrast, the marriage issue that dominates the discourse of African American women is that of interracial marriage: specifically, the issue of white women marrying African American men.

Scholars such as Patricia Hill-Collins and Orlando Patterson articulate the complexities of African American marriage under the oppressive structures of both racism and patriarchy, structures that leave African American men and women adrift as they attempt to create family life without the advantage of visible and accessible images to guide them (Hill-Collins, 2004).

In this chapter, we will examine data and patterns on marriage rates in the African American community. We will explore the variety of reasons for the fact that African Americans, and especially African American women, marry at a rate significantly lower than that of their white counterparts. We will offer some suggested solutions for creating stronger, more stable, and less poor families in the African American community.

Factors That Affect Family Form

We must begin this discussion by asking the question, "Why does it matter whether or not people marry?" First of all, we note that although most, but certainly not all, Americans assume that marriage to one partner for a lifetime is a "natural" phenomenon, data from other cultures suggest that it is only one of many patterns of adult intimate relationships that exist within the human population. There are many reasons why patterns of adult relationships vary across both space (culture/society) and time (historically). Here, we briefly examine the most important factors that contribute to the ways in which adult relationships are constructed: the economy and religion.

The Economy

The economy of a society plays a very important role in structuring family relationships. Agricultural economies are heavily dependent on both labor power and land. Therefore, fertility rates tend to be high and marriage patterns tend to follow certain prescribed rules. For example, in many agricultural societies, polygamy, or being married to more than one person at a time, is common. Even today, although polygamy is shunned by the Western world, in cultures as varied as China and Kenya, polygamy is still desired and practiced (Murdock, 1954/1983). Specifically, the polygamous pattern that is used is polygyny, or the form that allows a man to have more than one wife. This form is useful in agricultural economies because it allows men to father more children, who will provide the intensive labor that characterizes an agricultural economy. Another typical pattern of marriage in agricultural societies is the preference for marriage between families that allows for greater accumulation of land. So, for example, in many cultures, cross-cousin marriage is the preferred pattern. Cross-cousin marriage involves the sons in one family marrying their mother's brothers' (their maternal uncles) daughters (their cross-cousins). This pattern allows for the concentration of land and wealth within families.

These marriage and fertility patterns are strikingly different from those that we see in industrial and postindustrial societies across Western Europe, in Japan, and in the United States. In industrial and postindustrial economies, which are characterized by adults going to work away from home; in factories; in the service economy (health care, retail, food service); and so forth, there is no benefit to having large families. In fact, because the education and training to work in these economies is significantly greater than in agricultural economies, a family is more likely to be successful over time if they have few children and invest heavily in the development of each child's human capital (education, training, credentials). Thus, fertility rates decline significantly as societies industrialize. This is referred to as the "demographic transition" (Fehr, Jokisch, & Kotlikoff, 2003).

Because of the changing needs of the family—having fewer children and investing heavily in each—the most successful marriage patterns in postindustrial economies will be long-term monogamous marriages. In other words, one man and one woman marry for life and focus their investments on the one or two children they bear. Although this is the predominant marriage pattern, it does not preclude other patterns such as homosexual marriages, polygamy, and so on. There is very little reason why, for example, a same-sex couple would fare better or worse than a heterosexual couple, speaking in strictly economic terms.

Religion

Religious ideology also plays a significant role in shaping marriage patterns. In many cultures, for example, it is religion, and not the economic system, that is used as the rationale for the legal restrictions on marriage. For example, the Judeo-Christian doctrine that dominates both religious as well as political institutions across the European and the North and South American continents restricts marriage to monogamy. In the United States, marriage, in most states, is further restricted, legally, to a union between a man and a woman. The heated battle over homosexual marriage in the United States is generally framed in religious terms, citing the Bible as providing evidence for this restriction of marriage to heterosexuals.

Although most cultures are guided by either religious or economic principles, many are influenced by an intersection of the economy and the dominant religion. For example, many regions of the world that remain ensconced in an agricultural economy are coupled with hegemonic Christian religions (for example, much of Central and South America), and in these cultures, we see the power of hegemonic religion in dictating marriage patterns—monogamy is the only legal form of marriage despite the fact that the economic system would favor polygamy. Similarly, we have examples of postindustrial economies that are dominated by Islam. For example, some Middle Eastern countries, such as Saudi Arabia, meet this definition. In these countries, religion is more powerful in shaping marriage patterns; polygyny is still preferred, despite the fact that it may not be the most efficient family form for this type of economy.

Therefore, although the economy plays a powerful role in shaping family patterns (marriage and childbearing), it is more powerful in shaping fertility patterns than in shaping marriage patterns. Marriage patterns are, by and large, shaped by hegemonic religious ideology.

Functions and Purposes of Marriage

Marriage has a variety of functions or purposes. We will review here the primary functions and purposes that hold true across all cultures and across time.

Economic Function

Marriage has many economic functions. One purpose it serves is to allow for the accumulation of land, wealth, and power within families. Throughout the period of monarch rule in Europe, for example, marriages among the aristocracy were heavily constrained to maximize economic gain and political power. Much of the concentration of power in Western Europe was accomplished through marriages by the aristocracy that crossed national lines.

In fact, these same patterns persist today. There are several examples of the power of these social networks in the marriages of American politicians, such as that of Arnold Schwarzenegger (governor of California) and Maria Shriver (who is part of the Kennedy family), and the marriage of John Kerry (2004 presidential candidate) and Teresa Heinz (heir to the Heinz fortune and widow of powerful Senator John Heinz). In addition to the access to social networks and political capital that these unions provide, they also provide access to enormous amounts of money, or financial capital, that is necessary to successfully attain state and federal elected positions. At the individual level, marriage allows for two people to combine their assets and their networks. One outcome is clearly economic stability. Indeed, one of the most serious negative consequences of the low marriage rate among African Americans is poverty. Patterson also notes that one of the negative outcomes of low rates of *interracial* marriage is the exclusion of African Americans from the social networks of whites.

> But there is a broader, and more powerful way in which intermarriage has influenced both the successful integration of Euro-American and other immigrants and the vitality of American civilization. When we marry, we engage in an exchange of social and cultural dowries potentially far more valuable than gold-rimmed china. The cultural capital exchanged in intermarriage is considerably greater than that within ethnic groups. . . . The main intent and effect of segregation has been to deny Afro-Americans access to the nation's rich marital market, propinquity being one of the most important factors explaining choice of spouse. (Patterson, 1999, p. 155)

Sexual Access

One of the most important functions of marriage is to restrict with whom one can have sexual relations. There are many reasons for this, including paternity establishment, age of sanctioned sexual relations, and restrictions on marrying family members. In the United States, there is a minimum age requirement to marry. (This varies from state to state and has been as low as 12 in some southern and western states.) This restriction is clearly designed to prohibit sexual behavior among or with children. In contemporary times, this law has been used primarily to protect children from child molesters and is seldom used against the majority of teenagers who are sexually active. In most, but not all, states, one may not marry a relative who is closer than a second cousin. However, in some other cultures, first cousins are the preferred marriage partner. So, the restrictions can be used in different ways, to either prohibit or encourage certain marriage partners depending on norms of marriage in the particular culture. In the United States, until very recently (1967),[2] it was illegal in many states for whites to marry nonwhites. The purpose of these restrictions—known as antimiscegenation laws—was to prohibit interracial marriages, interracial sexual relationships, and the "mixing" of the races, as well as to prevent access to the social, economic, and political power that marriage can bring (as noted in the quote above by Patterson).

Establishing Paternity and Guaranteeing Childrearing

In most cultures, regardless of how much childrearing is shared by the community, the primary responsibility for supporting, caring for, and rearing children falls to the child's parents. Prior to the advances in DNA testing, paternity was nearly impossible to verify. This remains the case in virtually all parts of the world where DNA testing is expensive and not readily accessible. Therefore, one of the primary functions of marriage has always been to provide evidence of paternity. Because investing in raising a child is expensive, in terms of both financial support and time, marriage reassured men that the children born from their unions were, in fact, theirs, and worthy of such a significant investment. From the mother's perspective, the marriage also ties the father to the family and guarantees her the support of the father in providing for and raising her children. We cannot overstate the importance of this function. Because maternity is always certain but paternity can be established *only* through marriage (or now through DNA when it is available), marriage is used to both establish paternity and tie the father into the family. Because DNA has become available as a mechanism for establishing paternity only in the past 15 years or so, and because it is widely available only in industrialized societies, historically, marriage has established the legal relationship between fathers and their children. This legal relationship guarantees that children would be provided for economically and that property would be passed down to them through inheritance. However, relying on marriage to establish paternity, although useful, is not always accurate. Women can and do have sexual relationships with men to whom they are not married, and they can and do become pregnant by these men. We note that often these cases go unnoticed unless there are particularly obvious markers such as having a sexual liaison with a man who is of a different race from one's husband! Many social scientists (anthropologists, sociologists) note that this gender difference in parental establishment is one of the primary reasons why nearly all polygamous cultures allow men to have more than one wife but prohibit women from having more than one husband.

Finally, we conclude with an important distinction: Marriage is not just a ceremony but a legal contract that binds two people's lives together. In most states, a marriage contract means that each member of the couple has a legal right to the assets of the other: both those brought into the marriage as well as those acquired, together and separately, after the marriage. Furthermore, this means that upon the death of one member, the assets held both in common as well as separately by the deceased pass automatically and in most cases without being taxed to the surviving spouse. This legal contract can be dissolved only by another legal action: divorce. The implications of this legal contract are the most powerful of any contract most Americans ever enter.

Marriage Patterns

Now that we have examined some of the functions and purposes of marriage, we turn to an examination of marriage patterns in the African American community.

Looking carefully at the data in Table 3.1, we see that African Americans are far less likely to ever marry than are their white counterparts. African American women are twice as likely to have *never* married (41.9%) than are their white counterparts (20.7%). The gap is similar for men, although white men are *less* likely to marry than their female counterparts, so the race gap is not quite as great for men as for women.

> Afro-Americans are the most unpartnered and isolated group of people in America and quite possibly in the world. Unlike any other group of Americans, most of them will go through most of their adult lives without any deep and sustained attachment to a non-kin companion. Sixty percent of Afro-American children are now being brought up without the emotional or material support of a father. This is so because the great majority of Afro-American mothers have been seduced, deceived, *betrayed, and abandoned by the men to whom they gave their love and trust.* (Patterson, 1999, p. 4, emphasis added)

However, as any family sociologist knows, getting married does not necessarily mean staying married. Estimates are that nearly half of all marriages end in divorce, and this divorce rate has remained stable for nearly 20 years (Bumpass & Sweet, 1989; McLanahan & Sandefur, 1994). A closer examination of the data in Table 3.1 reveals that although whites are more likely to marry, they are also more likely to divorce. Thus, we agree with Patterson and others that African Americans are less likely to live in and raise children in married couple households, but when we consider the overall situation, the gap between whites and African Americans is not as great as the "ever

Table 3.1   Summary Table for Marriage and Divorce by Race and Gender
(for all ages, in percentages)

	White Men	African American Men	White Women	African American Women
Never married	27.4	43.3	20.7	41.9
Ever married	72.6	56.7	79.3	58.1
Married once	54.8	44.3	60.0	46.9
Still married	45.1	31.4	42.1	25.1
Ever divorced	23.3	18.8	25.4	20.1
Currently divorced	9.4	9.2	11.1	11.9
Ever widowed	3.8	3.7	12.9	10.5
Currently widowed	2.5	2.9	11.3	9.7

married" data would suggest, and much of the narrowing of this gap is driven by the higher divorce rate among white Americans.

One of the most important findings in these data is that there are differences in both race and gender. Although African Americans are less likely to marry than whites, and women are more likely to marry than men, there is virtually no gender difference for African Americans, whereas there is a significant gender difference for whites. This is another example of the importance of analyzing data through the lens of the race, class, and gender paradigm that allows the researcher to disentangle race and gender effects on marriage. We turn now to a detailed discussion of the marriage gap and its causes. A table with all of the data on marriage, broken down by age, is available in Appendix B.

The Marriage Gap

There have been a variety of explanations for the marriage gap between whites and African Americans, including "low morality" among African Americans, gender role ideology, welfare rules, the limited marriage pool for African American women, and even the race gap in the interracial marriage rate. In this section, we will explore the various explanations for marriage rate patterns.

"Low Morality" and Critiques

Many scholars, both African American and white, have often argued that the lower marriage rate among African Americans was driven by their lack of morality (Fogel & Engerman, 1974; Frazier, 1939). This belief is based

on the notion that African Americans were never socialized into understanding the importance of marriage. An important underlying assumption
is that the family structure in Africa was "uncivilized," polygamous, and
thus morally questionable.

However, other scholars argue that although there is a link between
slavery and trends in contemporary African American family form, it is not
the link that is purported by proponents of the "low morality" argument.
Gutman's work suggests that it is most likely that the descendants of
Africans, slaves and freed slaves, had a high regard for and valued family life.
Rather than seeing the failed attempts in creating families during slavery and
reconstruction, Gutman offers the argument that it is more instructive to
focus on the successes, the degree to which African Americans were able to
create and maintain family life in the face of institutional and legal forces that
prohibited family life, rather than focus on the inability of some enslaved
Africans and African Americans to successfully form families and keep them
together—a right to which they were not entitled anyway (Gutman, 1976).

Other scholars believe that trends in African American family form
are the result of the development of gender roles, coping strategies, and
resiliency in the face of employment and housing discrimination and strict
welfare rules, and that these phenomena provide the links between slavery
and contemporary marriage patterns.

Ideology and Norms

One of the strongest gender norms in contemporary American family life
is that of the male breadwinner (Hattery, 2001b; Kimmel, 1995, 2005).
Under patriarchy, men were crowned "king of the castle" and "head of the
household," and implicit in this distinction are the responsibilities to rule
the household and all of its members (Engels & Leacock, 1884/1972).
Engels argued that male power descends directly from patriarchy and is in
large part codified by the economic power men derive from employment.
Men worked in the public sphere, where they earned higher wages and had
access to other forms of power (Padavic & Reskin, 2002; Reskin & Padavic,
1994), and they brought that sense of power back into their families (Engels
& Leacock, 1884/1972; Hattery, 2001b). Women, because they did not start
working in the public sphere in vast numbers until 1970 or so,[3] have only
recently had access to the economic power to which men have had access for
150 years (since the beginning of the Industrial Revolution), and this results
in a gendered power differential within families and marriages.

Although seldom critiqued, this pattern is race specific. In the period
of reconstruction up through today, African American men have faced
significantly more employment and wage discrimination than their white

counterparts. As a result, women in African American families are and have always been more likely to be employed, and in many cases, they have out-earned their male partners (husbands) (see Coontz, 1992, 1997; Hattery, 2001b; Hill-Collins, 2004).

One of the results of this link between employment and marriage patterns is that when wives are the primary wage earners or they outearn their husbands, the marriages are more likely than not to dissolve (Franklin, 1997). Data on educational attainment and wages in the African American community demonstrate that this pattern of women being more highly educated and outearning male partners is highly probable in poor, working-class, middle-class, and even professional couples (see Tables 7.1 and 7.3 and Appendix H).

This is where ideology becomes a bigger problem than the earnings themselves. Hill-Collins (2004) notes, "This explanation is only plausible in a situation in which women and men accept prevailing gender ideology that grants men natural financial superiority" (p. 254). In other words, there is no intrinsic reason why men must be financially superior to women, but because the hegemonic gender role ideology dictates this set of gender relations when women are the breadwinners or outearn their male partners, they are less likely to (a) get married and (b) stay married. Therefore, gender role ideology and its consequent requirements shape marriage patterns.

Hegemonic and Alternative Ideologies

A brief discussion of hegemonic and alternative gender role ideologies is useful here. As Hill-Collins notes, it is the *belief* that men are supposed to be the breadwinners and the heads of their households that causes the problem in men's and women's attempts to negotiate relationships. This raises the question of the importance of dominant and hegemonic ideologies. In spite of the fact that African American women have always been involved in the paid labor market (see Hill-Collins, 1994; Rollins, 1985; Romero, 1992; Segura, 1994) and thus have always lived in relationships that are non-normative.[4] Hill-Collins argues that out of these lived experiences, women of color and mothers of color in particular developed alternative ideologies that matched their lived realities (Hill-Collins, 1994, 2004). Yet African American men and women continue to report that they are influenced by the dominant gender role ideology. Despite the development of these ideologies, they remained marginal and thus of little consequence in influencing individual behavior (see also Hattery, 2001b; Therborn, 1980).

African Americans, despite living in families that often appear different from the hegemonic images, make decisions and compare their lives to these images rather than to the lived realities in their families and communities. This practice is indicative of the extensive power that hegemonic ideologies have on individual actors. As Hill-Collins (2004) notes, the problem is not the fact that in many couples African American women would or do outearn African American men, but rather that they both *perceive* this to be problematic. She argues that if men and women were no longer constrained by these beliefs, then ideological barriers to forming family units would be dissolved (Hill-Collins, 2004). The mere fact that they cannot simply discard and move beyond these beliefs, even when they contradict their lives and the lives of those around them, demonstrates the power of hegemonic ideologies (Hattery, 2001b; Therborn, 1980).[5]

The Role of Welfare in Shaping Family Forms

Another significant impact on family formation in African American civil society, and especially among low-income and poor African Americans, were the many welfare programs that originated out of the period of the famous "War on Poverty" that President Johnson's administration launched in the 1960s. For example, one of the early requirements of AFDC (Aid to Families with Dependent Children) was that there be only one parent present in the home. Thus, poor mothers with children would refuse to marry the fathers of these children because to do so would result in the denial of the much-needed AFDC checks they received.[6] This practice was widespread among low-income African Americans and even had a name: "the man in the house rule" (McLanahan, 1985; Moffitt, 1997). As prohibitions against marriage became codified into welfare and public policy, norms around cohabitation evolved. Now, 30 years later, we see lower rates of marriage among African Americans, who are disproportionately likely to be receiving public assistance and/or to have grown up in households that were. It is possible that norms of cohabitation replaced norms of marriage. For example, research from the Fragile Families study concludes that increases in the receipt of welfare, although they do not necessarily encourage marriage, are correlated with the situation where parents in a nonmarital birth stay together (Carlson, Garfinkel, McLanahan, Mincy, & Primus, 2004). This finding suggests that researchers and policymakers may need to seriously consider the possibility that cohabitation has evolved as an alternative to legalized marriage that allows poor families, both African American and white, to continue to receive assistance (welfare, Medicaid, and so forth) while retaining much of the same stability and advantages of marriage.[7]

The Male Marriageable Pool: The Impact of Unemployment and Incarceration

Much of the scholarship on the lower rate of marriage among African Americans as compared to whites focuses on what is termed the *male marriageable pool.* The term refers to the fact that in order to be "marriage-able," men must have compiled educational credentials, they must be employ-able (and preferably employed), and so on. In 1995, according to Kiecolt and Fossett, there were 78 African American males for every 100 females in the general population. Termed the Male Marriage Pool Index, this ratio indicates that the pool of eligible African American men for marriage is significantly smaller than the pool of African American women presumably looking for marriage partners (Kiecolt & Fossett, 1995).

Education and Employment

Limited access to the male marriage pool occurs primarily because African American men face severe limitations in access to the opportunity structure: namely, education and employment. The barriers include everything from direct racial discrimination to the disproportionate likelihood of being poor. For example, African Americans are far more likely to attend underresourced primary and secondary schools (see especially Kozol, 2001, 2005), which leave them without the credentials to pursue higher education. Thus, removing barriers of race and class inequality, specifically with regard to education and employment, would result in a significant rise in the male marriageable pool. Finally, we strongly agree with Hill-Collins (2004) that, in addition, if African American men and women adopted alternative gender role prescriptions that did not restrict masculinity to being the breadwinner and femininity to being subordinate to men, then these discrepancies in educational attainment and employment between men and women in the African American community would not have a significant impact on the likelihood of marrying.[8]

Incarceration

Incarceration also plays a clear and obvious role in the marriageable pool explanation for lower marriage rates among African Americans. When any community has 25%–33% of its men incarcerated for any length of time, the likelihood of maintaining healthy, stable intimate and family relationships is severely affected. In the past 30 years, the rate of marriage for African Americans has declined while the rate of incarceration for African American men has exploded. We conclude that incarceration plays a major role in the marriage rates of African American men and women (Western, 2006).

Black-White Intermarriage

One of the biggest complaints of African American women is the "out-marriage" rate of African American men. African American women complain that white women are "taking their men." Data from the U.S. Census Bureau (2005b) confirm black women's complaints that white women were more likely to marry black men than white men were to marry black women. African American men had white wives 2.65 times more often than black women had white husbands. In other words, in 73% of black-white couples, the husband was black.

Looking at the big picture, an examination of trends confirms that there has been an overall steady increase in the rates of all interracial marriage (Wilson, 1987). In 1960, fewer than 4 in 1,000 married couples in the United States were interracial couples. By 1998, this proportion had increased by more than six times to slightly more than 24 per 1,000 couples (U.S. Bureau of the Census, 1999). Although still modest overall, interracial marriage has become particularly pronounced among some segments of the population, whereas it remains very uncommon in others. For example, it is important to note that among all interracial marriages, the highest rate by far is white-Asian marriages, with the most common arrangement occurring between white men and Asian women. In fact, more than 60% of Asian women are currently marrying "out" (Qian, 2005; U.S. Bureau of the Census, 1999).

With respect to black-white marriages, we note that these unions are also strongly shaped by the intersection of race and gender (see Figure 3.1). Those involving black men and non-black women, for example, have become increasingly more common since the U.S. Supreme Court ruled that laws prohibiting interracial unions are unconstitutional (Kalmijn, 1993). In 1970, less than 1.5% of married African American men were married to non-black women, and only 1.2% of African American men were married to white women (U.S. Bureau of the Census, 1972). In comparison, according to census data, by 1990, about 4.5% of the nation's married African American men had non-black spouses, with the majority of these being white women (U.S. Bureau of the Census, 1999).[9] In contrast, marriages between African American women and non-black men, especially white men, have historically been much less common than intermarriage between African American men and non-black women. For example, census data indicate that in 1990, less than 2% of the country's married African American women had non-black spouses (U.S. Bureau of the Census, 1999), up from just 0.8% in 1970 (U.S. Bureau of the Census, 1972).

In addition, Qian (2005) notes that there are other differences in marriages between African Americans and whites. Although overall, African Americans receive less education than all other race/ethnic and gender status groups, when they do attain high levels of education, they are more likely to marry outside of their race. For example, when white women marry African American men, they "marry up" in terms of educational attainment. In other words, there are more pronounced educational differences in marriages between African American men and white women than in African American

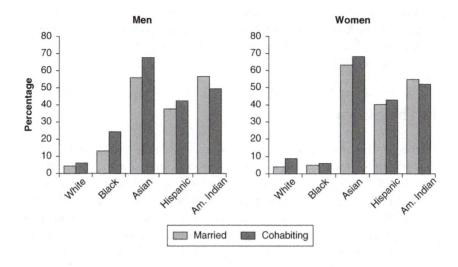

Figure 3.1   Interracial Marriage Among White and Black Americans
SOURCE: Qian (2005).

or white *intraracial* marriages (Qian, 2005). Qian goes on to suggest that this difference in educational attainment can lead to the presumption that white women are taking the best African American men out of the marriage pool, which is consistent with the beliefs that many African American women report (Qian, 2005).

Despite a variety of reasons we find for a decrease in marriage among African Americans (unemployment, incarceration, norms, and interracial marriage), interracial marriage has the *smallest* impact but is treated in the media and especially in popular magazines targeting African American women as the single most important explanation for why they remain single.

In reality, the impact of interracial marriage on the male marriage pool is relatively insignificant. Whereas 25 of every 100 African American men will spend time in prison, most during the years of family formation, only 4 in 100 will marry outside the race! Thus, the issue of interracial dating and marriage, although perhaps interesting in light of the long history of anti-miscegenation, has only the smallest actual impact on marriages between African American men and women; it contributes almost nothing to the marriage gap in the African American community. In fact, African American men and women who struggle against all of the odds presented above—male unemployment, male incarceration, female educational attainment, and female earning capacity—and do form loving, intimate partnerships overwhelmingly do so with other African Americans (Qian, 2005).

Although our sample of African American men and women is not representative of all African Americans, the reasons they give for not marrying are consistent with what the literature on marriage reports. Therefore, we use their voices to tell their stories.

In Their Own Words

Of the 40 African American men and women we interviewed, slightly more than half of the men we interviewed (11) were or had been married, whereas only 6 (30%) of the women we interviewed were or had been married. When we examined the data by including cohabitation, we found that 18 of the 20 men (90%) that we interviewed were married to or cohabiting with their female partners. Of the women, only 6 (30%) were still married to or cohabiting with their male partners. We grappled with how to explain these numbers, because they vary rather dramatically by gender, and in the case of the men, they vary dramatically from the data provided by the census.

We believe there are several structural reasons why the men in our sample were far more likely to be married and cohabiting than the women. First, our sampling technique in Minnesota was designed to identify couples. In fact, all of the women we interviewed who were married or cohabiting came from our Minnesota sample, and this is a direct result of our sampling technique. In contrast, the women we interviewed in North Carolina were all either living in the battered women's shelter or had only recently moved out. Thus, they were not likely to be living with men (they weren't living with anyone, otherwise they wouldn't be in the shelter). It's important to note here a unique aspect of conducting this kind of research. In North Carolina, when a domestic violence incident is entered into the criminal justice system or when a woman seeks shelter, one of the first things that happens is the issuing of a restraining order, a 50-B. One of the requirements of the restraining order, obviously, is that the woman not have any contact with the man and vice versa. Similarly, one of the conditions of the shelter is that the woman identifies and makes arrangements for a living situation that does not include her violent partner. Thus, like the "man in the house rule" that was an issue in welfare enforcement in the 1960s and 1970s, women in our North Carolina sample may have lied about their actual living arrangements. Although we assured them that we were not checking up on them, nor would we report their circumstances to the system (either the shelter staff or the criminal justice system), they may still have felt they needed to lie about their living situation. Thus, this measure is subject to various forms of systematic error.

Second, with regard to the men, certainly it is the case that the men in Minnesota were married or cohabiting because that's how we designed the study; thus, their overrepresentation among the married and cohabiting is a function of the study design. However, what is curious and is indeed more difficult to explain is the fact that the majority (9 out of 10) of the men we interviewed in North Carolina were also married or cohabiting. This overrepresentation stands as an intriguing question because couple status was not part of this research design, nor are there any obvious structural explanations for it (as the shelter is for the female sample). We propose that the answer lies in the influence women have on their male partners' behavior, specifically their likelihood of attending the intervention program. We know that only 50% of the men in Forsyth County, North Carolina, who are sentenced to the Time Out batterer intervention program attend (Hattery, Smith, & Williams, 2005). Perhaps those who are most likely to attend (and thus be available for our sample) are those who are still living with (either by marriage or cohabitation) the women they battered. It may be that one condition these women make for the relationship to continue is that the men attend the intervention program. This would explain the high rate of marriage and cohabitation among the men we interviewed in North Carolina.

In our interviews, we found that the lack of romantic relationships was a constant theme among the women. One would reasonably assume, as we did, that a woman who has survived one or even several battering relationships would have had enough of men, at least for a while, and would be content to get her own life together and be single. Yet without fail, when we asked, at the end of each interview, what the women saw in their future, every one of them answered that she would like to find a man.

AH: How would it be to not be with a guy? I mean, would you envision five years from now, you're still not with a guy? Or do you really feel like you're just one of those people that needs to be with a guy?

Sheri: That's how I feel 'cause I've always been with somebody. I've never been alone. (Sheri, 20-something African American woman, North Carolina)

Second, there is the issue referred to as the "feminization of poverty." As a result of many structural forces, from gendered wage discrimination to the responsibilities associated with childbearing and childrearing, even when women are employed full-time, they earn less, on average, than their male counterparts. Thus, women who are not in marital or cohabiting relationships with men are more likely to find themselves living in poverty (see Rich, 1980, 1995, for a lengthy discussion of the economic compulsion for marriage and heterosexuality).

The women in our study indicated that they wanted to be in a relationship with a man, and most of them were living in poverty and thus in need of the financial support of a male partner, so why didn't they marry or cohabit? The two primary reasons were male unemployment and incarceration. If, as Rich argues, it is "being attached to a man" and his wages that compel women to marry (or, as we argue in the contemporary United States, cohabit) then both male unemployment and incarceration (sometimes conflated) negate one or both of the reasons women marry in the first place. Thus, rather than propelling women toward marriage or cohabitation, these forces, as they exist in the world of African American men, exist as barriers to marriage and partnership.

This is different from thinking about the issue as one of an inadequate marriage pool in that Rich suggests something more pragmatic and rational. If what women get from marriage is primarily access to wages and status (in that no woman wants to be an old maid), and if neither of these can be conferred in a relationship, then the question is not "Why not marry?" but rather "Why bother marrying?"

For decades, some scholars have looked at the outcomes of not marrying, especially on women and children (e.g., see Gordon, 1988). More recently, however, research has focused specifically on two key outcomes of marital status for children: financial support and cohabitation. McLanahan and Sandefur (1994), in their study of single-parent, primarily female-headed households, note that the most significant negative outcome for children in female-headed households is poverty.

When children in female-headed households receive adequate financial contributions from their fathers, there are few significant differences between their own life chances and those of children raised in two-parent households. Furthermore, McLanahan and Sandefur (1994) note that legal marriage is not as strong a predictor of child well-being as is the involvement of the father or a male figure in the child's life. This involvement, coupled with his financial support, significantly reduces the childhood risks that are typically associated with single-parent households. Finally, they and others note that stable cohabitations may be as healthy for children as are legal marriages. This finding is important because the trend, especially among younger Americans and across most of Western Europe, toward long-term cohabitation indicates that in some geographic regions and among some populations, cohabitation is replacing legalized marriage. (We note, for example, that marriage rates in Sweden have dropped below 50%. Most adults enter long-term cohabiting relationships that look in every other way like marriages, except for the presence of the legal contract.)

We concluded every interview by asking the women what they saw in their futures, specifically with regard to male partners. We wondered if they would seek new relationships or if they would take some time to be single and get their lives together. We wondered if they planned to seek out relationships, and if so, what they would look for in a man. To a one, they all indicated that they wanted a man who was employed and had not been in jail. In their vernacular:

"A man with a J-O-B and NO FEL-ONY!"

Why did all of the women plan to seek out men who were employed and had not been incarcerated? When we probed, we learned that they associated the problems in their relationships, including the violence, with both unemployment and incarceration.

Unemployment and Underemployment: Ronny and Tammy

Most of the men and women we interviewed associated male unemployment with tensions and conflicts in their marriages and relationships. Ronny, who was caught in the cycle of fast-food employment, was often unemployed. Fast-food employment is tenuous at best; Eric Schlosser notes that the typical fast-food employee turns over every 6–7 months (Schlosser, 2002). Although Ronny rose to the ranks of assistant manager in one or two restaurants, his wages remained low and he was subjected to the rigid rules of fast-food employment. Ronny lost his job as assistant manager at a Wendy's because he ate a hamburger on the job. He clearly identified the relationship between his unemployment or underemployment and the conflicts in his marriage:

> Sometimes we didn't even have food to eat, so you know, we was eating like food she would bring home from work, or scrapping food like every day or something like that. And then you know, as them problems like that, we started to get into fights. (Ronny, 28-year-old African American man, Minnesota)

Incarceration, Drugs, and Unemployment: Will and Stella and Wanda and Chris

Men (and women) who have been incarcerated find it nearly impossible to find employment, especially the kind of employment we associate with the male role of breadwinner: employment that pays a living wage and is stable. Like Ronny, Will had a variety of jobs working in the fast-food industry.

Both Will and Chris struggled to remain employed because they both had prison records. (In fact, we interviewed Chris in jail.) In addition, both men struggled with drug addiction. Chris's was more mild in that he used marijuana, whereas Will's was very severe—he was addicted to crack and had been for 30 years. Both Will's and Chris's partners (Stella and Wanda, respectively) noted that the problems in their relationships were—as they perceived them—a direct result of the unemployment of their men.

For the first few years of their relationship, Will held down jobs in fast food, rising at one point to the rank of assistant manager at Kentucky Fried Chicken. However, as Stella notes, his drug habit got so severe that "Yeah, he was still working. But it was getting to the point where he was getting so bad that there were some days he couldn't go in to work." Within a few years of getting together, Will stopped working for good and spent his days focused on his next fix.

AH: Is he working now?

Stella: No. I pay everything. I pay . . . and I even said that out loud in front of him. I said, I said it to one of my friends. I said, why should he leave? He doesn't contribute anything to the house. I said, I pay the rent. I pay the rent. I pay the utilities. He drives my car. I put the gas in. I pay everything for the kids. I do the cooking and cleaning. Why should he leave? He's got it made. You know. And it's sad that I can realize that and I know I'm being used, but I just can't take that final step and I think it's because of the kids. They love him so much, but it's even gotten to the point where they'll say, dad's not here again. He's out with his friends. Or why can't dad do something with us? You know.

AH: But he's not working.

Stella: No. He's not working and even when he does, it's not going to make a difference 'cause his money is his money. He understands nothing about budgets, about this needs to be paid. This needs to be paid because he knows he's going to get paid tomorrow for this. He's already made plans with what he's going to do.

AH: He's pretty much just going to smoke up his money.

Stella: Yeah. Pretty much . . . (Stella, 20-something African American woman, Minnesota)

Wanda and Chris's relationship was similar. Chris blamed his inability to keep a job on his prison record. At one point, Chris had a job as a security guard. "I was working too, doing this little security job. Once they found I had a felony, they let me go." Chris is also partially blind as a result of glaucoma and this also affected his ability to find and keep a job. For example, he had worked for awhile at a car wash but was fired when he continued to miss entire sides of cars because of his visual impairment. His partner, Wanda, is very clear that his inability to contribute financially to the household is a source of conflict in their relationship. After a stint in jail, during which time Wanda developed friendships with other men, Chris returned home and told Wanda that he didn't want these men in their house. She responded,

> My house. I'm paying all the bills. I'm talking about rent, gas, light, phone, cable, everything. Everything. Everything. I even buy his deodorant, okay? So who are you? "I don't want nobody around my woman." All this and that, this and that. "What you want with my woman? Don't be calling my house!" But this is his house he say. I'm like, I said, "Mother fucker, this ain't your damn house. This is my mother-fucking house! You can get the fuck out!" So now I'm mad. Now I'm like get the hell out. So you know, now I really get angry. So now, you know, I'm not drinking at this point because there's no use to have a drink because when you so angry, you can't enjoy it. So now, really, I got hell in me now. I'm at, I'm at the end. Right. Okay. So now he got his people all up in Minneapolis, St. Paul, everywhere—Tennessee, calling me, please help Chris. Please help Chris. Please help Chris. I say, ya'll going, ya'll need to get Chris a place and pay him some rent somewhere. (Wanda, 40-something African American woman, Minnesota)

Thus, we argue that in the context of the "marriageable pool" identified by Wilson and others, and the context of compulsory heterosexuality identified by Rich, it is not surprising that we see such low rates of marriage in the African American community. The women we interviewed did not see anything positive that the men in their lives were bringing to the table, which is consistent with the belief that marriage has often been described as a system of economic exchange. And although the women obviously put up with the men despite their inability to get a job, their drug use, and their lack of contributions to the household when they were in cohabiting relationships, they did not see any reason to legally marry. The women understood the structural constraints of unemployment and incarceration on their relationships and on their probability of marrying in similar ways to the family sociologists who theorize about the living conditions of women like these.

Race, Class, and Gender Analysis

Here we underscore the importance of interpreting marriage data within the context of a theoretical framework such as the race, class, and gender paradigm. Although we argued in our previous discussion that interracial marriages have only a minimal effect on the marriageable pool problem identified by Wilson and others, we do note that there are distinct race/gender patterns in interracial marriage that must be considered. For example, the census data cited earlier demonstrate that African American men are five times more likely to marry outside the race than are African American women (10% compared to less than 2%). We also note that both unemployment rates and incarceration rates are significantly higher among African American men than any other race/gender segment of the population, which, as we noted, tend to depress marriage rates among African Americans. Thus, taken together, these two forces significantly influence the marriageable pool and significantly depress the marriage rates for African American women as compared to all other race/gender status groups.

If Rich is correct—that the primary reason most women have for marrying is economic security—then *in the aggregate,* women of any race who marry white men have, on average, a great deal to gain. But again, in the aggregate, women of any race who marry African American men have, on average, less to gain, and in fact, they may have something to lose. For example, the data in Table 8.5 illustrate that although marriage provides some insulation from poverty regardless of race, married African Americans are still significantly more likely to live in poverty than are married whites. In other words, race still matters. It is only when we analyze all of these illustrations through the lens provided by the RCG paradigm that the particular race/gender patterns in marriage in the contemporary United States can be understood.

Summary: Outcomes of the Low Marriage Rate

In summary, we conclude that there are several negative outcomes associated with the low rates of marriage in the African American community.

1. The first, as noted by Patterson (1999), is the fact that adult African American men and women are less likely to be partnered than their white counterparts. The loss or absence of relationship is significant and affects the majority of African American men and women.

2. Low rates of marriage in the African American community result in a high percentage of African American children growing up in single-parent households. There is no question that the absence of fathers has a negative effect on their children. Children who grow up without the presence of a father in their lives have a gap in terms of their relationships with adults (it reduces the number they may have), in terms of available role models, and so on.

3. The feminization of poverty is a real problem facing African American women. In fact, three fourths of households with children headed by single

African American women live in poverty. Thus, one of the clearest and perhaps most devastating outcomes of low marriage rates among African Americans is the poverty of the women and their children. Even with the severe job and wage discrimination experienced by African American men (women also experience this), the additional income that men could bring into a household would improve the life chances of their children.

However, we do want to draw attention to the fact that cohabitation may be replacing legalized marriage in the African American community as it is in countries like Sweden. If this is the case, the loss or absence of marriage may not be as significant as Patterson implies. Although there are differences in cohabitation as compared to marriage, these differences—such as rights of inheritance, slightly lower stability, and so on—do not seem to result in people being alone. This is true with regard to children as well. There may be very little difference for children if their father is present as a husband as compared to as a partner. The most important point is that fathers are present for their children. Furthermore, although a cohabiting partner may not have legal rights to financial resources, many cohabiting couples do share financial resources just as married couples do. The only exception may be that upon the death of one partner, the financial assets will not transfer automatically to the surviving partner, and thus legal documents, such as a will, must be prepared in order for this type of transfer to take place.

Therefore, we conclude this chapter by noting that much more attention needs to be paid to comparing the outcomes of long-term cohabiting relationships and legal marriages on the life chances of African American men, women, and children. We offer some recommendations to increase the rate of marriage among African American men and women.

Solutions

- Encourage and support marriages; make this an attractive family option.
- Increase the minimum wage to a living wage so that men and women who are employed can keep themselves and their families out of poverty.
- Reduce the number of African American men who are incarcerated for low-level drug offenses. This would improve the male marriageable pool as well as increase the likelihood that African American fathers would be able to be employed (because they would not be in prison) and thus they would be able to provide financial support for their children.

In the next chapter, we will continue our discussion of family formation by examining patterns of childbearing in African American families.

Notes

1. See, in particular, the remarks of public figures such as Rush Limbaugh and Newt Gingrich.

2. The Supreme Court ruling *Loving v. Virginia* (1967) rendered antimiscegenation laws unconstitutional. However, these laws still existed and were enforced in some states until the early 1970s.

3. We do not mean here that women did not work for pay; many did, but more often than not they were not employed in the public sphere. African American women, for example, were most likely to work as domestics in the homes of whites, and thus they did not have access to the power associated with the market economy of the public sphere.

4. We note here that it is typical that the lives, beliefs, and practices of minorities have constantly been compared to white Americans. We do not mean to imply here that we are making that kind of comparison. Rather, we note that among *all* women, historically, African American women have had significantly higher rates of labor force participation than any other group of women, thus the use of the term *non-normative*.

5. Hattery (2001b) discusses this at length in her examination of the disconnect between women's attempts at balancing work and family and the ideologies they hold about motherhood.

6. For a review of the struggles of welfare mothers to live by the rules of welfare, see Edin and Lein's *Making Ends Meet* (1997). They demonstrate that it is virtually impossible to live off of welfare while adhering strictly to the requirements of no man in the household, no employment, and so on.

7. However, we note that cohabiting couples clearly do not have access to many of the tax advantages and benefit advantages associated with marriage.

8. We suggest the same loosening of gender role ideologies for men and women of all races/ethnicities, including whites. Rigid gender role ideology is associated with many other negative aspects of intimate relationships, most notably violence (see Hattery, in press-a).

9. Wilson (1987) explores these trends using a different technique, examining marriage license data. His analysis confirms the same trend.

4

Childbearing and Childrearing Patterns

The centrality of children in this lower-class worldview of what is important and meaningful in life stands in striking contrast to their low priority in the view of more affluent teens and twenty-something youth, who may want children at some point in the future, but only after an education, career, and other life goals have been achieved. Putting motherhood first makes sense in a social context where the achievements that middle-class youth see as their birthright are little more than pipe dreams: Children offer a tangible source of meaning, while other avenues for gaining social esteem and personal satisfaction appear vague and tenuous.

—Edin and Kefalas (2005), p. 49

Objectives

- Use empirical data to examine the patterns of childbearing: marital, nonmarital, and teen among African Americans.
- Use the race, class, and gender paradigm to analyze differences in nonmarital and teen childbearing, between African Americans and whites.
- Understand the role that community norms play in contributing to higher rates of teen childbearing.

- Examine the outcomes, both positive and negative, of higher rates of nonmarital childbearing, especially to teens, in African American families.
- Identify solutions to the negative outcomes associated with high rates of nonmarital childbearing.

Introduction

Tied in with lower marriage rates for African Americans is a high percentage of African American children raised in single-parent, most often female-headed households. This high rate is a result of both divorce (more common in white families) and nonmarital childbearing. Bumpass and Sweet argued that by the early 2000s, half of all children in the United States would spend at least some time living in single-parent households (Bumpass & Sweet, 1989). What they may not have predicted was that nearly 3 out of 4 babies born to African American mothers would be born into single-parent households. In this chapter, we will explore childbearing and childrearing patterns in African American families.

Childbearing Patterns

One of the most frequently discussed and problematic issues surrounding the African American family is the issue of teen childbearing. Teen pregnancy has become problematized first with the implementation of mandatory schooling until age 18 and then with the overall rise in the age of first marriage, which is now around 24 years old for women.

In addition, we know that teens are getting pregnant earlier and earlier, some as early as age 14, as compared to the typical 18 or 19 years old that was common at the turn of the 20th century. Furthermore, most teen mothers at the turn of the 20th century were married; now, most who give birth are not. In fact, the issue that seems to trouble most Americans is not teen pregnancy itself, but the separation of childbearing from marriage, especially among young women. Although marriage and childbearing continue to co-exist in the contemporary United States, the low marriage rate among African American women results in a situation in which, more often than not, babies born to African American women are nonmarital births, whether the mother is a teen or an adult. Because there is some overlap in teen births and nonmarital births, people often use the terms interchangeably. However, this is problematic because each phenomenon has distinct causes and consequences. Thus, we use the term *teen pregnancy* when we mean teenagers who become pregnant, *teen childbearing* when we mean teenagers who give

Table 4.1   Teen Pregnancy Rates (Girls aged 15–19 years)

African Americans	Whites
58.8/1,000	27.4/1,000

SOURCE: Dye (2005).

birth, and *nonmarital births* when we mean births to unmarried women of any age. When the two co-exist, we will use the terms together.

We begin by examining the most controversial of the many issues involved in childbearing: teen pregnancy. The most current data available from the U.S. census (Current Population Survey) are listed in Table 4.1.

According to the Alan Guttmacher Institute (2004), teen pregnancy has been steadily declining over the past 30 years, but census data indicate that African American teenagers are still becoming pregnant at alarming rates and that African Americans are more than twice as likely to become pregnant as teenagers than are whites. To put these rates in context, we note that teen pregnancy rates, among both African Americans and whites, are significantly higher in the United States than in any other postindustrial society (Alan Guttmacher Institute, 1996). This is important because there are several negative outcomes associated with teen pregnancy and childbearing, some of which affect only the mother, some only the baby, and some both mother and child. In this section, we will examine some of the serious negative consequences associated with teen pregnancy and childbearing: medical outcomes, poverty, school completion, child abuse, and incarceration.

Medical Outcomes

There are several negative medical outcomes associated with teen pregnancy and childbirth. First, teenagers are far more likely to give birth to low birth weight babies. In 2002, 13.5% of infants born to mothers under age 15 years weighed less than 2,500 grams, compared with only 6.9% of infants born to women aged 25–29 years (Martin et al., 2002). Because low birth weight is associated with both physical and developmental problems, teen pregnancy poses a risk to the life of the baby as well as increasing the risk of long-term, costly problems for both the mother and the taxpayer. For example, many low birth weight babies require significantly longer hospital stays, and often in the neonatal intensive care unit (Martin et al., 2002). This type of specialized care is very expensive. Low birth weight babies are also more likely to develop more slowly, especially cognitively. As a result, they often end up in special classrooms or requiring educational services that are expensive (Maynard, 1996).

Finally, we note that low birth weight is also associated with infant mortality; thus, teen pregnancy contributes to the overall higher infant mortality rate that we see in the United States as opposed to other developing nations (Martin et al., 2002). (See Appendix C for international infant mortality rates.)

School Completion and Consequent Poverty

Second, teen childbearing is strongly associated with poverty. Girls who give birth in their teen years are less likely to finish high school and significantly less likely to get any postsecondary education, and as a result, they find it hard to secure employment that pays a living wage. Thus, they are more likely to rely on the bare bones that welfare supplies them (Hoffman, Foster, & Furstenberg, 1993; Moore et al., 1993; Rangaragan, Myers, Maynard, & Beebout, 1994).

> Just over half of teenage mothers complete high school during adolescence and early adulthood; many who complete high school do so with only an alternative credential—the General Educational Development (GED) certificate (Cameron & Heckman, 1993; Murnane, Willett, & Boudett, 1995; Webster & Weeks, 1995). . . . Among those who do complete regular high school, they have very minimal basic skills (Nord, Moore, Morrison, Brown, & Myers, 1992; Strain & Kisker, 1989). (Rangaragan et al., 1994, p. 18)

Because employment over the life course is significantly tied to education and experience, the likelihood of living in poverty does not decline as the mother herself ages. In fact,

> . . . more than 40 percent of teenage moms report living in poverty at age 27. . . . The rates are especially high among black and Hispanic adolescent mothers, more than half of whom end up in poverty and two-thirds of whom find themselves on welfare. (Moore et al., 1993, p. 393)

Also, "more than 80 percent of young teen mothers received welfare during the 10 years following the birth of their first child, 44 percent of them for more than 5 years" (Jacobson & Maynard, 1995, p. 10).

Reliance on Welfare and Problems for the Teen Mother and Her Children

The welfare reform bill signed into law under the Clinton administration (1996) was heralded as major progress for the poor and for society. It was designed to reduce the development of long-term, debilitating dependence on welfare. It was also designed to break the cycle of welfare families. The new welfare system, known as TANF (Temporary Aid to Needy Families), has had both positive and negative outcomes. Among the positive outcomes was the fact that welfare receipt was no longer tied to either gender or single parenthood. Low-income single fathers can now receive welfare benefits and two-parent low-income families can as well (thus negating the "man in the house rule" discussed in Chapter 3). However, it has also had some very problematic outcomes, among them the strict time limits on welfare receipt. Families are now limited to 24 months of continuous welfare and a lifetime cap of 5 years of total welfare receipt.

Tammy's Story

One of the authors saw firsthand the highly problematic outcome of this time limit through the eyes of a student on welfare. Her story serves to illustrate the effects not only on single mothers but also on those escaping intimate partner violence.

I met Tammy in August 1996 when I was teaching at a large state institution and she was just beginning her senior year. Tammy was enrolled in my sociology of gender course, and once she became comfortable, she began to share with me, and subsequently with the class, her struggles as a single mother who had escaped a battering relationship. She was raising two young children and going to school. Her dream: to get a good job and make a better life for her son and daughter. At the time, Tammy was on welfare. She received Section 8 housing, a voucher that allowed her to live in an apartment that rented for $500 per month (she paid only $125 of the monthly rent and the voucher paid the remainder). She received a child care subsidy that allowed her to put her two children into a high-quality day care while she attended classes and studied. Again, like the housing voucher, she paid only a small portion of the day care tuition. She also received food stamps and a monthly cash payment, what was referred to at the time as Aid to Families with Dependent Children. She was to graduate with a bachelor's degree in sociology in May 1997.

In early November 1996, as the cold weather settled in, Tammy arrived in my office one morning in a panic. Following the passing of the 1996 welfare reform legislation, Tammy had been called in by her caseworker to discuss the implementation of the new welfare policies (TANF). Because of the rule that limited continuous receipt of welfare to 2 years, the state in which we lived had passed a law that prohibited full-time students pursuing degrees in 4-year colleges from receiving any welfare. Why? The logic of the lawmakers was that a student who began a 4-year degree program while on welfare would need twice the limit (4 years rather than 2) of welfare support in order to complete the degree. Cutting students off after 2 years (of both welfare and college) would leave students without any credentials. Thus, they allowed welfare recipients to enroll in technical schools and 2-year colleges (that result in an associate's degree) but prohibited their enrollment in 4-year degree programs.

Despite the fact that Tammy had less than 7 months until she graduated with a 4-year degree and would presumably be able to move off of welfare and into work, the welfare office offered her a choice: She could stay enrolled and graduate in May but lose her welfare, or she could keep her welfare and enroll in a 2-year degree program or a technical school. She put it to me this way: "They'll let me keep my welfare if I enroll in cosmetology school, but if I stay here at XY University, I will lose my welfare!"[1]

Thus, the problem of teen mothers completing their education, a difficult task under the circumstances, becomes nearly impossible because of the welfare reform of 1996. Teen mothers, who are more than twice as likely to be African American, will find it virtually impossible to attend college and earn the credential that will ultimately lift them out of poverty and allow them to leave the welfare system. All of this is in the face of strong empirical evidence that shows that educational attainment is significantly correlated with higher wages and that this effect is even more significant for African American women than for other race/gender groups (Padavic & Reskin, 2002).

Child Abuse

Some evidence also suggests that teen mothers are more likely to engage in child abuse. This is most likely related to a variety of factors, including mother's education; her access to financial and stress-reducing resources (parenting classes, baby-sitting relief); her lack of training for parenting; and her own likelihood of having grown up in an abusive relationship (Gordon, 1988). As Maynard (1997) notes,

> Children born to young teen mothers are much more likely to be indicated victims of abuse and neglect than those born to non-teen mothers. And new families in which the mother's age was under 18 at the time of first birth are also much more likely to become an indicated case of child abuse and neglect than other families. . . . Data also show that once a child is in foster care, the duration of the foster care placement is higher for children of young teen mothers than for other children. (p. 205)

Some of the negative consequences or outcomes of teen childbearing are a result of the stresses involved with raising children. Many of the professionals who deal with teen mothers argue that outcomes such as child abuse are predictable when we consider the cognitive and emotional maturity of most teenagers, who are also more likely to engage in reckless behavior (binge drinking, unsafe driving, high-risk sex). These tendencies certainly play out in their childrearing practices as well.

Probability of Incarceration for Children Born to Teen Mothers

Finally, children born to teen mothers are "almost three times as likely to be behind bars at some point in their adolescence or early 20s as are the children of mothers who delayed childbearing" (Maynard, 1997, p. 18). Maynard notes that this finding remains even after controlling for "important" background factors. There are so many reasons why the children of teen mothers are more likely to go to prison, such as the higher probability that they are raised in poverty; that they may experience abuse and live in abusive households; and that they may spend time being shuffled from one household to another, even living in foster care. Prison has a devastating effect on families and communities, and we need to identify societal solutions to the current state of mass incarceration in our society. Reducing the prevalence of teen childbearing is one avenue to pursue.

Nonmarital Births

Nonmarital childbearing is not, in and of itself, terribly problematic. What is, as noted by McLanahan and Sandefur (1994), are the outcomes associated with the absence of the father. In other words, children who are raised with two parents who are not married are barely distinguishable from children raised in two-parent families. The distinction that really needs to be made is the presence or absence of a father figure.[2]

Today, 68% of African American babies are born to unmarried mothers (Alan Guttmacher Institute, 2004). Unfortunately, the majority of these babies are also born to women who have little to no contact with the child's father. Only about one third of the fathers in these situations have regular contact with their children, another third have intermittent contact, and the remaining fathers have no involvement whatsoever (Maynard, Nicholson, & Rangarajan, 1993). Moreover, the father's rate of contact and support declines substantially over time. This is problematic in two key ways: the lack of emotional support and socialization provided by a father and the lack of his financial support (McLanahan & Sandefur, 1994). The lack of contact with the father may lead to a lack of supervision for the child (while mothers are at work, for example, and can't secure child care), which increases the likelihood of deviant behavior on the part of the child[3] as well as the likelihood that young children will be in danger. It also leads to difficulties with discipline when only one parent is there to enforce rules. And, it reduces the available role models for the child, especially the kind of role modeling associated with work (men are more likely to be employed than women) and masculinity (see Hattery, in press-a).

Key to the issue of male role modeling is the fact that boys often rely on the men in their homes to teach them how to become men. Male role models play a very powerful role in the socialization of young men. When this role modeling is positive, it must be encouraged, and opportunities for it must be created. When it is negative, it must be eliminated, and other individuals must be identified who can provide positive role modeling. This confirms the findings of scholars who note the importance of father involvement on the socialization of children, especially boys (McLanahan & Sandefur, 1994).

The lack of financial support by fathers has devastating consequences for the children of unmarried mothers. As a result of this lack of financial support, 39% of female-headed households are below the poverty line, and 67% live 200% below the poverty line (DeNavas-Walt, Proctor, & Mills, 2004). Children who are born into and raised in single-parent households, especially when the financial support of the father is not present, are disproportionately likely to grow up in poverty. The data in Table 8.5 illustrate the role that family form has on the likelihood that children will live in poverty. We note that the probability that a child will live in poverty is shaped by both family form *and* gender. When children are raised in male-headed single-parent households, they are less likely to live in poverty than when they live in female-headed single-parent households.

Thinking about the poverty data another way, 4 out of 10 African American children will be on welfare and another 40% will be among the working poor—those who are not quite poor enough to receive welfare (DeNavas-Walt et al., 2004). In practical terms, this means that 8 out of 10 African American children will live in substandard housing, suffer from food insecurity, attend the poorest schools, and have only limited access to the opportunity structure (see Kozol, 1992, 2001, for descriptions of children raised in these conditions). When half of all African American children will grow up in poverty, having to depend on some type of social welfare for survival, and when 80% of African American children will suffer during *some period* of their childhoods with *some* of the outcomes of being poor, we are indeed in a state of crisis, and we argue that this crisis has become a national emergency.

Where Are the Fathers?

Although there are a variety of reasons why fathers choose not to be involved in the lives of their children, there are at least three structural causes that limit the involvement of African American men: homicide, incarceration, and unemployment. Homicide consistently ranks among the top 10 causes of death for all African American men, with the highest rate being for young men ages 18–34 who are also at the age when they are most likely to be the fathers of young children (National Center for Health Statistics, 2004). Furthermore, nearly one in three African American men spends some portion of their lives being incarcerated. They leave upwards of 5 million children behind, most of whom are living with the child's mother. Both of these phenomena leave African American men unable to have regular contact with their children, even when they desire to. Finally, all three of these situations—incarceration, homicide, and chronic unemployment, which stands at about 15% for African American men—seriously impede the ability of African American men to provide financially for their children.

We do note that these situations do not account for fathers who simply choose not to participate in their children's lives or provide for them financially, regardless of their marital status. And certainly, we acknowledge that so-called deadbeat dads exist among men of all race/ethnicities. We further acknowledge that there are many examples in all communities of fathers who are involved with their children; in fact, there has been a slight increase in the number of single-parent households that are headed by fathers (U.S. Bureau of the Census, 2003).

In order to explore this growing phenomenon, we interviewed many African American men who were very involved in raising their children. In some cases, they were even raising the children of their female partners.

Hank is a 30-something African American man living in Minnesota. He has fathered many children, and the oldest live with their mother in Chicago. Although he sends money to them, he is not able to be involved in their everyday lives. Like many men, he is attempting to reverse this trend and is currently raising his youngest two sons by himself. He is also raising the son of his female partner, who, at the time of the interview, was serving a 9-month prison sentence for check forgery.

ES: So you have three boys that you're raising, without this woman. You work at night?

Hank: Working night shift. [Hank is a security guard. He works the night shift in order to balance work and taking care of his family, a popular strategy in today's service economy as documented by Hattery

(2001a, 2001b).] The oldest kind of watch over my two sons. The oldest boy. The boy is smart as hell. Right now he's in his second year of high school and he's taking college classes. So, if I was to ask him. He got a D. Pull that D out. I don't, like, you're an A student. The next semester, it says A or B. It all depends on, why, I don't curse, I don't even understand his homework, so I can't help him with his homework. I mean, it's too advanced for me, algebra, I mean, I don't know none of that crap. You're done with your homework? Okay, good, fine. You know. I don't understand it. And he's book-bound. He's a book addict. Always in a book, always in the library. I don't have to worry about the oldest boy. The oldest boy does not get in trouble. He's like gold. All I do is give him his allowance a week . . .

AH: So you feel comfortable he can keep a handle on the others.

Hank: Right. I call home now. I definitely call home. And then, my younger son, he's thankful that I came and got him 'cause when I get home I see a poster that he made. Dad, I love you. Oh, my son, my son. Call me about eleven times a night. Dad, when you getting off of work and when you coming home and this that and the other. I mean, that boy he's something else. I'm so proud that he's with me you know. I'm not going to put him back in that environment again. They free from all that aggravation and misery they was, their momma was, and they know that the reason they don't want to go back is because they know what they going back to. (Hank, 30-something African American man, Minnesota)

Although we acknowledge the many good fathers in the African American community, what we are primarily concerned with is not the individual choices that men make to be involved or not as fathers, but rather the structural impediments to the father-child relationship that affect millions of African American men and their children. Together, these structural impediments account for a large part of the reason why too many African American children have only intermittent contact with their fathers. Thus, as we consider proposals designed to increase the role of African American men in the lives of their children, we must address issues of homicide, incarceration, and unemployment, all of which affect young African American men disproportionately.

Nonmarital Teen Childbearing

Not all teen mothers are unwed, and simultaneously, only a small fraction of nonmarital births are to teens, yet when these two situations occur simultaneously, the negative outcomes of each are compounded.

Many risks for mother, child, and community are associated with teen childbearing. Maynard (1996) notes that teen mothers are unlikely to wed the fathers because the fathers are typically older (not teens themselves) and in a different life stage. Although one might conclude that this means the fathers are more financially and emotionally stable, she notes that it does not necessarily translate into more support for the children. Statistics from the Congressional Budget Office (1990) are illustrative:

> They generally are not a consistent source of support for the teenage mothers or their children. Only 20 to 30 percent marry the mother of their child, and only about 20 percent of the nonresident fathers are ordered by the court to pay child support. Those with orders pay only a small fraction of the award amount. (p. 28)

Thus, the problems associated with nonmarital births to teens are more severe than to either teens who marry or single mothers in their 20s and 30s.

The data in Table 4.2 suggest that the major trend in the past 30 years is the shifting of teen pregnancy from marital to nonmarital births (Moore, Papillo, & Manlove, 2003; Wertheimer & Moore, 1998). There is some evidence that births to teen mothers are also occurring to younger and younger mothers. Whereas in 1960, teen mothers were more likely to be at least 17 years old, we now see a rise in the number of births to girls aged 14–16. In 1960, 16% of teen births were nonmarital, but by 1996, 76% of teen births were nonmarital (Wertheimer & Moore, 1998), and by 2003, this rate had risen to 80% (Moore et al., 2003). This is a disturbing trend because it intensifies the negative impacts associated with both teen childbearing and nonmarital childbearing.

Most of these mothers (and their children) end up on welfare, at a rate of 84%, with most remaining on welfare "for more than 5 of the 10 years following the birth of their first child" (Maynard, 1997, p. 18). The high poverty rates are accompanied by numerous other life-complicating factors,

Table 4.2   Marital Status and Childbearing, 2005

All Women	Percent of All Births
Marital Status	
Married	68
Unmarried	32
Race	
Nonmarital births to white women	25
Nonmarital births to African American women	68
Nonmarital births to Hispanic women	32

SOURCE: Dye (2005).

some caused by the poverty and some contributing to its perpetuation. Teenage parents are disproportionately concentrated in poor, often racially segregated communities characterized by inferior housing, high crime, poor schools, and limited health services (Maynard, 1997). Again, data from the Congressional Budget Office (1990) are illustrative:

> Teen mothers are also unlikely to be getting support from other family members or relatives, only 30% of single parent teens live with an adult relative and less than one-third receive any financial support . . . including informal support from the nonresident fathers of their children. (p. 20)

Finally, we note that data indicate that early childbearing is associated with higher fertility (Martin et al., 2002). The commonly understood reason for this is that women who begin childbearing early have more years of fertility ahead of them, and because they generally have less education and are less likely to be employed, they experience fewer barriers to continuing to have children. For example, women with more education and more involvement in the labor market often perceive additional children as inhibitors to their professional aspirations. These women have the lowest fertility among all women. (For a lengthier discussion of this, see Hattery, 2001b). This was confirmed by our interviews. Several of our respondents who had started their childbearing in their teen years had five or more children. Chris, for example, has 10 children, and Demetrius, at age 20, has six. C, who had her first child at 16, was, by her early 30s, a mother of six. This is yet another piece of evidence that suggests that the consequences of teen childbearing are long term and serious. And because women who begin childbearing early have higher rates of fertility, this suggests that the negative consequences of nonmarital teen childbearing will be experienced by many children.

Why Have a Baby?

All of this begs the question, Why do unmarried teenage girls have babies? The answers to this question are complex and often unpopular. As sociologists, we are concerned primarily with the structural rather than the individual answers to this question. We will examine the roles of sexual activity, the opportunity structure, norms, and finally the impact of sexual abuse and premature sexuality as explanations for the question, Why have a baby?

Sexual Activity

The obvious reason why teenagers are having babies is, first and foremost, because they are having sex, generally at younger ages and at higher rates than in the past.

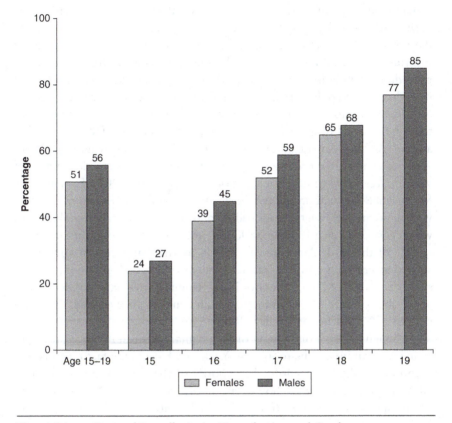

Figure 4.1   Rates of Sexually Active Teens by Age and Gender

SOURCE: Alan Guttmacher Institute (1994).

As the data in Figure 4.1 demonstrate, by the time they reach age 17, more than half of girls and 60% of boys are sexually active. By the late 1990s, the majority (78%) of teens were using contraception at the instance of first intercourse, but 20% were not. Furthermore, according to the Alan Guttmacher Institute (1994), teens are less likely than adult women to practice consistent, uninterrupted contraceptive use across the whole year. There are several predictors of teenage contraceptive use, including acknowledgment of sexual activity, access to contraception, knowledge about contraception, and religious beliefs. We note here that contraception is expensive and is not covered by Medicaid.[4] Thus, one explanation for the higher rate of teen pregnancy among African American girls (as compared to their white counterparts) may be the accessibility and affordability of contraception. That some of these sexually active teens get pregnant is not surprising.

Laws regarding the confidentiality of medical procedures, especially those performed on patients under the age of 18, make it difficult to estimate the rate of teenage abortions; however, according to the Alan Guttmacher Institute (1994), 40% of teens who become pregnant undergo an abortion procedure. Data indicate that African American teens are two to three times more likely to have had an abortion than their white counterparts (Centers for Disease Control and Prevention, 2000), but they are also two to three times more likely to get pregnant. In fact, data from the CDC indicate that among African American and white teens who get pregnant, African American teens are *more likely* to give birth to their children, indicating that they are *less likely* to have an abortion (Martin et al., 2002). Explanations for this race gap in abortion may be due to individual choice, norms[5] (which we will discuss below), religious beliefs, and access. First-trimester abortions, which cost between $400 and $800, are not covered by Medicaid (a consequence of the Hyde Amendment),[6] which means that access to abortion is shaped severely not only by social class but also by race. In addition, a recent survey finds that 87% of counties in the United States have no identifiable abortion provider, and when metropolitan counties are excluded, the figure rises to 97% (Mueller & Dudley, 2003).

Although we most often think of the pregnant African American teenager as living in an urban ghetto in New York or Chicago, the fact remains that according to the U.S. Census, the majority of the African American population (54.8%) lives in the South—primarily in Alabama, Mississippi, and Louisiana—where access to abortion and contraception is severely limited. For example, there is only one abortion clinic in the entire state of Mississippi (in Jackson). And because the South, especially the Deep South, is primarily rural, most African American women do not live in a county with an abortion clinic, and many, in fact, live hundreds of miles from the closest clinic. Therefore, these data suggest that one reason that African American teenagers may be having babies is because they have limited (or no) access to contraception or abortion.

The Economy/Opportunity Structure

Many scholars have explored the role that the economy plays in decisions about marriage and childbearing (e.g., see Wilson, 1987, 1996). For decades, sociologists have argued that when the economy is good, marriage and fertility rates are higher. Think of the Baby Boom generation that followed World War II. Soldiers returned to a booming industrialized economy, they went to college and bought homes under the G.I. Bill, and they married younger and had more children than those in their parents' generation.

For many poor African Americans, the likelihood of achieving any one of the markers for adulthood is low. This is especially true in areas where poverty is concentrated and segregated, such as in urban ghettos like Mott Haven, New York, or Lawndale, Chicago, and in rural counties such as Tallahatchie, Mississippi. In these communities, fewer than half of all young people graduate from high school, fewer than 10% will go to college, unemployment is at least 20%, welfare dependency in some areas is 50% or higher, and so on. When a young teenage girl realizes she is pregnant, she may conclude that becoming a mother may be her only chance at achieving a marker of adulthood (Edin & Kefalas, 2005). Similarly, if she hadn't planned to graduate from high school or attend college, then the argument that motherhood will derail her from her goals (a typical argument in more affluent communities) is irrelevant. Thus, whereas becoming a teenage mother in affluent communities may be a deterrent to goals or judged a "poor" decision, this decision may not seem so irrational for the poor teen (Edin & Kefalas, 2005).

Norms

Scholars such as Bette Dickerson and Linda Burton argued that in a community with norms that encouraged teen childbearing and that had the presence of social support for teen mothers, the result would be a greater number of teens bearing and raising their children. Furthermore, as Angela Davis (1983) and others have noted, a history of reproductive abuses, ranging from rape to forced sterilization, played a role in the development of strong pro-natalist and anti-abortionist ideologies among African American women. Researching from this perspective, Linda Burton conducted interviews with African American teen mothers to learn from them how they constructed motherhood. Their responses fell into four themes: (a) separation of marriage and childbearing, (b) accelerated family time tables, (c) compressed generations, and (d) intergenerational caregiving patterns (Burton, 1990).

Separation of Marriage and Childbearing These teens observed that the male marriageable pool was limited, and thus, they had already determined by their teen years that if they wanted to have children, they would do so without husbands. The dominance of this norm of behavior, which is different from the norm governing behavior in the white community, substantially increases the likelihood of nonmarital childbearing and makes teen childbearing seem rational.

Accelerated Family Time Tables African Americans understand that life expectancy for them is shorter than for whites (see Table 6.7). If one can expect to live only into her 60s rather than her 70s or 80s, then she will come to the conclusion that it is better to start childbearing earlier (rather than later) in life so as to be able to live long enough to raise her children and become a grandmother or even a great-grandmother. This logic follows the same pattern that was present in the United States until the middle of the 20th century as well as the pattern that we see in the developing world today, where life expectancies are shorter and, consequently, childbearing typically begins in the teen years.

Compressed Generations Multiple generations of teen childbearing result in younger and younger generational members. For example, if the average age at first birth is 25 (as it is in the United States today), then generations will be separated by 25 years or so. A child at age 1 will have a 25-year-old mother, a 50-year-old grandmother, and a 75-year-old great-grandmother. What we see in some segments of the African American community where teen child-bearing has been the norm for many years is that generations are significantly closer together, such that a child at age 1 will have a mother who is 15, a 30-year-old grandmother, a 45-year-old great-grandmother, a 60-year-old great-great-grandmother, and so on. Thus, a 10-year age difference in one generation, when it is continued, increases exponentially the age differences in subsequent generations, such that the mothers are 10 years apart (age 15 vs. age 25), but the grandmothers are 20 years apart in age (30 years old vs. 50 years old). Both the girls and their mothers told Professor Burton that compressed generations were preferable because of life expectancy (accelerated family time tables) but also because the older women (the grandmothers and great-grandmothers) wanted to be young enough to enjoy and keep up with their grandchildren and great-grandchildren.

Intergenerational Caregiving Patterns A common pattern in some segments of the African American community is that of sharing caregiving across generations of women. Grandmothers (who are in their 30s and early 40s) often raise their grandchildren, while their own daughters, who at 15 or 16 are considered too young to raise children, care for their own grandmothers and great-grandmothers as they age. This caregiving may involve cooking; helping with chores around the house; and driving grandmothers and great-grandmothers on errands, to appointments, and so on. Again, not only the daughters but also the grandmothers and great-grandmothers expressed a strong desire for teen childbearing so that this pattern could be continued.

Burton's work was important in identifying some of the norms that contribute to a culture of teen childbearing (Burton, 1990). Her findings, which are largely replicated by Edin and Kefalas (2005), may help us understand what is going on in low-income white communities as well, which are also characterized as having high levels of low-wage employment, lower rates of marriage, and higher rates of teen pregnancy.

Premature Sex Engagement

One of the risk factors associated with teen childbearing is a history of physical or sexual abuse in the life of the teen mother (Ellis et al., 2003). For example, studies of Washington State welfare recipients estimate that *half* of those women who give birth before age 18 have been sexually abused and another 10% or more have been physically abused (Boyer & Fine, 1992; Roper & Weeks, 1993). Data from the National Survey of Children indicate that 20% of sexually active teenagers have had involuntary sex and more than half of those who are sexually active before age 15 have experienced involuntary sex (Alan Guttmacher Institute, 1994).

In fact, somewhat higher rates of sexual abuse were reported among the women we interviewed.[7] Understanding the relationship between teen child-bearing and sexual abuse in childhood and adolescence is complex; however, because it is such an important and compelling relationship (Ellis et al., 2003), we will propose a mechanism for understanding it.

Among the women we interviewed, nearly *all of them* experienced at least one of two phenomena—sexual abuse in childhood and/or adolescence, and premature sex engagement. Therefore, although the relationship between premature sex engagement, sexual abuse, and nonmarital teen childbearing is complex, and despite the fact that our sample is not representative of the entire population of African American women, the strength of the relation-ship is compelling and thus requires that we examine it and use it to better understand nonmarital teen childbearing. Because our data are qualitative, generated from face-to-face interviews, they allow us to examine the *process* that underlies the national-level statistics.

Among the women we interviewed, premature sex engagement took on several different forms, such as first intercourse at a very young age (13 or 14) with much older men (in their 30s and 40s), as well as discreet and continuous experiences with prostitution, which occurred to a surprising number of women we interviewed.

Intercourse at a Very Young Age With a Much Older Man Veta, for example, told of her first sexual experience when she was 16. Her "partner" was a 42-year-old married man by whom she became pregnant. When we asked her if she *wanted* to be sexually involved with this man, she said "yes." When we asked her why with a man so much older than she, she replied that he gave her attention she was not getting at home. Clearly, the issue that arises is whether a relationship between a 16-year-old and a 42-year-old can be defined as consensual simply by virtue of the inherent power differential between an adult and a teenager. Indeed, this sexual experience constitutes statutory rape and could be prosecuted under today's legal code. In discussing the awkwardness of the age difference, Veta recalled telling her parents she was pregnant, and when they insisted that she bring the man to their home so they could meet him, she was forced to bring home to her mother and father a man who was not only married to someone else, but *older than her parents!*

For many African American women, sexual experiences at 14 or 15 almost invariably led to pregnancy and a birth before the mother turned 16. With rare exceptions, girls who had their first child by age 16 dropped out of high school and failed to earn a general education diploma (GED). In addition to the problems of poverty outlined above, this also left them even more vulnerable to violence in their intimate relationships because of their limited earning potential tied directly to their limited employment skills in the changing economy where low-skilled employment continues to disappear.

Preadolescent Prostitution: The Liquor or Drink House Of all of the African American women we interviewed, 15% (3 of 20) had experiences with childhood prostitution. Sally reports what may be a relatively common experience among poor women. Her experience is shaped by poverty and severe deprivation. We have no way of estimating how common Sally's experience is because it is "illegitimate" and because it is situational. Sally was not a "working girl"; she was a 12-year-old who found herself living with her aunt, who was a prostitute. Her aunt spent all of the money she earned turning tricks to support her drug habit. There was literally no food in the house. Sally had tried several ways of getting food, including sneaking food from neighbors and even stealing. She then admitted that on one occasion, she had had sex with one of her aunt's johns in order to get enough money to buy food for the house. This is, no matter how you define it, a horrible experience that left indelible scars on Sally. Although Sally's story was atypical of young girls, we did hear many, many stories of women who traded sex for drugs. Many of the women we interviewed began doing this in their mid- to late teens, and many continued periodically engaging in this behavior for most of their adult lives. Sally's experience is considered situational prostitution. We turn now to a discussion of systematized child prostitution as two women described their experiences.

We begin with a caveat. We do not want to imply here that childhood prostitution is a normative or even common experience for young African American women. We do suspect, however, that Winston-Salem, North

Carolina, is similar in many regards to other southern communities where the town has a single major employer. Often, there are relationships between the company, its executives, and the illegitimate economy that exist in all communities. When these conditions exist, the environment is primed for many exploitive and oppressive behaviors, among them prostitution. Therefore, we believe there is much to learn from the case of Winston-Salem, North Carolina.

We began our interviews by asking the women to describe the families in which they grew up.[8] In some cases, the women talked at length about abusive fathers or stepfathers. In most cases, as the women became more comfortable and we had established more rapport,[9] the stories would literally tumble out. These two women's stories fit each of these distinct patterns: One talked early on about the way that her father prostituted her out; the other woman made this disclosure only after an hour, or more, into the interview. Both these women grew up in liquor houses and were forced to work there as child prostitutes.

Liquor Houses: A Description One of the outcomes of conducting face-to-face interviews with men and women living on the margins is that the researcher is often able to learn of the varied life tragedies many of them experience. In this case, we learned about a phenomenon in some African American urban communities: liquor houses or drink houses.[10]

Liquor houses are a sort of unregulated social club. Typically, they exist in an apartment in the public housing projects. The "projects" in many communities, including Winston-Salem, North Carolina, have units that are designed so that the bedrooms are upstairs and the main living areas (living room, kitchen) are on the main level. In a typical liquor house, a man allows a woman (and often her children) to live rent free upstairs in exchange for her (and her children) running the liquor house on the main level of the home. This arrangement also typically involves sex with the woman whenever the man desires it.

Typically, drink houses are open very close to 24 hours a day. The women we interviewed told us that they were horrible places to grow up because customers, mostly men, come in at all times of the day and night to get a drink or a plate of food, to play cards and buy cigars or cigarettes. Evie talked, almost with pride, about how she could make the sandwiches and even pour a shot by the time she was 10. Her face turned dark and tears filled her eyes as she talked about the men she encountered there and what they made her do—coming up short of saying she had sex but that she "sat on their laps."

When we inquired about the men who frequented the drink houses, Evie told us that of course there were the locals, men who lived in the projects, but that the primary customers were white executives from RJ Reynolds Tobacco Company.[11] These men came during their lunch hour and at happy hour time (usually after 4 p.m.) to consume alcohol and smokes and to have sex before returning to their quiet, white, middle-class neighborhoods. And there were other middle-class men involved as well: city police officers. These police officers turned a blind eye to these unregulated social clubs through a system of pay-offs—in kind.

> Some of the Reynolds men got paid on Wednesday. They'll come in, maybe, and buy . . . give me a five, and maybe they done bought four drinks and I would have the change. Sometimes they would sell fish in there. And a lot of times, some of the guys would get the cigarettes and change cigarettes for drinks. And it was just like, I wonder that the people that lived out by a car [meaning out in the suburbs]. There was nice section. But they would come in *our neighborhood*, and drink, and buy women and stuff like that. (Evie, 50-something African American woman, North Carolina)

Both women who worked in (and, in fact, grew up in) liquor houses were initially lured into this work by their fathers, who told them they could earn a little money making sandwiches and pouring drinks. Evie recalls that by age 12 she was frying fish and totally managing the food side of the operation. Her father would give her $20 and she would buy the snacks and sandwich supplies at the community grocer. As she spoke, we sensed that she had a sense of mastery about her life. Within a few years, she was working full time in the drink house, much too busy to attend school.

The liquor house operation sounds a lot like a family business, until you realize that child and teen prostitution and other illegal activities were a major part of the scene. Evie admitted flat out that her father prostituted her in the clubs. She was required to "perform favors" for the men in the drink house. Incidentally, many of the women, and some of the men, we interviewed grew up in households where one or another of their female relatives—mothers, aunts, older sisters—worked as prostitutes in the drink houses. So, even if they themselves weren't working in the drink houses, they certainly grew up around it. Several women and men also talked about coming home to find johns in bed with their mothers.

Evie was very hesitant to talk about her life growing up in a drink house. She made indirect comments such as, "You can't even imagine what I saw by the time I was 10. No one should see what I was seeing." She said directly,

> You can't imagine what it's like to have to sit on the laps of men when you are a 10-year-old. *I hadn't even learned to ride a bike yet.* (Evie, North Carolina)

Of the 20 African American women we interviewed, two worked as regular child prostitutes in the liquor houses, one admitted to prostituting herself on occasion for food or drugs, and three or four spoke of being molested by their stepfathers and/or their mothers' boyfriends. Fully half of the African American women with whom we spoke had experienced sexual abuse in childhood. Virtually all of them had their first sexual experience, consensual or not, by the time they were 16 years old.

Race, Class, and Gender Paradigm

The experiences of these women can be interpreted using the lens provided by feminist scholars such as Susan Brownmiller (1975) and Peggy Sanday (1981, 1990). Sexual abuse is clearly an example of the overt devaluing of the female and the feminine (MacKinnon, 1991; Rich, 1980). Women are raped and abused sexually because they are already of low or lesser value than men, and because sexual violence further degrades women. Historically in the United States, and today in many cultures, a woman who is raped is no longer marriageable, and as a result, the punishment for the rapist often was that he was required to marry his victim.[12]

The sexual abuse experienced by these women illustrates a culture of misogyny. The abuse serves to teach and reinforce the lessons that women are of lower or perhaps no value relative to men, other than as sex objects. The abuse also serves to reinforce the masculine identities of the perpetrators. If we assume that girls learn many of their lessons about men from the men with whom they live, then the lessons in these households were (are) the lessons of patriarchy; women have no value, women are to be controlled and punished by men, and sexual abuse is normal and often defined as appropriate.

The lessons learned in the liquor houses are further shaped by race. One of the lessons learned by the girls who worked as prostitutes in the liquor houses is that the bodies of African American girls and women are of even less value than the bodies of white women. The white men who abused these girls and paid to rape them (how can a 12-year-old agree to sex in this situation?) engaged in this activity in the African American community, not in the white community. It appears that these white men assumed their race allowed them the privilege to abuse the young African American girls. Although rates of sexual abuse by stepfathers and mothers' boyfriends is also high in the white community, the *systematic* abuse of young white women by men from outside the community is not only less common, it simply does not exist.

The experiences of the liquor houses are also shaped significantly by social class. Middle-class and affluent communities typically do not have these outward manifestations of the illegitimate economy. African Americans who live in middle-class and affluent neighborhoods and communities are not likely to experience the type of abuse we heard about and detail here. However, this does not mean that middle-class African Americans are immune to this type of situation. Many middle-class African Americans who can afford houses in white neighborhoods and communities are red-lined and find they can purchase homes only in predominantly African American neighborhoods, which are typically fairly heterogeneous by social class (Massey, 2005; Massey & Denton, 1993; Shapiro, 2004), whereas white neighborhoods and communities are very homogeneous by race and social class. Therefore, although middle-class African Americans are not likely to be victims of the types of exploitation associated with the liquor houses, they may be aware of these establishments within their residential communities. Thus, the lens provided by the RCG paradigm allows us to examine how three distinct systems of oppression—race, gender, and social class—are interwoven.

Conclusions

In this chapter, we have explored and laid out the data with regard to childbearing patterns in the African American community.

We do not see the African American community as monolithic. Much of the data in this chapter reflect the situation in low-income and poor African American families more so than the situation in middle-income and affluent families. This is precisely the strength of using the race, class, and gender paradigm to examine the racial gap in teen childbearing and the reasons African American teenagers give for making what appears on the outside to be a poor decision (Edin & Kefalas, 2005). Finally, we note that the analysis that is conducted on this type of data cannot be used to make predictions about the success or failure of any individual and/or individual family. What we look at here are trends and relationships.

In the next chapter, we will turn our attention to one of the most devastating aspects of family life: intimate partner violence. Finally, we offer some solutions for improving family life.

Solutions

- Improve the public education system so that teenagers would have incentives to stay in school and not drop out.

- Make birth control and abortion affordable and accessible to teenagers.
- Rework the welfare laws so that unmarried teen mothers do not have to raise their children in poverty.
- Stop ignoring premature sex engagement and interrupt it when it occurs so that children can be children and not "children raising children."
- Improve the legitimate economy for teenagers so that young girls do not turn to prostitution as the only way to make money.
- Identify and interrupt the use of children and teenagers who are exploited in prostitution. Hold the adults who are exploiting them responsible.

Notes

1. Tammy did, in fact, forego her welfare check. She took out a series of loans and finished her degree.

2. We are not raising the issue here of same-sex parenting. All of these comments refer to heterosexual parents, who comprise the vast majority of parents in the contemporary United States.

3. We note that juvenile delinquency is not caused by mothers' employment, but rather results from a lack of adult supervision when fathers (or mothers) are absent or when appropriate supervision cannot be secured or afforded.

4. Birth control pills, the most effective and most popular form of birth control among teens (44% report using the pill), can run anywhere from $15–$40 per month depending on prescription insurance and access to low-cost birth control from agencies such as Planned Parenthood.

5. See Angela Davis's chapter "Race, Racism and Reproductive Rights" in Davis (1983).

6. Passed by Congress in 1976, the Hyde Amendment excludes abortion from the comprehensive health care services provided to low-income people by the federal government through Medicaid.

7. For an in-depth discussion of the relationship between sexual abuse in adolescence and intimate partner violence in adulthood, see Hattery (in press-a, in press-b).

8. Incidentally, the interviews with the men began this way as well.

9. When one conducts research on such a painful topic, it is critically important to establish trust and rapport with the subject. We have found that victims of gender oppression (rape, IPV) are ashamed of their experiences, and they have encountered people who are literally shocked by their story. Therefore, they tend to start out mildly and slowly drop more and more outrageous experiences on the table. It is critical that the researcher express sympathy but not shock at these revelations. By accepting the extraordinary experiences of these women, the researcher develops the trust necessary for the revelation of increasingly intimate and shocking events.

10. Virtually every interview with an African American man or woman in the South included a discussion of liquor houses or drink houses. The terms are used interchangeably.

11. For most of the history of Winston-Salem, RJ Reynolds has been the primary industry and employer. This town was literally built by Reynolds Tobacco Company.

12. Or, as told in the article "Sentenced to Be Raped" by Nicholas Kristof (2004), women in the developing world are often expected to commit suicide in order to deal with the impurities that result from rape.

5

Intimate Partner Violence

Violence against African American women, specifically intimate partner abuse, has a significant impact on their health and well-being. Intimate partner femicide and near fatal intimate partner femicide are the major causes of premature death and disabling injuries for African American women.

—Campbell, Sharps, Gary, Campbell, and
Lopez (2002), p. 1

When things were good, they were so good. Like I said, I was always secure with him. He might try to hit me and he might try to kill me, but nobody else was going to do it. Nobody else was going to talk bad to me or hurt me or talk bad about me. That just wasn't going to happen. I was secure in that sense with him. He was going to protect me from everybody else.

—Candy (20-something white woman,
North Carolina), emphasis added

Objectives

- Examine differences and similarities in intimate partner violence across race and ethnicity.
- Examine the ways in which intimate partner violence is shaped by other social problems, such as unemployment, incarceration, and health.
- Identify some solutions to intimate partner violence in African American families.

Introduction

Intimate partner violence (IPV) is an epidemic in the contemporary United States. Family violence accounted for 11% of all reported and unreported violence between 1998 and 2002, with violence between intimate partners accounting for half (49%) of all family violence (Durose et al., 2005). This translates into roughly 1.75 million acts of violence per year (Durose et al., 2005). A national probability survey of 8,000 women and men found that 3% of women who are married or cohabiting experience an assault *each year* (Tjaden & Thoennes, 2000). Estimates across the lifespan are, of course, significantly higher, with as many as a *quarter* of all women reporting physical abuse by a male partner during their lifetime (Tjaden & Thoennes, 2000). Minority women report higher rates of IPV: Twenty percent of minority and poor women reported an incident *in the past year* (Tjaden & Thoennes, 2000). At the "outer limits" (Browne, 1989) of lethal violence, 31% (http://www.ojp.usdoj.gov/bjs/homicide/gender.htm) or 1,272 (http://www.ojp.usdoj.gov/bjs/pub/press/ipv01pr.htm) of all female murder victims are murdered by their intimate (or ex-) partners (Rennison, 2003).

In this chapter, we will explore not only the nuances of IPV as it is experienced by African American women and perpetrated by African American men, but we will also examine the ways in which IPV in the African American community is tied up or woven together with the other social problems or ills we discuss in this book: poverty, unemployment, health, and incarceration. We argue that only when we see IPV as bound up with these other issues can we understand its impact on African American civil society.

Definitions

Intimate partner violence (IPV) refers to the physical, emotional, psychological, and sexual abuse that takes place between intimate partners. The focus of the discussion in this book is limited to a discussion of violence among *heterosexual* partners.[1] We choose not to use the term *domestic violence* because we are *not* referring to violence that occurs between other members of the domestic household, such as the abuse of children by parents. In addition, the term *domestic* implies a shared residence. Yet many of the casualties of IPV do not live together, and often when they do live together, the violence began before they moved in together or got married. Finally, we choose the term *intimate partner* rather than *domestic* in order to highlight the nature of the relationship—these are intimate partners who claim to love each other—regardless of their marital status. IPV is present in both marital and cohabiting relationships. We will not differentiate between this legal status, but rather will focus on the intimate nature of the relationship.

The Problem

Intimate partner violence is an epidemic problem. As we noted above, a series of large-scale, nationally representative studies finds consistently over time that as many as 3% of women report an incident of violence at the hands of their intimate partners in the previous 12 months, with as many as a quarter or more of women reporting at least one intimate partner assault in their lifetimes (Bureau of Justice Statistics, 2003a; Tjaden & Thoennes, 2000).

We should care about IPV because it affects our mothers, sisters, partners, and friends, and because it is our fathers, brothers, partners, and friends who are responsible for this violence—violence that kills 1,500 women per year (http://www.ojp.usdoj.gov/bjs/pub/press/ipv01pr.htm) and sends millions to local emergency rooms for medical treatment (Bureau of Justice Statistics, 2003a).

So, Will's at work one day and I'm, I'm home. Bri's at school. And I was sleeping up in my bedroom, and all of a sudden, my bedroom door came flying in. GW (Stella's ex-boyfriend) had broken through a window downstairs, come in and kicked open my door, and I was in T-shirt and panties and it was winter out, so I was barefooted. And he jumped on top of me and started choking me. Then he yanked me up, and started banging my head against a cement wall. And I managed to get my feet up against his chest and push him backwards, and I ran down the stairs, and got to the front door, but it's one of those, you have to turn the door knob and the thing at the same time. One of those old-fashioned locks. And he got me before I could get it out and he grabbed me around the waist and threw me backwards and I hit the banister to the stairs, which was solid wood, and I slid down. He ripped the phone out of the wall and then he was standing over me with a baseball bat. And I thought, this is it. I'm going to die. (Stella, Minnesota)

Up until very recently, domestic violence, as it has been referred to, was a problem to be dealt with inside the family. Furthermore, domestic violence was essentially legal—men were legally allowed to beat their wives as long as they didn't kill them or the violence didn't get out of hand[2] (Browne, 1987). In the late 1970s and early 1980s, second-wave feminists began to draw attention to the situation of domestic violence and its victims. The writings of these scholars (e.g., Browne, 1987; Kirkwood, 1993) were critical because they brought this common experience of IPV to the attention of the larger

American population. However, as awareness of IPV has grown, our discussions of it have remained narrowly focused on conceptualizing and defining IPV as a "women's" problem. Certainly, IPV is a women's problem. Many women are injured and even killed each year as a result of IPV. And certainly, there are many problems women face as they experience IPV: difficulties in leaving, difficulties in successfully engaging the criminal justice system, and so on. However, it is their male partners who beat them. We will argue in this chapter that we need to redefine and reconceptualize IPV as a "men's" problem and as a problem faced by couples and families in our society.

Although analyses from the data generated using large-scale surveys have allowed researchers to see the relative blindness of IPV to social demarcations of race/ethnicity, social class, or region of the country (Tjaden & Thoennes, 2000), the current literature on IPV has not adequately addressed the race and class differences in both the experiences and outcomes of IPV. In this chapter, we will focus our attention on the phenomenon of IPV in African American families.[3] First, we begin with a review of the theoretical approaches to understanding IPV.

The Family Violence Approach

The family violence paradigm was developed by researchers Murray Straus and Richard Gelles, who first published their empirical work in the mid-1970s. Their empirical research soon came to be organized under the rubric of the "Family Violence Approach." Their methods primarily consist of conducting telephone interviews with randomly selected men and women in the United States. They developed an instrument, the Conflict Tactics Scale, or CTS (Straus, 1979), that is designed to measure incidents of physical violence in couples. Theoretically, family violence theorists locate domestic violence (their term) in the larger framework of other forms of family violence such as child abuse, sibling abuse, and elder abuse (Gelles, 1974, 1997; Gelles & Straus, 1988; Straus & Gelles, 1995).

Family violence scholars examine these various forms of violence within families and among family members and identify patterns. They note, for example, that the most common factor across all of these various forms of violence is the relationship between the perpetrator and the victim: The perpetrator always has more power than the victim. Parents abuse their children, older siblings abuse younger siblings, male siblings abuse female siblings, adult children abuse aging parents, and husbands abuse wives. This pattern reveals at least two key elements to family violence, whatever form it takes. First, that power provides a license to abuse (powerful people are rarely held accountable for victimizing less powerful people[4]), and violence is an effective strategy for controlling the behavior of other family members. Moreover, Gelles argues that people in families "hit because they can" (Gelles, 1997). Family members with more physical power or status in the family hit because they are capable of doing so. We would add that because the consequences for violence in families are so mild and are seldom enforced, that family members *hit because they can get away with it* (see Harvey, 2002; Hattery et al., 2005).

The Feminist Paradigm

In contrast, feminist scholars note that IPV is better understood as a form of violence against women. Theorists ranging from Susan Brownmiller (Brownmiller, 1975) to Catherine MacKinnon (MacKinnon, 1991) to bell hooks (hooks, 2000) examine the ways in which patriarchy developed and was perpetuated in the contemporary United States.[5] Feminists argue that violence against women, such as sexual assault, battering, and sexual harassment, is an expected outgrowth of the power relations between men and women, just as lynching is an expected outgrowth in systems of racial domination.

Although some women beat their male partners, and although some families live with what can be best characterized as *mutual combat,* a term coined by Gelles and Strauss (1988), or *situational couple violence* (Johnson & Ferraro, 2000), in fact, IPV is a gendered phenomenon. The vast majority of batterers are men, and the vast majority of victims are women. Intimate partner violence is primarily a crime against women. For example, in 2001, women accounted for 85% of the victims of intimate partner violence (588,490 total) and men accounted for approximately 15% of the victims (103,220 total; Bureau of Justice Statistics, 2003b). Furthermore, the outcomes of IPV for women and men are quite different. Even family violence theorists Murray Straus and Richard Gelles note that male violence against women does much more damage than female violence against men; women are much more likely to be injured than men (Straus & Gelles, 1995).

Because feminists argue that IPV is a direct outcome of a social system dominated by patriarchy, one of the challenges is to explain mutual combat or situational couple violence—the times when women initiate the violence or hit back.

This type of violence is harder to explain using the feminist paradigm. However, we also note that it is relatively uncommon, existing in fewer than 10% of all situations involving IPV (Durose et al., 2005). Thus, it is an exception to the rule.[6] In interviews with women who were arrested for intimate partner violence, Stuart et al. (2006) report that "self-defense, poor emotional regulation, provocation by partner, and retaliation for past abuse were the most common reasons for violence perpetration" (p. 609).

Although both the family violence paradigm and the feminist paradigm help us to make sense of IPV, both perspectives are limited in several ways. First, neither perspective adequately addresses empirically verifiable differences in IPV across race/ethnicity and class lines.[7] Second, both family theorists and feminist scholars while recognizing differences in the experiences of men and women in terms of IPV continue to focus primarily on the experiences of women.[8] Although clearly identifying IPV as a form of violence against women was critical in moving our understanding of IPV forward, this perspective has become limited in its utility to solve the problem simply because IPV has been ghettoized as a "women's" problem: The almost total attention on women as victims has limited the discussion to things women can do to avoid IPV and escape it when they are confronted by it. Yet because the vast majority of violence is perpetrated by men, until we refocus on the role that men play in IPV, we will continue to flounder in our attempts at ending this serious social problem.

Race, Class, and Gender Approach to Studying IPV

In our analyses, we consider the ways in which IPV is experienced and dealt with differently by African American men *and* women, the poor, and to a lesser extent, the affluent. To the degree that there are sufficient data, this analysis examines the various ways that these systems—racism, sexism, and classism—intersect and become mutually reinforcing. For example, how do white, affluent men experience threats to their masculinity? In what types of IPV do they engage? How are they dealt with by the police? How are these experiences different from the experiences of African American men, who may, for example, experience different threats to their masculinity and are certainly treated differently in a criminal justice system that can only be characterized as racially unjust? (See Chapter 9 for further discussion on this topic.)

This attention to race, class, *and* gender is rather unique in the literature on IPV. Those who attempt to include the stories of a racially and ethnically diverse sample often fail to include variance by social class.[9] But perhaps the biggest flaw in previous research is that seldom do studies of IPV involve the experiences of both men and women, batterers and battered in the same study.[10] The approach of this chapter is also unique in that it is not limited to a discussion of IPV per se. The stories of men and women living with IPV will be presented and analyzed, but they will be woven together with the issues covered in other chapters: poverty, employment, HIV/AIDS, and incarceration.

IPV, a gendered phenomenon, and all of its causes and outcomes, must be located within the larger system of patriarchy. Patriarchy prescribes a certain set of gender relations as well as imposes limits and constraints upon educational attainment, labor force participation, and economic freedom for women. Patriarchy results in restricted constructions of motherhood and fatherhood and constrains women's reproductive lives. For example, women continue to be socialized to believe that it is better to have a man who beats you than no man at all (Doyle, 1999; Rich, 1980).

Women continue to earn 75 cents on the male dollar, leaving them economically disadvantaged (Padavic & Reskin, 2002). Until we address these fundamental, root causes, such as economic dependency, for staying in a battering relationship, battered women will continue to leave unsuccessfully or not leave at all. Only when we understand the ways in which patriarchy creates unequal gender outcomes can we begin to consider social reconfigurations that will eliminate (or at least reduce) the violence plaguing so many of our families.

But IPV is not simply structured by a system of patriarchy. It is also structured by a system of racial superiority and by the intersections of these two systems. We will argue later in the chapter that one of the triggers for men who batter is a feeling that their masculinity is threatened. One of the patterns that emerged from these interviews is that when men feel emasculated, often they will try to reassert their masculinity through violence. One of the outcomes of patriarchy is the requirement that men be the breadwinner in their families. But one of the outcomes of racial superiority is that this is a difficult, if not impossible, task for a large number of African American men, as we will discuss at length in Chapter 7. Thus, we will use the lens of race, class, and gender theory to analyze the differences that exist across race, class, and gender demarcations. Not until we understand better the nuances of IPV (or any phenomenon) as it is structured by interactions of systems of domination (racism, sexism, classism, and so forth) will we be able to work toward building a society free of violence and oppression.

The Dirty Little Secret: IPV in the African American Community

Although family violence is not something new to the American family (Gordon, 1988), what makes this a unique contribution is that we pay attention to African Americans. We're paying attention to a topic that doesn't get aired in the sociological literature, but it also doesn't get aired in the African American community either. Why?

As we noted at the beginning of this book, after the Moynihan report of the mid-1960s, focusing one's research on the problems facing the African American community was professional suicide (Moynihan, 1965). This type of research ran the risk of purporting to pathologize African Americans.[11]

Among African Americans, the subject is taboo as well. Although researchers are often focused on the fluctuations and seeming contradictions among different forms of oppression within communities, often members of these communities either are not aware of the issue of IPV or choose to remain silent. Black feminist theorists (Hill-Collins, 2004; hooks, 2000, 2004; King, 1988) have pointed out, for example, the ways in which sexism and gender oppression are rendered invisible in the African American community. For women, discussions of gender are often dwarfed by discussions of race. Furthermore, African American women often fear that discussions of gender oppression contribute to negative images of African American men. The consequences of this invisibility have been deadly for African American women.

> Currently, one of the most pressing issues for contemporary Black sexual politics concerns violence against Black women at the hands of Black men. . . . Much of this violence occurs within the context of Black heterosexual love relationships, Black family life, and within African American social institutions. Such violence takes many forms, including verbally berating Black women, hitting them, ridiculing their appearance, grabbing their body parts, pressuring them to have sex, beating them, and murdering them. (Hill-Collins, 2004, pp. 225–226)

> Black communities must begin facing up to the lethal consequences of our own sexism. The time is over for expecting black women to be silent about the sexual violence and personal suppression they experience in ostensible fidelity to our common cause. (Hill, 2005, p. 171)

Intimate partner violence in the African American community is both serious and controversial. Yet as both Hill and Hill-Collins note above, it is time to begin open discussions of the violence that African American women experience at the hands of African American men who proclaim to love them. And although patriarchy in the African American community is tied up in ideologies of racial superiority, we need to examine the intersections of race and gender, but we also need to deconstruct them and examine gender oppression as it exists singularly in the African American community.

African American Women as Victims/ Survivors of IPV: Statistics/Rates

Most, if not all, researchers who pay attention to rates of IPV across racial and ethnic lines note that IPV knows no boundaries: "Domestic violence is statistically consistent across racial and ethnic boundaries" (Bureau of Justice Statistics, 1995, p. 1). And yet, when we analyzed the data from the Violence and Threats of Violence Against Women Survey (Tjaden & Thoennes, 2000), we found that although the overall rates for experiencing IPV were the same for all women regardless of their race or ethnicity, African American women are more likely to report certain forms of IPV. Furthermore, the types of violence that African American women are more likely to experience are the more severe, the more near-lethal forms of IPV (see Table 5.1 and Figure 5.1).

One of the strengths of quantitative survey data like those reported below is that the data allow researchers to assess the prevalence of various types of violence among all Americans. One of the weaknesses, however, is that the numbers and statistics often do not provide the kind of detail that helps us

Table 5.1   Rates of IPV by Race (in percentages)

Types of Physical Violence	White	African American
Partner throws something at woman that could hurt her	10.1	9.3
Partner pushes, grabs, or shoves*	22.2	27.3
Partner pulls woman's hair	10.8	10.8
Partner slaps woman*	19.9	25.2
Partner kicks or bites woman*	6.2	8.6
Partner chokes or drowns woman	6.5	7.9
Partner hits woman with an object	6.8	7.9
Partner beats up woman*	9.8	14.7
Partner threatens woman with a gun*	4.9	7.7
Partner threatens woman with a knife	4.2	5.7
Partner uses a gun on woman	2.0	2.8
Partner uses a knife on woman*	2.2	3.8

*Indicates physical violence that is significantly *higher* among African American women than white women. All other forms of physical violence are *not* significantly different by race of the victim. χ^2 and p values < .10. (Analyses were performed using the data collected as part of the Violence and Threats of Violence Against Women survey, a national probability sample of men and women. Descriptions and data can be found at http://www.icpsr.umich.edu/cgi-bin/SDA.)

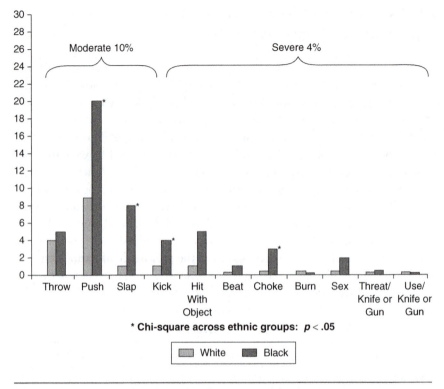

Figure 5.1   Types of Male to Female Partner Violence (in percentages)

SOURCE: Tjaden and Thoennes (2000).

to understand the process and outcome of the violence. For example, when we talk about the fact that African American women experience more severe, near-lethal forms of violence, it often helps to hear the stories that illustrate what constitutes such violence. When we began these interviews, we knew the statistics on violence and we knew that some of the women we would meet and interview would tell us of the horrors of IPV. We were both struck by how commonplace these stories were. Stella's story, which appears early in this chapter, of being hit with a baseball bat was typical of the violence described by the women we interviewed. Lara describes the night she was beaten up and hit in the head with a ball-peen hammer.

> He thought I had went somewhere. When he came here, I wasn't here, so I guess he thought I was out somewhere else. And he came in and we argued, and then, the pushing started. He grabbed me and hit me with a hammer . . . right here. And like across my head, whatever. . . . They [her kids] heard it. They didn't see it, but they heard it 'cause they were in the room. It was terrifying. So I went in the other room, locked myself in there, called the police and

whatever, and they came. By that time, he was gone. And they came, and I was just hysterical, I mean, bleeding everywhere, and the kids screaming and hollering. And it was just a terrible night. It really was. And I went to the emergency room and I had to get maybe twelve or thirteen stitches, cause they were in different spots. I had like six up here, I had maybe three over here, and like maybe half on my ear. It was like hanging down, ripped off, so a plastic surgeon had to come in and sew it back up. I called her [a friend] and she came to my house and picked them [her kids] up. (Lara, 20-something African American woman, Minnesota)

Lara's experience being beaten and hit in the head with a ball-peen hammer stands as a clear illustration of what constitutes near-lethal violence. As important as describing the violence is understanding the factors that contribute to IPV, in this case with special attention on the factors that are specific to African American families.

Women and Economic Dependency

One of the key issues involved with IPV in all families is women's economic dependency on men. As we noted in Chapter 3, and we will discuss at length in Chapter 8, Rich argues that one of the strongest compulsions for women to marry (or cohabit) is the fact that their economic standing is almost always enhanced by the economic contributions of their male partners (Rich, 1980, 1995). This dependency on men as breadwinners creates a sort of glue that prevents women from leaving their abusive partners. Because African Americans suffer from wage discrimination and low wages associated with a labor market that is characterized by race and sex segregation, they are significantly more vulnerable to economic hardship when they leave marriage and cohabiting relationships. For example, we know that when they are on their own, heading families, 70% of African American women are poor. Poverty data confirm that in African American families with two adults present, the rate of poverty drops to 28%. Although this figure is still well above that for whites, it does reflect the fact that, overall, African American women are better off financially when they are in committed relationships with men. (For a review of these data, see Table 8.5.) Thus, the ties to remaining in the relationship are strong.

As with so many issues that we have discussed in this book, the strength of the pull to stay with an abusive partner is also shaped by other forces, especially social class. For example, as we discussed in Chapter 3, African American women are more likely to be in the paid labor market in comparison with their white counterparts (Hattery, 2001b; Hill-Collins, 1994). As a result, middle- and upper-middle-class African American women may have fewer economic reasons to remain with an abusive partner than white women of the same social class who are less likely to be employed, and who may face a precipitous decline in economic well-being if they leave an abusive partner.

Finally, we note that there are several cases of African American women married to affluent, high-profile men who, when the men's battering is disclosed, usually through a phone call to the police, refuse to cooperate in the prosecution of their husbands and also refuse to leave, despite high levels of violence. An example that illustrates this point is the case of Felicia Moon, the wife of professional football player Warren Moon. Felicia Moon was so badly beaten up by her husband one night that she called the police, who arrested Mr. Moon for misdemeanor battering.[12] At the trial, the prosecutor produced photographs that demonstrated that Mr. Moon had beaten his wife into an unrecognizable state, yet Mrs. Moon stood by her man and in her testimony blamed his violent outburst on herself. As a result, Mr. Moon was not convicted and the couple remained together. Why? We would argue because in the balance, Mrs. Moon, like many wives of powerful, influential, affluent men, had a lot to lose, mainly money. Although Mrs. Moon could most likely have accessed the assets to exit, she chose not to.

On one hand, African American women may be better positioned to leave an abusive relationship because they are more likely to be employed. However, for all of the reasons we will discuss in Chapter 8 and those mentioned above, when African American women do leave, they are more likely to find themselves homeless and unable to meet the daily needs of their children. Many African American women initially rely on welfare, but because of the strict time restrictions, which we will discuss further in Chapter 8, welfare is not a long-term solution. Therefore, this situation can create additional pressure to find a new partner, especially one who is employed, and thus restore some form of economic stability to their lives and the lives of their children.

Our interviews revealed a common and dangerous cycle for low-income African American women. Before leaving, many of these women had been in the working class or lower middle class. But as the data on family form, poverty, and race confirm (see Chapters 3 and 8), these women often found that after they left, they were plunged into poverty, unable to pay the rent, feed their children, and provide or pay for child care while they worked. As a result, many of the women we interviewed began a frantic search for a new partner. Because they felt such pressure to establish a sexual relationship with another man (e.g., Rich's notion of compulsory heterosexuality; Rich, 1980), this search often resulted in a cycle of abusive relationships. Like a ping pong ball, these women reported that in an attempt to survive, they often found that they had simply traded one violent relationship for another.

This form of economic dependency, which is brutal and sometimes lethal, is more common in the experiences of African American women precisely because they have less education and fewer economic opportunities, they work for lower wages, and they often have more children to support (see the discussions in Chapters 4 and 7). Thus, African American women are particularly vulnerable to this type of dependency, one that leads to selling or trading one's sexuality in exchange for having one's basic (financial) needs met.

The stories we heard in the shelter serve to illustrate. Many of the women we met talked of moving out of the shelter (in North Carolina) and into an apartment with a man they had met at the mall only a few days or weeks before. Andi's story, although perhaps extreme in that it involves moving several hundred miles, is typical of the stories we heard from the women we interviewed.

Yeah, I got my older son, I got all my stuff and we went to Chicago. Um, with me working for the moving company, I knew this guy who drove a truck, and so he was up there and he had to go back to Chicago, so he took us to Chicago. I stayed in a hotel for about a week and then went to a shelter. I stayed in the shelter, but, mind you, I'm a hot girl, so, I don't know, but I stayed in the shelter for, like, three days, and then met this guy one day when I was outside of the shelter. And I do not know what was going through my mind, but I liked him; he was like, "Why don't you come to Minnesota with me." So I came to Minnesota. I'd been in Chicago for a week and a half. [AH: And how quickly did you move to Minnesota?] The next day after I met him. It was like, no, I didn't, it was like one of those stupid you're risking your life moves, but I was like, *"Hey, what do I have to lose right now? I have absolutely nothing."* So, he was, he had already came up here to Minnesota 'cause his brother got murdered and they couldn't stay in Chicago because the people who killed his brother were actually trying to kill him. So he were up here and he was supposed to be in Chicago picking up this girl who says she was pregnant by him but she said she didn't want to go, so he brought me back up here instead and told his family that I was her. I was living with him and his family, with him and his mom, and his grandma and younger brothers and sisters. I thought it was, I thought it was weird. Really, really weird. But, I mean, we talked to each other every day and we started getting involved with each other and everything. [AH: Were you sleeping with him?] Eventually, yeah. Yeah. The reason it's weird to me that we started getting closer, he started getting real close to my kids and my kids started getting close to him. So I kept working and he finally got a job. And he was working at [Simoniz] at first, 'cause he had never had a real job and he had always been hustling down in Chicago—that was the life out there. So he got his job at Simoniz in Apollo Air, and so we decided we wanted to get an apartment of our own. So we got an apartment of our own. Everything seemed pretty good for a minute. It was all right, I mean, but it was a two-bedroom apartment and everything. He got a job at Target, so that was a better job so we were living on our own, we got furniture and stuff 'cause we work hard to get furniture and everything, make sure the kids are okay, had day care set up; all that was good, but then one night he flipped out because he found out I had smoked a blunt, which I shouldn't have but it was a temptation. He found out I had smoked a blunt and that I had been around some guys. So he flipped out and we got into this fight and everything. . . . Well, first he had just grabbed me, and like, slammed me into the wall; and me, I'm not gonna just stand there, so, like, I try to shove him off me. And I grabbed his shirt up, like, roped it up, like that, and then I kept telling him "get off me," and stuff and . . . slinging me around and stuff and he ended up hitting my face against the wall. (Andi, 20-something African American woman, Minnesota)

What Andi's story illustrates is the cycle into which many of the battered women we interviewed fell. They often felt that their options were to live alone and be poor or take a chance to improve their economic conditions by moving in with a man. Although this may seem obvious and something that all women face, for many of the battered women we interviewed, leaving a violent relationship had plunged them into such severe poverty that they were homeless. In addition, moving out often meant that they lost their jobs because they either failed to come to work during the transition or they couldn't continue to go to work *and* care for their children. It is common in low-income families for parents to split shifts so that one parent watches the children while the other works, thus eliminating or significantly reducing child care costs (Hattery, 2001a, 2001b). Leaving the abusive partner often meant leaving behind the only child care that was available and "affordable." Therefore, the pressures these women felt to find a new relationship were significant and pressing. Most of the women we interviewed reported that after leaving an abusive partner, they often established a new relationship within weeks, often with someone they barely knew or with someone they knew had a reputation for violence, and more often than not, this relationship turned violent as well.

Early Experiences With Sex, Sexual Abuse, and Risk for IPV

Early sexual activity is one theme that runs consistently through all the interviews we did with battered women. So is the theme of prostitution. We refer the reader back to these discussions in Chapter 4. Our concern in this chapter is the link between early and abusive experiences with sex and risk for IPV.

Rape and sexual assault constitute a similarly common experience for girls and women in the United States, with studies conducted across a decade yielding stable estimates of 22%–25% of women experiencing some sort of nonconsensual sexual activity in their lifetimes (Fisher, Cullen, & Turner, 2000; Hattery & Kane, 1995; Koss, 1985; Koss et al., 1994; Tjaden & Thoennes, 2000; Warshaw, 1988).

The majority of victims of rape and sexual abuse are victimized before they turn 18 (Tjaden & Thoennes, 2000), and most are victimized by someone they know (Durose et al., 2005; Tjaden & Thoennes, 2000). For example, the Bureau of Justice Statistics reports that sexual assault and rape victims are three times more likely to be raped by a boyfriend than by a stranger (Durose et al., 2005).

Although women of any age can be raped, the majority of females (54%) who report being raped were raped before they reached the age of 18. Slightly more than a fifth (21.6%) were raped in childhood (before age 12), with the slight majority (32.4%) being raped in adolescence (ages 12–17; Tjaden & Thoennes, 2000). Compared with adult women, girls who are sexually assaulted during childhood and adolescence are more likely to be raped by someone they know (85.7%; Tjaden & Thoennes, 2000).

Women who were victims of child abuse are not significantly more likely to grow up to be battered in adulthood (46% are, but 53.3% are not); however, women who were victims of child abuse are *twice as likely* to experience IPV (46.7 % are battered) as women who were not physically assaulted in childhood (only 19.8% are battered); Tjaden & Thoennes, 2000).

In terms of sexual abuse, Tjaden and Thoennes (2000) also show a link between childhood and adulthood: Women who were raped as minors are twice as likely to be raped in adulthood (18.3% are compared to 8.7% of women who were not raped as minors), although as with child abuse, most women who are raped in childhood are not raped in adulthood (18.3% are, but 81.2% are not).

Finally, scholars have established the coexistence of rape and physical assault of women by their intimate partners (Browne, 1987; Russell, 1990; Tjaden & Thoennes, 2000). Seven percent of women report being sexually assaulted by their intimate partners, 22% report being physically assaulted by their intimate partners, and 25% report one or both of these events (Tjaden & Thoennes, 2000).

In summary, we have good estimates of both sexual and physical abuse in both childhood and adulthood, and we understand something about the increased risk that victims of both physical and sexual abuse in childhood have *for the same type of violence* in adulthood. However, there is little empirical research on the relationship between sexual abuse in childhood or adolescence and physical abuse in adulthood that allows us to consider the probability that female victims of childhood or adolescent sexual abuse are disproportionately likely to experience IPV in their adult relationships.

Because African American women are significantly more likely than their white counterparts to report being raped or sexually abused in childhood or adolescence (Tjaden & Thoennes, 2000), we suggest that these experiences leave them more vulnerable than their white counterparts to IPV in their adult relationships.[13]

The Pathway From Sexual Abuse in Childhood to IPV in Adulthood

> Many of the women in this study [of battered women] were raped, either as children or as young adults. Without a doubt these were traumatic experiences and they shaped or at least influenced much of the rest of their lives, particularly the ways in which they think about their own bodies and their self worth. (Lawless, 2001, p. 106)

For the women who had been sexually abused in childhood and adolescence, much of how they learned to relate to men was through the experience of sex. Thus, when they began to receive sexual attention, even though negative, from men who could be described as potential romantic partners, they often didn't define these experiences as abusive, even though in many cases they were. Recall that Veta was a 15-year-old having a sexually intimate relationship (by which she got pregnant) with a 45-year-old man. The stories from our interviews reinforce the findings of Browne (1987), who says that, often, caustic relationships seem at first to meet our definitions of passion and romance, of being in love. These women knew that sex with their stepfathers or mother's boyfriends or men in the liquor houses was wrong; that's why they were so ashamed to talk about it. However, in their early teens, when they entered sexual relationships with boyfriends, they defined this sexual attention as romantic and signifying love regardless of age differences or matters of consent. For the women who were sexually abused by men they also cared about (older boyfriends, stepfathers, and so on), they experienced both love and hurt in the same relationship, and this connection got cemented for them as one that was "normal." This is a key part of the problem. Women who are sexually abused in childhood and adolescence by men they care about conflate love and pain. From this, they learn a potent lesson: that those who love us can/will also hurt us, often deeply.

Valerie was molested by her stepfather from the time she was 12 until she was 15, when her mother signed permission for Valerie to marry a man in his early twenties. So, at 15, Valerie married for the first time a man who would ultimately batter her. For many women, "getting pregnant and married was practically the only avenue for their escape" (Lawless, 2001, p. 114)—or so it seemed!

> Well, I was excited [to get married]. I was excited. But then, you know, when the anger, when he'd lose his temper really easy, you know, maybe bust a hole in the wall or something. And then he was abusive to me but still, you know, that's the way it had been. So I still didn't have an example to go by to say, well this is not the way it's supposed to be. (Valerie, 50-something white woman, North Carolina)

The lack of positive models for a romantic, intimate relationship may, in fact, be one mechanism by which intergenerational transmission is occurring, although we would never suggest that this is the only mechanism or process at work. This finding reinforces an important finding in the literature that shows how a lack of positive relationship models leaves women unprepared to recognize the warning signs of a violent relationship (Browne, 1987; Lawless, 2001; Pipher, 1994). Lawless sums it up nicely:

> Nearly all the women in this study tell how they left home at a very young age; looking for an escape from the terror in their own homes. . . . Men would flatter them in order to gain their trust. The men . . . would treat them like "queens," notice them, look at them, and listen to their stories about their lives. The pull of that promise would suck them in every time. . . . They wake up, stunned, in abusive relationships with men who beat them, rape them, silence them exactly as their mothers, fathers, uncles, and brothers had done all the years of their lives. (Lawless, 2001, p. 116)

Lawless identifies very clearly the trap that pulls these women in, although it is hard to recognize. In the beginning, it is romance, even love—the love they are so longing for—but ultimately, they find that they have arrived yet again at the reckless world of degradation—violent beatings, rape, choking or worse, being sent to hospitals where they recover from near death—at the very hands of their newfound mates.

In sum, we have examined some of the factors, namely, economic dependency and sexual abuse, that leave women vulnerable to IPV. Both of these factors are significant because they affect African American women disproportionately, and they may account for part of the explanation for the higher rates of IPV that African American women experience relative to their white counterparts. We turn now to a discussion of the other side of the equation: African American men who batter.

Men and Masculinity

Just as early experiences with physical and sexual abuse put women at risk for IPV, there is a similar process at work for men. Men who were victims of physical child abuse are also twice as likely to batter in adulthood (Tjaden & Thoennes, 2000), but the strongest predictor of becoming a batterer for men *is growing up in a household in which there is IPV* (your father/stepfather beats your mother; Ehrensaft et al., 2003).

Yet overall, men who abuse their partners are not necessarily different from the typical American man. Rather, they are men who have been extremely well socialized into masculine roles and who are overly insecure and sensitive to threats to their masculinity.

What image do you envision when you think of a man who beats up his woman? Is he a factory worker who comes home, puts on a "wife beater,"[14] drinks a beer, and socks his wife in the mouth when the meatloaf she cooked for dinner isn't ready on time? The truth is, there is no description of a batterer. Men who batter are of all races/ethnicities, all ages, all levels of education, and all different occupations, and they live in all different regions of the country. We argue that if anything distinguishes batterers from men who don't batter, it is two things: Men who batter are well-socialized into hypermasculinity, and triggers to battering can be best understood primarily as threats to batterers' masculinity. In this section, we will explore constructions of masculinity and their specific iteration in the African American community.

What does it mean to be a man in our society? Masculinity is a set of characteristics that we often associate with men. From an early age, most children raised in the United States will ascribe qualities such as strength, power, height, and money to boys and men.[15] Kimmel (1995) traces the origins of the fusion of these masculine traits with being male. The sheer correlation between these qualities and being a man in this country illustrates the path through which masculinity has come to be associated exclusively with being male. Despite differences by race, ethnicity, sexual orientation, social class, and a variety of other factors that suggest there are really several "masculinities" (Kimmel, 1995), the image by which most men judge themselves and are judged can be boiled down to a few qualities or statuses as suggested by Goffman (cited in Kimmel, 1995):

> In an important sense there is only one complete unblushing male in America: a young, married, *white*, urban, northern, heterosexual, Protestant, father, of college education, fully employed, of good complexion, weight, and height, and a recent record in sports. . . . Any male who fails to qualify in any one of

these ways is likely to view himself—during moments at least—as unworthy, incomplete, and inferior. (p. 5)

Certain well-known men in our culture would be readily identifiable as "men's men," or "manly men." Most of the exemplars, or "ideal types," as Weber would call them, come from the realms of sports, entertainment, politics, and occasionally from the world of big business. What do these men have in common? They are successful, affluent, "strong," good looking, and mostly white, and according to popular discourse, they have multiple female sex partners.

African American Masculinity: The Cool Pose

Therborn (1980) argues that marginalized groups often develop alternative ideologies that are more in line with their lived realities. The most cited attempt at understanding African American male masculinity and the issues surrounding it comes from Majors and Bilson (1992), who argue that "Cool Pose" is an attempt to make the African American male visible.

Cool Pose is a ritualized form of masculinity that entails behaviors, scripts, physical posturing, impression management, and carefully crafted performances that deliver a single, critical message: pride, strength, and control. . . . It eases the worry and pain of blocked opportunities. Being cool is an ego booster for black males comparable to the kind white males more easily find through attending good schools, landing prestigious jobs and bringing home decent wages. (pp. 4–5)

If we correctly understand the path that Majors and Bilson (1992) take, they also argue that African American men are on a disturbing roller coaster ride through black male pathology. It is here that one finds not only failure in school but also extreme violence and criminality, drug use and abuse, and an illogical connection to parenting but without being a parent—absentee fatherhood of many children with many different mothers (Smith & Hattery, 2006). Majors and Bilson conclude that African American men construct their masculinity behind masks, worn to survive not only their second-class status but also their environment.

Therborn (1980) contends, as do others (see Hattery, 2001b), and we agree, that the behavior of members of marginalized groups is shaped both by these alternative ideologies and also by the hegemonic ideology. Furthermore, the construction of black masculinity is shaped not only by the lived realities of African American men but also in response to the constructions of masculinity more generally (read: "white" masculinity) and in response to institutionalized racism (see the description of Billy Black in Duneier, 1992).

Discourses of Masculinity

Regular men, masculine men, have access to images of the ideal man by watching ESPN, CNN, or most other cable television shows. For example, we saw the CEO of Tyco, Dennis Kozlowski, spend a million of his company's dollars on a birthday party for his wife. In the video images, what we saw was a successful American businessman flanked by beautiful women.

We saw America rally around Kobe Bryant as he endured a public rape charge (Katz, 2006). Many American men (and women) just wanted Kobe to be allowed to play in the NBA championship, reasoning that NBA players as "players" are legendary: witness Wilt Chamberlain and Magic Johnson (Smith & Hattery, 2006). Wilt Chamberlain bragged throughout his career that he had sex with at least 20,000 women, and Magic Johnson contracted HIV as a result of having unprotected sex with countless women he did not know. The public shunned him because of HIV but embraced his masculinity (as did his wife, Cookie, who stood by him). James Worthy (also a former Los Angeles Laker basketball player) got caught with a prostitute who was, in reality, an undercover cop. Kobe Bryant was, ultimately, just one more example of the sexual exploits of successful American men, especially those who are athletes.

Images of "regular" African American men also come across the television and radio wavelengths on a daily basis. The primary images we see of African American men are those of criminals and thugs (Glassner, 2000). The important point here is that a specific construction of masculinity is being transmitted to the young men (and women) who are watching. Men are supposed to be tough, strong, unfeeling, and most importantly, a "player" (hooks, 2004; Satcher, 2004).

No matter how many things are different about these men (e.g., Dennis Kozlowski and Kobe Bryant), such as their race, occupation, or education, they all share at least two traits: financial success and sexual prowess. Kimmel and Messner have argued that these two traits have come to signify manhood in contemporary America (Kimmel, 1995, 2005; Messner, 2002). And the key issues that both batterers and battered women identify as triggers to battering are men's successes in breadwinning and the bedroom—the two Bs.

Breadwinning

The first "B" is breadwinning. Breadwinning has long been defined by both popular discourse and sociological theory as one of the key roles that men in our society must play.

Structural-functionalists such as Parsons and Bales (1955) argued that men and women have evolved both biologically and socially toward distinct spheres of specialization. Based on this perspective, men and women are believed to be *biologically* suited for different tasks. As a result, men have come to dominate the instrumental sphere, whereas women have taken over the expressive sphere (Hattery, 2001b). The instrumental role, according to Parsons and Bales (1955), refers to the activities associated with providing for the basic needs of the family. In contrast, the expressive role refers to meeting the emotional needs of family members.

For example, in the traditional American family, the man is the bread-winner. He provides the economic support for the family, usually in the form of a paycheck. The woman, in contrast, nurtures and takes care of the children and comforts the man by providing a loving, quiet home, good food, and clean clothes in order to rejuvenate him before he heads back off into the stressful world of work.

Parsons and Bales (1955) construct a logical argument that traces our current division of labor from our existence in subsistence economies of the first tens of thousands of years of human existence:

> In our opinion the fundamental explanation for the allocation of the roles between the biological sexes lies in the fact that the bearing and early nursing of children establishes a strong and presumptive primacy of the relation of mother to the small child and this in turn establishes a presumption that *the man who is exempted from these biological functions should specialize in the alternative [occupational] direction.* (p. 23, emphasis added)

Parsons and Bales (1955) argue, for example, that a man's apparent greater ease at being away from his children for 40-plus hours per week, and even traveling away from home as part of his job, have evolved out of the time in human history when men went on long, extended hunting trips in search of meat. These hunting excursions encouraged a more detached masculine character (Hattery, 2001b). The important point here is that Parsons and Bales built an argument that the division of labor was *natural* and biological. Thus, it is the way things should be.

Breadwinning in the Current Economic Climate

Kimmel (1995) argues that one outcome of the contemporary political, economic, and social climate replete with declining real wages for men (Padavic & Reskin, 2002) and soaring unemployment (as high as 50% for African American men in places like New York City) is that establishing a masculine identity vis-à-vis success in the labor market is tenuous at best and leaves men feeling threatened by the possibility that they are not masculine enough.

> At the grandest social level and the most intimate realms of personal life, for individuals and institutions, American men have been haunted by fears that they are not powerful, strong, rich, or successful enough. . . . [As a result] . . . American men try to *control themselves;* they project their fears on to *others;* and when feeling too pressured, they attempt to *escape.* (Kimmel, 1995, p. 9, emphasis added)

Kimmel (1995) argues that this history of using economic success to establish a masculine identity—an experience that leaves men feeling threatened—created a landscape for the development of ideologies of masculinity that persist today. In many ways, he argues, as women gain more and more ground on men in the labor market, things have, in fact, gotten worse.

> American men feel themselves beleaguered and besieged, working harder and harder for fewer and fewer personal and social rewards. As they are struggling in order to define themselves as "real" men by economic success and having the right kind of woman, they see the rules changing. Suddenly they are competing *against* women for jobs they once held a monopoly on. They are working side by side with women who have no interest in dating them. Furthermore, they believe that the rules of sexual conquest have changed; men no longer have free sexual access. (Kimmel, 1995, p. 299)

Kimmel's point is clear: It isn't so important what advances women have actually made, nor is it important if they actually pose a threat to men. What matters is if men *perceive* these threats to be real, especially as they threaten their manhood and masculinity. Kimmel (1995) argues convincingly that this is, in fact, the social landscape of the contemporary United States.

Given Kimmel's argument that in this economic, political, and social landscape masculinity is already at risk, it seems that threats to a man's masculinity from his intimate partner—especially those related to the two Bs (breadwinning and the bedroom), the organizing principles of intimate partner relations—will be particularly powerful and, according to Kimmel (1995), would leave men feeling particularly vulnerable.

If this is true, and a man's reaction to feeling humiliated is "invariably violent," or if—in a less extreme interpretation—as Michael Kimmel notes, men's reaction to vulnerability is to *control,* then it seems that battering is a logical and probable outcome of threats to men's power.

The breadwinner role is perhaps the most significant identity for the typical American man. Most of the men whom we interviewed indicated that their identity as a provider was central. They identified this as their main contribution to their intimate relationships and to their households.

As central as this role of breadwinner is, being successful in this role is especially difficult for African American men (see our extended discussion in Chapter 7). Historically, African American men have suffered severe unemployment and wage penalties in the U.S. economy. Recent estimates of African American male unemployment, for example, hover in the 50% range in New York City, the symbolic center of capitalism (Villarosa, 2004). Thus, African American men will, because of structured inequality and differential access to the opportunity structure—especially education—find it inevitably more difficult to be successful breadwinners in comparison to their white counterparts.

In addition to inequality in the opportunity structure, African American men also face at least two other barriers to successful breadwinning: poor health and incarceration. In our discussion in Chapter 6, we will highlight the stories of Ronny and Demetrius. Both of these young men (at the time of the interview, Ronny was 27 and Demetrius was 20) were facing such serious health issues, including HIV, that neither is capable of working and neither expects to work again in his lifetime. Because HIV/AIDS now constitutes the sixth leading cause of death for African American men, and because HIV/AIDS is a disease that involves a long period of decline, more and more African American men will find it difficult to meet the first requirement of masculinity: breadwinning.

The second major obstacle in meeting the requirements of the breadwinning role is a direct consequence of incarceration. Our discussion in Chapter 9 will detail the impact of incarceration on African American men's employability. With one quarter to one third of all African American men being incarcerated for a period of time, mostly when they are young (18–35), it is fair to say that incarceration is a major and significant life event for African American men. It prevents them from ever making a living in the legitimate economy.

We note here that incarceration may be replacing other markers (such as breadwinning) of masculinity for African American men. This is logical for several reasons: (a) it is so common, (b) it is often related to making money in the illegitimate economy, and (c) going to prison is the mark of a "tough guy." However, we argue that regardless of the commonality of the incarceration experience for African American men, the power of hegemonic constructions of masculinity continues to create a standard—breadwinner—against which all men (and their female partners) judge their success.

Furthermore, our respondents confirm the importance of breadwinning to healthy intimate relationships.

We turn now to a discussion of the triggers to IPV that the men we interviewed identified. It is important to note here that we do not think that these triggers are justifications for battering. There are no excuses for striking one's intimate partner. Rather, these are the rationalizations that the men themselves identified and articulated as they described incidents of IPV in their own lives. In our analysis, we found that several key themes organized these rationalizations. Therefore, these themes organize our discussion.

Women as Nags, Spendthrifts, and Lazy, and Men's Failure to Provide

Threats to this provider or breadwinner role came in several different forms: men's own failure as providers, not being able to keep up with the demands of their wives or girlfriends, and frustration with wives and girlfriends who wanted to be "kept" when this was an unrealistic expectation given their financial circumstances. In other words, there were two distinct forms of failure in the breadwinner role. One form of failure was experienced as a problem with themselves: They could not get or keep good jobs. The other form of failure was experienced as external and was interpreted by the men we interviewed as a problem not with them, but with their wives and girlfriends. Because they described this situation as one of wives and girlfriends who nagged or spent too much money or who weren't willing to work to contribute financially to the household, they essentially blamed the women for threatening their masculinity, and thus their battering was, to some degree, in *their* eyes, justified.

Women as Nags

The majority of men we interviewed indicated that their wives and girlfriends failed to recognize their efforts in the provider role. Put in their terms, these men felt "nagged." These men reported that their wives and/or girlfriends nagged them about not earning enough money, about not being able to provide the standard of living they believed they deserved, and about not being able to allow them to keep up with their girlfriends and co-workers.

Eddie is an African American man in his late 30s who lives in North Carolina. In addition to owning his own painting company, he is a professional boxer. He has been involved in several violent relationships with ex-girlfriends as well as with his wife. When we asked Eddie to talk about conflict in his marriage, he indicated that they frequently argued about money.

Small stuff, you know. She's always complaining about that I don't treat her like a wife, because I don't buy her what she wants, things like I can't afford, she always throw up in my face like what her friend's husband, what kind of car he bought her and what kind of gifts he bought her. Of course he can buy her a brand new car when he the assistant chief executive at Wachovia. And uh, she a RN, got a master's degree at Wake Forest, you know, and she complain about, oh and he just bought this $160,000 house and you know you married me and you supposed to do this for me and my children, well what you, what you gonna do for yourself, and she always just nick nagging at me. (Eddie, 30-something African American man, North Carolina)

From Eddie's perspective, not only is this nagging unwarranted, he sees himself as a good provider who is doing the best he can,[16] but his wife is not contributing financially to the household.

My wife hasn't worked, man, right now she don't even work. She, we don't get no kind of assistance, we don't get no kind of assistance, I make the money. She just get a little small child support check from their father, that's it. (Eddie, North Carolina)

Eddie and his wife have had numerous arguments about her spending habits, the fact that she doesn't work, and her perception that he is not an adequate provider. These arguments often involve yelling and sometimes physical violence that is not limited to pushing and shoving.[17]

Failure as a Provider

Many of the men and women[18] we interviewed identified unemployment or underemployment as significant sources of conflict in their relationships. We illustrate with the case of Chris and Wanda. During the course of their 5-year relationship, Chris has repeatedly been incarcerated. He is unemployable because of his felony record and his stints in jail and prison. During his periods of incarceration, Wanda makes friends with other men who continue to call her and come by to visit her after Chris is released back into the free world. On a typical evening or weekend when he is out, other men call and drop by the house to see Wanda. This is a major trigger for Chris. He is jealous. When he tries to physically assert what he sees as "his right to his woman," Wanda reminds Chris that he is not the breadwinner in the household and therefore has no claim to enforce the rules. We include here a condensed version of Wanda's rant. The full quote is contained in Chapter 3.

My house. I'm paying all the bills. I'm talking about rent, gas, light, phone, cable, everything. Everything. Everything. I even buy his deodorant, okay? (Wanda, Minnesota)

This accusation of failure as a provider is interpreted by Chris as a threat to his masculinity. In an attempt to reassert his masculinity, the argument escalates and often becomes physical.

> This nigga got the biggest knife, it is in the house laying on the counter. So I looked at him, so I eased right? I eased back to the back door and I seen him walk toward the front door. I comes up in the house and I grabbed the knife. And I take the knife and I puts it behind my back in my panties right here, like this right, put my t-shirt over it. I say, do it make any sense for you to act like a fool like you do? Calling that lady house, acting a fool. I said, Chris, it don't make no sense. I said, you know what you need to do? You need to get your shit, get together and get your shit out of here, I said, 'cause you got exactly two hours. If your shit ain't gone, you ain't got a place to go, far as I'm concerned, its garbage. I'm not putting up with your shit no more. I'm just through. Oh, you just talking that shit, goddamn, 'cause you been over there drinking all night with Angela. She fooling your head full of bullshit. I said, no, you got my head full of bullshit. I said, I'm tired now. So, but no, he ain't listen. You is my wife till death till we die. So now that's when you start. That don't mean till death do you die like we done took no marriage vows. Till death do you die—either you're going to be woman or one of us going to be dead. You see what I'm saying. That's how I interpret it. Okay, so now wait a minute. So then, should I kill this mother-fucker? (Wanda, Minnesota)

This imbalance of economic power was a key justification for Chris beating his girlfriend (they were not legally married). He recognized Wanda's economic control as a threat to his masculinity, his sense of himself as a man. In short, Chris beat Wanda and threatened her with the knife when he felt his masculine identity, as defined by his (lack of) economic power in the household, was being threatened.

The Bedroom

The second "B" is the bedroom. The bedroom really encompasses several issues, from men's ability to satisfy their partners (sexual prowess) to men's success in the proverbial bedroom, often defined as the number of sex partners he is able to have (over his lifetime or, in the case of many of the high-profile athletes we mentioned previously, over a 24-hour period!), often through sexual conquest (see Sanday, 1990; Smith & Hattery, 2006).

As old as America, and perhaps most of the world, is the sexual double standard for men and for women. This double standard prescribes that men should or can have more sexual experiences and more sexual partners than women. The evidence for this is overwhelming and far reaching. Consider everything from the fact that polygyny (having more than one wife) was the dominant marriage form throughout history and across the globe (see the Human Relations Area Files at http://www.yale.edu/hraf/) and continues to exist in parts of Asia and Africa (Murdock, 1954/1983; Sanday, 1981). Typically, the only rule concerning multiple wives in these cultures is that the man must be able to provide economically for them. (The reader will recall our discussion of various family forms in Chapter 3.)

In the United States, despite a 30-year trend in a lower age at first inter-course and the declining percentage of newlyweds who are virgins at the time of marriage, American boys become sexually active a year or more ear-lier than their female peers, who are more than twice as likely to be virgins on their wedding day (Alan Guttmacher Institute, 1994). Furthermore, com-pare the language we use to describe men who have multiple sex partners to the language we use to describe women who do the same. We don't have to make a list here to demonstrate that virtually all the words for men are pos-itive (player, stud, sugardaddy) and all of the terms for women are negative (loose, whore, slut).

When taken together—the sexual double standard, a history of polygyny, and the acceptance and praise awarded men who engage in sexual conquest—it is clear that sexual prowess is an important part of masculinity in the contemporary United States, if not in the world more broadly. Clearly sexual prowess is important in constructions of hegemonic masculinity. Men were reluctant to discuss their failures in this area, although they were happy to share their successes in the bedroom! However, wives and girlfriends were not so close-lipped on this issue. In some cases, wives and girlfriends admit-ted to us that they were dissatisfied with their sex lives, and they often talked about how they expressed this dissatisfaction to the men in their lives.

Wanda: [Chris] don't appreciate nothing. Don't appreciate nothing, you know. They're living free, eating good, got a nice, I mean, a real nice hot water running in the shower in the bathtub. I mean, you know what I'm saying? But you know, a woman get tired. A woman get tired and then and I tried my best to figure out, why do we keep taking these men back?

AH: He isn't rubbing your feet anymore, is he?

Wanda: No! I put my foot up like this here, hmmph. Like they stink or something. Uh-oh, okay. So now you know, you're slacking up on everything, even the sex too now. Like sex, like it's a reward or something. NO way. And you know I'm a scuppy. I'm a freak, you know, I like my groove on when I want it. And you're going to tell

> me no? Oh, hell no. It's time for you to go 'cause I don't need you. 'Cause I got, I can go over here to Lovin' Fun [a lingerie store], I can buy anything, any toy I need and make love to myself 'cause I don't need you. And suck my own titty and everything. I'm just going to be frank. And so, all hell breaking . . . I am so serious! Ya'll laugh, but I'm so serious. (Wanda, Minnesota)

Although few men admitted to having problems in their sex lives, Eddie, the boxer, had this to say:

> We don't have a healthy sex life, because you have damage in the relationship, it takes the desire away from me. I sometimes come home and she touches me. Oh you can't hug, I say, I don't want to hug. Why, you got somebody. What she don't understand, she had damaged me so much. There's so much that's been said and done until I just, sometimes I don't even want to be bothered or talked to, I just want to come home, take a little shower, put on my stuff, and go to the gym. I don't want to talk, because maybe that morning before I left, she done told me you can just take your stuff with you. She been said something so damaging when I come home from work, she can just lovey dovey with me, like nothing never happened or said, and it just be so damaging to me. (Eddie, North Carolina)

Chris also talked about Wanda's complaints about their sex life. He identifies it as a major cause of the fights and physical violence in their relationship. In this case, however, he claims it is she who becomes violent.

> But, I got in here the first time, the mess with me and her. We was in the basement and she wanted more sex or whatever, and she was drinking her E&J [brandy]. She definitely, when she drink her E&J, that's when she gets physical. (Chris, 60-something African American man, Minnesota)

Jealousy

Scholars and practitioners have long identified jealousy as a major factor in couple arguments and in IPV (see Browne, 1987). Jealousy is an important trigger for IPV because it signals two key breakdowns in masculinity: ownership and sexual satisfaction. As noted at the beginning of this chapter, the crux of gender relations has been men's ownership of women. This is codified in both legal and religious codes. Violence toward women dates back centuries. "Throughout Euro-American history, wife beating enjoyed legal status as an accepted institution in western society" (Weitzman, 2001, p. 41). When John Adams was attending the Continental Congress in 1776, his wife, Abigail, wrote to her husband, whom she addressed as "Dearest Friend," a letter that would become famous: "In the new code of laws, I desire you would remember the ladies and be more favorable than your ancestors. Do not put such unlimited power into the hands of husbands" (Crompton & Kessner, 2003, p. 14). But John Adams and other well-meaning men were no more able to free the women than they were the slaves. When the founders of our country signed the Declaration of Independence, their own wives were still, in every legal sense, *their* property. Upon marriage, a woman forfeited the few rights she had, and her husband owned her just as he owned his horse.[19] As a result of this legal tradition of ownership of women by their husbands, Straus calls the marriage license a "hitting license" (Straus & Gelles, 1995).

It has long been taken for granted that access to sexual relations was a right of marriage. Men were entitled to have sex with their wives whenever and however they wanted it. This norm was so strong that it prevented women from accusing their husbands of rape. Marital rape was defined as a nonentity, an impossibility. Based on this belief that men own their female partners, if a woman engages in *any* interaction with another man (it need not be sexual), her husband or partner may interpret this as a threat. Just as we are justified in shooting a prowler who attempts to enter our homes, men feel justified in reacting violently if they think another man is about to "steal" his woman. It's interesting to note here that his rage is usually executed against his female partner—the possession—rather than the other man—the intruder. This is much like someone setting his or her house on fire when a prowler approaches rather than shooting the prowler to prevent his or her entry into the home.

Jealousy can also be interpreted as a threat to masculinity in that it signals a failure on the part of a man to satisfy his partner's sexual needs. This is strikingly similar to the threat men feel when they are unable to meet the requirements of the breadwinner role. Jealousy is such a powerful threat to masculinity and to the relationship itself that it is perhaps the most common justification men give for IPV. In fact, all or most of the men worried and/or believed that their female partners were sleeping ("talking") with other men.[20]

Sheri's boyfriend beat her up on at least six occasions. The first time he beat her up, she was pregnant and he kicked her in the stomach. The last time he beat her up, he knocked her head into a towel rack and she ended up in the hospital for a week. These episodes were always prompted by a fit of jealousy. Ricco was so jealous that he wouldn't leave Sheri alone at night, even following her around the *inside* of the house.

Basically, he would be controlling. I would get up at night and go to the bathroom, he'd follow behind me. He called, he'd come home, stare at the sheets and smell them, trying to see if anybody else been there. (Sheri, North Carolina)

Cindy described a similar situation with her boyfriend (she was 17 and he was in his late 20s). They had been to McDonald's—Cindy's first trip ever—for pancakes. After they had pancakes, he took Cindy into the woods and had sex with her against her will. Then, in a fit of jealousy, he beat her up.

> He, umm, beat me . . . he just got my nose and was like, beating me in my back, you know what I'm saying. It wasn't . . . I don't think . . . I don't even know that I was bruised 'cause I didn't want him to see. But see, he would be . . . he never checked my panties. But he checked other ones' panties. But I was in love with him. (Cindy, 40-something African American woman, North Carolina)

Eddie recounts the night that he caught his former girlfriend with another man, and probably engaging in an act of prostitution. He admitted to beating her that night to the point that she was unrecognizable. If the description isn't shocking enough, it is important to recall that Eddie is a professional boxer; a few weeks before our interview with him, he fought a man in a sanctioned boxing match, and later that day, the other boxer died. Eddie's fists are, indeed, lethal weapons.

> She was playing that role, you know, so what had happened was, come to find out she had got a hotel room, and what had happened was, I used to hang out on the street called 14th Street, you ever heard of that? I used to hang out on 14th Street a lot, and I seen her coming up and down 14th Street, that's a drug area, buying drugs. But I would call her and she would keep going in the car.
>
> So later on that Saturday night, because I couldn't catch up with her that Friday, later on that Saturday night she was coming up 14th Street and I seen her and her cousin was out there, and we was out there smoking rocks, 'cause we used to just behind trees and hit the pipe. That's how terribly it had gotten, you know, so I told him I would pay him if he would stop her when he saw her coming, when he catch her coming up the street. So he agreed, for a fee, for a small fee [laughter], so she fell for it. I gave him a rock. I gave him a rock. He took and stopped her, and when she stopped, I snuck up behind the car and jumped in the car and gave him the rock and told him to go ahead on and I told her to pull it off, and she was like, no, no get out of my car, and I was like if you don't pull off I will break your face, you know, I told her that. So she got scared and she pulled off.
>
> I didn't know that she had this room at the hotel, so I had scared her so bad when we was in the car, say where'd you been, when I got in the car I smacked her. You know I smacked her when I got into the car, and she said well I been

at the hotel, and that slipped out of her, and I said, what hotel you been in? She was like I got a room at the hotel because I wanted to be by myself, and now listen. Just before he called her, she was riding up the street with a guy on the passenger side. She didn't know that I was out there and I seen her, and when she came back down the street she had dropped him off and she was coming back down the street by herself when he called her. You see what I'm saying? So therefore I said, why did you let him out, who did you just let out. Blasé, blasé, and I knew who the fellow was and he got high.

When we got back to the room, you see, 'cause I got high with him before, I knew that he used to smoke those rocks inside the cigars, so we, she took me to her room, she had cigar butts in the ashtray, and I know she didn't smoke them like that, but I know he did, the one that she had just dropped off. Then I seen her underwear by the shower and her bra, as if she had took a shower and just slipped on something to come out to drop him back off, so when I got in there and seen that I lost my mind, man, and I beat her so badly, man. I beat her so bad until they couldn't hardly recognize her, man. Her eyes were swollen, her mouth was busted, I had chipped her tooth, but I didn't know that I had beat her that bad, because I had been up on 4 days straight, I had been on a mission, man, and you know I was like out of my misery you know, and so I went to sleep and when I went to sleep she snuck out of the room and went and called the cops, and they was flashing pictures, they were flashing pictures, and when I woke up they was shooting snapshots of me. (Eddie, North Carolina)

In summary, we have argued that hegemonic masculinity is essentialized by two core concepts: breadwinning and the bedroom, the two Bs. Because masculinity is defined by such a narrow range of behaviors, with the greatest weight resting on these two aspects (breadwinning and sexual prowess), many men construct most or all of their gendered identity (as masculine men) around their success (or failure) at these two roles.[21]

At an individual level, this may not seem so extraordinary. Men must simply get a job, work hard, make money, and satisfy their female partners. However, examining this from a structural or sociological perspective, we see that success and/or failure in this arena is not entirely up to individual effort. Especially with regard to successful breadwinning, individual performance is heavily structured by external forces such as the economy, returns on human capital, race discrimination, health status (the ability to work), and a history of incarceration.

As we will discuss at length in Chapter 7, because of a long history of underemployment and unemployment for African American men and ready employment (as domestics) for African American women, along with a history of sharing the provider role that dates back to slavery (see Hattery, 2001b; Hill-Collins, 1994), most African American men *expected* their wives and girlfriends to work outside of the home and contribute financially to the household, as noted by Eddie. For African American men, then, the frustration or trigger arises from a situation in which their female partners refuse to work yet desire a standard of living that the men cannot deliver on their own. Thus, the precise mechanism by which failure in the breadwinner role triggers violence among men is mitigated or shaped by race. For African American men, who have faced chronic wage discrimination and underemployment, the issue is centered on the situation in which their female partners refuse to contribute financially and expect their men to be able to adequately act as sole providers.

Similarly, sexual prowess is a major component of masculinity, especially for African American men. Many scholars, including Patterson (1999), note that African American men have the lowest marriage rates of all men in the contemporary United States (see our discussion in Chapter 3). Popular culture paints a picture of African American men as "players," on a sexual conquest for multiple female partners. Yet they too are especially threatened when they believe that their wives or girlfriends are being unfaithful. Ironically, in the case of African American men, the majority admitted freely that they had another woman on the side,[22] but they expected absolute devotion and faithfulness from their female partners, whom they admitted they suspected of cheating. This suspicion was the primary cause of a great deal of violence in their relationships. As with so many things, interviews with women confirmed this high level of jealousy to which African American women were subjected by their male partners, yet the vast majority of them confirmed that they were not having affairs, but that they were aware that their jealous male partners were!

Race, Class, and Gender Paradigm

As we and other scholars have noted, IPV knows no boundaries of race or ethnicity. Yet data from national-scale studies reveal that African Americans are more likely to be living in violent relationships than are other Americans. As we think across the data presented in this and the previous chapters, we argue that the reason why African Americans experience more violence in their intimate relationships is primarily because they are, in general, more at risk for violence.

Poverty

One of the key risk factors for IPV for women is poverty. Poverty is related to overall stress in families. As if the risk for IPV among poor women isn't enough, poverty exacerbates the problems of IPV because it creates serious barriers to leaving abusive relationships (see especially Brush, 2001; Brush, Raphael, & Tolman, 2003; Renzetti, 2001). Because African American women are disproportionately likely to be poor, they are at increased risk for IPV and will find it more difficult to leave relationships that become abusive.

Unemployment/Underemployment

As we will discuss in Chapter 7, African American men also face economic stresses, most often as a result of the consequences of unemployment and underemployment. The reasons for this are many. African American men face discrimination in hiring and wages, and they struggle for access to educational institutions that will offer them access to professional jobs, or access to unions that control the jobs that provide a middle-class standard of living. As a result, they have a very difficult time being successful in the role of breadwinner, a role that was constructed to match the experiences of white, middle-class men.

Incarceration

As we will discuss at length in Chapter 9, nearly a third of African American men will spend a portion of their lives incarcerated. Although there are many negative side effects to incarceration, with regard to IPV we have identified two significant risks: the consequent unemployment that follows incarceration, and the jealousies that arise while a man is incarcerated.

We argued here that constructions of masculinity for all American men revolve around two key issues: breadwinning and sexual prowess. We also argued that notions of masculinity are shaped by race. In the end, however, many African American men will fail to conform to the most central piece of hegemonic masculinity—breadwinning—as a direct result of structural forces that shape the lives and life chances of African American men.

Thus, in order to understand the increased rates of IPV in the African American community, one must understand the ways in which forces such as health, poverty, employment, and incarceration interact to put women at greater risk for victimization and men at greater risk for perpetration.[23, 24]

> Who, after all, can deny the endless and unspeakable power of so many desperate white schemes as American slavery, Jim Crow, the lynch mob, urban dispossession, and, most recently, the prison industrial complex to unman [read: dehumanize] the African-American male? (Wallace, 2002, p. 5)

Solutions

- Develop more inclusive constructions of masculinity that are not tied exclusively to breadwinning and sexual prowess. For example, develop constructions of masculinity that recognize being a good father, being a loving partner, and so on as part of being a "real" man.
- Design intervention and prevention programs that include practical advice for dealing with the triggers to IPV, including employment support programs, support for men who are re-entering the free world after a period of incarceration, and so forth.

Most important, as we will argue in the final chapter, is that the real solutions to IPV require radical and substantive transformation of institutions such as the labor market, the system of incarceration, the housing market, and the institution of education. African American women will remain at higher risk for IPV as long as they remain poor and unable to earn a living wage that provides support for them and their children. African American men will be at increased risk for engaging in IPV as long as they face discrimination in the labor market, as long as they, too, cannot earn a living wage, and as long as we lock them up at the rate that we do. Thus, we suggest that one consequence of improving the education, health, and employment of African American men and women will be a decline in rates of IPV.

We do note, however, that because IPV is also fundamentally rooted in patriarchy, improving the life chances of African Americans will not eradicate IPV entirely. Rather, African American men and women must create open dialogue about the gender oppression that continues to exist in African American families. When we see a coupling of both a reduction in gender oppression and improvements in economic and educational opportunities, we can expect a decline in the violence that is destroying African American families from the inside out.

Notes

1. We do recognize the serious problem of IPV within homosexual relations and refer the reader to Renzetti (2001).

2. In an examination of Palestinian women from the West Bank and Gaza Strip, Haj-Yahia (2000) found that even among fundamentalists, this seemingly universal truth holds for these women subjected by their mates to annual incidences of psychological, sexual, and economic abuse as well as physical violence. Battering, then, has been researched and argued by scholars to be legal, especially in legally constructed unions such as civil and religious marriage, in many countries,

including the United States, well into the 20th century (Browne, 1987; Leone, 2004; Weitzman, 2001). This finding correlates well with the early text by Engels (1884/1972), where he argues that women all over the world who enter into marriage become the property of their mates. Although originally contested, this "husband's right" (Murdock, 1954/1983) was confirmed by family scholars using the then-unique database of the Human Relations Area Files, located at Yale University.

3. We remind the reader that the data on IPV in African American families that are used in this chapter come from our interviews with 40 African American men and women who were living with IPV. We included a discussion of methodological issues in Chapter 1.

4. For example, data indicate that blacks who kill whites receive significantly longer sentences than when whites kill blacks or when blacks kill other blacks: Thus, the value of the black life is less than the white life (*Furman v. Georgia*, 408 U.S. 238; 92 S. Ct. 2726; 33 L. Ed. 2d 346; 1972 U.S. Lexis 169). Similarly, when women kill men, their sentences are significantly longer than when women kill other women (which is rare) or when men kill women. Again, these decisions and policies assign a value to a human life.

5. Some illustrations of the existence of patriarchy include the fact that until 1985, women could not charge their husbands with marital rape. Women continue to suffer wage discrimination, earning only 73 cents to the male dollar, and this wage discrimination persists when every conceivable factor is controlled (Padavic & Reskin, 2002). Women have limited economic power, serving as CEO of only two of the Fortune 500 companies. Women have limited political power, holding only 12%–15% of the seats in the U.S. Congress in 2005. Although they are allowed to enter the military, women are still banned from certain combat assignments, the very assignments that are required to enter the upper echelons of the military. In the United States, we've never had a female president. In addition, women have almost no power in religious institutions, especially in Catholicism and Islam.

6. *The exception to the rule:* Feminists have typically turned to interviews with battered women, and less frequently, their male partners, in order to gain a greater understanding of the phenomenon. Most of these studies (see Browne, 1987; Lawless, 2001) demonstrate two things. First, some couples really do engage in mutual combat or situational couple violence. They beat each other up. More commonly, however, is the finding that when women become physically violent with their male partners, it is most often out of either self-defense or in defense of their children (Browne, 1987; Lawless, 2001). Once these self-defense incidents of violence are removed, the level of female violence drops and becomes even rarer (Durose et al., 2005; Tjaden & Thoennes, 2000). We illustrate our point with the example of Valerie. We first encountered Valerie when she was in the batterers' intervention program, Time Out. When we arrived to interview her, we were curious to finally meet a woman who battered. As it turned out, Valerie's boyfriend had charged her with assault after she bit him. She bit him while he was driving and pummeling her at the same time. She was simply engaging in self-defense.

Um, he threw some water on me, ice and stuff. And um, he took my hand and I'm still having problems with it and, and bent it, like doubled it almost. He was driving and banging my head against the dashboard. [She gestures.] Well, so, when he did, I, uh, bit him. Bit down on him, but he jerked his arm, but when he did, of course, it broke the skin. And of course he charged me with assault. But anyway, and I've never had to go through anything like that, so that's still devastating. But anyway, you know it was just a constant battle. Always a battle. So finally, finally got here but it was, it was throwing things out the windows and you know he wasn't going to get out because he was going to charge me for this if I left him and all this stuff, power thing. (Valerie, North Carolina)

Clearly, Valerie's situation can only be described as self-defense, yet she was court-ordered to attend a batterer's intervention program.

7. In order to address this shortcoming, the primary theoretical framework employed in this discussion of IPV will be the race, class, and gender paradigm.

8. Feminist scholars are to be credited for identifying IPV as a form of violence against women, a gendered phenomenon.

9. A common problem that plagues much of the research on IPV is that most investigations have ignored its occurrence among the affluent. IPV is far more hidden in affluent families, who have more access to resources that result in their underrepresentation in social service agencies that are typically used to recruit subjects. For example, affluent women rarely use the battered women's shelter, and affluent men can afford legal representation that limits their required participation in court-ordered intervention programs. Similarly, the small financial incentive that is offered to subjects for interview is less attractive to affluent potential subjects. This study will not be able to deal adequately with IPV in affluent families, but there are a few affluent subjects in the sample, and their experiences will be analyzed with special attention to social class.

10. This sample, although small, is racially/ethnically diverse, but this is less the case when it comes to socioeconomic diversity. However, the inclusion of both men and women is perhaps the greatest contribution of this book.

11. We note that this same phenomenon is somewhat true of research that focuses on the social problems facing the poor, although less often is the researcher accused of pathologizing the poor.

12. For a fuller discussion of the Moon case, see Benedict and Yaeger (1998), pp. 130–133, and for a fuller analysis of IPV in intercollegiate and professional sports, see Smith (2007).

13. Because our sample is limited to women who have been battered, we are unable to use experiences with sexual abuse in childhood to predict the likelihood of being battered in adulthood. What we do in this section is examine the experiences of a group of battered women who were also victims of severe sexual abuse in their childhood or adolescence and illuminate the ways in which this early childhood sexual abuse led to poor partnering decisions and limited agency in ending IPV when it did occur.

14.   The origin of the term "wife beater," which refers to a white tank top, is from the stereotype that the shirts are worn predominantly by men who beat their wives. In the 1951 film *A Streetcar Named Desire*, the character Stanley Kowalski (played by Marlon Brando), who is frequently seen wearing tank tops, violently rapes his sister-in-law, Blanche. In the 1980 movie *Raging Bull,* the main character, a boxer, is commonly seen wearing tank tops around the house, including in one scene where he beats his wife.

15.   Emily Kane (2006) documents, using qualitative interviews, the mechanism by which parents teach their children "gender."

16.   Not only does Eddie own his own company, but he has accomplished this without a high school diploma and with a criminal record.

17.   We assert that even a push or a shove from a professional boxer can cause injury to a woman much smaller than he is.

18.   In this case, the women were talking about their perceptions of their male partners.

19.   This is ritualized in a tradition that continues into the third millennium. At a typical American wedding, the father of the bride walks her down the aisle and "gives her away." This ritual symbolizes the transfer of the woman from the ownership of her father to the ownership of her husband.

20.   An article in the *New York Times* on genital cutting summarizes nicely the motive behind this practice, one that remains widespread in Africa and the Middle East: to keep women faithful (Herbert, 2006).

21.   It is important to note here that femininity is also rather narrowly defined, primarily by one's ability to keep a good house and raise children.

22.   See the lyrics of the most popular rap music songs, as they clearly note that the male must have women on the side.

23.   We do not mean to excuse the individual choices that men of any race make when they engage in any form of abuse, be it physical, emotional, or psychological. We have developed a framework that explains a pattern that is bigger than differences in individual choice. Also, we do not believe that a tendency to be more violent with one's partner is biological. Therefore, our focus is on structural factors.

24.   Nowhere is this more clearly evident than in our own evaluation of Time Out, the batterer intervention program that is administered by Family Services, Inc., Forsyth County, North Carolina. At the end of each of our interviews with the men in North Carolina, all of whom were participating in the Time Out program, we asked about the utility of the program. Occasionally, we got an honest answer, but most often, we believe we were told what these men thought we wanted to hear— that they were learning a lot and that the Time Out program was affecting their behavior. However, as part of our arrangement with Family Services, we agreed to conduct an evaluation of the Time Out program. What we found was that the program was effective for white men who participated—it is important to note that only 49% of all men sentenced to Time Out ever attended a single session (Harvey, 2002)—but it was significantly less effective for African American men (who were more likely to attend than their white counterparts). For whites who participated in Time Out, there was a 50% reduction in recidivism (measured as a criminal charge

of battering), whereas for African American men, there was only a 20% reduction in recidivism (although we note that African American men had lower overall recidivism rates than whites). Thus, we conclude that any programs for dealing with IPV, be they programs designed to help women escape violent homes or programs designed to prevent and interrupt IPV, must be designed to be sensitive to the ways in which both race and social class shape experiences with IPV and the available options for dealing with it (Hattery et al., 2005).

6

HIV and Other Social and Health Issues

The growing inequalities we are witnessing in the world today are having a very negative impact on the health and quality of life of its populations. . . . When inequalities increase, some people's standard of living becomes much better, while others' becomes worse. It is within these latter groups that health indicators deteriorate.

—Dr. Vicente Navarro (2003)[1]

AIDS is now the leading cause of death among blacks aged 25 to 44, greater than homicide, heart disease, and accidents combined. The disease, long associated with white gay males, is slowly devastating black communities, claiming more men, women, and children every day. Yet among blacks, AIDS has been a silent killer . . . a culture of silence [that] surrounds this issue in the black community. The scourge will not end until people who looked the other way . . . begin to recognize and speak about the truths that lie behind the depressing numbers.

—"The Changing Face of AIDS" (1996), p. A10

Objectives

- Examine the overall state of health among African Americans with attention to health disparities in chronic illnesses such as diabetes and heart disease.
- Focus specific attention on the HIV/AIDS crisis that is devastating African American families.
- Examine differences in mortality, life expectancy, and infant mortality for African Americans.
- Identify some of the causes of health and mortality disparities, including poverty, access to health insurance, and access to health care providers.
- Explicate the ways in which poor health and premature death affect African American families, including the costs of poor health, the relationship between poor health and unemployment (lost wages), and the effects of early death on family structure.
- Identify solutions to the problems of poor health and well-being.

Introduction

In this chapter, we examine and analyze the state of health in the African American community. Despite living in the most advanced economy in the world with the most advanced health care system in the world, many Americans live with chronic disease and health crises that are similar to those of citizens in developing nations. Yet even within the United States, health and illness are not distributed randomly; in fact, African Americans are more likely to suffer from chronic diseases, lack access to health care, and die earlier than their white counterparts. Here, we explore outcomes of health disparities on the African American family, such as the expenses associated with illness, the ways in which health impedes gainful employment, and the ways in which premature mortality changes family structures. We also include two case studies: an examination of access to health care in Winston-Salem, North Carolina, and an illustration of the relationship between race, social class, and toxic industries (often known as "cancer alley") in Norco, Louisiana.

The State of Health and Well-Being in African American Civil Society

Early in the third millennium, the state of health of African American citizens living in the United States is grim indeed. For a variety of reasons, African Americans suffer from higher rates of many of the most lethal chronic diseases: cardiovascular disease (leading to heart attacks and strokes), diabetes, and certain forms of cancer. Although these diseases kill more Americans than other diseases or events (such as accidents or homicides), a matter of significant concern for health care practitioners and policymakers is the growing rate of HIV/AIDS and the tremendous racial disparities associated with this death sentence.

The power of these lingering disparities can be understood only when one considers some important facts about the U.S. economy and the U.S. system of health care, which is much more a "fee for service" health care system today than it was only 20 years ago. One of the reasons that the life expectancy for all Americans nearly doubled during the 20th century was because of the changing nature of the economy. During the long period of agriculture that dominated the economies of the 18th, 19th, and early 20th centuries, many laborers died in work-related accidents. Farming was and remains one of the most dangerous occupations (Bureau of Justice Statistics, 2004). Manufacturing occupations, such as mining and steel mills, which replaced agricultural work, were safer, but also dangerous.[2]

At the close of the 20th century, as the economy shifted to its current postindustrial or service phase, occupational fatalities continued to decline. Thus, as work becomes safer, and life expectancies grow longer overall, the life expectancy for African Americans, and African American men in particular, continues to lag behind. This leads to a higher probability that men, fathers, grandfathers, uncles, and brothers will die prematurely and be less likely to be part of their families, further disrupting African American family life (Stewart, Dundas, Howard, Rudd, & Wolfe, 1999).

It is also important to consider these racial disparities in health and life expectancy within the context of the U.S. system of health care. The United States continues to lead the world with medical advances, the rigorous nature of training and certification of all health care professionals, and the development of drug therapies. The affluent of the world flock to the small town of Rochester, Minnesota, where they receive treatment at the world-famous Mayo Clinic.[3] That Americans have the best medicine in the world is not disputed. However, access to this system of health care is significantly shaped by race and social class. In this context, these disparities are even more glaring and requiring of our attention.

Racial Disparities in Chronic Diseases

We begin by examining the data on the most serious and prevalent chronic diseases as they exist by race and gender groupings in the United States (all statistics on health come from the Centers for Disease Control and

Prevention [CDC] in Atlanta, Georgia). As noted above, these data are important because they tell us something about the overall health and well-being of Americans, because they allow us to identify race and gender differences, and because these diseases generate millions of dollars in medical costs that are borne by insurance companies and the government, but more often by individuals and families. Finally, these diseases have a significant impact on the daily lives of millions of Americans and result in millions of deaths per year.

Table 6.1   Stroke: 2002 Rates per 100,000 Population by Race and Gender

	White	Black
Male	54	82
Female	53	72

SOURCE: National Center for Health Statistics (2004).

The data in Table 6.1 indicate that stroke death rates are substantially higher for African Americans than for whites. Stewart and colleagues note that the incident rate for first stroke is twice as high for African Americans as it is for whites, even when age, gender, and social class are controlled (Stewart et al., 1999). But, as with many other diseases, our understanding of the impact of stroke must be examined through the race, class, and gender paradigm. Although stroke rates are significantly higher for African Americans, the gap between the rates for men and women is as important. In the case of stroke, there is no significant gender difference for whites, but there is a significant gender difference for African Americans; the rate for African American men is 10 points higher than for African American women.

Stroke is only one of the serious cardiovascular diseases that affect men and women. The leading cause of death for Americans, regardless of race and gender, is heart disease (see Table 6.2).

Table 6.2   Heart Disease Death Rates per 100,000 Population by Race

Blacks	206
Whites	259

SOURCE: National Center for Health Statistics (2004).

Heart disease is the only major disease in which the rate of death is higher for whites than for African Americans. We note, as will be evident in Table 6.5, that this is driven primarily by the extraordinarily high rates of heart disease among white *men*. And when the rates of heart attack and stroke are combined, the cardiovascular disease rates for African Americans remain higher than those for whites.

After cardiovascular disease, diabetes ranks as the next most significant chronic disease among Americans (see Table 6.3). Diabetes is of particular importance both for its prevalence and for the impact it has on people's lives. Type 2, or what used to be called adult-onset diabetes, has reached epidemic proportions in the United States, affecting nearly 20 million Americans (CDC, 2003). Diabetes, if it is not controlled through diet, exercise, and oral medications, afflicts many significant systems in the human body, most notably the circulatory and excretory systems. Possible outcomes for patients include lower body amputations (toes, feet, and legs) and kidney failure.

Table 6.3   Total Prevalence of Diabetes by Race Among People Aged 20 Years or Older, United States, 2005

Whites	3.1 million
	8.7% of all whites aged 20 years or older have diabetes
African Americans	3.2 million
	13.3% of all blacks aged 20 years or older have diabetes

SOURCE: National Center for Health Statistics (2004).

On average, African Americans are 1.6 times more likely to have diabetes than whites of similar age. The rate of diabetes is important because it is related to so many other diseases. Patients with diabetes are 2 to 4 times more likely to develop heart disease and 4 to 6 times more likely to suffer a stroke, and they account for 60% of all non-trauma-related amputations (CDC, 2003).

As the disease advances, many diabetics require dialysis that demands that they spend hours every week at a center having their blood cleaned while they wait for a kidney transplant. The consequences of this are far reaching. As diabetes advances, patients can no longer work—as is the case for 28-year-old Ronny, one of our subjects, who can no longer work because he has had most of his foot amputated—or because they are tethered several days a week to a dialysis machine. Furthermore, they may require near-constant care. How does this affect the African American family?

The *New York Times* did a series (Kleinfield, 2006) on the effects of diabetes in East Harlem, New York, a primarily African American neighborhood, where the rate is 20% (as compared to only 2% in the nearby Upper East Side). As with other crises that are concentrated in certain communities, certain patterns emerge. People (mostly African Americans) in this neighborhood die at twice the rate of diabetes diseases as people in other neighborhoods in New York City; the rate of amputations is higher, as is the rate of hospitalization. As a result, many of the adults in this community are unemployed as a direct result of their diabetes. Others are unemployed because they must care for parents or spouses who require regular dialysis. Families in these communities thus have lower incomes, and they have higher medical expenses. As we shall see later in this chapter, part of the problem in East Harlem is that it is a poor neighborhood, and as a result, two key institutions are absent, both of which would reduce the incidence and consequences of diabetes: medical clinics and healthy food stores. The absence of these key institutions makes preventing and managing the disease difficult (see especially Kleinfield, 2006).

Cancer is another serious disease that is nearly always fatal without treatment, and even with treatment, certain forms of cancer have a high rate of mortality. According to the American Cancer Society, lung cancer is one of the leading causes of cancer deaths among African Americans. Twenty-eight percent of all cancer deaths for African American men and 20% of all cancer deaths for African American women were attributable to lung cancer. This is the highest percentage of all cancers reported (American Cancer Society, 2006).

African American men have the highest rate of lung cancer, whereas African American women have the lowest rate (see Table 6.4). African American men have a rate of lung cancer that is more than twice that of their female counterparts (a ratio of 109/48) and a rate that is 1.25 times higher than their white counterparts (109/87). In contrast, although white women have a slightly higher rate of lung cancer than their African American counterparts, the rate is not significantly different (55/48). The American Cancer Society suggests two causes for these differences: smoking and treatment. They note that although African American men have the highest rate of

Table 6.4   Lung Cancer Incidence Rates by Gender and Race, United States, 2001

	White	Black
Male	87	109
Female	55	48

SOURCE: National Center for Health Statistics (2004).

NOTE: Rates are per 100,000 persons and are age-adjusted to the 2000 U.S. standard population.

smoking (27%) and African American women the lowest (18%), the *race* differences in smoking are negligible whereas the rates of lung cancer are significant (American Cancer Society, 2006). Their research also points out that diagnosis and treatment vary by race, with African Americans being diagnosed at later stages and receiving less treatment than their white counterparts. As a result, African Americans are more likely to die of lung cancer than their white counterparts. African American men have the highest rate of mortality as a result of lung cancer; 5 years after diagnosis, only 44% of all African American men are still alive (American Cancer Society, 2006). We will return to a discussion of disparities in diagnosis and treatment and the role that this plays in racial disparities in mortality.

Mental Illness

It is widely accepted that minorities and women are more likely to be misdiagnosed with mental illness and overprescribed drugs, especially antidepressants and psychotropic drugs (Matteo, 1988; Pi & Simpson, 2005). Research on gender differences in psychotropic drug use attributes the overprescription of these drugs to women to (a) women's greater likelihood of seeking help, (b) the greater likelihood of women being diagnosed by primary care providers, (c) the overreliance on drugs versus behavior therapy and counseling by physicians, and (d) physicians' belief that women are "overly emotional" (Matteo, 1988).

Research on race/ethnic differences in the diagnosis of mental illness indicates that the overdiagnosis of African Americans with mental illness, and schizophrenia in particular, is based on similar factors: beliefs about African Americans, utilization of mental health services, and "cultural" differences (Pi & Simpson, 2005). For example, Pi and Simpson note that African Americans often refer to intrusive thoughts as "voices." Although intrusive thoughts are not a symptom of psychosis, "hearing voices" is. Thus, a difference in the way that African Americans describe their symptoms can lead to a misdiagnosis as well as the inappropriate prescribing of dangerous drugs, such as Haldol.

In sum, research on gender and race/ethnic differences in the diagnosis of mental illness and in prescribing patterns indicates that most differences are not based on actual differences in the gender and/or race rates of disease, but rather on misunderstandings and false assumptions on the part of physicians and other mental health professionals.

With the exception of heart disease among white men, African Americans experience higher rates of each of the most prevalent chronic diseases and higher mortality rates as a result of these diseases. The effects of these diseases on the African American family are significant. Although most of the problems of disease are associated with older individuals, mothers, fathers, and grandparents, increasingly chronic disease among otherwise healthy children (those not born with congenital diseases) are affecting family life, especially in the African American community. Most notable is the rise of diabetes among poor African American children (Urbina, 2006). Most research suggests that this crisis is primarily a result of poverty—specifically, access to health care, access to healthy food, and access to a safe place for physical activity[4] (see below for an extensive discussion of the role poverty plays in shaping lifestyle). In short, the impact of chronic disease among children has a devastating impact on African American families.

Racial Disparities in HIV/AIDS

We started this chapter with a 1996 editorial from the *New York Times*. What's important about this editorial is that it was written a decade *after* the AIDS crisis began, and it foreshadowed quite accurately the situation of HIV/AIDS in the African American community 25 years after the first AIDS diagnosis was made public.

HIV/AIDS is an important health issue facing the African American community for a variety of reasons. First, as we shall see later, it is one of the leading causes of death of all African American men and women, and it is *the* leading cause of death among young African Americans (aged 15–44). Second, HIV/AIDS is a *preventable* form of death (Taylor-Gibbs, 1988a, 1988b).[5] Third, HIV/AIDS is directly linked to other issues that are explored in this book: namely, sexual practices (Chapter 4) and incarceration (Chapter 9). And finally, the rate of HIV/AIDS in the African American community can be examined not just as an outcome, but also as a symptom of other issues of well-being: drug use, poverty, and sexual practices such as multiple sex partners and the "down low."

More than half a million African Americans are HIV-positive. In the context of the U.S. population, we note that African Americans make up approximately 13% of the U.S. population, yet they make up nearly half (48%) of all HIV/AIDS cases that have been reported. Perhaps more important is the fact that HIV/AIDS is shaped by both race *and* gender. The race disparity, although great among men, is even greater among women. As we can see, African Americans make up 41% of the HIV/AIDS cases among all *men*, but 68% of the HIV/AIDS cases among all *women*.

HIV/AIDS provides a powerful illustration of the race, class, and gender paradigm because the rates exhibit strong disparities by both race and gender (see Figures 6.1 and 6.2). For example, the rate of HIV/AIDS among

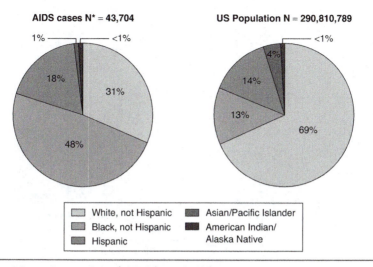

Figure 6.1   Proportion of AIDS by Race/Ethnicity

SOURCE: National Center for Health Statistics (2004).

NOTE: Excludes persons from U.S. dependencies, possessions, and associated nations.

*Includes 225 persons of unknown race or multiple races.

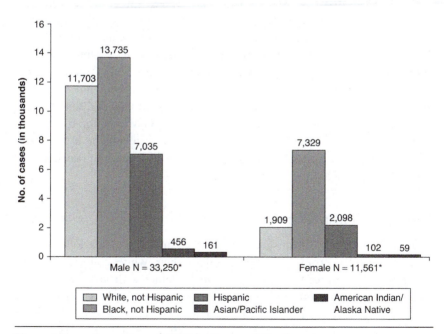

Figure 6.2   Proportion of AIDS by Race and Gender

SOURCE: National Center for Health Statistics (2004).

NOTE: *Includes persons of unknown race or multiple races.

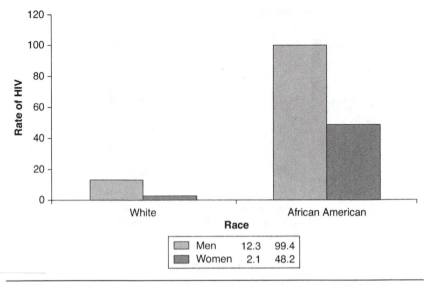

Figure 6.3   The Rates of HIV Infection by Race and Gender, 2004

SOURCE: Centers for Disease Control and Prevention (2004b).

African American men is seven times that of white men, and the rate among African American women is 21 times the rate for white women ("HIV Hitting Blacks Harder," 2006). In other words, there is a gender disparity (men are more likely to be infected than women) and a race disparity (African Americans are more likely to be infected than whites), but the biggest disparity occurs at the intersection of race and gender, with the gap being larger for women than for men. The rates of HIV infection by race and gender indicate that African American women remain vulnerable to systems of both the racism and sexism that play out in differences in transmission, diagnosis, treatment, and mortality (see Figure 6.3).

Modes of Transmission

In terms of mode of transmission, African American men are *more likely* to contract HIV from IV drug use than their white counterparts and *less likely* to contract HIV through sexual contact with an infected male. African American women are *more likely* to contract HIV through sex with an infected male partner than their white counterparts and *less likely* to contract HIV through all other modes of transmission than their white counterparts. This is important because it tells us something about IV drug use, males who have sex with males (MSM), incarceration, and so forth. The data in Figure 6.4 indicate that African American women are particularly vulnerable to HIV/AIDS specifically because they are in relationships with African American men, who have the highest rate of HIV/AIDS of all racial/gender groups in the United States. African American men contract HIV through IV drug use and through having sex (both consensual and non-consensual) with infected men during periods of incarceration. Because these men, both drug users and ex-offenders, are primarily heterosexual, they engage in sexual intercourse with their female partners, thus exposing them to the virus that causes AIDS. In order to develop more effective education and prevention programs for various race/gender groups, we must understand the ways in which risks for the disease vary by race and gender. For example, the highly effective programs that targeted white homosexual men in San Francisco are unlikely to be successful with African American men in prison or the partners to whom they return.

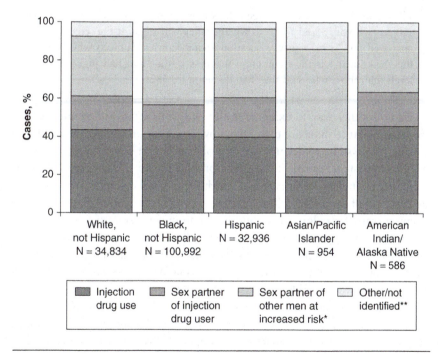

Figure 6.4   Modes of Transmission of AIDS by Race

SOURCE: National Center for Health Statistics (2004).

NOTE: Data adjusted for reporting delays and for estimated proportional redistribution of cases in persons initially reported without an identifying risk factor.

*   Includes sex with a bisexual male, a person with hemophilia, an HIV-infected transfusion recipient, or an HIV-infected person whose risk factor is not specified.

** Includes hemophilia, blood transfusion, perinatal, and risk factor not reported or not identified.

Leading Causes of Death

One of the problems with comparing levels of certain diseases across different race and gender groups is the fact that these statistics are based on official statistics that are generated by a diagnosis. An individual patient must have seen a doctor and received a diagnosis in order for his or her case to be counted. In addition, when survey methods are used to calculate the rate of particular diseases, the patient must understand the diagnosis and be articulate in the language of the medical field, or else his or her case will be underreported. For example, in a survey study by Schorling and Saunders, they found that many patients who had received a diagnosis of diabetes indicated simultaneously that they did not have "diabetes" but they did have "sugar" (Schorling & Saunders, 2000):

> There was a discrepancy between the survey and screening in that 31% of subjects who answered "yes" to whether they had sugar at the screening had answered "no" to the survey question about diabetes. Subjects who believed they had sugar felt their condition was less serious and had higher glucose levels than those who said they had diabetes. (p. 332)

Thus, another way to examine health and well-being is to examine causes of death, because these are determined by the physician signing the death certificate. These statistics are not free of problems either; however, they are often a more consistent source of data. The problems with this source of data are primarily related to the situation in which the medical examiner may not have access to all of the information. For example, a person who has been receiving chemotherapy for colon cancer but dies of an upper respiratory infection that is a result of a suppressed immune system will have listed as the cause of death "upper respiratory failure," not colon cancer. In fact, the medical examiner may not be aware of the colon cancer unless he or she has access to the medical records or to a reliable friend or family member of the deceased. However, unlike diagnoses that require a person to go to see a doctor, because the death certificate is required by law and must be signed by the medical examiner, there will be a record, no matter how imperfect, for every person who dies. Thus, "cause of death" is a more standardized measure.

Another reason it is important to examine causes of death is that they tell us something about how various individuals and groups cope with illnesses. For example, if 8% of whites have diabetes, but few die of the illness (or related complications), then we can assume that they have the support (financial resources, access to medical staff, and family support) needed to control the disease. Thus, causes of death tell us something more about health and well-being among different groups of Americans.

Table 6.5   Leading Causes of Death/Homicide (2002)

In 2002, 2.1 million white Americans died and 290,051 African Americans died.

Race/Gender	Cause	Number
White male	All causes	1,025,196
1	Diseases of heart	296,904
2	Malignant neoplasms	249,867
3	Unintentional injuries	58,467
4	Chronic lower respiratory diseases	55,409
5	Cerebrovascular diseases	52,959
6	Diabetes mellitus	28,110
7	Influenza and pneumonia	25,381
8	Suicide	23,049
9	Alzheimer's disease	15,874
10	Nephritis, nephrotic syndrome, and nephrosis	15,850
Black or African American male	All causes	146,835
1	Diseases of heart	37,094
2	Malignant neoplasms	32,627
3	Unintentional injuries	8,612
4	Cerebrovascular diseases	7,828
5	Homicide	6,896
6	Human immunodeficiency virus (HIV) disease	5,301
7	Diabetes mellitus	5,207
8	Chronic lower respiratory diseases	4,341
9	Nephritis, nephrotic syndrome, and nephrosis	3,427
10	Influenza and pneumonia	2,768
White female	All causes	1,077,393
1	Diseases of heart	309,972
2	Malignant neoplasms	232,614
3	Cerebrovascular diseases	86,760
4	Chronic lower respiratory diseases	59,986
5	Alzheimer's disease	39,184
6	Influenza and pneumonia	32,965
7	Unintentional injuries	32,399
8	Diabetes mellitus	30,349
9	Nephritis, nephrotic syndrome, and nephrosis	16,765
10	Septicemia	15,191

(Continued)

Table 6.5 (Continued)

Race/Gender	Cause	Number
Black or African American female	All causes	143,216
1	Diseases of heart	40,527
2	Malignant neoplasms	29,990
3	Cerebrovascular diseases	11,028
4	Diabetes mellitus	7,480
5	Nephritis, nephrotic syndrome, and nephrosis	4,061
6	Unintentional injuries	
7	Chronic lower respiratory diseases	3,901
8	Septicemia	3,490
9	Influenza and pneumonia	3,434
10	Human immunodeficiency virus	3,103
	(HIV) disease	2,534

SOURCE: National Center for Health Statistics (2004).

The data in Table 6.5 suggest several important things. First, that for all the discussion about race and gender differences, the leading cause of death for women and men, African Americans and whites, is heart disease.[6] Death by heart disease crosses both race and gender boundaries. That said, these data also indicate that there are *important* race and gender differences. The key difference between African Americans and whites is the likelihood of dying of HIV/AIDS, which is the 10th leading cause of death for African American women and the 6th leading cause of death for African American men. In contrast, HIV/AIDS is not among the top 10 causes of death for white men or women. Obviously, this is partly a result of the significantly higher rate of HIV infection among African Americans, but as we will explore later, because of racial disparities in treatment for HIV/AIDS, African Americans who have the disease die sooner than whites.

Finally, we note an important race/gender difference in causes of death: violence. The fifth leading cause of death for African American men is homicide. Although African American men are five times more likely to die of heart disease than by homicide, 5% of all African American men who die in a given year are murdered. (We note that the eighth leading cause of death for white men is suicide. This is, perhaps, violence, but it is distinct from homicide in that the death is a result of one's own decision.)

What becomes clear in these data is that whites die of diseases related to aging: heart disease, cancer, even Alzheimer's (the fifth leading cause of death for white women), but African Americans die *prematurely*. HIV/AIDS is not a disease associated with aging, nor does it cause death after decades of struggle. Rather, it is a disease that takes the lives of people who are much too young to die. And the most profound death, of course, is homicide. Homicide is a violent death that is *always* premature.

The effects on African American families and on African American civil society are profound. African American families and communities are being devastated by premature death and shortened life expectancy events that are associated with preventable causes of death. In practical terms, this means, as we have discussed throughout this chapter, that the implications on the daily lives of African Americans are profound. For example, in economic terms, premature death frequently removes a wage earner from the family. We know from the data in Chapters 4 and 8 that African American children raised in female-headed households are extremely vulnerable to poverty, and that three-quarters of these children live below 200% of the poverty line. They are poor. When an African American child loses his or her father to homicide or HIV/AIDS, typically that child is plunged into poverty. He or she no longer has access to the economic inputs of his or her father.[7]

As we will discuss in Chapter 9, both HIV/AIDS and homicide are often related to incarceration. Therefore, when a father or mother dies of HIV/AIDS or is murdered, it is highly likely that the other parent is also dead or incarcerated. For example, as we noted earlier in this chapter, the most common form of transmission of HIV/AIDS for African American women is from having sex with an infected partner. Therefore, the likelihood that the other parent is also infected and may already be dead or may be unable to care for the child is high. Similarly, as we discussed in Chapter 5, most female homicide is committed by the woman's abusive partner. So, for an African American child losing his or her mother to homicide, the likely per-petrator is the father, who will most likely be incarcerated for the murder. Thus, both HIV/AIDS deaths and homicide often result in children being put into foster care or being raised by their grandmothers, aunts, or other relatives. Although we pass no moral judgment on these arrangements, we do note that premature death is extremely disruptive to family life and fre-quently results in both poverty and a significant change in family structure.

Infant Mortality

One measure of health and well-being is the infant mortality rate, which refers to the probability that a child will die before his or her first birthday.

The rate represents the number of children/infants who die before their first birthday per 1,000 live births. Thus, an infant mortality rate of 7.1 (the U.S. average) means that of every 1,000 babies born alive, 7 will die in their first year of life.

The infant mortality rate is considered by researchers to be a good measure of poverty and access to health care because of what it represents as well as the fact that it is (a) a clear measure, and (b) it is comparable across geographic regions. What do we mean by "clear measure"? We mean that unlike many other measures of poverty, such as literacy or hunger, it is clear whether an infant has lived or died by his or her first birthday. Second, unlike measures of income that are difficult to standardize because of variance in cost of living and other factors, infant mortality, the death or life of an infant, has the same meaning across all geographic regions and all cultures and societies on the planet.

Finally, although some infants die accidentally or because of genetic birth defects, or sadly, some are murdered by one of their parents, the majority of infants die because of preventable causes such as infections that go untreated, birth defects that are preventable through prenatal care, and so on (see http://www.cdc.gov for a list of causes of infant death).

Internationally, infant mortality rates vary from a low of 2.28 deaths/1,000 in Singapore to a high of 192.5 deaths/1,000 in Angola. To put the infant mortality rate in perspective, the United States ranks 36th of the 208 countries for which there are infant mortality data. We are outranked by all of the western European countries as well as many countries in Asia such as Singapore, Japan, and Hong Kong. Our infant mortality rate is slightly higher than the rate in the countries of the former Soviet bloc and slightly lower than the rate in many Caribbean nations. Specifically, an African American child born in the United States is as likely to die before his or her first birthday as a child born in the developing economies of the Caribbean and more likely to die before his or her first birthday than children born in former Soviet bloc countries such as Latvia and Estonia. (For a full table of all of the infant mortality rates of each of the 208 countries reporting, see Appendix C.)

As with many of the other issues we have discussed in this book, and in this chapter more specifically, many different factors contribute to something as complex as the infant mortality rate. As noted, infant mortality is affected primarily by poverty and access to health care. The role that poverty plays in infant mortality is related to at least two key factors: maternal diet and infant diet. Women who do not have adequate nutrition during pregnancy are more likely to deliver low birth weight babies as well as babies with particular birth defects (mostly related to the consumption of folic acid). These low birth weight babies are more likely to die in their first year of life. Second, new mothers who do not have adequate nutrition during the period of lactation will be unable to produce enough nutrition-rich breast milk to nurture their infant. Third, mothers who are unable to produce enough nutrient-rich milk may need to rely on formula. If they cannot afford formula or do not have access to a clean water supply, their infants will be at serious risk for death during the first year.[8]

As with many other phenomena, infant mortality rates are not uniform across the United States. Not only are African American babies twice as likely to die in their first year as white babies, infant mortality rates for African Americans are also significantly higher in segregated, poor, southern counties (Hattery & Smith, in press).[9] In fact, an African American infant born in parts of the Deep South is more likely to die before its first birthday than one born in many developing nations. At the extreme, only four *countries* in the Western Hemisphere have infant mortality rates *higher* than Tippah County, Mississippi: Dominican Republic (41), Guyana (45.2), Bolivia (66), and Haiti (88.9)! (For a full table of all of the infant mortality rates of each of the Mississippi counties, see Appendix D.)

Infant mortality is not simply a measure of well-being; as with other types of premature death discussed above, it is disruptive to family life. Parents whose child dies in the first year of life often incur tremendous medical bills during the short time the child is alive. Added to this, one or both parents may be required to take a leave of absence from their job in order to provide the round-the-clock care and attention that a sick infant requires. Finally, it is difficult to estimate the emotional costs for a family whose child dies in the first year of life. This premature death is likely to be very disruptive to the family, it may cause a decline and break-up of the parental relationship, and it may put additional stresses on extended family relationships as the parents rely on their own parents for financial and emotional support during this event. Although infant mortality affects a relatively small number of families in the United States, rates of infant mortality are twice as high for African Americans as for whites (see Table 6.6), and thus are a significant disruption to African American family life.

Table 6.6   Infant Mortality Rates per 1,000 Live Births, by Race, 1999

U.S. Population	African American	White
7.1	14.6	5.8

SOURCE: National Center for Health Statistics (2004).

Outcomes of Poor Health: Premature Death

We have already discussed the primary outcome of poor health in the African American community, and that is death. Because we will all die someday, what becomes important, as noted above, are the causes of death that (a) are preventable and (b) result in premature death.

One of the standardized measures of health and well-being is life expectancy. Life expectancy is a statistic that represents the *average* number of years remaining for a person of a given age to live. Life expectancies are calculated for each new cohort. Thus, the life expectancy for a child born in 2006 is significantly longer than the life expectancy of a person born in 1940.

Many scholars talk about the cumulative stress associated with racism[10] (Livingston, 1985; Shapiro, 2004; Williams, 1999). One outcome of that accumulated stress as well as of poverty (lack of access to health care, poor nutrition, etc.) is a lower life expectancy. This relationship between race, poverty, and health is nowhere more clear than in life expectancy data (see Table 6.7 and Figure 6.5). For Americans born in 2002, whites can expect to live longer, as can women. White women have the longest life expectancy and African American men have the shortest; in fact, African American men can expect to live nearly 12 years less than white women. What is also interesting about Table 6.7 is the interaction effect of race and gender. We see, for example, that the gap between African American and white women is narrower (white women can expect to live 5 years longer than their African American counterparts) than it is for African American and white men. Thus, African American women, for example, share some of the protections that all women have relative to men, but they suffer some of the negative health outcomes that we associate with racism and poverty. In other words, as was the case in our earlier discussion of HIV, the relationship between life expectancy and race can be understood effectively only when we also examine gender. This is yet another example of the strength of using the race, class, and gender paradigm for understanding inequalities.

Table 6.7   Life Expectancy, in Years

	White	*African American*
Male	75.1	68.8
Female	80.3	75.6

SOURCE: Arias (2002).

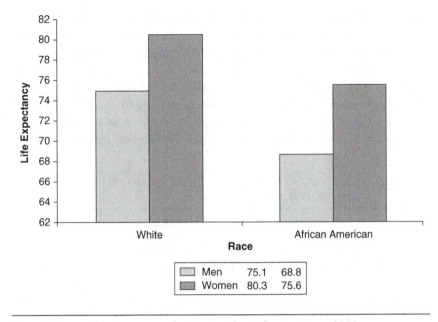

Figure 6.5   Life Expectancy by Race and Gender, in Years, 2002

SOURCE: Centers for Disease Control and Prevention (2004b).

Another measure of premature death is years of life lost. Years of life lost is a mortality statistic that attempts to measure or estimate the likelihood of a population to die early. Given that the average life expectancy for all Americans (averaging life expectancy across men and women and all racial and ethnic groups) is 75, the statistic is based on the number of people in a given demographic group who die *before* age 75. Thus, years of life lost captures *premature death*. In this country, premature death is due primarily to a small number of factors: homicide, suicide, HIV, and accidents. When analyzed by race, we see that African Americans have twice as many years of life lost as whites, which reflects the stresses associated with racism (Shapiro, 2004), as well as higher homicide rates and rates of HIV/AIDS.

Years of life lost is an important statistic because it is somewhat different from life expectancy. Life expectancy is an average; it measures how long the average person lives. In contrast, years of life lost captures the variance around this average (life expectancy). This is important when we consider the impact of premature death on African American families because it allows us to capture the severe premature nature of deaths caused by homicide and HIV/AIDS in addition to the "milder" effects of premature death caused by chronic diseases. To illustrate, let's consider the fact that the single greatest cause of death for white men is heart disease. Yet most white men who die of heart disease, although they die premature, may die only a few years earlier than they are "expected" to. In contrast, African American men who die of homicide and/or HIV/AIDS often die *decades* before they are expected to. Nearly 10% of all African American men die as a result of homicide or HIV/AIDS—preventable causes of death that are always premature. This type of variation is not captured as well by the life expectancy statistic as the years of life lost statistic, and yet this type of difference has devastating consequences for African American families (see Table 6.8).

Table 6.8   Years of Potential Life Lost, 2002 (Years lost before age 75 per 100,000 population under age 75)

Whites	6,949.5
African Americans	12,897.1

SOURCE: National Center for Health Statistics (2004).

NOTE: Years of potential life lost (YPLL) is a measure of premature mortality. Starting with *Health, United States, 1996–97*, YPLL is presented for persons under 75 years of age because the average life expectancy in the United States is more than 75 years. YPLL-75 is calculated using the following eight age groups: under 1 year, 1–14 years, 15–24 years, 25–34 years, 35–44 years, 45–54 years, 55–64 years, and 65–74 years. The number of deaths for each age group is multiplied by years of life lost, calculated as the difference between age 75 years and the midpoint of the age group. For the eight age groups, the midpoints are 0.5, 7.5, 19.5, 29.5, 39.5, 49.5, 59.5, and 69.5. For example, the death of a person 15–24 years of age counts as 55.5 years of life lost. Years of potential life lost is derived by summing years of life lost over all age groups. For more information, see National Center for Health Statistics (2004).

Ronny

Perhaps one of the best examples of years of life lost is a man we interviewed in Minnesota named Ronny. We conducted our interview with Ronny in the hospital. He is a 27-year-old African American man with serious health issues. He has had quadruple bypass surgery, has eight bullet holes in his body, and was in the hospital having most of his right foot amputated as a result of uncontrolled diabetes. He is also HIV positive. Not only will Ronny most likely die young (at 27, he has the body of a man 40 years his senior), but his potential is already destroyed. At the end of the interview, we asked him what he planned to do in the next few years with regard to employment (he had worked for 10 years in the fast food industry, eventually holding assistant manager positions at two different restaurants). He indicated he will probably not be able to work again. As a result of his amputation, he can't even stand up. Even after extensive physical and occupational therapy, it is unlikely that he'll ever be able to stand for the extended periods of time that are associated with the kinds of jobs for which he is qualified (with only a high school diploma, those jobs are in food service or perhaps retail). Ronny's story serves as a real-life example of the impact of poor health on both life expectancy and years of life lost.

Losing one's father or grandfather is traumatic for almost anyone and is disruptive to family life. Yet we argue that losing one's father prematurely at age 65 is qualitatively different from losing one's father prematurely at age 35. The statistics on life expectancy, years of life lost, and causes of death tell us very clearly that this is, in fact, the difference between white and African American families. African American families are far more likely to experience the death of men (fathers, grandfathers, and sons) while these men are still contributing to the economic and social well-being of their families. The loss of income, social support, companionship, and male role models is devastating to African American families.

Causes of Poor Health and Death

There are a variety of causes of poor health and death for all Americans. Many experts argue that obesity is the number one health problem of all Americans. Today, 65% of Americans are overweight or obese, a 16% increase over the rate just a decade ago (Flegal, Carroll, Ogden, & Johnson, 2002). African American women have the highest rate of obesity of all race/gender groups: 77.1% are overweight, and they are 20% more likely to be overweight than white women (57.2%). Both African American and white men fall between these two extremes, with white men being somewhat more likely to be overweight (69.4%) than African American men (62.6%; http://www.cdc.gov/nchs/data/hus/hus04trend.pdf#069). Overweight and obese individuals are at increased risk for many diseases and health conditions, including hypertension; Type 2 diabetes; coronary heart disease; stroke; and some cancers (endometrial, breast, and colon).

Comparing the health conditions associated with being overweight or obese and the leading causes of death for Americans, it is clear that one of the major causes of poor health (and even death) in the United States is lifestyle: eating too much, eating an unhealthy diet, and not getting enough exercise. Although this is less of a problem for African American men, it is a serious problem for African American women.

Poverty

The relationship between lifestyle causes of poor health and illness and race is confounded by social class. In order to disentangle this set of relationships, we will begin with a brief discussion of the relationship between social class and lifestyle. The relationship is complex and occurs at both the individual level and the societal level.

Lifestyle

At the societal level, America is the land of wealth and abundance. Americans eat more meat, for example, than people in most other nations, both developed and developing. Fewer and fewer Americans have jobs that require much, if any, physical activity, and as the literal land of the automobile, except for those Americans living in our major cities (New York, Chicago, Washington DC), few Americans walk anywhere. Thus, compared to citizens in other countries, both developed and developing, Americans eat more, especially calorie-rich foods, and get less physical activity.

Like almost everything else, however, even this is shaped by social class. The affluent, for example, are the least likely to have jobs that are physically demanding, but they are the most likely to own memberships to exclusive gyms and country clubs where they can exercise, play golf, and so forth. Similarly, although the affluent have the resources to purchase more meat and "rich" foods, it is the poor who find it difficult to afford healthy food such as fresh fruits and vegetables, leaner cuts of meat and fish, and low-fat dairy products. Thus, in this land of plenty, social class shapes lifestyle, in particular, access to healthy food and exercise.

Because African Americans are disproportionately likely to be poor, they are less likely to eat healthfully and exercise and more likely to suffer diseases such as stroke, diabetes, and heart disease. The rates especially of diabetes bear this out. Thus, Americans almost never die of the diseases the world's poor die of, such as malaria and cholera; instead, they die of diseases of overconsumption, such as diabetes and heart disease. And just as the poor in other parts of the world are more vulnerable to diseases such as malaria and cholera, the poor in the United States and especially, African Americans, are more vulnerable to the diseases associated with an unhealthy lifestyle.

Access to Health Insurance

In the United States, unlike most of the other nations in the developed world, health insurance is linked primarily to employment. The government provides health insurance for the very poor (Medicaid)[11] and the retired (Medicare). Despite the millions covered by these two programs, by far the majority of Americans live with the reality that health insurance is attached to and disbursed by employers. Pitting corporate interests against individual interests with few government guidelines, the availability of health insurance is widely variable. Wal-Mart,[12] for example, engages in a popular practice of employing its workers fewer than the 40-hour mark that requires health insurance benefits, and as a result, the majority of its employees do not have health insurance (Greenhouse, 2005). As a result of unemployment, under-employment, and these sorts of corporate strategies, nearly 40 million Americans are without health insurance. We provide an extensive table on this topic in Appendix E, and we summarize it here:

- African Americans are almost twice as likely to be uninsured as whites; nearly 20% of African Americans are uninsured compared to only 11% of whites.
- Whites are more likely to have private health insurance (86%) than African Americans (66%).
- African Americans are 2.5 times more likely to be on Medicaid (government insurance for the poor) than are whites (70% compared to 32.6%).
- African Americans are only half as likely to receive Medicare (government insurance for those over age 65) than are whites (30% compared to 63.2%).
- African Americans are about equally likely to be on Medicaid as to have employer-based insurance, whereas whites are eight times more likely to have private, employer-based insurance as they are to be on Medicaid.

The two key issues that are raised in this data are (a) the likelihood of being uninsured and (b) the type of insurance that individuals have. In the United States, as hospitals, preferred provider networks, insurance companies, and health maintenance organizations engage in heated wars over sharing the costs of delivering health care, the costs continue to rise, making health care a virtually unattainable luxury for all but the insured. For example, a simple office visit for a check up at a local medical office will run at least $100. (A chart with the costs of many preventative procedures is including in Appendix F.) For a minimum-wage worker, this single visit is 12% of his or her take-home pay for a month. It is something he or she is simply unable to afford. Thus, when 20% of African Americans have *no* health insurance, we know that they are unlikely to seek medical care unless it qualifies as an emergency, in which case they cannot be denied treatment. In practical terms, this means that many African American women give birth having had little or no prenatal care; African American children are less likely to have regular check-ups (which means they may not receive childhood vaccinations); and many of the African Americans who are at risk for or have chronic diseases such as heart disease and/or diabetes receive little, if any, regular medical care. The outcomes are obvious: At-risk individuals are less likely to receive the kind of preventive care that will lead to better health, and when they do develop chronic diseases, they are less likely to receive the regular medical care necessary to control these diseases.

The issue of access to health insurance is inextricably woven with employment (as we will discuss in Chapter 7) and specifically with employment that is full-time, stable, year-round, and generous enough to offer benefits. However, an additional barrier to health insurance is the cost of the premiums. Even on our own campus, staff and some adjunct faculty report that they cannot afford the monthly $375 premium that provides health insurance for them and their dependents. Add to this the fact that insurance companies have a history of charging higher premiums to African Americans. In July 2005, an insurance company in North Carolina settled a class action suit on behalf of 70,000 African American citizens who were charged higher premiums ("Insurance Settlement," 2005). The result is that even for employed African Americans, health insurance premiums may simply be too expensive to afford, and this is exacerbated by discriminatory premium practices that target them. The lack of health insurance clearly has serious, long-term consequences for African American families.

The second issue that these data raise is the distinction between private health insurance and Medicaid. Private health insurance has the most flexibility; patients find that they can see any physician they choose at any hospital or clinic. The costs may vary, but will always be reasonable (co-pays may range from $0 to $50 per visit). More popular in the past 15 years or so are health insurance plans that are run through health maintenance organizations or preferred provider organizations. Both have less flexibility than private insurance but are typically cheaper for both employer and patient. Although patients have somewhat more limited choice, they are typically restricted to seeing physicians within a network or on a preapproved list, the costs are generally very low (co-pays of $0 to $25), and the quality of care is generally as high as that available with private insurance plans.

In serious contrast, we find the government health insurance system of Medicaid. Medicaid insurance has severe limits on hospital and physician reimbursements, and as a result, many of the highly ranked hospitals and clinics will not see Medicaid patients. Therefore, many Americans who receive Medicaid find that they can see physicians only at clinics that are specifically Medicaid practices. We are not arguing here that Medicaid practices are inferior, but rather that our system of private versus public health insurance creates a system of health care that is segregated by social class, and as a result of the conflation of race and social class, the system is racially segregated as well. The vast majority of Medicaid recipients (70%) are African American, and African Americans are about equally likely to be on Medicaid as they are to have private, employer-based insurance, and this, in and of itself, leads to a health care system that is racially segregated.

The famous U.S. Supreme Court decision in 1954, *Brown v. Board of Education,* dictated that separate, segregated facilities are, by definition, not equal. Thus, these data on health insurance raise the question of whether or not African Americans and their families are, in fact, receiving "equal" health care, and suggest that they are not.

Access to Health Care

There are many racial and gender disparities in the type of medical care that Americans receive. For example, as a result of differential access to private practices and clinics as opposed to Medicaid clinics, urgent care clinics, and emergency room treatment, African Americans are twice as likely to report having difficulty accessing specialists when compared to whites (Collins, Hall, & Neuhaus, 1999).

> We found that the physicians whom the black patients visited were less likely to be board certified (77.4 percent) than were the physicians visited by the white patients (86.1 percent, P=0.02) and also more likely to report that they were unable to provide high-quality care to all their patients (27.8 percent vs. 19.3 percent, P=0.005). The physicians treating black patients also reported facing greater difficulties in obtaining access for their patients to high-quality subspecialists, high-quality diagnostic imaging, and nonemergency admission to the hospital. (Bach, Pham, Schrag, Tate, & Hargraves, 2004, p. 575)

Thus, access to health insurance directly affects access to health care. Although most Americans believe that the issue turns on whether one has health insurance, these data suggest that the type of health insurance that one has is causally related to the type of care to which one has access. African Americans, who are more likely to have chronic diseases such as cardiovascular disease (stroke) and diabetes, are less likely to have access to the types of specialists (endocrinologists, cardiologists, and so forth) who have the training necessary to treat these diseases (Jha, Fisher, Li, Orav, & Epstein, 2005).

Another layer of access is physical proximity to a clinic or hospital. Although this is less of an issue in urban settings that have many clinics and hospitals that are on public transportation routes (buses and trains), this is a serious and significant issue in smaller communities and in rural counties where many African Americans live. For example, in rural Mississippi, there are counties that have no hospital beds (Hattery & Smith, in press)—not even one. In the poorest parts of the country, such as rural counties in Mississippi, African Americans may have to drive 50 miles or more to find a hospital or clinic (Hattery & Smith, in press). And this assumes that they have access to a car, which the poorest often do not. Yet we do not have to look further than our own community to see this same situation.

Winston-Salem: A Case Study

Winston-Salem is a medical community. The town leaders boast that the health care industry employs more local citizens than any other.[13] We have two major hospitals, Forsyth Medical Center and the North Carolina Baptist Hospital, at Wake Forest University, which is also one of the four medical schools in the state. We have an entire section of town devoted to doctor's offices, rehabilitation compounds, and medical research labs. One would think that access to health care in Winston-Salem would not be a problem.

But like so many southern cities, Winston-Salem is deeply segregated. With a total population of just over 185,000, African Americans make up 37.1% of the city's population, most of whom live in East Winston—a section that is separate from what is simply referred to as Winston-Salem—by Highway 52. In order to clarify when we mean the entire community and when we mean the "white" section of town, we will refer to the white section as West Winston. Maps of East Winston confirm that neighborhoods in this part of town are 75%–95% African American, whereas neighborhoods in West Winston are 85%–90% white.[14]

We decided to examine the prevalence of clinics and physicians in both East and West Winston.[15] Although there are private practices in Winston-Salem, the "clinic" market is dominated by Aegis, which is affiliated with North Carolina Baptist Hospital, which is affiliated with Wake Forest University. We found that there are eight Aegis clinics in Winston-Salem; six of the clinics are in West Winston and only two are in all of East Winston. This is despite the fact that both areas of town are of similar geographic size. Both of the clinics in East Winston are located very near the racial boundary, in the westernmost part of East Winston. And like so many cities of its size, Winston-Salem's public transportation system (buses) is very limited. As a result, the majority of residents in East Winston do not live within walking distance or an easily accessible bus route to either clinic.

One of the wonderful features of the Internet is that it allowed us to see pictures of the staff at each of the eight clinics in Winston-Salem. We were actually stunned to discover that all of the physicians in the West Winston clinics are white and all of the nine physicians in East Winston clinics are African American. With even the most rudimentary training in statistics, it is obvious that the probability of this being a random event is zero. There was not a single case of a physician crossing racial boundaries and working in a clinic that serves a population that is racially different from him- or herself.[16] Our overall conclusion is that access to health care in Winston-Salem is shaped by race, and it is a segregated system. African Americans are served in clinics that are segregated and staffed by physicians who are African

American, and whites have the same segregated experience. We strongly suggest that the situation in Winston-Salem results in differential access and inequalities in the type of health care received, and that this is in clear violation of the *Brown v. Board of Education* decision.

Delays in Treatment

There are serious racial and gendered disparities in the ways that treatments for various acute and chronic diseases are dispersed.[17] For example, African Americans and women of all races presenting with acute cardiovascular symptoms were significantly less likely to be offered interventions, and they were also less likely to be offered surgical procedures such as bypass. The disparities exist even when all other factors associated with assessment for surgery are held constant. In an extensive review (meta-analysis) of delays in treatment, the studies reported in an Institute of Medicine book note that delays extend to virtually all areas, from cancer to cardiovascular disease to diabetes to analgesia (Smedley, Stith, & Nelson, 2003).

Delays in treatment are important because the likelihood of surviving cancer or living long term with a chronic disease is significantly affected by the time of diagnosis. When diagnosis is delayed, lifestyle changes (such as diet and exercise) and treatments are delayed; and when treatment is delayed, morbidity is higher. Delays of treatment occur for many different reasons. First, treatment may be delayed because the patient may not be diagnosed. Diagnosis may be delayed because the patient fails to present his or her symptoms to a health care professional either out of fear or mistrust, or because he or she lacks health insurance, financial resources, and/or access to health care. Diagnosis may also be delayed because of biases on the part of the health care professional. For example, it is well known that physicians are less attentive to symptoms of heart disease in women than they are in men, and this is directly related to delays in treatment according to the Institute of Medicine (Smedley et al., 2003). Third, treatment may be delayed because the health care professional whom the patient sees is underqualified or undertrained. Because African Americans are far less likely to have health insurance at all—and when they have health insurance, it is typically Medicaid—they are far less likely to get regular health care. When they do receive it, it is more likely at the hands of uncertified physicians, in lower quality clinics, and in family clinics and emergency rooms that are rarely staffed by specialists. Thus, delays in treatment may be directly related to access to health insurance and health care. Finally, delays in treatment may be a result of prejudice and discrimination. For example, a health care professional may deny a medical procedure because he or she believes that the patient will not make the lifestyle changes that are necessary to accompany the treatment. Again, there is strong evidence for this. Diabetics are refused treatment because health care providers do not believe certain patients will adhere to dietary changes and exercise programs (Kleinfield, 2006). We illustrate this phenomenon using the example provided by HIV/AIDS.

HIV/AIDS

As we have noted throughout this chapter, one of the major health issues facing the African American community is HIV/AIDS. For a variety of reasons, we turn our attention to this disease. First, HIV/AIDS is lethal. The past decade or so has brought drug therapies that extend life such that what used to be a virtual immediate death sentence has moderated, and we now find some HIV-positive (HIV+) patients living 20 or more years without developing AIDS or Aids Related Complex. However, unlike cancer, which in many cases can be "cured," there is no such cure for HIV/AIDS, only treatments that extend life. Second, HIV/AIDS is now among the leading causes of death for African Americans, and it is a top cause of premature death (death between ages 25 and 44). Third, it is a preventable disease. Unlike many other terminal diseases, there are a limited number of specific ways that HIV can be transmitted: (a) blood exposure (contaminated needles, blood transfusion, etc.); (b) semen (sexually transmitted); and (c) exposure at birth (through the birth canal and/or breast milk). Fourth, HIV/AIDS is embedded in the African American community and is devastating African American families.

Delays in Treatment

As with so many other diseases, delays in treatment for HIV/AIDS are both critical and racialized. Because there is no cure for AIDS, the very best that an HIV+ patient can hope for is an aggressive treatment that will extend life.[18] The longer the delay in treatment, the more quickly the patient will develop full-blown AIDS. Several studies note delays in anti-retroviral treatment for African Americans (Bennett et al., 1995; Shapiro et al., 1999). This remains true even when there is no difference in the stage of HIV at the time of presentation (Moore, Stanton, Gopalan, & Chaisson, 1994). Part of the racial disparity in the role that HIV/AIDS plays in causes of death for whites and African Americans results from the fact that rates of infection are higher among African Americans. But these data on the delays in treatment indicate that this form of discrimination also contributes to earlier deaths for African Americans with AIDS. In North Carolina, for example, African Americans with AIDS are twice as likely to die as whites (Deayer & Ingram, 2004).

Finally, we note that anti-retroviral treatment costs $1,200–$1,500 per month, and if it is not paid for by insurance companies, the cost itself will be prohibitive for many African Americans who are HIV+. In context, this treatment cost is nearly twice the take-home pay of an individual earning minimum wage. But without these drug therapies, an HIV+ patient will soon develop full-blown AIDS and be yet another premature death, thus leaving his or her family with medical bills and without the income that he or she had previously provided, which only adds to the devastation of the disease.[19]

Incarceration

The relationship between incarceration and HIV/AIDS is complex. We will devote an entire chapter (Chapter 9) to the issue of incarceration, but here we note two key issues. First, rates of HIV/AIDS are higher inside prisons than in the "free world" (C. Greene, personal correspondence, 2005; Solursh, Solursh, & Meyer, 1993). As noted earlier in this chapter, IV drug use is the most common way for African American men to be infected with HIV. Because the incarceration policies in the United States focus on illicit drug use, many of these men end up spending some time in jail or prison. Yet prisons and jails vary in their procedures for dealing with HIV+ inmates. In many instances, including our local jail (Forsyth County Jail), HIV+ inmates are housed in the general population. In contrast, at the Mississippi State Penitentiary at Parchman, HIV+ inmates are also housed in the general population, but when/if they develop full-blown AIDS, they are housed in a special AIDS unit. This practice has less to do with concerns about HIV transmission and more to do with the serious medical requirements needed to treat AIDS patients.[20]

Because HIV+ men are housed in general prison populations, and because the rate of consensual and nonconsensual sex among the inmates and between guards and inmates is estimated to be very high (Staples, 2004), many inmates who enter prison without HIV are released from prison HIV+. This phenomenon is exacerbated by the fact that because prisons have an official ban on sex between inmates, "condoms are banned or simply unavailable in more than 95 percent of the nation's prisons" (Staples, 2004, p. A22). These men then re-enter society, most often returning to their home communities and resuming relationships with their wives or girlfriends or forming new relationships, usually with women. We illustrate with the story of "Louise," who was profiled in a story on HIV/AIDS in North Carolina.

Newly released prisoners often plunge immediately into dangerous sexual behavior. "Many inmates who have been locked up for a while want two things when they come out," said Dr. Wohl, who regularly sees current and former inmates in his clinical practice. "One of them is a Big Mac. The other is sex. If you're going to get to them with condoms or health messages, you have to be quick." . . . "When you think about the things that might happen, you think as long as you don't have a baby you're O.K.," Louise said. "You think about the guy you're dating, how he might violate probation and go to jail again and you'll be alone. But you never think that he could have this disease. You never think about that." (Clemetson, 2004)

The issue of HIV transmission and reentry is exacerbated by the fact that, as with so many other phenomena, incarceration is not spread evenly across the population. As we have noted, 25%–33% of all African American men are incarcerated in their lifetime. However, the probability of incarceration is not spread evenly across other status variables, such as social class and educational attainment (see Chapters 7 and 9). As a result, in low-income neighborhoods and housing projects, the majority of African American men will have been incarcerated.

"H.I.V. is an opportunistic disease that thrives on disruptions of social networks," said Dr. David Wohl, an infectious disease specialist at the University of North Carolina, where several studies on the subject are under way. "You can hardly get more socially disruptive than removing double-digit percentages of men from communities for extended periods of time." (Clemetson, 2004)

And because these men return to their neighborhoods of origin, and because many of them bring HIV with them, the women and families who live in these neighborhoods and projects are extremely vulnerable to HIV/AIDS (Clemetson, 2004).

Second, delays in treatment are significantly greater in prison. Greene notes that societal problems are magnified within the prison setting and then magnified many times over in their impact on people living with HIV/AIDS. She concludes that entering prison HIV+ *cuts the time to death in half* (C. Greene, personal correspondence, 2005).

Finally, we note that sometimes the tragedy of nonconsensual sex in prisons and HIV/AIDS results in men dying in prison. We illustrate with the story of a young man at Parchman that was told to us by an inmate named Walter Lott. One of Walter's jobs is to help bury the dead (there are three cemeteries inside the prison farm) and to sing at the funerals. He recalled for us the recent funeral of a 15½-year-old boy. This young man had been sentenced to Parchman at age 14. Shortly after arriving, he was gang raped and, as a result, was infected with HIV. Eighteen months later, at age 15½, he had died of AIDS and was buried on Parchman Farm. This young man was not sentenced to life in prison, nor did he receive the death penalty. But with the current state of prisons in the United States, and especially with regard to HIV/AIDS, any sentence can become a death sentence.

Ignorance/Denial: Men Having Sex With Men, or "the Down Low"

Both scholarly literature (social epidemiology) and case studies (see the North Carolina College Student Study in Altman, 2004) suggest that the rapid rise in HIV infection among heterosexual African American women may be related to the "down low" phenomenon of African American men (Altman, 2004; Barnshaw, 2005).

African American men report at least three reasons for being on the "down low": (a) male-to-male prostitution; (b) habitual men-having-sex-with-men (MSM) behavior that begins in prison and may (or may not) be continued after release; and (c) the desire to "reject a homosexual identity and maintain a façade of heterosexuality within African American culture, where homosexuality is a highly stigmatized identity" (Barnshaw, 2005, p. 5; see also King, 2004).

What remains to be seen is if the recent public attention[21] on men on the "down low" will open up the door for honest discussions of sexuality in the African American community. Men who are having sex with men need to realize that this behavior puts them at risk, and they must adopt safe-sex practices. If, as the public discussions suggest, this phenomenon of men who have sex with men and also women has become relatively common, then women must be encouraged to find out about the past and current sex practices of their male sex partners and require the adoption of safe-sex practices themselves. If the North Carolina College Student study is any predictor, then rates of HIV are significantly higher than previously believed in the African American male population, and college enrollment is no indicator of immunity from HIV (Altman, 2004). African American women also need to be honest about the fact that there is a high probability that the African American men they are with have been to prison (25%–33% have), and that if he has done time, then there is a very high probability that he has had at least one consensual or nonconsensual sex act with another man, putting both him and her at risk for HIV/AIDS.

No one is saying that black people don't care about long-term, stable relationships. . . . But the lower number of economically viable black men destabilizes marriage and long-term partnering. One pattern is the man who has sex with one girlfriend, goes back to a previous girlfriend and then returns to the new one. This kind of pattern can increase H.I.V. spread. (Altman, 2004, p. 18)

The negative effects of this pattern are devastating to African American families. The burdens of living with HIV/AIDS are tremendous for families. The treatment for HIV/AIDS is expensive and often not covered by insurance; the patient typically reaches a point when he or she can no longer work. We illustrate from a case in North Carolina that was published in the *New York Times*. The story is of "William," a man living on the "down low."

> [There were two letters on the coffee table.] One was from the Social Security Administration, informing him that although he had AIDS, he did not qualify for financial benefits. The other was from the Guilford County Department of Social Services, explaining that because he had been denied Social Security, he was ineligible for Medicaid, a benefit he needed to pay for his twice-daily regimen of five AIDS medications. The side effects of those same drugs, he said, made it difficult to work the physically demanding jobs he was qualified for with only an eighth-grade education. (Clemetson, 2004)

Finally, the emotional toll of living with an ill family member and living without that person after he or she dies is immeasurable. We illustrate the problems with denial as they arose in our interviews with African American men, in which we learned about another mask for HIV/AIDS: sickle cell anemia.

Demetrius Demetrius is a young African American man whom we interviewed in Minnesota. (We mentioned Demetrius briefly in Chapter 4 because by age 20, he had already fathered six children.) Demetrius is a small man who appears emaciated and weak. He is clearly in poor health. When we asked him about his job or what he thought he would do with his life, he indicated that he was too sick to work. He claimed to have sickle cell anemia, which is probably true, but he later hinted that he is also HIV+. His denial of his status is severely affecting his help-seeking behavior. When we asked him about his medical care, he indicated that he doesn't go to the doctor because he doesn't like hospitals. For Demetrius, the issue is not access. Living in Rochester, Minnesota, he has access to the very best medical care that is available, even if only on an emergency basis. Yet his dislike of hospitals prevents him from seeking help for either the sickle cell or the anti-retroviral drugs that are essential for his long-term well-being.

What happens in the trajectory of HIV/AIDS cases in the African American community is dependent upon pulling away the shroud and having open and honest discussions about these issues.

Religion, Homophobia, and HIV/AIDS in the African American Community

Nothing is more misunderstood in African American civil society than religious beliefs and the HIV/AIDS illness. Although the comparative research has not been done that answers the question of whether African Americans are more homophobic than all other race and ethnic groups in America, there is strong speculation that African Americans have a high intolerance for male and female homosexuality (C. Cohen, 1999; Constantine-Simms, 2001). A good part of this perspective is embedded within the whole of religiosity among African Americans.

Historically, African Americans are a deeply religious people. Some of that religious belief tends to block empathy for those millions of African Americans living with HIV/AIDS. Summarizing that African American leaders have shunted their responsibilities as leaders, C. Cohen (1999) also shows that in the African American faith community there is the same neglect by the clergy to address the issue of HIV/AIDS. Looking closely at one of the most highly visible African American reverends, Dr. Calvin O. Butts, III, minister of the Abyssinian Baptist Church in Harlem, New York City, we find the following:

> The response of the church is getting better. At one time the church didn't respond and when the church did respond it was negative. Ministries thought that a negative response was in keeping with the thinking that AIDS was transmitted by homosexual transmission, drugs, you know. But as more thoughtful clergy became involved, issues of compassion entered the discussion and we used Jesus' refuge in the house of lepers as an example. (C. Cohen, 1999, p. 286)

Once African American reverends, pastors, and preachers became cognizant of the fact that their churches are, in fact, also businesses (Richardson, Williams, & Harris, 2006), what Rev. Butts alludes to above became a reality. The stance by clergy of the National Baptist Convention has begun to change from what it was: "Seventeen years ago, some pastors were actually afraid to get into the same baptism pool with people who had AIDS. The deadly disease and its causal virus, HIV, were taboo conversations—even in the pulpit" (Edney, 2006).

Today, although not wholly embracing the people who suffer from this deadly disease, African American churches have begun to join in on the fight against HIV/AIDS. This response clearly could not have come from just criticizing the African American faith community for putting its collective head in the sand. The new response comes from discussions and meetings between clergy and HIV/AIDS activists, who are coming together to understand the connections that they have in trying to help African Americans suffering from HIV/AIDS (Peterson, 1998).[22]

Environmental Injustice

Whether it was the racing car track at the Freeport Stadium; the city dump; the place men took rags, bottles, and even lead from the bullets used at the police firing range that were lodged in the earth pit behind the targets; or the old automobile junkyard with the fearsome "junkyard dog," one author always asked why all of these eyesores were located on the African American side of town.

Research on environmental degradation by Robert Bullard and colleagues in the southern United States has documented[23] the existence of chemical sites in places such as Alabama, Louisiana, Oklahoma, South Carolina, and Texas. The total capacity of these toxic landfills represents 60% (76,226 acre-feet) of the nation's total hazardous waste landfill capacity (Bullard, 1990).

Unique in all of this is the identification of concentrated sites that house the chemical plants and factories that produce toxic chemicals that are released in the air and water of surrounding *minority* communities. The rates of diseases—including asthma (Kozol, 2001), cancer, and birth defects—in these areas are statistically significantly higher than in any other region of the United States. The CDC refers to these areas as "cancer alley" (CDC, 2006). Just like the statistical improbability that rates of cancer and birth defects are unrelated to the environmental hazards, equally as improbable is the relationship between the location of these plants and the racial composition of the surrounding communities.[24] We illustrate with a case study: Norco, Louisiana.

Environmental Causes of Poor Health: Norco

Diamond, Louisiana, has a history that dates to slave times. Free blacks set up this community, and it has existed as a community for African Americans for hundreds of years. However, in the late 1950s, Shell Oil came in and not only began to move the residents out but renamed the town to its current name, Norco (for New Orleans Refinery Company).[25]

Today, Norco, a small community of just several city blocks, is literally sandwiched in between the Shell Oil Refinery on one side and the Shell Chemical Plant on the other. The refinery and chemical plant, which bound Norco, are no more than 300 yards apart. In this 300-yard-wide swath of land live Norco's residents.

Residents with whom we spoke,[26] including a woman named Iris, told of health conditions such as asthma, lung cancer, miscarriages, and higher-than-average rates of birth defects and various other cancers, all of which they attribute to the environmental hazards associated with Shell Oil. We note that we were in Norco for only a few hours, and during our time there, most of us reported that it was like walking behind the exhaust pipe of a city bus. We could hardly breathe, and we all found it impossible to imagine living in this environment.[27]

The Politics of Health Care

The locations of chemical plants, hazardous waste dumps, and incinerators are not random; rather, they are highly correlated with the race and class composition of the surrounding community. The decisions about where to locate these environmental hazards are political. In this final section of the chapter, we examine some of the lingering effects of racial mistreatment by the medical profession as well as some current issues at the intersection of race and health. We begin with some current issues.

The Genetics (and Politics) of Race/Ethnicity and Health

As we discussed at length in Chapter 2, sociologists have been arguing for decades that race is a social rather than a biological concept. In Chapter 3, we also described the common and long-practiced experience of white men having consensual and nonconsensual sexual intercourse with African American women. This practice began during slavery and continues today. The fact that there was much more racial "mixing" than has been acknowledged plays an important role in the science of medicine in the 21st century. The mapping of the human genome (DNA) (http://www.ornl.gov/sci/tech resources/Human_Genome/research/research.shtml) has brought about some clarity in an area that until just recently many refused to accept: the belief that race is a social rather than a biological or genetic construct.[28]

DNA testing has provided a way to discover evidence for racial ancestry. Since the discovery of the human genome and the burgeoning of DNA companies, both African Americans and whites have used DNA testing to explore possible kin relations that had formerly been restricted to the realm of myth or speculation (Harmon, 2005). When Americans have their "racial maps" constructed via DNA, more often than not they learn that although they always believed they were exclusively of one racial group ("black" or "white"), they learn that they are, in fact, of mixed race heritage. All of this is in the face of our belief that we can tell our race by the way we look (the complexion of our skin, the texture of our hair, etc.).

What does all of this have to do with health and illness? Essentially, this means that looking at race differences in health and illness is a tenuous proposition at best because this analysis assumes a stable construct of race when, in fact, race is a fluid construct. Many of us who are classified as being of one race ("black" or "white") are actually of mixed ancestry. Thus, any analyses of disease and/or treatment based on differences by race are inherently flawed.[29]

Racial disparities in the delivery of health care are, however, an entirely different situation. Because access to health care is shaped by what we look like (our external presentation of race) and how people perceive us and treat us, we absolutely argue that racial disparities in health and illness that are related to access to health care, access to diagnosis and treatment, and so forth are indisputably shaped by race.

It should be quite clear as we are deep into this discussion that much about health in the United States is about politics. People do not die in the United States because of things such as famine or war. (Certainly, soldiers die every day in Iraq and Afghanistan, faraway places that many Americans cannot locate on a map.) Americans do not die because the drugs needed to fight the disease are too expensive for import (although they may be too expensive for purchase by individual patients), as is the case with anti-retroviral drugs in Africa. Americans do not die of preventable diseases like dysentery or cholera, as so many do in Africa and Asia. Americans have poor health and die early because of politics that are largely shaped by race and social class. In this section of the chapter, we will highlight two distinctly political issues: first, the new controversy over the development and marketing of drugs specifically to African Americans; and second, the role that past discrimination plays in African Americans' attitudes toward, and thus utilization of, health care.

Drugs Targeted at African Americans

In June 2005, the Food and Drug Administration (FDA) approved a drug called BiDil to treat cardiovascular disease specifically in African Americans (Stein, 2005). In clinical trials, BiDil proved to be successful in treating heart disease among self-identified African Americans, whereas it showed little promise treating heart disease in those self-identifying as white. The decision to approve and market this drug—the first time in U.S. history that a drug has been approved for a specific racial group—is not without controversy.

On one side are physicians and scholars interested in health disparities, who note that this is finally a move in the right direction in that it brings attention to the fact that 700,000 African Americans have chronic heart disease, and they seem somewhat less likely to respond to traditional therapies.[30] In contrast, however, others view the decision as just another step in reversing the gains of the civil rights movement and moving back toward the Jim Crow era, when there were certain things that were appropriate for whites only and others appropriate for African Americans only. They argue that this is especially dangerous because the marketing of this drug is based on the presumption that there are basic biological differences between African Americans and whites, which is the same argument that was used to keep African Americans, for example, out of swimming pools[31] (see Smith, 2007).

In brief, the controversy over BiDil both relies on and is contradicted by the logic of race, as we detailed in Chapter 2. The development of BiDil relies on DNA or genetic coding. Basically, the pharmacology is based on the fact that an individual's genetic make-up will make him or her less or more receptive to specific drug therapies. The basic logic is that racial variations in our genetic make-up will mean that African Americans are more receptive to certain drug therapies and less receptive to others, and that the opposite will be true for whites.[32]

Yet the very same DNA research that we summarized earlier demonstrates clearly that racial phenotype and racial genotype are not always consistent. To put it in lay terms, some proportion of Americans who *appear* to be clearly either "black" or "white" have DNA that confirms that they actually trace their ancestry to both the European and African continents. Thus, prescribing (or not prescribing) a drug based on *phenotype* will be fraught with error precisely because the science of BiDil depends on a *genotype* relationship. Although we applaud the attention that heart disease in the African American community is receiving, we are skeptical that this new race-based medicine will indeed be successful, especially when it relies on phenotype rather than genotype.

A History of Mistrust

For a variety of reasons, African Americans have a long and justified history of distrust of the medical community. Although most Americans do not know the details of the racial disparities in disease, treatment, and death that we have detailed here, many African Americans have had personal experiences with discrimination in hospitals and clinics, and many still remember when hospitals, clinics, and even blood banks were segregated. Furthermore, as the facts about the Tuskegee experiments and the eugenics movement come into the public discourse, African Americans and whites have to confront the realities of racial discrimination and even genocide that have been part of mainstream medicine in the United States.[33]

Segregated Medicine

Scientists studying issues related to how African Americans interact with the medical establishment have uncovered several facts about these interactions. Several research findings suggest that, more than other Americans, African Americans fear not only doctors but the medical establishment itself, including the research arm. Corbie-Smith, Thomas, Williams, and Moody-Ayers (1999) found that mistrust of doctors, scientists, and the government was reported consistently by the participants. Many participants described concerns about the ethical conduct of clinicians and investigators when poor or minority patients are involved and cited examples of exploitation as supporting evidence for their mistrust of the medical establishment.

A recent study by Schnittker, Pescosolido, and Croghan (2005) notes that African Americans were not less likely to seek medical treatment, expect less from medical treatment, or have less faith in the institution of medicine. They did note, however, that African Americans were more likely to refuse treatment. They suggest that this "treatment refusal may have more to do with the actions of physicians than with the expectations of patients" (Schnittker et al., 2005, p. 267). They identify several possibilities for this refusal, such as the amount of time the physician spends with the patient, the responsiveness of the physician to the patient's needs, and the degree to which the treatment is negotiated between patient and physician.

> Finally, the results would seem to diverge from research that finds African Americans are less trusting of their physicians. Yet, it is not uncommon to observe differences between beliefs about institutions and beliefs about actors within those institutions. . . . In the case of medicine, *African Americans may be skeptical of their personal physicians or believe that physicians treat other African Americans poorly. But, nevertheless, they may remain optimistic about what medicine can provide, at least in the abstract* [emphasis added]. Indeed, African Americans may be more optimistic, despite the fact that whites have disproportionately benefited from modern medical improvements. (Schnittker et al., 2005, p. 267)

Empirical research shows it is still the case that African Americans, and especially lower-class African Americans, fear institutionalized medicine in the United States (Carlos & Chamberlain, 2004). Some researchers report that African Americans also find the medical establishment reminiscent of bygone days when African Americans were barred from access to any type of medical care unless it was in those segregated establishments. This would include, among other things, being turned away from a hospital and sent to other institutions that allowed African Americans to get care.[34] The most famous case of the debilitating effect of segregated hospitals, and one reason African Americans today fear not just doctors but the entire medical establishment, is that of Dr. Charles Drew.[35] Whatever the actual cause of Dr. Drew's death,[36] it is clear to us that segregation in U.S. hospitals did not further the cause of adequate and accessible health care for African Americans. Rather, it contributed to a strong belief among African Americans that the medical establishment participated in racially discriminatory practices and that the institution itself could not be trusted.[37]

In the autobiography by historian John Hope Franklin, he recounts from his days at Fisk University that in 1931, Professor Juliette Derricotte had taken two students with her to Georgia for a short vacation. While they were driving on a rainy afternoon, they had a head-on collision with a white couple in Dalton, Georgia. The professor and one student traveling with her were seriously injured, but they were denied admission to the local tax-supported hospital. "They were sent to the home of an African American woman who provided beds for sick or injured black patients" (Franklin, 2005, p. 43).

The Tuskegee Experiments

Distrust of the medical establishment by African Americans was strongly shaped by two other important events as well: the Tuskegee syphilis experiments and the eugenics movement. The Tuskegee experiments involved letting poor African American men with syphilis go untreated in order to study the long-term effects of the disease.

For 40 years, between 1932 and 1972, the U.S. Public Health Service (PHS) conducted an experiment on 399 black men in the late stages of syphilis. These men, for the most part illiterate sharecroppers from one of the poorest counties in Alabama, were never told what disease they had, nor were they informed of its seriousness. They were told that they were being treated for "bad blood," but their doctors had no intention of curing them of syphilis at all. The data for the experiment were to be collected from autopsies of the men, and they were thus deliberately left to degenerate under the ravages of tertiary syphilis—which can include tumors, heart disease, paralysis, blindness, insanity, and death. "As I see it," one of the doctors involved explained, "we have no further interest in these patients until they die" (Jones, 1981, p. 134).

The Eugenics Movement

The eugenics movement of the early 20th century is another example of institutionalized racism.[38] Proposed by national leaders like President Theodore Roosevelt (forever ensconced on Mount Rushmore) and academic leaders like Wake Forest's very own president William Louis Poteat, the eugenics movement was a social movement for the improvement of the races that relied primarily on the sterilization of potential "unfit" parents. The policies had both social class and racial overtones (for a detailed account, see Schoen, 2001).

Davis (1983) details both forced and nonconsensual sterilizations practiced on the African American and Native American communities. An example of forced sterilization comes from the South Carolina Board of Obstetrics and Gynecology. Until 1973, the official stance of the South Carolina Board was that in cases in which a (black) woman presented to give birth, if she was on "welfare," the physician was to refuse to deliver the baby until she "consented" to having a tubal ligation (a sterilization procedure) performed during the delivery procedure (Davis, 1983). Here is the account of a North Carolina woman in just this situation:

> Nial Cox Ramirez remembers every detail of what happened to her in 1965, even though she has been trying hard to forget. Ramirez had a choice to make, and it was a wrenching decision for an 18-year-old who had just had her first child. Her options? Sign a form from the Eugenics Board of North Carolina "consenting" to be sterilized, or have welfare payments for her mother and six brothers and sisters cut off. (Begos & Railey, 2002, p. 1)

This procedure was so common that in North Carolina alone, "the records of the N.C. eugenics program, which ran from 1929 to 1974, are in the state archives in Raleigh with the names of about 7,600 people who were sterilized" (Begos & Railey, 2002, p. 1). Davis (1983) estimates that, nationwide, more than 65,000 women, mostly African American and Native American, were sterilized without their consent.

The tragedies of the eugenics movement are many. The program itself was designed to effect a near-genocide of African American and, to a lesser extent, Native American *citizens* living in the United States. Although it was obviously unsuccessful, the human costs were significant. In short, the outcomes of these discriminatory practices inside the institution of medicine continue to have adverse effects in African American families.

Race, Class, and Gender Paradigm

In this chapter, we have provided an overview of issues related to health and well-being in the African American community. Unfortunately, on nearly every front, the story is dismal. African Americans are more likely to suffer from many chronic diseases, such as cardiovascular disease and diabetes. They are more likely to be among the uninsured, and when they are insured, they are often relegated to the rolls of Medicaid rather than having private, employer-based health insurance. This situation seriously limits their access to all kinds of health care, but especially the kinds of preventive and ongoing care that would reduce the incidence and severity of chronic diseases.

African Americans die earlier than white Americans and for different reasons. Whereas 90% of the leading causes of death for whites are diseases of lifestyle and age, 20% of the leading causes of death for African Americans are preventable and premature: HIV/AIDS for both African American men and women and homicide for African American men. African Americans now comprise half of all of the HIV/AIDS cases in the United States. And because they face discrimination in treatment (as they do for nearly all medical conditions), they die sooner.

The African American community is being devastated by illness and premature death. And the effects on African American families are extraordinary. Because African Americans are more likely to face health crises and live with chronic diseases, the burdens on family members are tremendous. These burdens include both financial and emotional strain as well as the burnout associated with long-term caregiving. But clearly, the greatest impact is the disruption that premature death causes in families. Children grow up without parents and grandparents; partners are widowed and live out their lives alone. It is impossible to measure the impact of this on African American families.

African Americans face greater problems with regard to health and illness for a variety of reasons: poverty, lack of health insurance, lack of access to clinics and hospitals, stress, and discrimination in treatment. Perhaps the most serious aspect is the strained relationship between African Americans as a community and medicine as an institution. We discussed here two key events, the Tuskegee syphilis experiments and the eugenics movement, that created a sense of distrust and fear among African Americans. Medicine was used to *severely harm* them rather than help them. Although solutions can be implemented to increase the health of African Americans, repairing the hurt and rebuilding the trust of a century of abuse will be difficult.

The utility of a race, class, and gender lens is perhaps best illustrated by the discussions of health, well-being, and death that we focused on in this chapter. For example, almost every disease, from heart disease to HIV/AIDS, that we discussed is significantly shaped by race, gender, and social class. Access to health insurance and treatment is similarly shaped. Perhaps the most vivid example of this is provided by the discussion on HIV/AIDS. Rates of infection and mode of transmission are heavily shaped by race and gender, and access to treatment is shaped significantly by social class. Without considering the impact of all three systems of oppression and privilege, we remain entrenched in a limited understanding of health and well-being in the contemporary United States. Finally, we remind the reader to examine the essay on Dr. Wright, written by his son Kai, who poignantly demonstrates, through the premature death of his father at age 57 from complications of diabetes, the impact of race, class, and gender on the health and well-being of individual African Americans and their families.

This theory holds that black folks carry a legacy of disease that isn't genetic but that nonetheless is transferred from one generation to the next—and eventually catches up even with those who clamber up the socioeconomic ladder. Wright's father died, according to this theory, from the side effects of racism (Wright, 2006).

Solutions

Although there is much to be addressed, we offer some suggested solutions:

- Create a high-quality national insurance program that provides health insurance to all uninsured Americans.
- If the first cannot be accomplished, require that all employers provide affordable, high-quality health insurance for all of their adult employees and their dependents.
- Dismantle *Plessy v. Ferguson* as it relates to clinics and hospitals. Separate has never been equal, and that remains true in the 21st century.
- Encourage African American community leaders to have frank and honest discussions about sexuality and HIV/AIDS.
- Provide condoms in prisons and enforce laws that prohibit the rape of inmates by other inmates and staff.
- Expose the health effects of environmental hazards and construct a disposal plan in which no single group bears the burden.
- Enforce laws that prohibit race-, gender-, and social class–based medicine unless doing so would be harmful to the patient.[39]

The institution of medicine and the white community need to take seriously the devastating impact of the Tuskegee syphilis experiments and the

eugenics movement and move beyond apology to the hard work of rebuilding trust, which begins by listening to the fears and concerns that African
Americans express.

Notes

1. Dr. Vicente Navarro, Professor of Public Policy, Sociology, and Policy
Studies at the Johns Hopkins Bloomberg School of Public Health. This address was
to the 2003 graduating class of the Johns Hopkins Medical School.

2. Within a month of completing the revisions for this book (2006), approximately 13 miners were killed in mining accidents in West Virginia. To be clear, we
do recognize that there has been a long history of workplace violence. Recently, a
postal worker, Jennifer Sanmarco, killed eight co-workers in Oleta, California. This
is the most deadly serial murder of co-workers by a woman, and in 2003, Doug
Williams shot 14 co-workers, killing 6, at a Lockheed Martin aircraft plant in
Meridien, Mississippi.

3. For example, the king of the United Arab Emirates comes annually to the
Mayo Clinic for his routine physical examination. He brings with him an entourage
of more than 300 royalty, who also receive their health care in the United States.

4. Namely, the CDC reports that one of the primary risk factors for diabetes is
a parent with diabetes. Diabetes, as a lifestyle disease, is highly correlated with
poverty. Children who grow up poor—and 40% of African American children are
poor—have less access to exercise and healthy food. In part, this access is a direct
result of living in poverty. Segregation also has an effect on poor African American
children. They typically live in neighborhoods that have understocked grocery stores
across the street from fast food restaurants that serve unhealthy but affordable food.
They attend underresourced schools that may not have playgrounds and that have
often seen cuts in their physical education programs. The typical African American
student in an underresourced school gets no more than 50 minutes per week of
physical education. Finally, poor African American children often live in neighborhoods that no longer have usable parks and playgrounds. In effect, exercise and
healthy food, not to mention regular health check-ups, become luxuries that only
the affluent can afford.

5. Although we talk about many forms of disease as being preventable—
diseases such as heart disease and diabetes—we argue that HIV/AIDS is distinct for
several reasons. First, it is the only one of these diseases that has no genetic component. In contrast, heart disease, stroke, diabetes, and even cancer seem to have some
risk that is transmitted genetically. Second, whereas these diseases have multiple
causes and thus require multiple modifications of behavior in order to reduce one's
risk (not smoking, eating a healthy diet, exercising, reducing stress, and so on), one
needs to modify only two behaviors in order to reduce one's risk for HIV/AIDS:
engage in safe-sex practices with a minimum number of partners, and refrain from
IV drug use.

6. We note here that this does not mean that the disease process itself is the same across gender and race groups. Indeed, one of the biggest critiques of the medical community is the lack of research on heart disease in women (African American or white) and African American men. As we will discuss later, we do not mean to argue that African Americans and whites or men and women receive the same treatment for the disease. In fact, there is a plethora of studies that demonstrates that white men are more likely than either African American men or women of any race to receive treatment and to receive it more quickly when they present to the emergency room with chest pain (see Daumit, Hermann, Coresh, & Powe, 1999; Gregory, Rhoads, Wilson, O'Dowd, & Kostis, 1999; Hannan et al., 1999).

7. The same can be said for losing one's mother, although the data on poverty that were reported in Chapters 2 and 4 indicate that father-headed single-parent families are far less vulnerable to poverty.

8. Access to health care, both pre- and postnatal, is also significantly linked to infant mortality. Mothers who receive prenatal care are more likely to deliver healthy babies of normal birth weight. Similarly, when mothers and their babies receive health care, check-ups, and vaccinations in the first year of life, the babies are far less likely to die in the first year. Finally, mother's age is also a significant predictor of low birth weight and, ultimately, of infant mortality. As noted in Chapter 4, babies born to teenage mothers are at significantly higher risk for low birth weight and infant mortality. Because teen childbearing is significantly more likely among African Americans than whites, this stands as another factor in the racial disparities in infant mortality.

9. The results of an analysis of census data for counties in the Deep South indicate that counties in which African Americans are disproportionately represented (greater than 40% of the county population) have infant mortality rates that are many times greater than the rates for counties in which African Americans are not disproportionately represented. Furthermore, in many cases, the infant mortality rates of these counties are more similar to those of countries in the developing world than to the rate in the United States.

10. We highly recommend Kai Wright's essay on his father's early death at age 57 (Wright, 2006). His father, a surgeon, suffered from many of the hidden costs of being African American that Shapiro describes.

11. Medicaid is a program that has shared funding between the federal and state governments, but the programs are administered by the states. Eligibility varies by state, but in general, Medicaid covers pregnant women, children and teenagers, adults with disabilities, and some very-low-income women.

12. Wal-Mart is an important company to examine because it employs more American workers than any other single corporation.

13. The irony here is that only a few decades ago, most citizens were employed in the tobacco industry, and R.J. Reynolds Tobacco was a cornerstone.

14. Mapping was done using the census program "American Fact Finder," available at http://www.census.gov.

15. We note here that we did not examine either of the two hospitals, both of which are centrally located, but we note that both were racially segregated until the

1970s, and in fact, Baptist Hospital participated enthusiastically in the eugenics movement by sterilizing 7,600 people (women, men, and children), mostly African American, without their consent and against their will (see http://againsttheirwill .journalnow.com/).

16. We do note here, as we are acquainted with some of the African American physicians, that although they serve patients in their own racial group, they live on the "white" side of town.

17. We note that the *New England Journal of Medicine* recently reviewed the issues of inequities in medical care and concluded that grave inequities still exist between African Americans and whites (see Volume 353, Number 7, August 18, 2005).

18. We note that the treatment protocols are extraordinarily expensive, they are often not covered by health insurance, and they have serious side effects. Many HIV+ patients experience severe nausea, exhaustion, facial wasting, and neuropathy. And this is before they develop the debilitating diseases that together make up AIDS.

19. We reiterate: Diseases like HIV/AIDS that result in premature death are terribly disruptive to family life. The effect is similar to that seen shortly after periods of heavy war, such as the Civil War, World War II, and the Vietnam War. Because of serious casualties in these wars, entire generations of women were widowed in their twenties, and generations of children grew up without their fathers. Now that HIV/AIDS is in the top 10 causes of death for African Americans, we know that a similar phenomenon is happening in African American families: A whole generation of people is watching spouses or partners die of this disease that ravages the body; parents are burying their children, who die prematurely in their twenties and thirties, and children are growing up with only the memory of a parent they watched waste away. The vacuum this leaves in families is similar to that left by wars. It is devastating and has long-term effects. And because there is no end in sight to the HIV/AIDS war, we wonder how many more lives will be ruined before it is all over.

20. For the medical staff, it is simply easier to deal with all of these men in the same unit as opposed to having to make rounds to different units (or camps, as they are called at Parchman). Currently, there are approximately 275 inmates with AIDS housed in this unit at Parchman. The prison population as a whole is approximately 6,000, so about 5% of the inmate population has full-blown AIDS.

21. For example, Oprah hosted J. L. King in a discussion on African American men on the "down low."

22. Several good, insightful online articles about the African American community and the African American faith community can be found at the Black AIDS site: http://www.blackaids.org/

23. There is much controversy over the exact nature of "cancer alley." Some call it a myth, and government agencies like the CDC even spent time to set up an agency that keeps track of "cancer alley." Our purpose here is to follow the science and report that in places like "cancer alley," there is overrepresentation of low-income African Americans. The CDC also reports that there are large "cancer alleys" in West Virginia, populated by low-income whites. For a more complete discussion of "cancer alley," see the National Program of Cancer Registries at http://www.cdc.gov/cancer/npcr/

24. See the work of activist Majora Carter at Sustainable South Bronx: http://www.ssbx.org/

25. In the book *Diamond: A Struggle for Environmental Justice in Louisiana's Chemical Corridor* by Professors Steve Lerner and Robert Bullard (2006), we are exposed to the social history of Diamond, Louisiana, and its struggle with the Shell Oil Company. According to Lerner and Bullard's account, the mega-oil company reneged on almost all promises except the relocation. In a move unprecedented in U.S. history (except in the later relocation moves under the Urban Renewal Program that destroyed many minority communities in major urban centers and sent minorities elsewhere), Shell and its side company Motiva pushed residents out, without ever acknowledging that their central nervous system problems and lung cancer were caused by the environmental hazards produced by the refining methods.

26. We visited Norco as part of a course we teach, taking Wake Forest students for 2 weeks through the Deep South. For a description of the course, see our course Web site: http://www.wfu.edu/academics/aes/social_stratification/. We have also published two papers on the pedagogy of teaching this course. See Hattery and Smith (in press), as well as a paper, "Home Grown Poverty," we published on the course as part of Sociologists Without Borders. It can be retrieved at http://sociologistswithoutborders.org/contributions/hattery-smith_-_homegrown_activism.pdf

27. One group that is working on the environmental hazards of Norco is the Louisiana Bucket Brigade. If you would like to learn more about the Louisiana Bucket Brigade, you can check out their Web site: http://www.labucketbrigade.org/communities/norco/profile/index.shtml

28. Since 1992, 160 individuals have been exonerated of crimes of which they had been convicted. Most of these exonerations have been the result of DNA testing that excluded conclusively the person convicted of the crime.

29. We note that in examining health differences by race, we consulted data provided by the CDC. The CDC itself notes that when compiling death statistics and analyzing these by race, there is some degree of error because these statistics rely on the reporting of race as indicated on the death certificate. Because of errors in accurately reporting race on death certificates, there is inherent error in the compilation of statistics. We argue here that in light of the new genetic science of race, any correlations between race and health and illness are inherently flawed.

30. The FDA said the approval marked "a step toward the promise of personalized medicine" (Stein, 2005, p. 15) and was based on research that found the drug could significantly improve the quality of life for black heart disease patients and markedly reduce their chances of being hospitalized and dying.

31. "It invites people to think there are significant biological distinctions between racial groups when in fact the evidence shows nothing of the sort," said M. Gregg Bloche of Georgetown University. "There's a risk of casual thinking that can shade over into discrimination—there's a substantial risk" (Stein, 2005).

32. Of course, this logic should work for any racial group, including Asians and Native Americans.

33. Some of the negative reaction of some African Americans to the "BiDil Experiment" is no doubt reminiscent of Tuskegee.

The old Negro in me, raised on hardship and always on guard for racist enemies, was struck with wariness when I saw a news article about a drug that is being tested specifically for blacks with heart failure. As a friend similarly struck said, "Why? What special physical attributes do we have? . . . Why do you think that we would be the ones who could use this? Does this tie in with sickle cell, because we have a particular genetic trait? Why is it not good for everybody?" The old Negro that lives in me and many of my friends knows about Tuskegee. It's one of the first things to come to mind. (Shipp, 2004)

34. For example, according to the newsletter *Medicine at Michigan,* the more generously endowed facility, James Walker Memorial, maintained about 25 beds for black patients in a ward that had only two toilets and was completely separate from the main hospital building. In order to reach the delivery room, operating room, or other diagnostic facilities, the black patient had to be wheeled or walked 30 yards across an open space. The medical staff didn't just deny black physician applications for privileges; the hospital actually had by-laws that restricted staff privileges to white physicians. Yet Walker Memorial paid no taxes and received public dollars for its support.

35. Dr. Drew was famous for his work with blood and directing the National Red Cross Blood Bank, so it is ironic that stories surrounding his death center around and focus on at least two events. It is widely believed that he died because he was refused a blood transfusion by a white hospital after being in a car wreck. The second belief is that he was badly injured in a car accident, possibly killed, and when he was brought to a white hospital he was refused admission. According to the news reported at the time of Dr. Drew's accident, the nearest hospital refused to treat him, and the time delay in taking him to another hospital that would treat blacks contributed to his death.

36. On the CDC Web site, there is a warning that death certificates often contain faulty information, especially if the person who died is not white. What we don't know about Dr. Drew is this: Could he have been saved if racial discrimination were not a factor in who did and who did not receive medical care in America?

37. We return here to remind the reader of the case study presented earlier in this chapter, noting that although hospitals and clinics are no longer officially segregated (that would be prohibited by law), establishment segregation (see Chapter 7) often exists in health care. Although this is not legal segregation, the outcome, segregated health care, is the same.

38. It is widely accepted that many of the eugenics techniques used by Joseph Mengel in Nazi Germany were developed by and borrowed from the United States. Under Mengel, some 450,000 Jews and other "unfit" people were sterilized.

39. For example, we are not advocating that men and women be given the same treatments if there is clear evidence that doing so would be harmful. What we are advocating is the demise of discriminatory practices that delay treatment protocols for African Americans and women.

7

Access to Opportunity

Educational Attainment and Occupational Segregation

I have never known a man who died from overwork, but many who died from doubt.

—Charles Horace Mayo (1865–1939),
American surgeon and cofounder of the Mayo Clinic

Nonetheless there are few areas in which the value we attribute to a child's life may be so clearly measured as in the decisions that we make about the money we believe its worth investing in the education of one person's child as opposed to someone else's child.

—Kozol (2001), p. 144

I have yet to hear a man ask for advice on how to combine marriage and a career.

—Gloria Steinem

Real education means to inspire people to live more abundantly, to learn to begin with life as they find it and make it better, but the instruction so far given Negroes [and still today] in colleges and universities [and elementary and secondary schools] has worked to the contrary. In most cases such graduates have merely increased the number of malcontents who offer no program for changing the undesirable conditions about which they complain. . . . If you control a man's thinking you do not have to worry about his action. When you determine what a man shall think you do not have to concern yourself about what he will do. If you make a person feel that he/she is inferior, you do not have to compel him/her to accept an inferior status, he/she will seek for it. If you make a person think he/she is a justly outcast, you do not have to order that person to the back door, that person will go without being told, and if there is no back door, the very nature of that person will demand one.

—Woodson (2000), pp. 197–198

Perhaps the most plausible speculation is that those who break through the glass ceiling may be wounded—even destroyed—by the shards.

—Greenwood and Peterson (2006), p. 1B

Objectives

- Examine African Americans' experiences with education and levels of educational attainment, including barriers to educational attainment such as legacy.
- Examine the labor force participation of African American men and women from slavery to today.
- Examine the causes of a race-segregated labor market, including discrimination, legacy, racial disparities in educational attainment, and incarceration.
- Identify solutions to the barriers that African Americans face in higher education and the labor market.

Introduction

A major concern in all societies is the economy. As we outlined in Chapter 3, the economic system of a society structures many other institutions, among them the family unit. Education is perhaps the most important institution that shapes work, income, and inequality. Furthermore, education is believed by most Americans to be the panacea, the miracle solution for all social class inequality that currently exists in the United States. In this chapter, we will examine these two institutions, education and work, that play such an important role in shaping so many other parts of social life. We consider these two institutions together because they are so intertwined and because both are shaped significantly by one's ability to access these institutions.

A Brief History of Race and Education

Denying African Americans access to education has been a fundamental part of their experience for the 400-plus years they have been in the United States. One of the primary mechanisms for keeping slaves on the plantation and totally exploitable by whites was the prohibition against teaching African Americans to read (Washington, 1963). Although slaves did learn to read, according to Williams (2006), they were taught mostly by slave mistresses who believed it was their Christian duty to teach slaves to read the Bible. The penalties for teaching slaves to read involved flogging the slaves and heavy fines for the teachers (Williams, 2006).

Shortly after emancipation, freed blacks began setting up schools all over the South (Gutman, 1976), a move that Williams (2006) argues transformed education in the southern region of the United States. How? The South had never established a system of public education. Instead, wealthy whites, not wanting to pay taxes for public education, had always sent their children to private schools in the Northeast to be educated. Soon after African Americans set up schools to educate their youth, observers including Du Bois noted that African American children were outpacing poor whites in terms of education (Williams, 2006). The response of white citizens was to establish a system of public education in order that poor whites, who could not afford to have their children educated in the private schools in the Northeast, would not fall behind African Americans. Of course, this system of education was segregated and would be challenged on a regular basis until the historic U.S. Supreme Court case of *Brown v. Board of Education of Topeka*, 348 U.S. 886; 1954 U.S. LEXIS 1467, Nov. 22, 1954; *Brown v. Board of Education*, No. 1, 349 U.S. 294; 75 S. Ct. 753; 99 L. Ed. 1083; 1955. The challenges continue in various forms in many parts of the South even today (Boger & Orfield, 2005).

African Americans were also swift in setting up institutions of higher learning. Less than 15 years after emancipation, Booker T. Washington founded the Tuskegee Institute in Tuskegee, Alabama. Across the latter part of the

19th century and into the early part of the 20th century, many more historically black colleges and universities were founded. Many of these institutions
offered undergraduate as well as graduate and professional degrees and
programs. Literally thousands of African Americans were educated and
trained in these segregated colleges and universities, including many of the
most prominent African Americans of the 20th century, such as John Hope
Franklin.

Despite an excellent system of higher education for African Americans,
the majority of African Americans attended inferior grammar and secondary schools. Those seeking to attend white schools, including colleges and
universities, were often denied access. Some schools in the north desegregated
voluntarily and, in some cases, early in the 20th century, but schools in
the South resisted integration severely and systematically (Douglas, 1995). In
some cases, movements to integrate under court order erupted into violence.[1]
The integration of Central High School in Little Rock, Arkansas, was so contentious that President Eisenhower sent National Guard troops to protect the
eight young men and women attempting to attend school there. Similarly,
when James Meredith attempted to integrate the University of Mississippi a
near war broke out, forcing President Kennedy to send in armed troops.
Governor Ross Barnett closed the Ole Miss campus in response.

The *Brown* decision, which guaranteed African Americans the right to
attend any public school, was intended to offer access to the institution of
education in the United States. Yet it has been only partially successful. First
of all, the Supreme Court decision was resisted. It was intensely resisted in
the Deep South, so much so that many southern school districts were not
integrated until the early 1970s, nearly 20 years after the historic decision
(Douglas, 1995). The most severe resistance to school integration was in
Mississippi. The resistance movement resulted in the development of a set
of private, often religiously affiliated, academies that were not required by
the *Brown* decision to integrate (Douglas, 1995; Rubin, 2002). The development of what Rubin (2002) refers to as "segregated academies" has been
the most successful of all strategies employed to resist integration, and it continues today (Rubin, 2002).

We also note that following the period of real progress in school integration (the 1970s to 1990s), over the past 15 years, we have seen a serious
reversal of that trend—a 13% decline in integration, according to Boger and
Orfield (2005)—such that African American children today are more likely
to attend schools that are more highly segregated than the schools their
parents attended (Boger & Orfield, 2005; Kozol, 2001, 2005). Boger and
Orfield (2005) note that although minority enrollment in public schools is
now nearly 40% nationwide, the typical white student attends a public

school that is 80% white. Furthermore, a high percentage of African American students (actual rates vary depending on the region of the country) attend schools that are 100% African American (Boger & Orfield, 2005). Consistent with the U.S. Supreme Court case of *Plessy v. Ferguson* (1896), Jonathan Kozol has demonstrated repeatedly across the past two decades that separate education is never equal (Kozol, 1992, 2001, 2005).

Educational Attainment

Given this long history of a struggle for equal education, it is not surprising that education remains a site of inequality for African Americans. The data on educational attainment for African Americans and whites are dismal. (A full table of educational attainment that includes data on graduate and professional degrees is available in Appendix G.)

One of the most controversial parts of Table 7.1 is the data on high school graduation rates. The table shows only a minor gap (5% or 6% difference) in the high school graduation rates for African Americans and whites. Yet other studies note that there is a wide disparity in the graduation rates of white and minority students, especially with regard to the type of diploma earned.[2] In the class of 2002, about 78% of white students graduated from high school with a regular diploma, compared to 56% of African American students and 52% of Hispanic students (Greene & Winters, 2005).

There is also a significant race/ethnic difference in the percentage of students who leave high school eligible for college admission. About 40% of white students, 23% of African American students, and 20% of Hispanic students who started public high school graduated "college-ready" in 2002 (Greene & Winters, 2005; Greene, Winters, & The Manhattan Institute for Policy Research, 2005; Herbert, 2005a). We will assume that the real racial disparity lies somewhere between the government estimate of 5–10 percentage points and the 20 percentage points that policy researchers report. We do note

Table 7.1   Educational Attainment by Race for Americans Age 25 and Over (summary, in percentages)

Race	No HS	HS	Less Than BA	BA or Higher
White	14.2	85.8	71.8	28.2
African American	19.4	80.6	82.4	17.6

SOURCE: U.S. Bureau of the Census (2004).

that there is reason to believe that the government estimates of high school graduation are inflated. Why? Because George W. Bush's education policy, No Child Left Behind, links school funding to test scores, the percent of students promoted from grade to grade, and graduation rates. Because public school funding is so low, schools rely heavily on the financial incentives that are provided by No Child Left Behind. As a result, schools may report slightly inflated data in order to maximize their financial rewards. In contrast, because the findings of the policy research have no bearing on funding, these numbers may be more accurate. At any rate, the fact remains that African Americans are less likely to graduate from high school than whites, and the racial disparity in college and postcollege education is even greater.

These differences in high school graduation rates translate into a series of parallel problems. First, the high school degree or its equivalent remains a requirement for many jobs that pay above minimum wage. Thus, not having a high school diploma means one will be eligible only for the lowest paying jobs in the service sector (fast food shops and discount retail stores; Schlosser, 2002). The authors of the Manhattan Institute study sum up the outcomes for those not graduating from high school (Greene & Winters, 2005; Greene et al., 2005):

- High school dropouts, on average, earn $9,245 less per year than high school graduates.
- The poverty rate for families headed by high school dropouts is more than twice that for families headed by high school graduates.
- Dropouts are much more likely to be unemployed, less likely to vote, and more likely to be imprisoned than high school graduates. This is particularly true for African American men.

New York Times columnist Bob Herbert made a very sociological observation on the deeper meaning of the impact of dropping out of high school on America and on African American civil society in particular:

> For those concerned about the state of leadership in America, and who wonder where the next generation of leaders will come from, I can tell you it's not likely to emerge from the millions upon millions of dropouts we're setting loose in the land. (Herbert, 2005a, p. A10)

Second, if the quality of the high school education differs, and we know that it does at the level of the state, the county, the individual school, and the track within the school (Kozol, 1992, 2001, 2005), then the opportunities to pursue postsecondary education will differ. And to the degree that the quality of the high school education is tied specifically to race and social class, which it undoubtedly is (Kozol, 1992, 2001, 2005), then the opportunities to attend college *will differ by race and social class*.

The data in Table 7.2 confirm that African Americans are significantly less likely to earn postsecondary degrees (college, master's, professional, and doctoral degrees) than their white counterparts. In fact, African Americans are half as likely to earn a PhD as white women, and only 20% as likely to earn a PhD as white men. There are mild gender effects for African Americans, but significant gender effects for whites. In the case of advanced degrees, such as those earning professional and doctoral degrees, white women are only slightly more likely to earn these degrees than African Americans (men or women) but are significantly *less likely* to earn advanced degrees than their male counterparts. Therefore, educational attainment is yet another important issue that is best understood using a race, class, and gender framework. Omit race or gender and one omits an important part of the story.

In addition, when we examine the prestige of the institutions of higher learning that African Americans and whites attend, we see yet another layer of difference and inequality. For example, African Americans are grossly underrepresented at schools ranked by *U.S. News & World Report* as the "best" colleges and universities in the country (Harvard, Yale, Princeton, Stanford, and even our own Wake Forest University; Smith, 2007; Smith & Hattery, in press-b). We know that the prestige of one's degree is highly correlated with one's opportunities for careers and further education (Bowen & Bok, 1998). Thus, differences in the prestige of the degree-granting institution will contribute to "establishment segregation"—a type of occupational segregation that we will describe later in this chapter. In short, graduates from Harvard and Yale Law Schools, for example, are more likely to be offered clerking positions with the highest courts, and they are also more likely to be offered partner track positions in the most prestigious firms in the country than are graduates of Howard University, which remains one of

Table 7.2   Individuals Earning a Professional or Doctoral Degree by Race and Sex (in percentages)

Race/Gender	Professional Degree	PhD
White men	1.8	1.5
White women	0.8	0.7
African American men	0.7	0.4
African American women	0.5	0.3

NOTE: See the full data in Appendix G.

the most prestigious of the historically black colleges and universities yet is ranked in the third tier of law schools (approximately 125th).

Access to Education: Legacy

One of the major systems of exclusion or "social closure" as defined by Parkin (1979) is the system of legacy. In brief, legacy refers to the passing on of access. Typically, scholars discuss legacy with regard to education: Most colleges and universities offer preferential admission to applicants whose parents, grandparents, or other relatives are alumni (Karabel, 2005).

We argue here that preference for legacies can be considered the ultimate in affirmative action, precisely because it gives preference based on status rather than qualifications. Furthermore, legacy is primarily a benefit that accrues to whites, and white men in particular. What is particularly insidious about legacy is that it is often associated with institutions that refused admission to African Americans until relatively recently, and thus African Americans have been completely locked out of legacy preferences. For example, we will use our own institution to illustrate. Wake Forest University, like most colleges, gives preference to legacies during the process of admissions. Yet Wake Forest University did not admit African Americans until the late 1960s. Thus, a cohort of children of African American alumni, the potential beneficiaries of legacy preferences, didn't even exist until the mid-1990s at the earliest. (Consider that it takes 20–30 years for an alumnus or alumna to have a child who is old enough to apply to college.) In contrast, the children of white alumni have benefited from this practice for at least 150 years. Similar arguments can be made with regard to other institutions, such as politics and trade unions, which only recently became accessible to African Americans. We now examine the ways in which access to education shapes work.

The Economy

The United States is a relatively young country, and the economic transitions in this country have been relatively rapid. Therefore, there are a limited number of economic systems and transitions that we must address. Before the arrival of the European colonizers, the Native Americans lived in two basic economies: subsistence (or hunting-and-gathering) and agriculture. Because western Europe had already transitioned into a full-blown agricultural economy by the arrival of the colonists, they would have brought with them the notion of using the New World as part of an expansion of agriculture. We note here that the land that now constitutes the United States was not the only land colonized for this purpose.[3]

Therefore, although some Native American nations continued to engage in a subsistence economy, this was relegated primarily to the Midwest and western regions of the land, and agriculture quickly dominated the colonies. This historical fact is confirmed by the fact that almost immediately upon the arrival of colonizers in Virginia, the slave trade began bringing Africans to the colonies (see Chapter 2 for a lengthier discussion of the plantation slave economy). The United States was dominated by an agricultural economy until the middle of the 19th century, when the Industrial Revolution, which began in western Europe, arrived in the United States. It spread very quickly in the northern regions of the United States. And for a period of about 100 years, the United States was really two economies: industrial in the North and plantation agricultural in the South. However, by the mid-20th century, the South had industrialized and the transition across the entire United States to the postindustrial service and technology economy had begun. This is the economy in which we live today.

Leaders of every country on the planet pay attention to the health of their nation's sociopolitical economy. Although individual citizens talk vaguely about "the economy," the major concern for these citizens is at the microlevel: work. Work shapes nearly every part of our lives. It provides structure to our days. It provides, in many cases, a sense of gratification and self-fulfillment. It can also provide a social group where many of us find friends and even our romantic partners. Work defines us. We talk about ourselves in terms of the work that we do. I am a carpenter or a teacher or a waitress or a lawyer.

Most importantly, work provides the money we need to pay for all of our material needs, from housing to food to clothing to education for our children. Work and family life are inextricably woven together. Work allows us to provide for ourselves and our family members, but it is also the primary activity that keeps us away from our family members for 40 or 60 or even 80 hours per week (Hattery, 2001b). Thus, work and the economy are very important parts of any discussion of family life.

The absence of work also defines our lives, our families, and even our communities. For example, as we discussed at length in Chapter 5, work is a mark of masculinity, and when men are unemployed, it can lead to the kind of stress in their intimate relationships that often erupts into violence. When work is absent in a community, in what Wright (1997) and others refer to as ghettos, it is the absence of work that defines the community (Wilson, 1996). In a society where adults go to work on a regular basis, it is increasingly clear that in those communities where this model is absent, where there is a high rate of joblessness, young men and women fail to learn that working is normative and unemployment is nonnormative. For example, Wilson (1996) argues that one of the most serious and negative outcomes of chronic unemployment in a community is the "culture" of not working that is created. On the other side of the coin, sociologists have argued that steady employment defines a community and shapes the values that are held by community residents and passed down from one generation to the next (Kasarda, 1993).

Although many sociologists have focused their research on various aspects of work, the work of two prominent sociologists who studied unemployment among African American men is of particular importance to our discussion here. One study was done recently (Wilson, 1996), and the other was conducted about 40 years ago (Liebow, 1967/2003). We review the findings of both studies here because they provide a context for understanding the impact of chronic and widespread unemployment that characterizes many low-income African American communities.

In his book *When Work Disappears* (1996), Wilson is attempting to explain the long-term structural effects of high rates of unemployment for those African Americans, primarily men, living in inner cities. In these socially disorganized neighborhoods and communities, the impact of not working exacts a heavy toll. For Wilson, the inhabitants of these ghettos face grim prospects.

For example, it is important to understand and communicate the overwhelming obstacles that many ghetto residents have to overcome just to live up to mainstream expectations involving work, the family, and the law. Such expectations are taken for granted in middle-class society.

> Americans in more affluent areas have jobs that offer fringe benefits; they are accustomed to health insurance that covers paid sick leave and medical care. They do not live in neighborhoods where attempts at normal child-rearing are constantly undermined by social forces that interfere with healthy child development. And their families' prospects for survival do not require at least some participation in the informal economy (that is, an economy in which income is unreported and therefore not taxable). . . . I argue that the disappearance of work and the consequences of that disappearance for both social and cultural life are the central problems in the inner city ghetto. (Wilson, 1996, pp. xviii–xix)

Some 30 years prior to the arrival of sociologist Wilson and his important work reemphasizing that sociologists should get out and talk to citizens if we are at all interested in understanding their life circumstances from their point of view, Elliot Liebow conducted his ethnographic study in inner-city Washington, DC. For Liebow, who asked a different set of questions, he, too, was interested in the cycle of poverty and the relationship of work to well-being. In an interesting chapter in *Tally's Corner* devoted solely to work (Chapter 2, "Men and Work"), he gives us this poignant portrait of an event that, like Wilson's observations, points out the complexities that come with trying to understand the human condition, and especially joblessness.

> A pickup truck drives slowly down the street. The truck stops as it comes abreast of a man sitting on a cast-iron porch and the white driver calls out, asking if the man wants a day's work. The man shakes his head and the truck moves on up the block, stopping again whenever idling men come within calling distance of the driver. At the Carry-Out corner, five men debate the question briefly and shake their heads no to the truck. The truck turns the corner and repeats the same performance up the next street. . . .
>
> Let us look again at the driver of the truck. He has been able to recruit only two or three men from each twenty or fifty he contacts. To him, it is clear that the others simply do not choose to work. Singly, or in groups, belly empty or belly-full, sullen or gregarious, drunk or sober, they confirm what he has read, heard and knows from his own experience: these men wouldn't take a job if it were handed to them on a platter. (Liebow, 1967/2003, pp. 19–20)

Part of what is remarkable about these two excerpts is their similarity, which suggests the persistence and embeddedness of chronic unemployment in some low-income African American communities and the consequent culture and norms that develop.

Historically, African Americans have been relegated to the low-wage sector of the American economy. The relegation of African Americans to low-wage work has several important implications that will shape the discussion of work and employment in this chapter. First of all, this relegation, based on ideologies that arise out of centuries of slavery, results in a hyper-segregated labor market. Most African Americans and whites do not work together. Second, low-wage work produces a class of people referred to as the "working poor." The working poor work one and sometimes two jobs, but they do not make enough money to stay out of poverty. Thus, low-wage work contributes directly to poverty. Finally, low-wage work that leaves the worker and his or her family in poverty is difficult to sustain in the presence of a welfare system that pays benefits that, taken together, result in a better standard of living than that which can be accomplished on the income associated with low-wage work. This produces a culture that discourages work and encourages dependency. Therefore, in order to understand the current state of work in the lives of African American families, we must begin with a brief examination of the role that slavery played in restricting access to occupations for African Americans.

Slavery and Occupations

The peculiar socioeconomic history of the United States has significantly shaped images of who does what kind of work as well as created racial segregation in the labor force. Because we spent a good deal of time in Chapter 2 talking about slavery as the historical context for race relations in the United States, we will not reproduce that discussion here. However, we note that there are some critical ways in which slavery shaped work and occupational patterns.

The Work Done by African Americans

During the more than two centuries of chattel slavery in the United States, African Americans did all kinds of work. Americans are probably most familiar with the agricultural work that slaves were required to do, primarily the work required for the production of cotton and tobacco, and the other agricultural products that we associate with the plantation economy of the South. However, slaves were also trained in many of the trades, such as blacksmithing, and many accounts of the time note that they were not only masters of these trades but quite gifted in many of the artisan trades (Blassingame, 1979). Historian Kenneth Stampp, in his book *The Peculiar Institution,* pays attention to the varied use of slave labor, including their work as skilled laborers (Blassingame, 1979; Stampp, 1956). One striking piece of evidence we have of this mastery of the trades by African Americans is the Tuskegee Institute in Tuskegee, Alabama.[4] Tuskegee was built using the various trade skills of former slaves, including carpentry, masonry, and glass work. Further evidence comes from the fact that in immediate response to the racial oppression of segregation that followed emancipation, African Americans established every type of school and training program that prepared individuals to perform every type of craft and profession, from blacksmiths to physicians, so that African Americans could service their own communities.

Slaves were also used extensively in the home. Slave women were required to do the cooking and cleaning for the master's family. They were also required to care for the master's children, a task that went so far as to involve wet-nursing the infants.[5] The main point we have made here is that African Americans were involved in literally all of the types of work that whites in the same historical period did. They were skilled artisans, hard-working field hands, and wet-nurses. Despite this fact, African Americans were (a) deemed lazy and (b) denied access to membership in these trade organizations from the Civil War until today. We explore the myth of laziness below and will return to this blocked access in the trades later in the chapter.

The Myth of Laziness

Despite overwhelming evidence to the contrary, several negative stereotypes of the African American laborer have persisted since slavery to today. African American women and men have been portrayed in every possible medium, including motion pictures, across all time periods from slavery to freedom, as lazy, shiftless, and incompetent (Blassingame, 1979; Bogle, 1973; Davis, 1966).[6] This insidious stereotype is captured in Bogle's research.

Certain aspects of the slave relationship were specifically cited by whites as evidence that African Americans are lazy. For example, during slavery, the slave often had to be cajoled to work, sometimes with the whip (Fogel & Engerman, 1974). Furthermore, resistance on the part of pregnant slaves, in the end stages of labor, to work (which any woman who has been pregnant can fully understand) fueled the stereotype that African Americans were lazy (Amott & Matthaei, 1991).[7]

Most white Americans believe that the civil rights movement improved whites' attitudes toward blacks. However, the 2004 General Social Survey (a nationally representative sampling survey) conducted by the National Opinion Research Center included items designed to measure attitudes and beliefs whites held about African Americans. These data confirm the persistence of stereotypes of the laziness of African Americans. The survey found that a majority of the white, Hispanic, and other non-black respondents (78%) said blacks are more likely than whites to "prefer to live off welfare" and are less likely to "prefer to be self-supporting." Furthermore, 62% said blacks are more likely to be lazy, 56% said they were prone to violence, 53% said they are less intelligent, and 51% said they think blacks are less patriotic (Carlson & Chamberlain, 2004).

In the face of mounting evidence that African Americans provided the bulk of the labor that built the United States, we find the persistence of these myths of the laziness of African Americans to be particularly insidious. In fact, large fortunes, both individual and collective, were amassed on the backs of "free" labor provided by African and African American slaves. In the past few years, evidence for this outcome of slavery has become public. For example, as part of the recent requirement the city of Chicago placed on corporations wishing to do business there, corporations must disclose any evidence of their involvement in the slave trade. In 2005, Wachovia (a banking and financial institution) disclosed the following:

Through specific transactional records, researchers determined that the Georgia Railroad and Banking Company owned at least 162 slaves, and the Bank of Charleston accepted at least 529 slaves as collateral on mortgaged properties or loans, and acquired an undetermined number of these individuals when customers defaulted on their loans. (Williams, 2005)

In another illustration that is perhaps more germane for those of us in academic settings, evidence has surfaced that prestigious Ivy League Brown University was built on the fortunes the Brown family amassed in the slave trade.

Slavery was an integral part of the developing economy of colonial and post-Revolutionary Rhode Island. In the early and mid-1700s, members of the Brown family participated in the slave trade while simultaneously developing other enterprises. Slaves were employed at the family's spermaceti candle works and iron foundry, among other businesses, and almost certainly were used for farm work and household labor. In addition, while managing the 1770 construction of the College Edifice (later renamed University Hall), Nicholas Brown & Company apparently used some slave labor. In addition, at one time or another, ships owned by Brown engaged in the triangle trade that brought slaves to the Caribbean and to America (Nickel, 2001). In light of this overwhelming evidence for the hard work of African American slaves, we find the myths of laziness that much more disingenuous.

The relationship between race, gender, and work is also important for two key reasons: First, in research about gender and work, most respondents describe workers as male; and second, the myth of "lazy African Americans" has been grievously and prejudicially applied to African American women through the wholesale dissemination of the term *welfare queen,* coined by President Ronald Reagan (1985).

Race, Class, and Gender: African American Women's History of Work

Perhaps more than any other chapter in this book, there are important and powerful interactions of race and gender that need to be explored and analyzed here. For example, although many slave women worked in the fields alongside men (and children), the tradition of a slave domestic was a powerful force in southern households. Whereas plantation size varied widely from those with only a few slaves to those with thousands, nearly every white household that was *not* poor, regardless of whether it was classified as a plantation or not, had at least one female slave who worked in the house. Slave women were responsible for all of the domestic labor in the white households: cleaning, cooking, and, of course, taking care of the children. This pattern certainly did not end with slavery; in fact, it persists today. For example, when we talk about this phenomenon in our classes, the majority of our white students who are from the South smile and share their fondest memories of the black woman who was their housekeeper or nanny. We note that although nannies and housekeepers are popular in other regions of the country, primarily in the Southwest, where they are mostly Hispanic (Segura, 1994), and in the Northeast, where they are primarily Caribbean immigrants (Waters, 1999), there are two key differences in the South. First, because wages for domestic labor are so low, this phenomenon is not limited to the affluent; in fact, middle-class families often employ a domestic. And second, the patterns are deeply rooted in the historical landscape of slavery.

African American women's labor force participation has also played a different role in their households than white women's participation ever has. As a result of their male partners' unemployment, underemployment, and wage discrimination, African American women sought work as domestics and in other industries in order to provide for the economic needs of their families.

> We only got seven dollars a week. We worked from eight a.m. to five p.m. Monday through Saturdays. Of course, the cost of living [in the 1930s] wasn't what it is today. You could kind of survive. We thought, "Well, that's what the pay is, so . . . ." And, there wasn't any other kind of work. (Rollins, 1985, pp. 109–110)

Thus, the history of slavery set the stage for distinct employment niches for African American women and men. As a result of slavery and continuing through the Jim Crow era, African American men were viewed as strong but intellectually slow. Thus, they were denied access to an education and they were restricted to occupations that required brawn rather than intellectual training. In contrast, whites with any social class standing were educated and pushed toward occupations that were paraprofessional.[8] They were educated and trained to work in education, the trades, and financial occupations such as bookkeeping.

This long history of domestic work resulted in the fact that, in the South at least, domestic work came to be identified with African American women. Not only did they *not* face discrimination with regard to finding domestic work, whites actually preferred to hire African American women to work in their homes. However, as we shall see, overrepresentation in one occupation typically means there is serious underrepresentation in other occupations. And in the realm of work, this is the case.

Occupations and Work

Americans conjure up specific and surprisingly similar images with regard to who does what type of work. When we think of medical doctors, lawyers, investment bankers, and college professors, most Americans see images of white men. When we think of elementary school teachers and secretaries and nurses, we think of white women. When we think of garbage collectors and road crews, we think of African American men, and when we think of food service workers, cleaning "ladies," and, especially in the South, nannies, we think of African American women.

Occupations are highly segregated by race and gender. Many scholars (Maume, 1999; Padavic & Reskin, 2002) agree that occupational segregation is perhaps the most central and critical piece in shaping everything from the work we are offered; to the likelihood that we will face discrimination; to the overall perceptions we have of people (as industrious, smart, or lazy); and perhaps most importantly, the amount of money that can be earned (Pattillo-McCoy, 1999).

Where do these images come from, and how do they shape issues such as aspirations, role-modeling, discrimination, and other aspects of work? Many of these images are, in fact, based in reality; for example, 97% of elementary school teachers are women (Bureau of Labor Statistics, 2005c). But many of these images are either partially false or misleading. For example, when we ask our students to name the top 10 occupations for men, the list they generate typically includes medical doctors, lawyers, college professors, and bankers. When we ask them to name the top occupations for African American men, the list they generate typically includes professional athletes and entertainers.

Social Class Bias: White Men as Doctors, Lawyers, and College Professors

The lists of common occupations that students (and most Americans) typically produce are instructive in what they demonstrate about perceptions. When students generate this list of occupations for white men, they are doing so through a lens that is shaped by biases of social class—this reflects both their own experiences with white men and also the images they see in the media. Although white men are overly represented in these occupations (medical doctor, lawyer, and college professor), these industries do not employ *most* white men. In fact, none of these occupations even makes the top 10 list. Surprised? The reason is because most white men are not professionals. Only 30% of white men work in occupations that can be described as "professional," and the occupations identified by our students comprise only a very small set of occupations within this occupational class. Most white men drive trucks; work in construction; and work in the trades as plumbers, electricians, and so on (Bureau of Labor Statistics, 2005c; Padavic & Reskin, 2002).

All African American Men Are Professional Athletes

Our students, and most Americans, make similar mistakes when they are asked to think about the jobs that African American men do. Most African American men are not professional athletes or entertainers.

Few Americans are aware that there are only 1,600 or so African American men making money playing professional sports, but there are 1,700 African Americans who earn a PhD every year, and there are more than 41,000 African American medical doctors—25 times more than the number playing professional sports (Smith, 2007).

Again, are the students wrong? Yes and no. African American men are overrepresented in the professional sports of football and basketball (Smith 2007),[9] but most African American men *do not* make a living playing professional sports. In fact, African American men are also overrepresented in occupations such as garbage collector, janitor, and unskilled construction worker (Bureau of Labor Statistics, 2005b).

So what if most Americans misunderstand what most people do for a living? The problems with these myths are many. For example, if African American boys grow up surrounded by images of African American men as NBA stars and without images of African American men as corporate professionals, then they are likely to set their aspirations in line with what they see, foregoing an education while they work to develop their skills as basketball players (Smith, 2007).

In fact, the odds that an African American man will become a medical doctor are 25 times higher than the odds that he will play professional sports. Yet because of the media focus on professional athletes (not medical doctors) and because of the glorification of the career (we can credit shows such as MTV's *Cribs,* which allows us to see the lives of players such as Shaquille O'Neill), young African American men "study" to become the next Michael Jordan rather than the next Floyd J. Malveaux, MD, PhD, who specializes in the treatment of and racial disparities in asthma.[10]

We also concur with Wilson that the effect of high rates of unemployment in low-income African American neighborhoods has a similar and equally devastating effect on the aspirations of young African American boys and men (Wilson, 1996). When young men of any race grow up without images of the men in their community going off to work, they are less likely to develop work and professional aspirations themselves. The effects of this are devastating to African American civil society and on African American families.

How? Why? Because African Americans, especially young men, fail to develop their intellectual talents and instead put all of their energy into pursuing an athletic dream that, although more glorious, is riddled with negativity (short career span, crime, drugs, sexual promiscuity) and is also significantly less likely to become reality. (For a longer discussion of the high rates of violence and sexual promiscuity, see especially Smith & Hattery, 2006.) Hence, it is especially important for African American males who look to athletics as the "ticket out of the ghetto" not to be fooled when they see that three of the first five or six first-round picks in the NBA draft come directly out of high school, delivering the message that schooling is far less important than playing a sport. The odds that they will be among the high schoolers who make it out are more remote than winning the multimillion-dollar lottery. Certainly, their chances to escape the life of poverty in which they grew up are far higher if they complete high school and get some post-secondary education in the form of technical training or a college degree. That is the real ticket out.[11]

The image myths also create problems on the other side of the desk. When white men who do the hiring in corporate America see African Americans as athletes rather than professionals, they will inevitably overlook credentialed job applicants who do not fit their image of a new colleague. An African American with a college degree may find that the white man interviewing him assumes he went to college on an athletic scholarship rather than purely for an education. This may lead to doubts about his training and ultimately lead to the decision not to hire him.

Thus, beliefs about what men and women, African Americans and whites, do for a living shape both our individual aspirations as well as the way that we see potential colleagues and job candidates. And these images, although often based in reality, are perpetuated by the media in a way that seriously distorts the truth.

The racial (and gender) segregation in work that began 400 years ago persists today. Why? Because of the persistence of beliefs (held by whites) about their own abilities as well as the abilities of African Americans (Bonilla-Silva, 2001, 2003), legacy (the passing of jobs), differential access to education, differential access to trade/craftsman guilds, and so forth. We turn now to a deeper, empirical discussion of occupational segregation.

Occupational Segregation:
The Impact of Race and Gender

As noted above, the area of work and occupations cries out most strongly for a race, class, and gender analysis. Occupational segregation draws lines using both race and gender such that there is almost no integration in the workplace along lines of either status category. White men work with white men, and African American women work with African American women. This pattern has remained consistent over time. In addition, this segregation crosses all social class lines, thus persisting from the lowest level service work all the way up through the most prestigious professions.

There are two different types of occupational segregation that need to be differentiated. The first is called *industry segregation,* and the second is known as *establishment segregation.*

Industry Segregation

Industry segregation refers to the fact that there are gendered and racialized jobs (Maume, 1999; Tomaskovic-Devey, 1993). In other words, there are jobs that African American men do, jobs that white women do, and so on. This is the type of segregation with which most people are familiar. White men are physicians, white women are teachers, African American women are housekeepers, and African American men are professional athletes. In other words, each industry is dominated by one status group at the exclusion of the others. To illustrate, we note, for example, that 97% of all elementary school teachers are women (sex segregation), and 85% of all U.S. senators are white men (racial and sex segregation).

Establishment Segregation

Establishment segregation is a term that describes the segregation within otherwise integrated (and we use the term loosely) occupations. In the chapter on health (Chapter 6), for example, we used Winston-Salem, North Carolina, as a case study. We noted that 100% of the physicians in West Winston clinics are white, and 100% of the physicians serving the African American community in East Winston are African American. The common illustration when we talk about establishment sex segregation comes from Padavic and Reskin (2002), who provide the example of waiters and waitresses. Sit down in any café, and more than likely a woman, usually white, will serve your food. Sit down in an upscale restaurant in a major city and the odds are your server will be a white male. Thus, to the degree that the occupations of physician or waitstaff are integrated, the establishments in which they work are not. And, not surprising, the places women and minorities work are of lower prestige and pay less, whereas those establishments (or specialties) in which white men are concentrated are of higher prestige and are more lucrative.

The data in Table 7.3 demonstrate the high degree of race and sex segregation in occupations. African American men and women are significantly more likely to work in the service economy, which can be characterized as the low-wage economy. In contrast, white men are more likely to work in the professions and in construction-related occupations; the latter is an occupation we associate with low education but high wages. Furthermore, we note that white women are most likely to work in the professions. Do not be misled. This does not mean that women have begun to dominate professions such as law and medicine. In fact, the Bureau of Labor Statistics categorizes occupations such that the "pink-collar" occupations such as teacher and secretary are classified as "professional occupations". In terms of wages, the pink-collar occupations often pay less than many blue-collar occupations, such as the trades and construction.

Finally, we note that the statistic that sociologists and economists use to measure segregation is called the index of dissimilarity. The index of dissimilarity represents the percentage of people who would have to change occupations in order for the occupation to be integrated. The sex index of dissimilarity is .57, meaning that more than half of all men and women would have to change jobs in order for occupations to be integrated (Padavic & Reskin, 2002). Similarly, the index of dissimilarity for race is .53, meaning that more than half of all whites and African Americans would have to change jobs in order for the labor force to be integrated (Wells, 1998). There is no doubt that the labor market is sex and race segregated. The question is, why?

Table 7.3   Employed Persons by Occupation, Race, and Sex (in percentages)

Occupation	White Men	African American Men	White Women	African American Women
Professional and related occupations	16.5	12.8	25.0	20.7
Service occupations	12.3	20.0	18.8	27.0
Construction and extraction occupations	11.9	7.9	0.4	0.3
Installation, maintenance, and repair occupations	6.7	5.1	0.3	0.5

SOURCE: Bureau of Labor Statistics (2005b, 2005c).

NOTE: A full table with all occupations by race and sex can be found in Appendix H.

Causes of Occupational Segregation

Occupational segregation is severe and complex. Examining the factors that cause it will allow us to see some of the issues facing African American civil society and African American families in particular.

Education and Human Capital

One of the major causes of occupational segregation is differences in education and other forms of human capital. Human capital refers generally to the skills that a worker has to "sell" in the labor market. These include educational attainment, credentials, training, and experience. For example, one of the reasons that white men are more likely to enter the professions than African Americans and women is that they have the education necessary to do so. One cannot enter medical school without a bachelor's degree, one cannot practice medicine without a medical degree, and so on. Thus, if one group is able to obtain credentials, then members of that group will gain access to the occupation. Our lengthy discussion of education and educational attainment highlighted the high levels of variance in education (both quantity and quality) by race and gender.

Access to the Opportunity Structure: Occupational Legacy

Although we don't typically use the term *legacy* to refer to handing over a business from father to son (the usual pattern), when a parent hands over a business to the next generation, this is, in effect, an example of occupational legacy: the son (or daughter) is given preference in "hiring" or "selling" over others. Although some occupational segregation is a result of this form of legacy, we argue that much more common is a pattern of legacy that mimics the tradition in college admissions: handing down the actual job to one's son or daughter. This particular pattern of legacy is present along the entire occupational spectrum from professional to blue-collar work. Here we illustrate with some examples.

Coaching

Many men, especially "retired"[12] or ex-athletes, aspire to continue their lives on an athletic field (or court) in the ranks of coaching. The competition for these jobs, especially at the collegiate and professional ranks, is tight; there are many applicants for every position. And yet there is an extraordinarily high rate of "families" who dominate in this profession. In fact, although an opening in the coaching sphere, especially at a public university, would seem to require an open search, when one looks at the changes in coaching over many decades, we see examples of fathers virtually handing down head coaching jobs to their sons in the same way that businesses are handed down (Smith, 2007). For example, there are two NCAA Division 1 basketball programs, each with one of the winningest coaches of all time: Bobby Knight at Texas

Tech (formerly at Indiana University) and Eddie Sutton at Oklahoma State. Both have sons who have already been given "title" to the team. Eddie Sutton's son Sean's official title is "head coach designate." The cases of Patrick Knight, who will "inherit" the head coaching job at Texas Tech, and Sean Sutton, who will take over Oklahoma State, are perhaps the most glaring examples, but there are many, many more. We recommend examining the legacy of legendary college football coaches Joe Paterno (Penn State) and Bobby Bowden (Florida State) for further illustration (Smith, 2007).

Medicine/Law/Business/Academics

Again, as sociologists, what we are examining is a rate of correlation that is not random. In the case of the professions, there is an extraordinarily high rate of "keeping it in the family" that is greater than we would predict by chance. This is true in both private practices, where sons and daughters enter medical and law practices with their parents (fathers), but it is also true in terms of the wider profession if not the actual job. In other words, we see a high rate of physicians, lawyers, and academics whose parents are or were in the same profession, although they do not work together in the same firm, clinic, or college. One of the primary ways in which this type of legacy works is by exposure. Children who grow up in professional families are exposed earlier and more often to these professions, and this makes them seem more accessible. For example, children of college professors often literally grow up on campus. Although they may not enter the professional world of academia, their college attendance rates are disproportionately high, and this is a clear reflection of their early and repeated exposure to college. In contrast, children who grow up in a low-income, segregated neighborhood may rarely, if ever, set foot on a college campus. This lack of exposure certainly reduces the probability of attending college, in part because college is a foreign environment. (For a wonderful description of this, see Suskind, 1998.)

Politics[13]

Politics is one of the areas in which the evidence for legacy is crystal clear. A brief tour of the U.S. legislature (House and Senate), governors' seats, even the presidency itself illustrates a much higher rate of correlation than we would ever expect by chance. There are many examples from the earliest part of our history, including John Adams and John Quincy Adams both serving as president, and Teddy Roosevelt and Franklin Delano Roosevelt doing the same less than 100 years later. However, in both of these cases, the population of the United States was relatively small, the number of educated citizens was even smaller, and many Americans, including women and African Americans, did not have the right to vote. Furthermore, the country was vastly smaller in terms of geography. Therefore, we would expect our leadership to come from a small subset of the people eligible to serve.

What is perhaps more surprising is the continuation of this trend well into the 21st century. The Kennedys are an excellent example. Their dominance in national politics (John F. Kennedy as president, Ted Kennedy as senator, and Bobby Kennedy as attorney general) was not limited to the 1960s. Today, some of the children, grandchildren, and in-laws of this power family are serving in the national government (Mark Kennedy Shriver, D–Maryland) and in the position of governor (Arnold Schwarzenegger, R–California).[14] Finally, there is the example of the Bush family. During the 1990s, two brothers were serving simultaneously as governors of very powerful states (George W. Bush in Texas and Jeb Bush in Florida). Consider that in the span of little more than a decade, father and son were both elected to the highest office in the country (perhaps in the world) as President of the United States (George H. W. Bush in 1988 and George W. Bush in 2000). The statistical probability of this is so remote that there is no other way to explain it besides legacy.

Skilled Labor Unions

Most of the research on legacy and social closure has focused on the "glass ceilings" that African Americans face in their climb up the corporate or professional ladders (Maume, 1999). As interesting and intriguing as it is to consider family ties as they relate to the highest and most powerful professions, the vast majority of Americans will never hold these offices, nor, as noted earlier, will they enter these professions. Most Americans work in skilled and unskilled labor—manual labor as well as service labor—and thus we turn our attention to legacies in these occupations. In much the same way as young, middle- and upper-middle-class *white* men and women find their way into the professions of their parents (medical doctor, lawyer, etc.), *white* young men who grow up in blue-collar households have a similar path into the skilled trades. Although we think of labor unions as organizations that protect workers from management, they also served as a system of social closure—much like limiting the number of seats in medical school and giving preference to legacy applicants—thus limiting access into these lucrative jobs to white men.

For years, trade unions functioned like whites-only fraternal organizations where insiders helped ease the way for certain applicants. That's why there are so few blacks in unions today, said Rev. Anthony Haynes, director of the Building Bridges Project, a free program that prepares mostly minorities to take union entrance tests (Taylor, 2004).

Furthermore, "The only union in which African-Americans made signifi-cant gains is in the laborer's union, which is the least skilled and pays less than most other trades" (Taylor, 2004, p. 1). This is a clear example of establishment segregation. Although African Americans are admitted to the union in some cases, they are segregated in the trades that are the least skilled and that pay the lowest wages.

This type of social closure, occupational legacy, has resulted in one of the most important forms of occupational racial segregation because it affects so many Americans. Whether they are working in fields where power and financial security are concentrated, such as law, medicine, politics, and head coaching, or in fields that employ most Americans, including the trades, the impact is felt across all social classes, regions of the country, and levels of education. This form of social closure is also important because it is not a form of segregation that results from interest in a particular occupation, talent, access to education, or anything else. The cause of this segregation is simply discrimination.

Discrimination

Occupational legacy is perhaps a more subtle, less easily identifiable form of discrimination. Yet there is no doubt about its power in shaping both industry and establishment occupational segregation. We also know that familiar, long-standing forms of discrimination exist as well. For example, in 2004, the Equal Employment Opportunity Commission (EEOC) received 27,696 charges of race discrimination. The EEOC recovered $61.1 million in monetary benefits for charging parties and other aggrieved individuals. The EEOC reports that color bias filings have increased by 125% since the mid-1990s (http://www.eeoc.gov/types/race.html). Huffman and Cohen (2004) note the presence of race-based discrimination in hiring practices, promotion practices (see also Maume, 1999), and pay.

Perhaps more chilling are the specific contemporary examples of racial discrimination, and unfortunately, there are many: from the dragging of African American James Byrd behind a truck in Jasper, Texas (Bragg, 1999), to the continuation of discrimination in coaching at both the intercollegiate level and in the professional game of football (as noted above; Lapchick, 2006), to racial discrimination at multinational corporations such as the Texaco Corporation. All of these examples indicate that we have entered the 21st century carrying forward patterns of social interaction reminiscent of the 19th and 20th centuries.

Racial discrimination in America has lasted a long time. What is troubling for many Americans is that it continues. For example, in the state of Georgia, the pension plan for police officers has been structured along race lines. In a finding at the end of 2005, we learn that

> . . . because of Jim Crow policies that barred them from the fund as shamefully late as the mid-1970's, many of these African American police officers are facing troubled and underfunded retirements, with benefits substantially lower than those of their white colleagues. ("The 'Whites Only' Retirement Fund," 2006, p. A10)

Another example of the continuation of racism is the case (lawsuit) recently settled at the Texaco Corporation. Executives at Texaco (especially those in the Finance department) collaborated to deny non-white employees, especially African Americans, the standard route to promotions and access to upper-management positions (Roberts & White, 1999). In fact, high-level executives were caught on tape in an official meeting in a company boardroom discussing African American employees and describing them as "black jelly beans" clustered at the bottom of the jelly bean jar (a euphemism for the promotion pool; Roberts & White, 1999).

This example compares to that of Reggie Clark. Clark, a professor at Claremont College, overheard his department colleagues collaborating to bar him from the regular route to tenure and promotion. His colleagues agreed not to vote on his advancement for the sole reason that Clark is African American. Clark filed a lawsuit and won a judgment of $1 million in back pay and damages (McCurdy, 1990).

Thus, racial discrimination in hiring continues to shape the labor force participation of African Americans, and particularly African American men, as well as the racial composition of workplaces. In order to examine the presence of racial discrimination more broadly, outside of individual cases such as that of Professor Clark or Texaco, several experiments have been designed in order to detect racial discrimination in hiring. Researchers Bertrand and Mullainathan (2003) found that job applicants with names that *sounded* white elicited 30% more callbacks than did applicants with names that sounded African American—even with high-quality, *identical* resumes showing their capabilities. (Actual names in the study included Kristen and Tamika, and Brad and Tyrone.)

These cases highlight the fact that on-the-job discrimination still exists with regard to access to upward mobility. Other types of on-the-job discrimination continue to persist as well. In one of the most celebrated cases of the latter, Tyson Foods Inc. was found responsible for maintaining segregated bathrooms and breakrooms in its Ashland, Alabama, chicken processing plant. African American employees were locked out of the restrooms, which were adorned with signs reading "Whites Only," and when they complained, they were told that they were not allowed into the restrooms because they were dirty (Buncombe, 2005). These examples of contemporary racism are, in fact, reminiscent of the Jim Crow era in America, a time when separate institutions—from schools, to churches, to work facilities, to neighborhoods—were more the norm than exceptions to the rule (Bonilla-Silva, 2001).

Social Capital and Employment

One of the many barriers to employment for African Americans that scholars have identified is the lack of social capital. Many of us get access to jobs through social networks. Thus, one explanation for the lack of access African Americans have to jobs was the belief that the social networks of low-income African Americans were weak and removed from the mainstream, and that this contributed to the barriers low-income African Americans faced in access to employment (Smith, 2005). Smith's study, based on interviews with 105 low-income, urban African Americans, revealed that, in fact, it was not the lack of social networks that posed barriers to employment, but rather a reluctance on the part of individuals to refer friends for employment. In fact, she found that 80% of respondents indicated that they were reluctant to refer a friend for employment based on the belief that the applicant was lazy, lacked motivation, or might bring the business of the streets to work (Smith, 2005). This finding is discouraging because it suggests that at least among low-income, urban African Americans, one of the primary conduits to employment is blocked not by structural discrimination or employer attitudes, but rather by the individuals themselves.

When we consider this finding along with the fact that there are few African American–owned businesses, we see the importance of economic and capital development in the African American community. This type of economic, human capital, and social network development could go a long way in improving the employment and economic conditions of African American men, women, and families.

Incarceration

We briefly summarize here the data that we present in Chapter 9 that expose employment discrimination based on the presence or absence of a felony record. Devah Pager designed an experiment in which she sent out a series of job applications to employers. In this classic 2 × 2 design, she varied both the race of the applicant (white or African American) and the felony status (had a felony or did not have a felony). As Pager's data clearly demonstrate, African American men face outright discrimination like that identified in the "name" experiments. White men were significantly more likely, in both conditions, to be called back for an interview than African American men. In addition, she found that African American men face further discrimination when they have been incarcerated. Perhaps the most important finding by Pager is the interaction effect between race and incarceration status. African American men *without* a felony record are less likely to be called back than white men *with* a felony record (Pager, 2003). In the context laid out in Chapter 2, with the reality that 25%–33% of African American men will be incarcerated in their lifetimes, the impact of incarceration on the employment of African American men is significant and profound.

The cycle between unemployment and incarceration is like a feedback loop. For example, recidivism rates are significantly related to unemployment (Smith & Hattery, 2006b, in press-a). In our interview with Chris, whose quotes are presented in Chapters 3 and 5, he talked about the difficulty he has in keeping a job. He is able to get low-level service jobs, but he remarks that once his employer finds out about his felony record, he is fired. In our visits to the penitentiary at Parchman, we note that the issue of employment is a constant theme among the inmates. Those who are still hoping they may one day be released wonder what they will do for work in the "free world." Calvin, serving a 30-year sentence for drug convictions, told us he would dig ditches if he had to; he would do anything for work. But during his previous foray into the free world, when he was out after his first stint in prison, he recalled that he was unable to find a job and quickly fell back into the illegitimate economy of drugs. He lasted only 4 months on the outside before he returned to Parchman.

We further illustrate this concept with the comments by Mr. Darryl Hunt of Winston-Salem, North Carolina, whose individual case will be explored in much more depth in Chapter 9. Two years after being released from prison (having served 19 years) and *exonerated* on all charges (as a result of DNA evidence that excluded him as a suspect), Mr. Hunt reports that he still cannot find work. Although he has no felony record, he has a nearly 20-year gap in his employment history. When asked to account for that, he has to disclose that he was in prison. Even though he was exonerated, many employers are not willing to offer a position to Mr. Hunt. In fact, in a recent conversation with him, we learned that shortly after being released from prison, he applied to work for a nonprofit organization that provides re-entry assistance for ex-convicts returning to the community. He was not hired and was told that the reason for this was that he "lacked experience." Thus, the case of Mr. Hunt illustrates that the simple *perception* on the part of whites that many African American men have been to prison will also result in racial discrimination in hiring practices. Thus, incarceration, both real and perceived, affects hiring practices and thus contributes to occupational segregation.

Outcomes of Occupational Segregation

Occupational segregation is important for a variety of reasons: (a) it is a direct indicator of where we are in terms of racial and gender equality; (b) it reflects lost opportunities for African Americans and women who fail to develop their potential; (c) it is a major process by which other resources (such as income, wealth, and education) are hoarded by the privileged; and (d) it is the primary cause of wage discrimination for both African Americans and women. In this section, we explore the outcomes of occupational segregation.

Unemployment

Perhaps the biggest form of occupational segregation is what happens *outside* the labor market: the experiences of those individuals who are unemployed. Erik Wright, a neo-Marxist sociologist, argues that in order to operate as efficiently as possible, a capitalist economy must eliminate waste. According to Wright, one source of waste is individuals with no human capital to contribute to the economy. They are defined as a waste because they require inputs from the culture and government, but they do not contribute to the economy. Wright argues that one modern strategy to eliminate waste is to cordon off the nonproductive and nonexploitable into ghettos and prisons (Wright, 1997). His main argument is that ghettos are structured so that unexploitable, expendable individuals do not clog the wheels of capitalism. Another outcome of this ghettoization is the removal of employment opportunities from low-income neighborhoods (Wright, 1997). We point out here that Wright is not advocating the cordoning off of individuals into either ghettos or prisons, nor does he believe that individual people are expendable or unexploitable. Rather, he is analyzing, from a neo-Marxist perspective, what he considers to be one of the most dangerous parts of capitalism: the cordoning off of members of society.

Drive through any low-income urban or rural area and you will see the effects of ghettoization as described by Wright. The primary businesses in these areas are of the fast food, "dollar store" genre. They provide limited consumer products, but perhaps more importantly, they do not provide jobs that pay a living wage.[15] The limited number of jobs that these businesses do create are minimum-wage jobs, and there are not enough to employ the number of people who live nearby. Thus, we argue that the unemployed are completely outside of the world of work, and this is perhaps the greatest form of occupational segregation.

The data in Table 7.4 demonstrate that the unemployment rate for African Americans is more than twice the rate for white Americans. Although this gap generally holds across gender and age configurations, the effects are devastating for young African American men, nearly a third of whom are unemployed. Data on unemployment, of course, do not capture those who are "underemployed"—those people who are working in jobs for which they are grossly overqualified. In addition, unemployment data include only those people who are looking for work. In other words, those men whom Liebow (1967/2003) describes standing on Tally's Corner, the chronically unemployed, are not counted. Thus, the unemployment rate is a *gross underestimate* of the number of people who are not working and thus not earning a wage.

In our interviews with African American men and women, we saw this phenomenon firsthand. In our sample, 40% of the men we interviewed, and many more of the men we learned about from their female partners, were unemployed. A typical response when we asked women what their male partners did for a living was that they "hustled." We note that "hustling" is not an occupational category on which data are collected by the Bureau of Labor Statistics. Technically, these men would be measured as "unemployed," or if they have been unemployed for a long period of time and have stopped looking for work, they would not be counted at all. However, these men were, in many cases, making a living in the illegitimate or underground economy. Evie's situation illustrates a way of life in this underground economy. Evie revealed that she did not hold her first legitimate job until she was nearly 50 years old. However, it is also important to note that Evie never relied on welfare. She earned money by engaging in various aspects of the

Table 7.4   Unemployment Rate (in percentages)

Whites	4.4
African Americans	10.4
White men	5.5
White women	4.6
Whites (16–19 years old)	15.0
African American men	11.0
African American women	9.3
African Americans (16–19 years old)	29.0

SOURCE: Bureau of Labor Statistics (2005a).

illegitimate economy. Her "jobs" ranged from prostitution to writing numbers to shoplifting to selling drugs.

More typical, and equally significant, were the men we interviewed who could have been on Tally's Corner. Will, for example, who has a chronic crack habit (he's been using crack for 30 years), has not held a job in more than 5 years. When he and Stella first met, he was employed in the fast food industry, but his crack habit got the better of him. Furthermore, Stella was willing, if reluctantly so, to support him financially, and as a result, he has not worked since. Chris is another example of chronic underemployment. Chris worked for 20 years in the local carwash but lost his job there once he developed glaucoma and could no longer see the cars he was washing. (For more on the relationship between health and employment, see Chapter 6.) As noted above, Chris also had difficulty holding a job because of his felony record. Luckily for Chris, he has a partner who reluctantly supports him.

Male Marriageable Pool

In Chapter 3, we talked at length about the relationship between employment and marriage. We return to that discussion here. Many of the women whom we interviewed noted that there was no reason for them to marry when the men with whom they were involved remained unemployed. In the context of compulsory heterosexuality (and exchange theory), there is no reason for these women to marry because they will not gain the typical advantages that come to married women via their husbands' salaries. Thus, the high rate of unemployment among African American men contributes to lower marriage rates in African American civil society. (For a longer discussion of this relationship, see Chapter 3.)

Intimate Partner Violence

As we discussed in Chapter 5, there is a significant relationship between unemployment and intimate partner violence. In brief, unemployment creates an economic power imbalance in the household. The person earning the money typically has more power in a variety of household decisions ranging from how to spend the money to the allocation of household labor. However, when the unemployed person is the male, there is often an attempt to re-establish the power differential and restore masculinity. Hochschild (1989) notes, for example, that when women outearn their husbands (who may or may not be employed), the men do *less* housework and the women do more in an attempt to reestablish what the couple perceives as the "normal" gendered power balance. Beating up one's female partner is another way that men can and do attempt to reestablish their masculinity. Our male and female respondents articulated the relationship between unemployment and violence. We illustrate with the story of Kylie and Jon.

> So Jon had lost his job—and I get very cranky when that happens—and, well, just, I guess, not regularly, but it's happened too many times since we've been together, I guess. I've had the same job for this many years and he's, he's changed jobs so many times and, well, some of it's—a lot of his work is seasonal so then he gets laid off and unemployment just doesn't cut it. So, then, he'd have to find a new one and the new one and then he'd get like a—I'd complain so much, he'd get, like, a telemarketing job. No. Six-fifty an hour, we can't pay bills on that, you gotta look. So he'd just get like these stupid little jobs in between the bigger couple year jobs, or whatever. (Kylie, 20-something African American woman, Minnesota)

The rest of the story for this couple on this night involves a physical fight. Kylie confronted Jon about his being unemployed again. He had been drinking heavily (anticipating this confrontation), and after being nagged, he exploded. He threw Kylie on the floor, threw her on the couch, and put his hands around her neck, all while their 2-year-old cowered in the corner. Thus, one of the most negative outcomes of unemployment in African American families is the intimate partner violence that often erupts as a reaction to the stresses of male unemployment. (See Hattery, in press-a, for a lengthy discussion of the relationship between masculinity, employment, and intimate partner violence.)

Financial Outcomes: Lower Earnings

Scholars of sex (Padavic & Reskin, 2002) and racial (Huffman & Cohen, 2004) occupational segregation argue that of all of the causes of the wage gap, occupational segregation is the biggest contributor. As these scholars detail, the relationship between occupational segregation and wages arises from the fact that for a variety of reasons, those occupations in which white men are overrepresented have higher wages than those in which African Americans and women are overrepresented. It is far too complex to detail this entire relationship, but there are a few key factors that we will illustrate here.

First, one of the typical ways of ensuring social closure is establishing job requirements. Typically, these requirements are based on credentials and training. So, for example, one way of limiting the number of physicians and thereby keeping the demand for them high but the supply of them low (which will drive up wages) is to control access to the occupation via complex credentialing (bachelor's degree, medical degree, board exams, etc.)

and by limiting the number of students who are admitted to earn the credential (seats in medical schools are highly controlled) and sit for the board exams. A second piece of this relationship, and one that affects many more American workers, is the presence of unions. The trade occupations that employ white men (as illustrated by the data in Table 7.3 and comments by Taylor, 2004) are unionized, whereas the occupations that employ African Americans and women are not. For example, many African Americans and women work in the low-wage service economy characterized by employers such as McDonald's and Wal-Mart, both of which prohibit the unionization of their employees. And much research has documented the fact that unionization drives up wages and significantly increases the likelihood that employees will receive costly benefits such as health insurance. Finally, gender plays an important role in setting industry wages. The occupations in which women congregate—nursing, teaching, cooking, domestic work—are all "professionalized" versions of housework. The low-status, low-prestige image that is attached to housework remains when these forms of work become "professionalized," and this image translates directly into low wages (Hattery, 2001b). We devote a portion of Chapter 8 to the most extreme outcome of unemployment and low wages: welfare.

Race, Class, and Gender Paradigm

The institutions of education and work, and access to these institutions, are significantly shaped by race, social class, and gender. Although we have pointed out these relationships throughout this chapter, we summarize briefly here. Both African Americans and women of all races face discrimination, blocked access, and a glass ceiling with regard to both education and work. The particular forces that shape individuals' experiences with education and work are shaped by their particular race, class, and gender identities. For example, there are race/gender gaps in employment. African American men are the most likely to be unemployed but white, middle-class women are the most likely to *choose* to be out of the labor market, a choice they make under the constraints of the hegemonic ideology of stay-at-home motherhood (Hattery, 2001b).

The data we have presented in this chapter, derived primarily from the census, illustrate the ways in which race and gender shape the educational and work experiences of all Americans. These patterns began in the early 17th century, when African Americans and whites entered into the economic relationship of chattel slavery. From the very beginning, whites made money by having work done for them and *not paying for it*. This laid the groundwork for the economic relationship we continue to see today.

This exclusion of African Americans from a way to make a living continues today, but under the more palatable guise of social closure and credentialism. It is no longer legal, for example, to prohibit African Americans from applying to law school, earning a law degree, and practicing the lucrative occupation in the most prestigious firms. However, because the road to law school requires quality education from kindergarten through college, and because higher education is often extremely expensive—out of the reach of most Americans, and African Americans in particular—the road itself serves to keep the profession, at least at the most prestigious incarnation (reaching the Supreme Court, being a partner in a major law firm in Manhattan) lily white and predominantly male. The story about unionized jobs, the trades, is the same. At every turn, although a few African Americans (and a few more women) will be offered access, the majority of African Americans find that their access to the opportunity structure is blocked at every turn. In terms of education, these blocks begin with kindergarten (Kozol, 1992, 2001, 2005), when African Americans begin education in a segregated setting that will continue for the rest of their lives. (Whites are also educated in a segregated system, but consistent with the arguments in *Brown v. Board of Education* that overturned *Plessy v. Ferguson,* separate is anything but equal, and the segregated system in which whites live is superior.)

These exclusionary practices result in a labor market that is highly race and sex segregated by both industry and establishment. This occupational segregation is the major cause of wage discrimination in the contemporary United States, and as we noted throughout the chapter, wage discrimination leads to poverty and all of its attendant consequences. Finally, as we have argued throughout this chapter, the race, class and gender paradigm is the most useful in explaining the variations we see in educational attainment and occupation patterns in the United States today.

Solutions

The most obvious solution is equal access—equal access to education, equal access to job training, equal access to jobs for African Americans and women. If occupations were to integrate, the wage gap would narrow.

Affirmative action has been one approach to addressing issues of blocked access and income inequality for racial and ethnic minorities as well as for women. We note that the primary beneficiaries of affirmative action have been white women. We also remind the reader of our argument throughout this chapter, and indeed, this entire book, that in order to truly address racial disparities, in everything from education to income to health to incarceration, we must address the structures that underlie each of these institutions.

Affirmative action policies, which are typically applied only in the institutions of education and work, will fail to adequately address the wide range of inequalities faced by African Americans.

A second solution we offer is that companies and multi-billion-dollar corporations like Wal-Mart (which employs more Americans than any other single company) pay their employees a living wage and provide health insurance for them. These kinds of changes would affect millions of American workers. Third, we need to address the rights of ex-convicts. When people (men) emerge from serving their sentences, if they are not allowed to work, they will likely end up right back in prison. Finally, we need to recognize that diversity in the workplace is the genesis of new ideas. Just as a population with a small gene pool will eventually be destroyed because of its inability to adapt, the same can be said for businesses and governments. A diverse workforce brings with it a wider variety of talents and perspectives that, when allowed to develop and flourish, will be the incubator of innovation.

- Create equal access to education and work opportunities.
- Enforce equal opportunity/nondiscrimination laws.
- Recognize legacy, be it in education or occupations, as affirmative action for whites, and particularly for white men, and develop standards for admission and hiring that are based on qualifications, not legacy.
- Address the inequalities that characterize the system of education in the United States and dedicate resources to guarantee that all children have access to high-quality education. This will go a long way toward opening doors of opportunity in higher education and occupations.

In the next chapter, we will examine two sides of the same coin of privilege and oppression we've discussed here: wealth and welfare.

Notes

1. Some of the more contentious desegregation fights included Central High School in Little Rock, Arkansas, in 1957–1958; the University of Mississippi (Ole Miss) in 1962; and the University of Alabama on June 11, 1963.

2. Many states as diverse as New York and North Carolina have moved to a system of tracking that leads to different types of high school diplomas, ranging at the high end a diploma that reflects a student's readiness to attend college to a diploma that signifies simply that a student is ready to enter the low-wage labor force.

3. Many European countries colonized much of South America and Africa for these same purposes. In fact, the main reason the British colonized Kenya was for the production of tea. The highland region in Kenya is some of the world's best agricultural land (the soil and the climate together) for the production of tea.

4. Recall that we discussed Tuskegee in Chapter 6 as the site of the infamous Tuskegee experiments.

5. We explore the contradictions of allowing African American women to wet-nurse white infants, a practice that was popular well into the 20th century, while prohibiting these same women (and other African Americans) from drinking from the same water fountain and other symbols of Jim Crow segregation in our paper titled "Cultural Contradictions in the Southern Mode of Segregation: Black Tits, White Only Water Fountains, Bad Blood, and the Transmission of Semen" (Hattery & Smith, 2004).

6. David Brion Davis, in his magisterial *The Problem of Slavery in Western Culture* (1966), tells us that everything associated with Africans was seen as "black."

> Black was the color of death, of the River Styx, of the devil; it was the color of bad magic and melancholy, of poison, mourning, forsaken love and the lowest pit of hell. . . . Edmund Burke told of a blind boy who had suddenly acquired vision as a result of surgery: "The first time the boy saw a black person it gave him great uneasiness. . . . Some time after, upon accidentally seeing a negro woman, he was struck with a great horror at the sight." (p. 448)

7. The belief in black incompetence was widespread and initially emerged via the racial theories that came into prominence during the 1800s (Gossett, 1963, provides a nice review of these theories). The theories were embraced by people around the whole country—northerners, southerners, and defenders of slavery as well as abolitionists.

8. As we will demonstrate using data on all occupations, only a very small number of people of any race enter the prestigious professions.

9. We note, however, that they are *underrepresented* in other sports, such as golf, tennis, swimming, and alpine skiing (see especially Smith, 2007).

10. Floyd J. Malveaux, MD, PhD, is Vice Provost for Health Affairs, Howard University Hospital, and Dean, Howard University College of Medicine.

11. For a lengthier discussion of these issues, see Smith (2007).

12. "Retirement" may occur at any time, whether it comes after finishing one's career at the end of high school or college or after a paid career in the professional leagues.

13. See Zweigenhaft and Dumhoff (1999, 2006) for a thorough discussion of African Americans and other minorities in the power elite.

14. For more information on the Kennedys in politics, see http://www.time .com/time/covers/1101010813/cover.html

15. Worth watching in the future is Earvin "Magic" Johnson, the former professional basketball player who controls the Johnson Development Corporation. Johnson has a network of corporate partnerships with Loews Cineplex Entertainment, Starbucks, Burger King, 24 Hour Fitness, and Washington Mutual, and he is building the Johnson Canyon-Johnson Urban Funds. They are hoping to become a major player in the underserved urban housing market. Johnson plans to grow his movie theater business and connect with the housing business, serving largely low-income African Americans in cities such as Chicago, Houston, Boston, and New York.

8

Welfare and Wealth

The first thing you see on entering the Arbordale welfare office is a large red banner, 12 feet long, 2 feet high, reading, "HOW MANY MONTHS DO YOU HAVE LEFT?" Underneath that banner is a listing of jobs available in the area—receptionist, night clerk, fast-food server, cashier, waitress, data entry personnel, beautician, forklift operator. In most cases, the hours, benefits, and pay rates are not listed. The message is unmistakable: you must find a job, find it soon (before your months run out), and accept whatever wages or hours you can get.

—Hays (2003), p. 33

Residents work in stable middle-class jobs, and many have single-family homes with a backyard and a two-car garage. Some send their children to private schools and are able to retire with solid pensions. Yet despite these privileges, they face unique perils. Continuing inequities in wealth and occupational attainment make these families economically fragile. Racial segregation confines many middle class African Americans to neighborhoods with higher poverty rates, more crime, fewer resources, less political clout, and worse schools than most white neighborhoods.

—Pattillo-McCoy (1999), p. 5

Objectives

- Examine the degree to which African Americans and their families have access to the American Dream via their ability to accumulate wealth.
- Examine the relationship between the labor force participation of African Americans and income, poverty, and wealth.
- Examine the role of welfare and welfare reform in shaping African American families.

Introduction

Poverty is one of the most important and pressing issues facing African American families. In previous chapters, we have alluded to its persistence and its prevalence. We have also noted that poverty shapes many of the experiences of African Americans, from their experiences with marriage and childbearing, to violence in their intimate relationships, to their experiences with health and health care, and finally, to their experiences with education.

In this chapter, we will examine two very different sides of the same coin: the presence and absence of wealth. Its presence guarantees access to the American Dream and reduces the risk of many crises facing African Americans and their families. At its absolute extreme, the absence of wealth or access to it can result in families living on the outer margins of the economy: on welfare. We will analyze the degree to which African Americans and their families have access to the American Dream (via wealth), and we will examine the experiences of those living on the margins—those cut out of the American Dream who must rely on welfare to raise their families.

Income Versus Wealth

In Chapter 7, we discussed occupations and work and the degree to which occupational segregation shapes wages. Wages are the primary source of income for individuals and families. Yet income is only part of the equation when we consider access to the American Dream. Income is defined as any money that is earned by performing work or a service. Reports on income are typically expressed in annual terms in part because this is the figure we report on our income taxes, and thus, most of us know this figure. Sometimes, income is also reported in dollars per hour or in monthly salary. Wage workers are generally more familiar with their income in terms of dollars per hour, whereas salaried and professional employees are generally more familiar with their income expressed as their monthly salary. The census collects and reports income data for individuals, households, and families. Generally, the census reports income data in terms of the median rather than the mean because the median is less likely to be skewed by significant outliers, namely, very high incomes and zeros (those receiving no income).

In contrast to income, wealth refers to the total value of one's assets minus the cumulation of one's debts. Net worth refers to assets such as property, homes, stocks, retirement accounts (401(k) and/or IRA), savings accounts, etc. *minus* all debts (mortgages, credit card debt, student loans, etc.). Whereas most Americans can easily report their income in both annual and monthly (or hourly) figures, few can report their total wealth without consulting a series of documents.

When examining African Americans' financial well-being compared to individuals of other race/ethnicities, the usual comparisons are made along the lines of annual income. When done this way, African Americans have demonstrated significant gains over the past three decades.

Today, African American individuals and their families work in all sectors of the U.S. economy. This is the good news. In the American workplace, you can find African Americans working inside the post office as well as delivering the mail, as secretaries, supervisors (including supervising whites), managers, architects, physicians, and lawyers. With the dismantling of segregation in schools around the country, you find them as schoolteachers and college professors, and with the dismantling of segregation in sports, you find pitchers, linebackers, and basketball centers (indeed, of the National Basketball Association's players, 78% are African American). More recently, with the development of a "diversity" training program in NASCAR, there are African American race car drivers "in training."

At the corporate level, there are now six or seven African American Fortune 500 CEOs, and a handful of Division 1A universities have presidents who are African American (e.g., Adam Herbert, Indiana University; Ruth Simmons, Brown University; and Shirley Ann Jackson, Rensselaer Polytechnic Institute).

Income and Income Disparities

Despite the fact that African Americans have made significant gains in terms of access to occupations, we remind the reader that we concluded our discussion in Chapter 7 by noting that occupations remain highly race (and sex) segregated, and that one of the most important and significant outcomes of occupational segregation, resulting from legacy, blocked access, discrimination, and inadequate preparation—educational attainment—is disparities in income.

The data in Tables 8.1 and 8.2 demonstrate the devastating financial outcome of occupational segregation on African American families. First, we note that the difference in median household income for African Americans and whites is 62% (Table 8.1). In other words, African Americans earn, on average, only 62% of what whites earn. And because these data are based on employed individuals and thus do not include a $0 figure for those who are unemployed, the figure for African Americans is not artificially deflated by their higher rate of unemployment.

Table 8.1   Median Income Among African Americans and Whites

	African Americans	Whites
Median household income	$30,000	$48,000
Earnings of full-time, year-round workers	$15,775	$24,626

SOURCE: DeNavas-Walt et al. (2004).

Although the median income is an important statistic, and it is quite a good measure of disparity at the lower end of the income distribution, it suffers from a flaw based on the way income is distributed in the population. The median income measure masks the incredible disparity at the *top* of the income distribution. Thus, we turn to the numbers in Table 8.2. First, we note that in every income category less than $50,000, African Americans are overrepresented in comparison to whites. Furthermore, at every income category greater than $50,000, whites are disproportionately represented. To summarize, these data demonstrate that African Americans are twice as likely to be *poor* (27.4% of African American households earn less than $15,000 whereas only 13.4% of whites live in households with such low

Table 8.2   Income Distribution by Race (% of individuals in each income category)

	African American	Whites	Ratio
Under $5,000	6.9%	2.5%	6.9/2.5
$5000–$9,999	10.7%	4.6%	10.7/4.6
$10,000–$14,999	9.8%	6.3%	9.8/6.3
$15,000–$24,999	16.0%	12.2%	16.0/12.2
$25,000–$34,999	13.3%	11.3%	13.3/11.3
$35,000–$49,999	14.9%	14.8%	14.9/14.8
$50,000–$74,999	14.8%	18.8%	14.8/18.8
$75,000–$99,000	7.0%	12.1%	7.0/12.1
$100,000 & over	6.8%	17.3%	6.8/17.3

SOURCE: DeNavas-Walt et al. (2004).

incomes). At the other end of the income distribution, we see that whites are more than 2.5 times more likely to be affluent (earning more than $100,000 per year) than are African Americans.

Most of the research on race and economic inequality focuses on the poor, noting the fact that African Americans are twice as likely to be poor as whites. In contrast, few scholars or policymakers are concerned with the fact that the gap is actually greater among the affluent—where whites are 2.5 times more likely to earn high salaries than are African Americans. Yet this race gap is also important in understanding the ways that race shapes inequalities of social class. For example, it is important to examine the effects of wage discrimination and occupational segregation on the accumulation of wealth (Conley, 1999). This type of analysis allows us to examine disparities at the upper end of the income bracket that lead to differences in wealth and ultimately in access to the American Dream.

Wealth and Wealth Disparities

According to Shapiro (2004), "Wealth has been a neglected dimension of social sciences' concern with the economic and social status of Americans in general and racial minorities in particular" (p. 33), so much so that wealth disparities are hardly found in the social science literature. Shapiro argues that this neglect is important precisely because wealth is so important.

> Wealth represents a more permanent capacity to secure advantages in both the short and long term, and it is transferred across generations. . . . We have been much more comfortable describing and analyzing occupational, educational, and income inequality than examining the economic foundation of a capitalist society, private property. (p. 33)

The data in Table 8.3 demonstrate some very disturbing facts.

- White households have *10 times* more wealth (net worth) than African American households.
- Among the wealthiest Americans, the top 20% of the income distribution, white households hold three times as much wealth as African American households in the same income bracket.
- Among the poorest Americans, the bottom 20% of the income distribution, white households hold 420 times more wealth than African American households in the same income bracket.

What these last two points illustrate is that when social class is controlled, when we compare affluent whites and affluent African Americans (or poor

Table 8.3   Wealth Disparities

Household Median Net Worth (2000)	
African Americans	Whites
$7,500	$79,400

Household Median Net Worth Among the Highest *Quintile (top 20% of the income distribution)*	
African Americans	Whites
$65,141	$208,023

Household Median Net Worth Among the Lowest *Quintile (bottom 20% of the income distribution)*	
African Americans	Whites
$57	$24,000

SOURCE: Orzechowski and Sepielli (2003).

whites and poor African Americans), a racial disparity persists. In other words, the wealth disparity we see between African Americans and whites cannot be explained by the fact that whites are congregated in higher-earning occupations whereas African Americans are congregated in lower-earning occupations, and if we simply moved people around a bit things would equalize. Rather, these disturbing facts suggest that something far more powerful is at work (Conley, 1999).

When we consider just the richest Americans, whites are at the top of this category and African Americans are at the bottom. Conversely, when we examine the poorest category of Americans, whites are among the most well-off of this group whereas African Americans are clustered at the bottom. In other words, each social class stratum is internally stratified by race.

How can we explain this internal stratification? Among the affluent, the explanations hinge on at least two differences between African Americans and whites. First, because of the history of slavery and Jim Crow segregation, whites have been able to work in the professions, build businesses, and accumulate wealth over several hundred years (many generations), whereas African Americans have been able to do so only recently (Darity, Dietrich, & Guilkey, 2001). Because you "need money to make money," as the saying goes, African Americans have arrived later at the money-making game than whites. Second, among the affluent who *work* for a living—the professional classes—as opposed to those living on an inheritance—African Americans are more likely to have come from lower- and middle-class backgrounds than their white counterparts, and thus, they have had to personally invest more in preparing for entry into their profession. For example, African American physicians typically arrive at the profession with greater student loan burdens than their white counterparts. Because debt is a part of the wealth equation, this difference explains part of the disparity in wealth among the affluent. This is illustrated time and time again in scenarios similar to that described by Kai Wright, who writes about his father, a prominent African American physician, who died at age 57 without a pension and with no real assets:

> At least we held our ground: Troy and Grandma got my father to college, and my parents did the same for us. But none of us [African Americans] will take part in the historic wealth transfer now under way in America: According to another study Shapiro likes to cite, parents will pass on a total of more than $10 trillion to their adult kids between 1990 and 2040. (Wright, 2006)

Karger (2005) argues that part of the explanation lies in the predatory lending practices that target the poor and, disproportionately, African Americans:

> Without question, the fringe debt economy targets the poor, including especially immigrants, and those who are not poor but living from paycheck to paycheck. Many of these people are the "unbanked," those without bank accounts of any kind. Most of them have yearly incomes below $25,000. . . . As many as 56 million adult Americans—about 28% of all adults—don't have a bank account. Almost 12 million U.S. households (one-fourth of all low-income families) have no relationship with a bank, saving institution, credit union, or other mainstream financial provider.

Shifting our attention back to the lower end of the income distribution, it is terribly concerning that poor African Americans hold, on average, $57 in assets (or wealth) compared to $24,000 (a gap of 420 times) held by their white counterparts. Although the reasons for this internal stratification are similar to the explanations laid out for the affluent, the consequences are more severe. Because the poor live on the proverbial economic edge, living paycheck to paycheck, any emergency, be it medical (see Chapter 6 for a discussion of health insurance and health costs), a layoff, a short trip to jail, or even something as routine as having to miss a shift at work because the baby-sitter is sick, can plunge these families over the edge, into homelessness, for example. Thus, many African American families live every day with severe threats to their very existence.[1]

Wealth Disparities and Access to the American Dream?

> The American dream promises that Americans who work hard will achieve success and just rewards. But, of course, this depends in part on your starting point. (Shapiro, 2004, p. xi)

According to Block and colleagues, there are four key components to the "American Dream": (a) owning a single-family home, (b) being able to afford quality child care, (c) being able to afford a college education for one's children, and (d) being able to afford full health insurance. In Figure 8.1, they demonstrate the incredible inflation over the past three decades of these building blocks of the "American Dream"—what they refer to as "the four Hs" (Block, Korteweg, & Woodward, 2006).

Block and colleagues demonstrate that the coupling of incredible inflation in the four Hs with the decline in real wages—minimum wage has doubled in value in the past 25 years, whereas the value of the four Hs has quadrupled—has

Price Rises for the Four Hs

	Housing	High-quality child care	Higher education	Health insurance
1973 (annual cost)	$1,989	$978	$736	$509
2003 (annual cost)	$10,245	$7,200	$5,000	$8,933
Percent increase	515%	736%	679%	1755%

When the Dream Line is compared to the federal poverty line or to the income that a two-parent family would earn if both parents were working full-time at the minimum wage, it is clear that the dream has become increasingly distant for millions.

Figure 8.1   The Price for "the Four Hs"

SOURCE: From Block, F., Korteweg, K., Woodward, Z., Schiller, I.M., The compassion gap in American poverty policy, *Contexts*, copyright 2006. Reprinted with permission of The University of California Press.

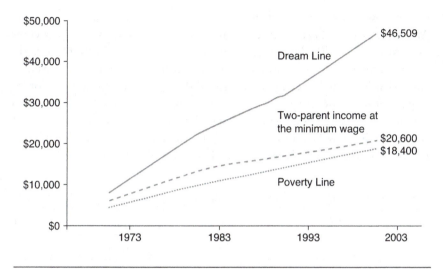

Figure 8.2   The Dream Divide

SOURCE: From Block, F., Korteweg, K., Woodward, Z., Schiller, I.M., The compassion gap in American poverty policy, *Contexts,* copyright 2006. Reprinted with permission of The University of California Press.

severely limited the access of working Americans to the American Dream. They argue that the dream that was within the reach of working Americans during the 20th century is out of reach for all but the affluent in the 21st century. Through much of the 20th century, working families, even those working at the bottom of the salary ladder, could afford a portion of what they call the American Dream. As the data in Figure 8.2 illustrate, a conscientious working family could achieve the American Dream in 1973 by taking on a few extra hours at work, saving carefully, and so on. Today, the typical working-class family living on two minimum wage incomes earns less than half of what is necessary to achieve the American Dream. The inability to buy into the American Dream, especially buying a home, has significant consequences for wealth attainment.

Housing

Homeownership is one of the most important elements of the American Dream because it is so central to the definition of the American Dream and because it is one of the most common forms of wealth. Disparities in rates of homeownership are a powerful illustration of differential access to the American Dream. Furthermore, because homeownership is the most common form of wealth, homeownership rates are a good proxy for wealth. Homeownership also provides the type of security against crises that we discussed earlier. Families can borrow against the equity in their homes in order to pay college tuition for their children or to provide the money necessary to weather a crisis such as a layoff or illness. Finally, homes are one of the most commonly inherited forms of wealth. Thus, homeownership contributes significantly to the accumulation of wealth across generations.

Table 8.4   Homeownership Rates, 2006 (in percentages)

Total	Whites	African Americans	Affluent	Poor
68.5	75.5	47.3	83.7	52.4

SOURCE: Callis and Cavanaugh (2006).

NOTE: Affluent households are those with incomes greater than the median household income; poor households are those with incomes less than the median household income.

The data in Table 8.4 reveal that both race and social class shape homeownership. In terms of race, whites are 1.5 times more likely to own their own homes than are African Americans. The affluent—defined as those with incomes above the median household income—are also 1.5 times more likely to own their own homes than are those with incomes below the median— the poor. The fact that African Americans are disproportionately likely to be poor is reflected clearly in the data on race, social class, and homeownership. However, it is interesting to note that among all Americans living below the median household income, whites, as a group, are *more likely* to own their own homes than are African Americans as a group. We suspect that this disparity in homeownership explains the huge racial disparity in wealth (a gap of 420 times) among low-income whites and African Americans.

We note that the *value* of one's home is also critical to understanding disparities in wealth. Owning a home that is of little value is not much better than not owning a home at all, because in a time of crisis or when it is time to pay college tuition, a home with little equity cannot be liquidated or borrowed against in order to provide the cash necessary to address the crisis.[2]

Housing Discrimination

African Americans face discrimination with regard to access to housing. In fact, Feagin (1999) estimates that 2 to 10 million individual incidents of racial housing discrimination occur each year. Discrimination includes red-lining—refusing to show or sell homes in predominantly white neighborhoods to African Americans—refusing to rent or sell to African Americans, and unfair mortgage practices.

A recent study by the Center for Responsible Lending (Bocian, Ernst, & Wei, 2006) shows that despite legislation against housing discrimination, it still exists. The primary victims of housing discrimination in the United States are racial minorities and especially Hispanics and African Americans. The Center for Responsible Lending study also showed that African Americans face discrimination in lending practices as well, especially when they are looking to borrow money for mortgages. As a result of predatory mortgage practices, African Americans lose upwards of $25 billion annually.

Borrowers of color are more likely to get higher-rate, subprime home loans—even with the same qualifications as white borrowers. After accounting for credit scores, African Americans and Latinos are 30% more likely to get the most expensive financing (Bocian et al., 2006).

These illegal practices lead to a situation in which more African Americans end up renting at high prices per month rather than buying their homes because they cannot afford the exorbitant interest charged on their mortgages.

There have been many studies of racial discrimination with regard to renting. The typical design involves sending white and African American "testers" out into local markets to see if they experience discrimination in access to units or price. Carpusor and Loges designed a study in which they e-mailed inquiries to rental companies in Los Angeles, California. They found significant effects for both availability and price when they varied the name of the potential renter. Potential renters with white-sounding names were significantly less likely to be told the unit had already been rented, and they were also less likely to be quoted an inflated rent. Potential renters with African American–sounding names were the most likely to be told that the unit had already been rented, and they were also the most likely to be quoted inflated rents. Potential renters with Middle Eastern–sounding names fell in between whites and African Americans (Carpusor & Loges, 2006). This was particularly surprising given the post–September 11 climate (the study was conducted in 2003) and thus serves to reinforce the overall finding, replicated many times, that African Americans continue to face severe housing discrimination, more so than all other race and ethnic groups.

Housing Segregation

Scholars have continued to document the fact that long after the *Brown v. Board of Education* decision in 1954 that effectively outlawed legalized segregation, the housing patterns in the United States remain highly segregated (Massey, 2005; Massey & Denton, 1993). Analysis of census maps indicates that most Americans live in neighborhoods that are composed of 80%–90% of people of one racial group. Whites live in white neighborhoods and African Americans live with African Americans. As we noted in Chapter 4, one outcome of severe housing segregation is that whites are more likely to live in neighborhoods that are also homogeneous by social class, but African Americans, even those who are solidly in the middle class, are more likely to live in socioeconomically diverse neighorhoods that include low-income residents. Because whites do not buy homes in African American neighborhoods, and because middle-class African Americans are restricted to buying homes in segregated, socioeconomically diverse neighborhoods, housing values in African American neighborhoods remain deflated. Shapiro (2004, pp. 13, 97) argues that racial segregation in housing is one of the primary reasons why African Americans lag so far behind whites in terms of wealth—because the value of their primary asset, their home, remains deflated.

The situation of housing for African Americans, regardless of class status, is precarious (Pattillo-McCoy, 1999). In the ethnographic research by sociologist Pattillo-McCoy, we learn from her Groveland, Chicago, study what previous sociologists who examined housing patterns found (Wilson, 1984), and that is that of African Americans who do manage to escape poverty and blighted neighborhoods, many end up in middle-class neighborhoods and communities side by side with poorer African Americans (Pattillo-McCoy, 1999). Recall the quote from her study that opens this chapter. In short, she notes that African Americans who have entered the middle classes through professional occupations are still denied access to the American Dream as a result of racial housing segregation.

A Clear Illustration: Hurricane Katrina

Although sociologists don't pay a lot of attention to the racial disparities in wealth, our discussion above demonstrates that severe racial disparities in wealth persist (Conley, 2001; Oliver & Shapiro, 1995). Like most African Americans who have limited access to opportunities, there is a real hidden cost to being African American.

> I maintain, however, that exclusively focusing on contemporary class-based factors like jobs and education disregards the currency of the historical legacy of African Americans. A focus on wealth sheds light on both historical and contemporary impacts not only of class but also of race. Income is an

indicator of the current status of racial inequality; I argue that an examination of wealth discloses the consequences of the racial patterning of opportunities. (Shapiro, 2004, p. 36)

These disparities in wealth were played out clearly and in plain view in the fall of 2005 as images of Hurricane Katrina were broadcast into our living rooms and offices. It can be argued that, based on firsthand accounts shown across American television sets, African Americans were hit the hardest when Hurricane Katrina devastated New Orleans. Hundreds of thousands of African Americans were left homeless or dead. People lost their property; loved ones; pets; and access to normal, day-to-day living arrangements. As a consequence of the mishaps of the Federal Emergency Management Association, people found themselves scattered all over the country waiting for the signal that it was safe to return home.[3]

The TV scenes from New Orleans after Hurricane Katrina were horrific. The American public saw devastation and hopelessness in front of their very eyes. The poor, mostly African American women, men, and children were literally crying out for help and assistance live on TV. Months later, we finally got the rest of the story, and it was not just the poor, unable, homebound, and those without cars who were stranded in flood-devastated New Orleans. With the return of Mardi Gras in February 2006, we learned that middle-class and professional African Americans, many of whom were dentists, lawyers, medical doctors, and corporate managers, were also flooded out of their neighborhoods. Most lost not only their homes but also their businesses and professional careers. This piece of the story was not mentioned in news reports.

Why? Because we want to believe that there is a separate place for middle-class and affluent African Americans, away from those we did see on the news. What we forget is that as a racial group, African Americans of means are more likely to live with or near those who are poor. This is not the case for whites. The African Americans in the professional class living in what has been described as New Orleans East—a racially segregated community—lost their livelihoods and their businesses and clients not only because of Hurricane Katrina but also because of racial segregation. Willard Dumas, a dentist, recounts what happened to him and others he knows in New Orleans East:

You spend 45 years building a life and then it's gone. Your home was flooded; your business was flooded. And this happened not only to you but to practically everyone you know, so your patients or clients are gone, your friends are scattered, and your relatives are somewhere else. (Cass, 2006, p. A1)

The media had us believing that the reason we saw so many black faces on TV was because Hurricane Katrina disproportionately affected the poor, most of whom were African American. In other words, the conclusion was that this social problem was more about poverty than about race. What we learn is that, in the final analysis, *it is about race.* The middle class and affluent of New Orleans who were most affected by Hurricane Katrina were, in fact, African Americans living and working in the racially segregated city alongside their poorer African Americans brethren. Racial disparities persist across class boundaries (Wilson, 1987).

In concluding this section on wealth, we have to underscore the fact that wealth differences are more unequal than income differences for African Americans and whites. Although pronouncements have been made about the decline in the meaning (and mostly negative meaning) of race in American society, it is still important to note that our review of survey research on race relations tells us that, for most of the big important decisions that African Americans and whites make, such as where to live, where to send our children to school, what careers to pursue, which YMCA to join, and even for what sports to prepare our children, all are, in the final analysis, shaped by race (Bonilla-Silva, 2003).

Poverty

Research on and discussions about poverty remain contentious (Wessel, 2006). Although many people believe they know what poverty is, it is important to contextualize our discussion with an understanding of the ways in which poverty is measured. The official poverty rate is based on the number of Americans who live below the official poverty line. In the United States, the poverty line is established as three times the cost of a minimally nutritional diet.[4] The actual poverty line is adjusted each year—although the formula for establishing the line has never been revised—and in 2006, the poverty line for a family of four was approximately $18,500 per year. Furthermore, the poverty line is not adjusted for differences in cost of living by region of the country or rural or urban settings. Finally, we note that the formula for calculating poverty in the United States is radically different from the way in which most countries report poverty, which is to set the poverty line at 50% of the median income (Wessel, 2006). If we were to adopt this model, the actual poverty line in the United States would be closer to $22,000 per year, and the number of Americans who are counted as poor would jump dramatically.[5] For this reason, researchers often consider the poor to be those who live below 200% of the poverty line.

Although the largest number of poor in the United States are white Americans, African Americans are the most likely to live in poverty. Nearly one quarter of all African Americans live in poverty. This is often attributed to family form, based on the assumption that most African American households are single-parent and female-headed, but the data in Table 8.5 indicate that the disproportionately high rates of poverty for African Americans hold regardless of family form.

For both whites and African Americans, marriage provides some protection from poverty; yet married African Americans are more likely to live in poverty than are married whites. In addition, among single-parent households, African Americans are significantly more likely to live in poverty than their white counterparts. For African American women heading single-parent households, just less than half (40%) live below the poverty line.

As noted above, the rates are dismal when we consider who is actually poor—those who live below 200% of the poverty line. Based on this definition, nearly half of all African Americans living in families are poor; more than one quarter of all African Americans living in married couple households are poor; and more than two thirds of African Americans living in female-headed, single-parent households are poor.

Table 8.5   Poverty Rates Among African Americans and Whites

Below 100% of the Poverty Line	African Americans	Whites
% of people in families	23.1	8.7
% of people in married couple households	8.5	5.8
% of people in male-headed, single-parent households	23.7	11.8
% of people in female-headed, single-parent households	39.0	25.6

Below 200% of the Poverty Line	African Americans	Whites
% of people in families	47.2	24.9
% of people in married couple households	28.0	20.1
% of people in male-headed, single-parent households	50.0	33.6
% of people in female-headed, single-parent households	67.7	54.1

SOURCE: http://www.census.gov/hhes/www/poverty03.html

NOTE: Two-parent households are less likely to live in poverty regardless of race. However, African Americans are more likely to be poor regardless of family structure (two-parent and/or gender of head) than whites.

We indicated earlier that for the poor as well as for anyone living in the bottom quartile of the income distribution, any crisis—a layoff, an illness, a move, or a divorce—may plunge this individual and his or her family into poverty. And because African Americans in the bottom quartile have significantly less wealth than similarly situated whites, they are significantly more vulnerable to these types of crises. Thus, we turn now to a discussion of families who live on the extreme margins of poverty, those who are so poor that they are receiving public assistance (welfare).

Welfare

Welfare, now referred to as Temporary Aid to Needy Families (TANF), is a complex set of public assistance programs that was designed as a safety net for Americans who fell below the federal poverty line. Most of these programs, originated under the social reforms of President Franklin D. Roosevelt, were greatly expanded as the "Great Society Programs" under President Lyndon B. Johnson, and were reformed in 1996 under President Bill Clinton. The oldest and largest of all welfare programs is one from which most of us will eventually benefit: Social Security. Because of this, Social Security does not have the negative stereotypes associated with it, and most Americans do not even think of it as "welfare".

One of the purposes of establishing the official poverty line is to determine who is eligible for public assistance. As individuals and families get close to the poverty line, they become eligible for some sorts of public assistance, and when they fall below the poverty line, they are typically eligible for all forms of public assistance. Public assistance programs cover food (food stamps), housing (section 8 housing subsidies and units in public housing complexes), child care (child care subsidies), and health care (Medicare), as well as cash assistance.

The data in Table 8.6 confirm that whites comprise the largest number of those who are receiving welfare. In fact, there are more than twice as many whites receiving welfare as there are African Americans. This is an important statistic because it debunks the widely held belief that African Americans dominate the welfare rolls (Seccombe, 1998).

However, when we compare the *rates* of welfare receipt, these data indicate that African Americans are *more than twice* as likely to be receiving some form of cash public assistance as whites, and the rate of receiving public assistance is so high that just under half of all African Americans live in families that are receiving some form of cash public assistance. Many of these families

Table 8.6	Number and Percent of Individuals Receiving Public Assistance (cash)
Whites	44.1 million (19%)
African Americans	17 million (47%)

SOURCE: Current Population Survey (2004).

are among the working poor—working 40 or more hours per week, but not earning enough to pull themselves and their families out of poverty (Ehrenreich, 2001). As we noted in Chapter 7, there is a strong relationship among employment, underemployment, occupational segregation, and welfare receipt. Because African Americans are more likely to work in the low-wage economy and to be denied access to work that pays a living wage, their families live in poverty and are eligible to—*but do not necessarily*—receive public assistance or welfare. This has devastating consequences for African American children, 1 million of whom, according to the Children's Defense Fund, live in extreme poverty.

Welfare Reform

Perhaps the primary intended purpose of the 1996 welfare reform signed into law by President Bill Clinton was to discourage dependency by moving people off of the welfare rolls. There is no question that this goal was met. A decade after the welfare reform, the number of Americans receiving welfare has declined 60% (Committee on Ways and Means, 2006). With the decline in the welfare rolls, the U.S. government has also decreased its spending on welfare. Figure 8.3 illustrates the trends in welfare spending from 1980 to 2006. As one can see, welfare spending (AFDC/TANF) peaked in 1999 and has been dropping since then.

Figure 8.4 confirms this finding by illustrating that the average spending on poor individuals has declined precipitously since 1995 or so, such that in 2006, the U.S. government spent about the same per poor individual as it did in 1980. In fact, in 2003, the average monthly TANF benefit was $393, compared to $490 in 1997 (Block et al., 2006).

Perhaps more importantly, Figure 8.3 demonstrates one of the primary changes in the way welfare is distributed. In the 1980s and 1990s, the bulk of welfare spending was cash assistance (AFDC/TANF); currently, however, the proportions have shifted so that very little of the welfare budget goes into cash assistance. This has been replaced with the Earned Income Tax Credit

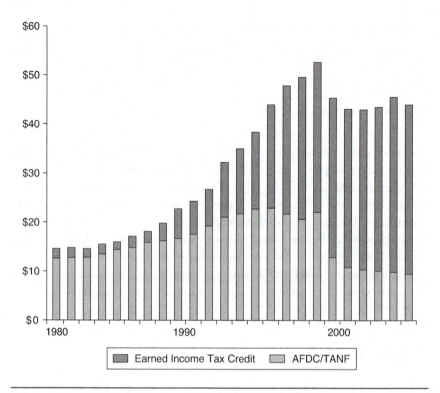

Figure 8.3   Assistance to Those in Poverty, 1990–2004

SOURCE: Block et al. (2006).

(EITC), a several thousand–dollar tax credit for which poor families are eligible. The EITC is designed to pull working families who are living in poverty above the poverty line. What is important about this is that only working adults (and their families) are eligible for EITC. Those who are unemployed and thus do not pay taxes are not eligible. Block and colleagues argue that each year, millions of poor families are not eligible for EITC because of unemployment, illness, lack of child care, and so on (Block et al., 2006). Finally, we refer the reader back to Chapter 4 and our discussion of the role that time limits on welfare play in the lives of single mothers and how these time limits block their attempts to complete their education and stay off of welfare permanently.

Stereotypes About Welfare and Poverty

As if to add insult to injury, as if being poor and living your life constantly looking into a world you can see but cannot access isn't difficult enough,

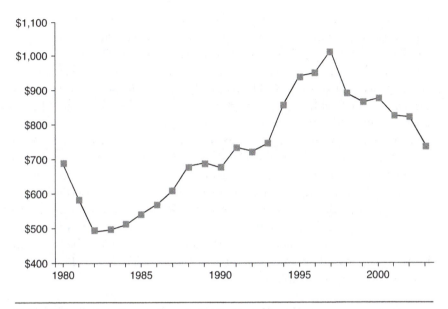

Figure 8.4   Spending on Poor Individuals per Person

SOURCES: Block et al. (2006), DeNavas-Walt et al. (2003), and Orzechowski and Sepielli (2003).

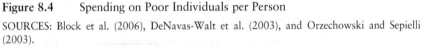

many Americans hold very negative attitudes about the poor, and especially about those who receive welfare. This is decidedly different from the beliefs in many other cultures, where poverty is not seen as the mark of an individual failure, as it so often is in the United States. Weber argues that this tendency to blame the poor for being poor is deeply rooted in the ideals of hard work and salvation that characterize the Calvinism that the early Puritans brought with them when they settled the colonies. These ideals have simultaneously become secularized and deeply embedded in the hegemonic ideology of work and poverty in the United States (Weber, 1996).

Like the stereotype of the "Welfare Queen,"[6] who is most often thought to be an African American single mother who is lazy and promiscuous (Seccombe, 1998), the stereotype is that African Americans have less than whites fiscally because they are careless with their money. This belief often surfaces in discussions about homeownership. There is, in the popular culture, the belief or stereotype that African Americans would rather purchase a Cadillac than a home (Adelman, 2001; Adelman & Morgan, 2006).

This set of beliefs about African Americans, which fits conveniently with white Americans' beliefs about African Americans as lazy (see Chapter 7), found support in the research of urban sociologist Banfield. In a highly successful book titled *The Unheavenly City* (1970), Banfield put forth the notion that African Americans would have a hard time re-engaging the gutted urban formations for the simple reason that they did not know how to delay gratification. That is to say, according to Banfield, African Americans had an inherent disposition for what he termed *immediate gratification*. According to authors like Banfield, African Americans are extremely present-oriented with a penchant for preferring cash now rather than a greater sum in the future. As this belief entered the mainstream, it was picked up by scholars and social commentators, who attached it to other social behaviors, namely, unprotected sex and dropping out of high school and/or not attending college, thus using this ideology of instant gratification to explain African American teenage mothers and high school dropouts.

In contrast, research scholars who study wealth disagree with this assertion and have published work that addresses the social stereotype of the welfare cheat as well as the notion that African Americans would be better off if they only behaved differently when it comes to saving money (Blau, 1990; Conley, 1999; Shapiro, 2004).

> We hear about "poor future orientation," excess consumption, and the lack of deferred gratification on the part of African Americans resulting in lower savings. The facts speak otherwise. It is not clear whether any deficit in the African American saving rate has played a role in the racial wealth gap. (Shapiro, 2004, p. 96)

Shapiro goes on to note that savings rates are higher when you have a higher income, and as we noted earlier, African Americans have lower overall incomes than whites. Thus, according to Shapiro, income, not race, clearly emerges as a causal factor in the debate about wealth.

Welfare Versus Work

The debate over the role that welfare plays in the economy is contested terrain. On one side of the debate are those who argue that welfare is too easy and that it results in laziness and produces dependency (Tanner, Moore, & Hartman, 1995). Others argue that welfare pays such a pittance that those who are forced to live on it endure a standard of living that is dramatically below that of other Americans (Edin & Lein, 1997).[7] We contribute to and fuel this debate by asking the question a slightly different way. We consider the choices that a single mother raising children must make as she negotiates the complex web of work and welfare. This is not such a different question as posed by others on both sides of the debate. However, we raise the question within the framework of the ideologies of motherhood.

When women have a child, they immediately enter the debate about whether or not they should stay at home or go back to work (Hattery, 2001b). Although we live in a time when women with young children are more likely to be employed than not employed, this change in our culture, which has been viewed positively by some and negatively by others, is primarily a change for white, middle-class families (Hattery, 2001b). As we noted in Chapter 7, African American women have always worked (Hill-Collins, 1994). Despite these differences in mothers' labor force participation across race/ethnic lines and time, the dominant motherhood ideology in the contemporary United States is that of the stay-at-home mother (Hattery, 2001b; Hirshman, 2006). In both survey research and qualitative studies, women are far more likely to say that being a "good" mother means staying at home and raising one's children than they are to say that being a "good" mother means providing financially for one's children (Hattery, 2001b). It is in this context, then, that we compare welfare to work.

Tanner et al. (1995) report that "in 40 states welfare pays more than an $8.00 an hour job" (p. 2). This translates into roughly $16,640 per year. And because these benefits are not taxable, this payment is not reduced. Furthermore, this report notes that in addition to the cash payment, welfare recipients typically receive additional support, including food stamps (typically $250–$300 per month), housing assistance (typically $350–$500 per month), and child care subsidies. Child care subsidies typically reimburse parents on average $50–$80 per week for the care of a single child. (For the full report, see Tanner et al., 1995.) In contrast, a minimum wage job pays $5.15 per hour, which translates into roughly $10,000 annually or $800 per month take-home pay after taxes. Even in states that passed minimum wage laws in the 2006 midterm elections, most states settled on an average minimum wage of $6.50, which is approximately $13,000 per year or less than $1,000 per month in take-home pay. Although these increases in the minimum wage will make a real difference in the daily lives of low-wage workers, they will still leave many families living below the official poverty line. Although a minimum wage employee who is a single parent raising one or more children will be below the poverty line, and thus eligible for other benefits, such as food stamps and housing assistance, we can see how difficult this decision becomes. In our community, even in public housing at the lowest end, monthly rent will run a *minimum* of $300; child care, at the lowest end, will run a *minimum* of $50 per week per child or $400 per month for two children. Thus, a single mother raising two children, after she has paid for child care and rent, will have only $100 left over for the month for food, utilities, transportation, and other items not easily budgeted. Finally, we again underscore the fact that most minimum wage workers do not have health insurance (see our discussion in Chapter 6).

Thus, the dilemma—a single mother raising two children will be better off financially by being on welfare, and she will also have access to health insurance for her children and higher-quality child care (Brush, 2001). When we consider this dilemma within the context of the ideology of a good mother, it seems clear that the proper, *rational* decision to make is to use the welfare programs available in order to stay at home raising one's children.

Most Americans polled would not agree with this decision. And this is where we see the emergence of race and class bias. When a white, middle-class woman makes the decision to opt out of the labor force and become entirely *dependent* upon her spouse's or partner's income so that she can stay at home and raise her children, we applaud her for the sacrifices she is making.[8] But when a single African American woman with limited employment options chooses to rely on welfare so that she can stay at home raising her children rather than seek minimum wage work—often the only work she can obtain but that would leave her, in the end, living deeper in poverty—we denigrate her and call her a lazy, remote-clicking welfare queen. Yet both mothers want to do the best they can for their children.

Let us be clear. We are not arguing that welfare should be revamped so that families receiving it get fewer benefits. This would only result in plunging even more children into poverty. And because half of all African American children live in poverty, the results would be especially devastating on African American families. What we are arguing for are the following:

- Increased access to education
- Equality in public schools
- Increased access to jobs, especially in the trades
- Affordable child care
- Affordable housing
- A living wage for all workers

We believe that we will continue to see high rates of welfare utilization by African Americans until they have access to the same opportunities as whites and until working in the strongest economy in the world yields a paycheck that translates into enough money to provide for a family.

Welfare Reform and Family Values

Clearly, much of the welfare reform passed under President Clinton was a reaction to the belief that poor African American women would rather receive welfare than work. This set of reforms was believed by many to resolve some of the inadequacies of the previous welfare program initiated under the Johnson administration. One of the most obvious changes was the renaming of welfare from Aid to Families with Dependent Children (AFDC) to Temporary Aid to Needy Families (TANF). TANF eliminates the "man in the house" rule associated with AFDC and allows for intact families to receive welfare. However, Hays (2003) argues that, in fact, welfare is still designed to allow the government to interfere with and shape poor, mostly African American families:

> Ever since the inception of government-funded programs for the poor, policy-makers have believed that the giving of benefits comes with the right to inter-fere with the families of the poor. . . . All the most blatantly discriminatory policies have been struck down by the courts. A few questionable family regu-lations have remained, however, and welfare reform has strengthened those and added more, reasserting the right of the government to interfere in the familial life of the poor. (p. 66)

According to Hays (2003), welfare reform created a system designed to reinforce traditional marriage and limit fertility. Although many conserva-tives applaud these tenets of welfare reform, others find that they are inva-sive and oppressive. For example, we argued in Chapter 4 that one of the major negative outcomes of teen childbearing is child poverty. Teenagers who give birth are less likely to marry, and thus their children are vulnera-ble to the poverty associated with female-headed households.

Although few scholars or policymakers are advocates of teen childbearing, many believe that tying welfare to marriage and fertility decisions is social engineering for the poor. For example, Hays (2003) describes the case of an infant named Tony. One of the restrictions on welfare receipt that is designed to limit family size and control fertility renders children conceived while the mother is on welfare as permanently ineligible for welfare benefits. As a result of conceiving Tony while on welfare, Tony's mother will never be able to col-lect a cash payment or food stamps for Tony, nor will Tony be eligible for health insurance (Medicaid) or any other benefits. Tony is what the welfare system refers to as a "capped" child (Hays, 2003). We wonder if, ultimately, the social engineering couched in welfare reform is very much different from the eugenics movement of the early 20th century (see Chapter 6)?

Hays (2003) and others argue that one of the consequences of welfare is the ability of the government to enforce white, middle-class family values. "The kinds of families that Congress has in mind, in other words, must include breadwinner husbands—ideally the type with sufficient earnings to allow mothers to stay at home" (p. 64).

Finally, we note that the changes in family form that we discussed in Chapters 3 and 4, primarily the decline in marriage and the rise in nonmarital births, begin at the same time as the Johnson administration's Great Society programs, most notably welfare. When welfare became more lucrative than working in the low-wage economy, and when intact families were ineligible for welfare (the "man in the house" rule), the African American family, an institution that had survived centuries of slavery and decades of Jim Crow segregation, was decimated.

Welfare Reform and Incarceration, or African American Mothers Are Crackheads

One of the prevalent stereotypes of poor African American women is that they are addicted to both welfare and crack (Edin & Lein, 1997; Seccombe, 1998). Studies of differential treatment of pregnant women find that regardless of *similar* or *equal* levels of illicit drug use during pregnancy, African American women are *10 times* more likely than white women to be reported to child welfare agencies for prenatal drug use (Chasnoff, Landress, & Barrett, 1990; Neuspiel, 1996).[9] This racial disparity can only be explained by the power of hegemonic ideologies in shaping perceptions. Simply put, when a pregnant African American woman is discovered using drugs, this confirms our stereotype of African American women as crackheads, and therefore, she and her children are referred to child welfare agencies. In contrast, when a pregnant white woman is discovered using drugs, this appears to be an isolated event, it doesn't match the stereotype, and so she is not referred to child welfare agencies. Thus, stereotypes are powerful in shaping the overall incarceration rates of African Americans and whites.

One of the most politically palatable parts of welfare reform was the enactment of a series of bans on welfare receipt for convicted drug felons. Because African American women who use drugs are disproportionately likely to be arrested for, charged with, and convicted of a drug felony (Chasnoff et al., 1990; Neuspiel, 1996), their children are disproportionately likely to suffer the consequences. This set of bans has resulted in one of the most devastating effects on African American children.

Most states (38) impose a ban on the receipt of cash assistance (TANF) and food stamps to individuals with a felony drug conviction. Nearly half of these states (17) impose a *lifetime* ban on cash assistance and food stamps. The remaining 21 allow for the reinstatement of eligibility for these social welfare programs if certain conditions, such as successful treatment or a waiting period, have been met (Mukamal, 2004). We underscore here the impact of these bans. Given the fact that individuals with a felony record face serious obstacles to employment (Mukamal, 2004; Pager, 2003), we ask the question, upon release from prison, struggling to find a job, facing a ban on cash assistance and food stamps, how will the ex-convict eat? Furthermore, as we will discuss at length in Chapter 9, the changes in drug possession laws mean that possessing 5 grams of crack cocaine can bring a felony conviction. Thus, the ban extends to those whose conviction is for *possession*. In contrast, no similar ban is imposed on individuals with felony convictions that are not drug related. The ban does not extend, for example, to those convicted of felony rape, murder, or child molestation. We wonder, then, about the integrity of these bans, but also about their purpose, especially in light of the fact that African Americans are disproportionately likely to be convicted of a drug felony (which carries the ban), whereas white men are disproportionately likely to be convicted of child molesting (which does not carry the ban).

The federal government also allows public housing authorities to use evidence of a criminal record in determining eligibility for public housing. Furthermore, the federal government imposes lifetime bans on eligibility for public housing on two groups: (a) those convicted of the production of methamphetamine and (b) those required to have lifetime registration on the state's sex offender registry. In addition, Mukamal's research of housing authority guidelines found that the majority of housing authorities do consider a person's criminal record when determining his or her eligibility for public housing. The most common bans were for felony drug convictions and violent offenses. Furthermore, her research noted that more than half, 27, of housing authorities "make decisions about eligibility for public housing based on *arrests that never led to a conviction*" (Mukamal, 2004, p. 16, emphasis added). Because children are most likely to live with their mothers, children of mothers with a drug felony will be ineligible to live in public housing. Therefore, this ban poses a serious threat to the safe housing of more than 1 million African American children. We will explore the issue of incarceration on African American families in greater depth in Chapter 9.

Race, Class, and Gender Paradigm

In practical terms, African Americans are far more likely to live in poverty and receive welfare than are whites. The median household income for whites is 1.6 times that of African Americans. But perhaps most disturbing are the racial disparities in wealth. Not only do whites have significantly more wealth than African Americans, this racial disparity holds at every income level. Even among the poorest of Americans, whites have 420 times more wealth than do African Americans, whose average wealth is $57. And because social class is related to educational attainment, health, and incarceration, and because income and wealth are central to the well-being of individuals and families, we conclude that this has a devastating effect on all aspects of African American family life. Specifically, we note that as a result of the decline in the value of real wages; the static nature of the federal minimum wage; and the increasing costs of housing, health care, education, and child care, African American families increasingly find that even when they are working, they are all but shut out of the American Dream.

We have also argued here that welfare reform can be interpreted as an assault on what is perceived as negative behaviors on the part of African American women and an attempt to impose the values of white, middle-class motherhood on them. Regardless of what one thinks about women who choose to rely on welfare, we point out that, in fact, many African American families are forced to rely on welfare in response to a crisis that they do not have the wealth to address. We also note that the impact of welfare reform, including bans on welfare, has a devastating effect on the millions of poor African American children who can no longer rely on the welfare receipt of their mothers to provide food and housing security and access to medical care.

Debates about welfare and welfare reform are important because they illustrate one of the most powerful ways that racism and discrimination have changed in response to the civil rights movement of the 1960s. Bonilla-Silva (2003) talks about this as "color blind racism." For example, it is no longer socially or politically acceptable to shape a debate about the behavior and family practices of African Americans, but it is perfectly acceptable, and common, to shape a debate about the behavior and practices of *poor* Americans. Yet when African Americans are disproportionately represented among the poor and those receiving welfare, the debate most certainly is about race and gender and about the desire of many whites to assert white, middle-class values onto African Americans, especially African American women. One clear illustration of this is the way that welfare reform is used to transmit judgments and values about what it means to be a "good" mother based on white, middle-class motherhood ideology. We reiterate here that the race, class, and gender paradigm allows us to decode these "reforms" by allowing us to compare the choice that a poor African American mother makes to go on welfare and stay at home raising her children and the choice that an affluent white mother makes to exit the labor market, become dependent on her partner's (usually husband's) income, and do the same. One is a "good" mother and one is not. And this assignment of value is clearly shaped by expectations associated with race, class, and gender.

Solutions

In terms of solutions, consistent with our analysis throughout, we propose structural solutions. Shapiro (2004) articulates the problems related to wealth:

> The typical black household earns 59 cents for every dollar earned by the typical white household. This income comparison closely matches other national data and is the most widely used indicator of current racial and ethnic material inequality. . . . However, changing the lens of analysis to wealth dramatically shifts the perspective. The net worth of typical white families is $81,000 compared to $8,000 for black families. This baseline racial wealth gap, then, shows that black families possess only 10 cents for every dollar of wealth held by white families. The issue is no longer how to think about closing the gap from 59 cents on the dollar to a figure approaching parity but how to think about going from 10 cents on the dollar to parity. (p. 47)

- We need to first recognize and then seriously address inequities in wealth that are a direct result of discrimination and blocked access to the opportunity structure that African Americans have faced over the 400 years they have lived in the United States.
- We need to end the types of discrimination that African Americans face in terms of access to wealth—namely, red-lining, other forms of housing discrimination, and unfair lending practices.
- We need to acknowledge that discussions of welfare reform are really code for discussions of African American women and their children. We need to end this type of racist discussion.
- We need to restructure wages so that working families are no longer living below the poverty line.
- We need to reframe welfare as a system that provides a safety net for vulnerable members of our society—namely, the elderly and the young. Reforming TANF as an entitlement for poor children, much as Social Security is an entitlement for the elderly, would ensure that all children in this country have the food and housing security as well as the access to health care that they deserve.

Notes

1. We explore this issue at length in Hattery and Smith (in press).

2. For a lengthier discussion of this, we point the reader to our analysis of these data in Hattery and Smith (in press).

3. This event reminds us of a similar natural disaster with racialized outcomes that occurred in the state of Mississippi in 1927. African American men were dragged from their homes or while walking down the street in cities like Greenwood and taken to fight back the massive flooding of the Mississippi River (Barry, 1997).

In 1927, African Americans in all of Mississippi had no rights that whites respected. African Americans were literally being used as human sandbags in the attempt to stop the Mississippi River from ruining lucrative crop land in the Delta.

4. This formula was developed by Mollie Orshansky and published in a research paper in 1965. She came up with the formula of calculating the poverty line based on the minimum threshold of three times the cost of food during an era when economists believed that the average American family spent one third of its income on food. This formula has never been modified despite the fact that economists estimate today that low-income Americans spend at least one half of their budget on housing.

5. Clearly, the U.S. government is resistant to adopting this new formula for calculating the poverty rate because no president wants the poverty rate to rise under his administration.

6. This "Welfare Queen" stereotype was given credence by then-candidate Ronald Reagan on the 1976 presidential campaign trail. During that election campaign, Reagan often recited the story of a woman from Chicago's South Side who was arrested for welfare fraud. He would repeat that she had 80 names, 30 addresses, and 12 Social Security cards, and she collected veteran's benefits on four nonexistent deceased husbands. He repeated that she collected Social Security on her cards, noting that she received Medicaid and food stamps and regularly collected welfare under each of her names. She was, of course, African American (Zucchino, 1997).

7. We encourage the reader to view HBO's documentary *Lalee's Kin* for an honest visual portrayal of life on welfare in rural Mississippi.

8. In fact, the competing paradigms of what we call the "Cultural Wars of Motherhood" (Hirshman, 2006) has pitted stay-at-home "soccer moms" against "super moms" who are embedded in fierce battle for the right construction of motherhood in contemporary American society. The "war" is so big it has been captured in the editorial pages of the *New York Times* (Brooks, 2006).

9. More recently, debates have erupted over laws that would charge mothers who deliver drug-addicted babies with child abuse, neglect, child endangerment, and even murder if the child subsequently dies.

9

African American Males and the Incarceration Problem

Not Just Confined to Prison

As long as Nina could remember, the prison system held uncles and cousins and grandfathers and always her father. Nina, like Toney and Lolli, was raised in the inner city; for all three, prison further demarcated the already insular social geography. Along with the baby showers of teenagers, they attended prisoners' going-away and coming-home parties. Drug dealing and arrests were common on the afternoons Nina spent playing on the side-walk as she and her parents hung out with their friends. People would be hauled away, while others would unexpectedly reap-pear, angrier or subdued. Corrections officers escorted one hand-cuffed cousin to Nina's great-grandmother's funeral; her favorite uncle had to be unshackled in order to approach his dying grand-mother's hospital bedside. The prison system was part of the tex-ture of family life.

—LeBlanc (2003)

Corporations that appear to be far removed from the business of punishment are intimately involved in the expansion of the prison industrial complex.

—Davis (1998), p. 16

Jails and prisons are designed to break human beings, to convert the population into specimens in a zoo—obedient to our keepers, but dangerous to each other.

—Davis (2003), p. 23

Dear Sister:

One might have hoped that, by this hour, the very sight of chains on Black flesh, or the very sight of chains, would be so intolerable a sight for the American people, and so unbearable a memory, that they would themselves spontaneously rise up and strike off the manacles. But, no, they appear to glory in their chains; now, more than ever, they appear to measure their safety in chains and corpses. And so, Newsweek, civilized defender of the indefensible, attempts to drown you in a sea of crocodile tears ("it remained to be seen what sort of personal liberation she had achieved") and puts you on its cover, chained. You look exceedingly alone—as alone, say, as the Jewish housewife in the boxcar headed for Dachau, or as any one of our ancestors, chained together in the name of Jesus, headed for a Christian land. . . . If we know, then we must fight for your life as though it were our own—which it is—and render impassable with our bodies the corridor to the gas chamber. For, if they take you in the morning, they will be coming for us that night.

—Baldwin (1971), pp. 19, 23

Objectives

- Examine the rate of incarceration and growth of prisons in the United States over the past century.
- Examine the demographics of the prison, particularly in terms of race and gender, including the rise in the incarceration of mothers and the special issues this creates for women but also for African American families.

- Examine the various ways in which prisons have entered the global economy with goods for sale on the world market.
- Examine the impact of incarceration on African American family life and African American communities.
- Examine the relationship between felony records and employment and other rights (housing, welfare, and voting).
- Examine the links between incarceration and other issues addressed in this book: employment, poverty, health, family life, and intimate partner violence.
- Identify solutions to the "incarceration addiction"[1] in America.

Introduction

In this book, we have already discussed some of the most pressing issues facing African American civil society. In our discussions of family formation, health (HIV/AIDS), employment, and intimate partner violence (IPV), we have made references to the role of incarceration in shaping those problems. African American women remain unmarried, raising their children alone in part because the fathers of their children are in prison. African American men are contracting HIV/AIDS in prison and dying there, or, upon release, they are bringing HIV/AIDS back into the communities from which they came, infecting their female partners along the way. A criminal record makes it difficult to find employment, and one of the major risk factors for IPV is male unemployment. We are not arguing in this chapter that incarceration is the root of all of these problems, but we are noting that incarceration is a key piece of the web of entanglement that traps many African American men and women in a life of struggle, poverty, ill health, violence, and limited life chances.

Definitions

The U.S. prison population, incarcerated in all types of institutions from county jails to the new supermax prisons, has grown exponentially. We acknowledge that one of the most confusing aspects of writing and reading about prisons are the distinctions in various kinds of institutions. These distinctions, although common parlance for those who work directly in the criminal justice system, are often a bit hazy for the rest of us. Therefore, we begin with a few definitions. In this chapter, we tend to use the term *prison* as shorthand for a variety of types of institutions. But it is important for the reader to be able to distinguish the different kinds of incarceration institutions that are present in the contemporary United States.

Jails. Jails are administered at the county level. Jails exist to fill three primary functions. Jails hold inmates who (a) are awaiting trial and either cannot make bail or have been denied bail; (b) are required to make a court appearance for any reason—this is because jails are connected to court-houses, whereas prisons generally are not; and (c) are serving sentences of 364 days (1 year) or less.

Prisons. Prisons are administered at both the state and federal level. State prisons hold inmates who (a) are convicted of state crimes[2] *in that state;* (b) have sentences of more than 1 year; and (c) are of all custody levels: mini-mum, medium, maximum, and death row (if the state has the death penalty). Some facilities hold all custody levels in the same prison, and others house only one or two custody levels in the same facility. Federal prisons hold inmates who are convicted of federal crimes. Inmates may be housed in any state that has an appropriate federal prison.[3]

Private Prisons. Private prisons are administered by corporations. The largest, Corrections Association of America (CAA), trades on the New York Stock Exchange. In 2005, CAA's total revenues were $1.2 billion. Private prisons incarcerate inmates with sentences longer than 1 year but who are convicted of either state or federal crimes. Private prisons are essentially a "leasing" system whereby states that have fewer prison beds than they need can ship prisoners to other states for the term of their sentences. Most pri-vate prisons are in the economically depressed South and Southwest regions of the country. Most of the inmates who are shipped out of state come from states in the Northeast and the Midwest.

Supermax Prisons. The supermax prison is relatively new and houses two main types of inmates: high-profile inmates who pose a serious security risk, and those who have exhibited such serious disciplinary problems that this is the "end of the line" for them. For example, the supermax prison in Florence, Colorado, is home to the September 11th terrorist Zacharias Moussaoui and Oklahoma City bomber Terry Nichols.

> In this supermax prison, 1,500 inmates are locked two to a cell for twenty-three hours a day in a space measuring 14 feet by 8 1/2 feet. The only time they will leave their cells will be for "recreation" alone in an attached outdoor "kennel" half the size of the cell. Food is pushed through slots in the door, and the only human interaction an inmate has is with his "roomie." (Wray, 2000, p. 16)[4]

Prisons as Total Institutions

Every American interested in the U.S. prison system should read the explo-sive text by Russian author Aleksandr Solzhenitsyn (1973/2002) titled *The Gulag Archipelago.*[5] This book reveals how similar the U.S. prison system is to the gulag. It is, in fact, a mirror image of the U.S. prison system in all of its details. American prisons are horrible places. They resemble the *worst* in "total institutions" described brilliantly by Goffman (see McCorkel, 1998), who developed the term based on his participant observation[6] in a mental hospital. He defined the term as follows:

> Their encompassing or total character is symbolised by the barrier to social intercourse with the outside and to departure that is often built right into the physical plant, such as locked doors, high walls, barbed wire, cliffs, water, forests, or moors. (Goffman, 1961, p. 227)

A basic social arrangement in modern postindustrial society (as compared to agricultural economies) is that individuals tend to sleep, play, and work in different places with different co-participants, under different authorities, and without an overall rational plan. *The central feature of total institutions can be described as a breakdown of the barriers ordinarily separating these three spheres of life.* Goffman (1961) identifies four specific features of total institutions:

> First, all aspects of life are conducted in the same place and under the same central authority.

> Second, each phase of the member's daily activity is carried on in the immediate company of a large batch of others, all of whom are treated alike and required to do the same thing together.

> Third, all phases of the day's activities are tightly scheduled, with one activity leading at a prearranged time into the next, the whole sequence of activities being imposed from above by a system of explicit formal rulings and a body of officials.

> Finally, the various enforced activities are brought together into a single rational plan purportedly designed to fulfill the official aims of the institution.

Thus, we argue that although prison experiences vary widely by type of institution, length of incarceration, custody status, and so on, any period of incarceration significantly shapes the individuals who are incarcerated, and these experiences shape the social relations of inmates both during incarceration as well as during re-entry into the free world.

The Growth of Prisons: Institutions and Population

The number of prisons has grown, as has the number of Americans incarcerated (see Figure 9.1). In 2005, more than 2.3 million[7] Americans (or 0.7% of the U.S. population) were incarcerated, in nearly 1,700 state, federal, and private prisons, with many more under other forms of custodial

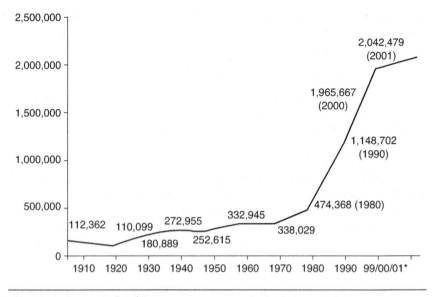

Figure 9.1   Growth of Prisons

SOURCE: Justice Policy Institute analysis of U.S. Department of Justice Data.

*1999, 2000 and 2001 are Bureau of Justice Statistics estimates of what could be the year end totals.

supervision, including probation and parole. (A table that details the size, number of inmates, staff ratios, and so on for all state, federal, and private prisons is available in Appendix I.)

Furthermore, despite the fact that we think of certain other countries as being dominated by incarceration, in relative terms, compared to other countries, the United States incarcerates a higher proportion of its population than all other developed countries and many in the developing world (see Table 9.1).

The Role of Drug Laws in the Growth of Prisons

Why do we incarcerate so many of our citizens? There are many answers to this question, and we will be exploring a variety of them throughout this chapter. However, the most straightforward answer is the changes in drug laws (Western, 2006). In summary, the "War on Drugs" officially began in 1972 with a formal announcement by President Richard Nixon. The War on Drugs officially heated up under the administration of President Ronald Reagan, who added the position of "Drug Czar" to the President's Executive Office. The War on Drugs was not so much about criminalizing substances, because that had been happening across the early part of the 20th century.

Table 9.1   Incarceration Rates for Selected Countries

Country	Incarceration Rate
United States	702
Russia	628
South Africa	400
England and Wales	139
Spain	125
China	118
Canada	116
Australia	112
Italy	100
Netherlands	93
Germany	91
France	85

NOTE: Incarceration rates are the number of incarcerated persons per 100,000 population.

What it did do was put into place stiffer sentencing guidelines that required (a) longer sentences, (b) mandatory minimums, (c) moving some drug offenses from the misdemeanor category to the felony category, and (d) instituting the "Three Strikes You're Out" policy (Mauer, 2003; Roberts, 2004).

Longer Sentences Today, most of the crack cocaine defendants receive an average sentence of 11 years (King & Mauer, 2006).

Mandatory Minimums The most frequently cited example is the sentencing guidelines for possession of crack cocaine. As part of the War on Drugs, a conviction of possessing 5 grams of crack now mandates a 5-year minimum sentence (Meierhoefer, 1992).

Felonizing Drug Offenses Small possession convictions, particularly of crack cocaine, were recategorized from misdemeanors to felonies in the 1986 Drug Abuse Act (this distinction is important for both "Three Strikes You're Out" and bans that we will discuss later in the chapter; King & Mauer, 2006).

"Three Strikes You're Out" This law allows for life sentences for convicts receiving a third felony conviction. Coupled with the recategorizing of some drug *possession* offenses (i.e., crack cocaine) as felonies, the result has been that many inmates serving life sentences are there for three drug possession offenses; in effect, they are serving life sentences for untreated addiction (Haney & Zimbardo, 1998).

One of the clearest outcomes of these changes in drug sentencing is the rapid increase in the number of inmates (recall the data in Figure 9.1). Along with the increase in the number of inmates has been the rise in the number of prisons built to house them.

Again, we use an international comparison in order to contextualize the situation in the United States. Currently, 450,000 of the more than 2 million inmates (45%) in state and federal prison are incarcerated for nonviolent drug offenses. In contrast, this is more people than the European Union—an entity with a population of 100 million more people than the United States— has in prison for *all crimes combined*. States and the federal government continue to spend about $10 billion a year imprisoning drug offenders, and billions more on the War on Drugs, and these costs do not include the impact that incarceration has on the economic and social life of the country, individual states, and communities. In addition, because inmates incarcerated for nonviolent drug offenses are disproportionately likely to be African American, the impact on the African American community is devastating (Roberts, 2004). What this means is that young men (and increasingly women[8]) now have a higher chance of landing in jail at some point in their adult years than ever before.

As with any accumulation of disadvantage, such as the steep rise in incarceration for African American men, comes an accumulated advantage for someone else. For example, whites, implicitly or explicitly, benefit from the sending of hundreds of thousands of African American men to prison. One big advantage that can be measured empirically is that these high levels of incarceration effectively remove these men from the competitive labor force, and upon release, they are disenfranchised in the political system. Thus, whites can hoard jobs and political power for themselves.

Second, advantage can accrue to communities. For example, the prison boom, in terms of both the number of prisons built and the escalating numbers of citizens sent to prison, as well as the locating of prisons in deindustrialized communities and rural communities is an economic advantage that accrues to whites in the form of jobs—as prison staff—and in terms of building contracts and other services that are necessary when a town builds a prison. These advantages by and large do not accrue to African American communities.

Furthermore, the prison boom is devastating to the lives of individual African Americans, but perhaps more serious is the effect on the African American community. Later in this chapter, we will explore both the individual outcomes of incarceration and its effect on the African American community, with specific attention to the loss of various forms of capital— physical, human, and social—within these communities.

The Purpose of Prison: Rehabilitation or a Tool of Capitalism?

Interestingly, whereas prisons used to be hidden institutions, tucked away in the backwaters of American society, today they are found everywhere. This deliberate implementation over the past two decades of sentencing policies designed to lock up more and more people can be interpreted as society using prisons as catchments for the undesirables in our society.[9] Wisconsin sociologist Professor Erik Olin Wright (1997) put it thus:

> In the case of labor power, a person can cease to have economic value in capitalism if it cannot be deployed productively. This is the essential condition of people in the "underclass." They are oppressed because they are denied access to various kinds of productive resources, above all the necessary means to acquire the skills needed to make their labor power saleable. As a result they are not consistently exploited. Understood this way, the underclass consists of human beings who are largely expendable from the point of view of the logic of capitalism. Like Native Americans who became a landless underclass in the nineteenth century, repression rather than incorporation is the central mode of social control directed toward them. Capitalism does not need the labor power of unemployed inner city youth. The material interests of the wealthy and privileged segments of American society would be better served if these people simply disappeared. However, unlike in the nineteenth century, the moral and political forces are such that direct genocide is no longer a viable strategy. The alternative, then, is to build prisons and cordon off the zones of cities in which the underclass lives. (p. 153)

According to Wright, prisons can be seen as a form of modern-day genocide, a strategy for removing unwanted, unnecessary, nonuseful members of a capitalist society. It is a system whereby the privileged can segregate or cordon off these unwanted members of society without the moral burden of genocide. It is easy to see how prisons accomplish this goal: They remove individuals from society, and they permanently (in many states) disenfranchise them from the political realm. Prisoners and ex-convicts become virtual noncitizens, unable to challenge the economic, social, or political power structures. And the very fact of cordoning off some individuals means that the goods and riches of society are accessible only to those citizens who are *not* cordoned off, who benefit from the consequent limits on competition for power. As Zinn and Dill (2005) note, every system of oppression has as its reflection a system of privilege: That which cordons off some, cordons in others.

We note here that many first-time readers of Wright interpret his comments as suggesting that he is advocating the cordoning off of poor, primarily African American citizens, those with few skills that can be used by capitalism, from the opportunity structure. Nothing could be further from the truth. As a neo-Marxist, Wright is arguing that this desire to rid society of individuals who have no skills to contribute to the insatiable and ever-expanding capitalist machine resulted in genocides such as that of the Native Americans in our own country and the Jews in the Holocaust. Today, with genocide being deemed morally objectionable, capitalism seeks new ways in order to accomplish this same goal. Wright argues that in the United States, prisons have provided a mechanism to meet this goal.

The Demographics of the Prison Population: Gender and Race

In the largest context, this chapter is about the effort by academics to rethink the race issue in rising imprisonment in the United States. As we show above, the prison system has, on many measures, grown in the past two decades. In this section, we examine the demographics of the prison population: a story of race and gender. We begin with the more obvious variable: gender.

Gender

Across all of U.S. history, and this holds globally as well, men are far more likely to be incarcerated than are women. Depending on the type of facility, women constitute 6%–10% of the prison population, or of the 2.6 million Americans who are incarcerated, 150,000 or so are women. The probability that a woman will be incarcerated in her lifetime is 11/1,000 or 1.1% (Bureau of Justice Statistics, n.d.; Harrison & Beck, 2005). The incarceration of women raises special issues that are not required in the incarceration process for men. As a result, jails and prisons are sex segregated. Typically, jails house both men and women who are segregated by unit or floor. In most states, prisons are segregated by institution; in other words, there are men's prisons and women's prisons.

Gender differences in incarceration are primarily related to reproductive health, childbearing, and childrearing. For example, the practices at our local jail, which are typical (Liptak, 2006; Rogers, 2000), involve special procedures for pregnant inmates; nationally, 6% of all women entering prison are pregnant (Rogers, 2000). In an interview with prison specialist Mr. Steven Dobson, Forsyth County, North Carolina Detention Center, we learned that when a pregnant woman enters the final stages of labor, she is transported by ambulance, shackled and with leg irons, to the local birthing unit. She remains shackled while the baby is delivered, and as soon as she is cleared out of recovery, she is transported back to her cell in the Forsyth County Detention Center. When we inquired about the baby, we learned that the baby is immediately taken into foster care by either a relative or a foster family and is under the supervision of Child Protective Services and the Department of Social Services.

It is critically important to note that there is wide variation in the treatment of female inmates. This is in large part because there are very few federal or state laws that set policy for the treatment of pregnant inmates or their children. For example, Liptak (2006) reports that only two states, New York and Illinois, have laws that prohibit the shackling of inmates during labor and delivery. Some counties and states have informal policies that recommend that inmates not be shackled during labor and delivery, but others require it.

Many people wonder about the justification for shackling women during labor and delivery.[10] Britton (2004) argues that the policy or practice of shackling women while they are laboring and delivering arises out of the practice of shackling male prisoners any time they are transported, such as to court or to a local hospital, a practice that is consistent with the "sameness" debate that infuses not only feminism but also the theoretical debates in the area of criminal justice. Furthermore, the explicit justification for shackling women during labor and delivery is that because they are being transported during that experience, they pose a flight risk (Britton, 2004; Liptak, 2006). Liptak (2006) notes that shackling during labor and delivery poses a health risk to both the mother and the baby.

What is important for our discussion here is the fact that more and more women are being incarcerated, and thus, jails and prisons are finding that they have more and more gender issues to address. With no national policies on the treatment of mothers or their minor children, the practices vary tremendously, but many of the practices leave both mother and baby at risk for health problems and even death. Later in the chapter, when we consider the effects of incarceration on the African American family, we will return to a discussion of what may be the biggest tragedy of all: the children left behind.

Race

Of the 2.6 million Americans who are incarcerated, one million (43%) are African American men. In other words, more than 40% of *all* American prisoners, men and women, are African American *men*. Controlling for gender, African Americans comprise nearly two thirds (62%) of the male prison population, yet they make up just 13% of the U.S. male population (Roberts, 2004; see Figures 9.2 and 9.3).

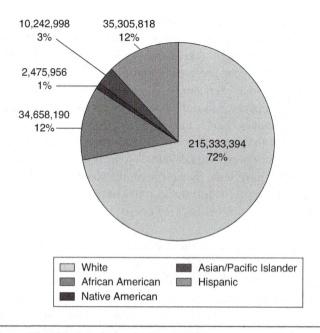

Figure 9.2   The U.S. Population by Race, 2005

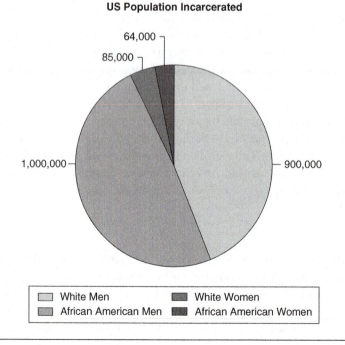

Figure 9.3   Prison and Jail Inmates by Race and Gender

SOURCE: Harrison and Beck (2005).

In terms of probability, 90 out of every 1,000 men in the United States will be incarcerated in their lifetimes. When we break down the data by race, only 44 out of every 1,000 (4%) white men will be incarcerated, but 285 out of every 1,000 (28.5%) African American men will be incarcerated in their lifetimes[11] (Harrison & Beck, 2005). Put another way, *nearly 1 in 3 African American men will be incarcerated during their lifetimes.*[12] (See Appendix J for probability statistics by race and gender.)

Explaining Racial Disparities in Incarceration

The data on incarceration are clear. African American men and women have much higher rates of incarceration than any other racial/ethnic group, especially when compared to the rates for white Americans (Cose, 2000; Roberts, 2004). There are many beliefs, myths, and stereotypes that are invoked to explain these differences. We will briefly discuss some of the explanations for these racial disparities, noting that entire volumes are devoted to this issue (see especially Elsner, 2006; Western, 2006).

African Americans Commit More Crime African Americans do commit certain crimes more often than whites. For example, as we noted in Chapter 6, homicide is now one of the leading causes of death for African American men. And the data on homicide indicate that, more often than not, the perpetrator in these homicides is also African American. In fact, an examination of the data on all violent crimes (rape, homicide, assault) demonstrates that violent crimes are primarily intraracial; in other words, both the victim and the offender are of the same race (LaFree & Drass, 1996). However, when one examines the range of crime statistics, one finds that just as African Americans are disproportionately likely to commit certain crimes (homicide), whites are disproportionately likely to commit others. Although some of these are nonviolent, financial crimes like those of which executives such as Martha Stewart, Bernard Ebbers (WorldCom), Dennis Kozlowski (Tyco), and Kenneth Lay (Enron) were convicted, these crimes harm millions of Americans who have lost their pensions, their paychecks, their health insurance, and indeed their livelihood. But whites are also more likely to be serial murderers, child molesters, and school shooters. In fact, the primary demographic description of the perpetrators in these horrible crimes is not just white, but male. White men commit these crimes at disproportionate rates. Furthermore, our analysis suggests that child molesters, who are primarily white men, serve shorter average sentences than crack offenders, who are primarily African American men. Child molesters serve an average of 6 years and only 43% of their full sentences, whereas the average inmate serving a sentence for possession of crack serves 11 years and 80% of his or her sentence. Thus, the racial gap in incarceration rates cannot be explained entirely by racial differences in the rate of committing crime. Part of the incarceration rate is driven by differences in sentencing that keep certain people in prison for longer periods of time than others.

Racial Profiling Over the past decade or so, significant attention has been paid to the catch-all category of "racial profiling." Typically, racial profiling refers to the targeting of African Americans; Hispanics; and, since the tragedy of September 11th, Middle Easterners, in "pulling over" a person for no apparent reason, searching private property such as a car or home, and arrest. Anecdotal evidence suggests that since September 11th, non-whites are more likely to be subjected to more extensive searches in airports and train stations. But the most reliable data come from the Bureau of Justice Statistics. Beginning in the mid-1990s, the law required that local law enforcement agencies collect data on the race, ethnicity, and gender of all people involved in traffic stops. The latest report, released in April 2005, noted that there were no racial differences in the probability of being stopped, but that African Americans (and Hispanics) were more likely to be subjected to "forced search" of their cars and more likely to have "force used against them" (Lichtblau, 2005, p. A14). The relationship between racial profiling and racial disparities in incarceration is significant and clear. Part of the higher rate of incarceration for African Americans is a direct out-come of the higher probability that they will be searched, arrested, and charged with a crime. Furthermore, we note that the discussion of racial pro-filing is politically charged. In August 2005, the director of the Bureau of Justice Statistics, Lawrence Greenfeld, was *fired* over a dispute regarding their research on racial profiling. The Bush administration did not want data on racial profiling released and sought to repress it. When Greenfeld refused to suppress this important information, he was fired (Lichtblau, 2005). Thus, the business of racial profiling and its relationship to incarceration is a hot-button issue for American politicians.

Sentencing Disparities Along with differences in traffic stops and arrest, there is also substantial evidence to support the argument that African Americans receive stiffer sentences than their white counterparts who com-mit the same crime. Among persons convicted of drug felonies in state courts, whites were less likely than African Americans to be sent to prison. A report by the U.S. Department of Justice on sentencing in state courts found that 33% of convicted white defendants received a prison sentence whereas 51% of African American defendants received prison sentences (Durose & Langan, 2001). In addition, in a review of 40 recent and methodologically sophisticated studies investigating the link between race and sentence severity, many of the studies, especially at the federal level, found evidence of direct discrimination against minorities that resulted in significantly more severe sentences for African Americans than their white counterparts (Spohn, 2000). Therefore, we conclude that part of the explanation for differential rates in incarceration is racial disparities in sentencing. More African American men are in prison than their white counterparts because when they are convicted of the same crime, they are more likely to receive prison sentences (Durose & Langan, 2001) and more likely to receive longer, more severe sentences (Spohn, 2000). One of the most egregious cases that received a lot of attention recently is that of Wilbert Rideau. Wilbert Rideau was released in 2005 after serving 40 years of a life sentence for murder at Angola (the Louisiana State Penitentiary). His case is interesting in that he has been so successful as a writer and spokesman on prisons that he has been allowed to travel (chaperoned by armed guards, of course) to speaking engagements. He was released in 2005 after lawyers agreed that he had served *twice* the sentence that a similarly situated white convict would serve in Louisiana.

The Relationship Between Ideology and Incarceration Those who defend racial profiling note that if African Americans are more likely to commit crime, then it makes sense for law enforcement agents to target African Americans with surveillance, police presence, and traffic stops. Unfortunately, in some cases, the targeting or treatment of a population is based more on myths or stereotypes about that racial/ethnic population than on empirical evidence. In other words, the hegemonic ideologies around race and crime are so powerful that they create perceptions about African Americans and crime that significantly influence the behavior of whites reporting crime, identifying suspects, and, in the case of police officers, engaging in racial profiling.[13] We illustrate our point here with two very different examples.

African American Mothers Are Crackheads As we noted in Chapter 8, one of the prevalent stereotypes of poor African American women is that they are addicted to both welfare and crack (Edin & Lein, 1997; Seccombe, 1998), and as a result, they are treated more harshly by social service agencies and the criminal justice system when they do use drugs. Thus, stereotypes such as this are powerful in shaping the kinds of behavior that affect the overall incarceration rates of African Americans and whites. (We refer the reader back to our lengthy discussion of this stereotype in Chapter 8.)

Our second example is based on a long-standing myth of the unregulated nature of African American male sexuality. Angela Davis refers to this as the "myth of the black rapist" (Davis, 1983). Davis argues that this myth led to a widespread belief that African American men were propelled toward the desire to rape white women. Because whites believed that African American men wanted to and could rape white women, the protection of white women fell to white men. It was a duty that they took seriously. Thousands of African American men were accused of raping white women, but they were lynched by mobs long before they were ever tried in court (Apel, 2004). The power of this accusation without the requirement of evidentiary support provided the justification for the vast majority of the lynchings of 10,000 African American men during the period from 1880 to 1930 (Apel, 2004; Davis, 1983). We argue that this myth of the black rapist persists, it contributes to the incarceration of African American men, and it is the primary reason for the high rate of false rape convictions that African American men experience.

We argue that it is not simply that white Americans are more likely to mistake one black person for another, but it is also an outcome of the long-held myth of the black rapist. As stated, although only 10%–15% (Bureau of Justice Statistics, 2003b) of all rapes are perpetrated by an African American man on a white woman, because this scenario matches the myth, African American men are more likely to be accused, charged, and convicted than are their white counterparts, who account for 70% (Bureau of Justice Statistics, 2003b) of the rapes of white women. Thus, ideologies about crime and offenders affect the incarceration rate.

The racial mix of those exonerated, in general, mirrors that of the prison population, and the mix of those exonerated of murder mirrors the mix of those convicted of murder. But whereas 29% of those in prison for rape are black, *65% of those exonerated of the crime are.* Interracial rapes are, moreover, uncommon. Rapes of white women by black men, for instance, represent less than 10% of all rapes, according to the Justice Department. But in *half* of the rape exonerations where racial data was available, black men were *falsely convicted* of raping white women. "The most obvious explanation for this racial disparity is probably also the most powerful," the study says. "White Americans are much more likely to mistake one black person for another than to do the same for members of their own race" (Liptak, 2004).

When we talk about incarceration, we need to be clear that although there has been a dramatic increase in the number of women who are incarcerated, and they are disproportionately African American, incarceration can only be characterized as a phenomenon that is shaped by *race and gender.* Thus, we will turn our focus to the impact of incarceration on African American men and their families. Because the primary impact of incarceration on African American women is the impact on their children, we will return to that discussion later in the chapter.

The Effects of Incarceration on the Lives of Young African American Men

Taking a closer look, we see that not only do African American men make up a disproportionate percentage of the prison population, but this is exaggerated at particular age categories: specifically young men aged 18–34 who are at the height of their economic productivity and family involvement. Nearly 10% of all African American men aged 25–29 are incarcerated in the prison system. This statistic does not include those African American men who are in local jails, either awaiting trial or serving sentences less than 1 year in length, nor does it include those African American men under custodial supervision: those on parole or probation.[14] (For a detailed table by race, gender, and age, see Appendix K.)

These are young men serving lengthy sentences primarily for drug-related crimes.[15] They enter the state and federal prison system, prisons like Parchman in Mississippi, Angola in Louisiana, or Sing Sing in New York, at the prime of their economic and reproductive lives, and when they emerge, they will be behind in these life stages if not aged out of them entirely. When the rest of American young men are finishing school, starting careers, earning seniority at work, and marrying and having children, these men are in prison, their human capital decaying.

If they are released, they enter the labor force a decade after their peers, which will have irretrievable consequences on their lifetime earnings and on their retirement savings—if they are able to accrue any at all. In addition, these men—who reflect the prison rather than the jail population—if they are released, return back to their communities with a felony record, which as noted by Pager (2003), is devastating to their employment prospects. In addition, in most states, these men are either temporarily or permanently disenfranchised, and by not being able to vote, they lose all political power (Mauer, 2002; Uggen & Manza, 2002). Across the lifecourse, fully 25%–33% of African American men will be in the criminal justice system.[16]

Due to harsh new sentencing guidelines, such as "three-strikes, you're out," a disproportionate number of young Black and Hispanic men are likely to be imprisoned for life under scenarios in which they are guilty of little more than a history of untreated addiction and several prior drug-related offenses. . . . States will absorb the staggering cost of not only constructing additional prisons to accommodate increasing numbers of prisoners who will never be released but also warehousing them into old age. (Haney & Zimbardo, 1998, p. 718)

Finally, many people talk about the "fact" that there are more African American men in prison than in college, and the data on this topic are complex. Indeed, as the data in Table 9.2 show, there *are* more African American men in prison (1 million) than in college (less than 500,000). In contrast, with only 600,000 white men in prison and 3.5 million in college, there are 5.8 times as many white men in college as in prison. But perhaps the comparison that is more relevant is the relationship between prison and college for young men aged 18–24.

Table 9.2   American Men Aged 18–24 in College and in Prison

	Population Total	*In College*	*In Prison*	*Ratio*
White	10,739,000	3,522,392 (32.8%)	125,700 (1.1%)	28:1
Black	1,885,000	469,000 (24.9%)	179,500 (9.5%)	2.6:1

NOTE: Data for this table were taken from various portions of the 2000 U.S. census.

When we compare data on these young men, what we find is that although African American men in this age group are more likely to be in college than in prison, there is a substantial and significant race gap in the ratio of men in college to men in prison. Whereas African American men are 2.6 times more likely to be in college than in prison, white men are 28 times more likely to be in college than in prison—a 10-fold difference in the ratio.

Education and race also work together to shape the likelihood that one will end up in prison. For example, 11.5% of all African American men between the ages of 20 and 40 were in prison in 2000, but 32.4% of African American men of the same age who had dropped out of high school were incarcerated (Western, 2006). Thus, the probability that an African American man will go to prison is increased threefold if he is a high school dropout.

What are the consequences of this on the African American community? The consequences are far-reaching, especially the political consequences. If 25%–33% of a population is disenfranchised, the whole community loses its already limited access to the political structure. The economic consequences are endemic. Those who emerge with a felony record face chronic unemployment and underemployment. Those who can find a job nevertheless enter the labor market with depleted human capital. They emerge from prison as constantly evolving technology has rendered what skills they have obsolete. They become, to use Professor Wright's term, *unexploitable* (see also Pager, 2003).

Those who emerge in the best of possible situations, with no felony record and with human capital still intact, nevertheless enter the labor market behind their same-age peers. This affects layoffs, seniority, wages, and retirement accumulation. And all of this assumes that these ex-cons can even obtain a job, given that they will have a several-year "gap" in their work history.[17]

We have already noted, in Chapters 3 and 4, that incarceration is terribly disruptive to family life. It significantly reduces the probability that men will marry, and it removes them temporarily, if not permanently, from their relationships with their children. The fact that men with a felony record face such significant barriers to employment means that even when they do form stable, long-term relationships, they are often literally handcuffed in their ability to provide financial support for their families. Finally, as we discussed in Chapter 5, they are far more likely to be involved in intimate partner violence. Thus, the consequences of incarceration on the African American family are devastating. How we can better understand the overincarceration of young African American men and the wider consequences of incarceration on their families and communities is a question that sociologists and others have been asking but for some reason have not paid a lot of attention to.[18]

Loss in the African American Community: Economic Costs

The economic and family consequences of incarceration affect more than just the individual and his or her family. As a result of hyper-residential segregation (Massey & Denton, 1993), communities of African Americans (either rural or urban) will, by default, have higher rates of male incarceration than white communities. As noted by Jonathan Kozol, in Mott Haven, New York, half of all the children in the local elementary schools routinely make visits to prisons like Rikers Island to visit their fathers (Kozol, 2001, 2005).

Furthermore, incarceration has a social class component as well. The 25%–33% of African American men who are incarcerated in their lifetimes are not spread evenly across all social class categories. The rates are much lower among middle- and upper-middle-class and professional African American men, and they are much higher among low-income and poor African American men. Thus, in a poor African American community, perhaps as many as 50% of the men will have been in prison. If 50% of men in a single community have been incarcerated and have felony records, then half the families in this community will face the consequences of their chronic under- and unemployment. This produces a situation in which poverty is far-reaching. With little human capital, entire communities will struggle just to have enough income to survive, and there will be little to no chance of owning homes or establishing businesses in the community, thus leaving the entire community vulnerable to other oppressive forces such as slum lords and the requirement to leave the community to find work.

Loss in the African American Community: Human Capital

A major part of the prison problem is that an enormous amount of human capital is lost with the incarceration of African American men during their most productive years. These men learn few transferable skills while they are in prison, and when they are finally released, they are useless to themselves and to others. Becker (1975) provides a working definition of human capital:

> Schooling, a computer training course, expenditures of medical care, and lectures on the virtues of punctuality and honesty also are capital. That is because they raise earnings, improve health, or add to a person's good habits over much of his lifetime. Therefore, economists regard expenditures on education, training, medical care, and so on as investments in *human* capital. They are called human capital because people cannot be separated from their knowledge, skills, health, or values in the way they can be separated from their financial and physical assets. (p. 1)

One of the most obvious and devastating outcomes of incarceration on human capital is seen in the labor market. Protected by law, employers are allowed to ask prospective employees if they have an incarceration record. Although the inquiry of a felony record is legally justified, in some states and in some industries, we note that employers can also ask about misdemeanor records as well as arrest records (with no conviction). In order to examine the impact of felony records on employment (Mukamal, 2004), Pager (2003) designed an experiment to test the effect of race and incarceration history on the likelihood of getting a "call back" after submitting a job application (the details of her research design can be found in Chapter 7). What she found was terribly disturbing.

In her study, which included only men, whites were more likely than blacks to be called back for an interview regardless of incarceration history. And white men without a felony were, not surprisingly, the most likely to be called back of all groups. But the shocking finding from her research is that whites *with* a felony record were more likely to be called back than African Americans *without* a felony record (see Figure 9.4). Less than 5% of African American men with a felony record were called back (compared to 15% of whites with a felony record). Incarceration is problematic for anyone, but the effects are devastating on the employability of African American men.

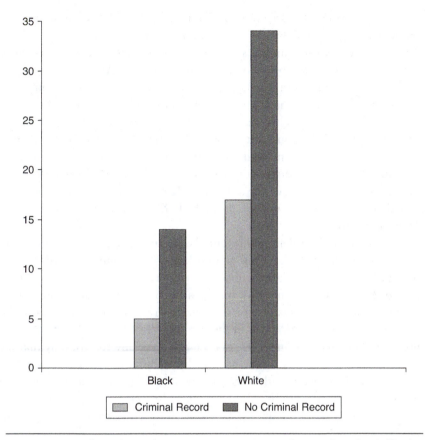

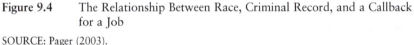

Figure 9.4   The Relationship Between Race, Criminal Record, and a Callback
for a Job

SOURCE: Pager (2003).

We illustrate the effect of incarceration on employment with the case of a
man with whom we work, Mr. Darryl Hunt.

An Illustration: The Case of Darryl Hunt

One case from the South is especially illuminating. Darryl Hunt was
convicted in 1984 of the rape and murder of a white female employee of
the afternoon newspaper *The Sentinel* in the city of Winston-Salem, North
Carolina.[19] The case against Mr. Hunt is precisely the kind that was built
on the myth of the black rapist (Davis, 1983) that we outlined earlier. The
rape-murder divided the southern city, as expected, and the racial division
between African Americans and whites continues in the early 21st century.

After spending 18 years in prison for a crime he did not commit, Darryl Hunt was exonerated by the governor of North Carolina in February 2004. Exoneration is unique, as compared to a pardon or an overturned conviction, in that it is based on absolute innocence. After many years of struggle in the courts, in 2003, a judge finally considered the results of a DNA analysis that originally had been conducted a decade earlier. The DNA analysis was conclusive: Mr. Hunt was excluded with 100% accuracy from the DNA found at the scene. Furthermore, after the DNA was compared to a list of convicted felons in North Carolina, a perfect match identified the rapist and murderer: a man named Willard Brown who was incarcerated at the time of the analysis. (He has since been tried and convicted of the rape and murder for which Mr. Hunt served more than 18 years in prison.)

In a talk Mr. Hunt delivered to our classes and in response to a question from one of the students, Hunt stated that no one would hire him, even though he is now (officially) publicly not guilty. Mr. Hunt has no felony record. Yet despite this, he still cannot find a job. He says that when asked about his employment history for the previous 18 years, he has to acknowledge that he was in prison. From the perspective of the employer, it seems not to matter that he is innocent, that he has no felony record, only that he has been in prison. His attorney of record for all the 18 years he was incarcerated, Mark Rabil, says that the only way Mr. Hunt can start over is to move away from the South. This case illustrates the real impact of Pager's (2003) study, that although the felony itself is a barrier to employment, incarceration or even the perception that one has been (or will be) incarcerated also limits the employment of African American men, especially those in the working class.

What is unique and interesting in this case is both the fact that Hunt is not guilty and the years of life lost from his teenage years to adulthood. As we noted above, one of the most tragic outcomes of the overincarceration of African American men is that they miss out on realizing their own personal goals and growth. This loss is great in that not only does Hunt fall behind his age cohort in education and training for specific job-related skills, but also the ever-changing world of technology, the Internet, the laptop computer, ATM machines, and all advances in our society since the 1980s and 1990s have passed by him. His family lost their son for 18 years of his life. Although he married in prison and now lives with his wife April and her children, he lost out on the opportunity to start a family in the ways that most Americans believe they have a right. This example is a good illustration of how individuals, families, and communities can lose human capital at the onset of involvement in the criminal justice system.

Social Capital

Related in many ways to the human capital loss is also the loss of social capital. The loss of social capital to the African American community and to African American families is immense. We employ a definition of social capital offered by Harvard political scientist Robert Putnam (1995):

> Social capital refers to connections among individuals—social networks and the norms of reciprocity and trustworthiness that arise from them. In that sense social capital is closely related to what some have called "civic virtue." The difference is that "social capital" calls attention to the fact that civic virtue is most powerful when embedded in a sense network of reciprocal social relations. (p. 67)

These very important "reciprocal social relations" are lost when African American men are sent to prison. We illustrate this loss through the words of inmates with whom we've met as well as with a thought exercise based on our home state: North Carolina. We begin with the perspective of an inmate.

Twice, during the summers of 2003 and 2005, we taught a course in which we take 20 students on a 2-week, off-campus course through the Deep South. A significant part of the course is a discussion of social justice in the South. Central to this discussion is a visit to the Mississippi State Penitentiary at Parchman. "Parchman Farm" is located right in the heart of the Mississippi Delta. Parchman is a 20,000-acre men's prison with the capacity to house 6,000 inmates. It holds all death row inmates in Mississippi and has executed prisoners using a roving electric chair, a notorious gas chamber, and now by lethal injection. Parchman was founded more than 100 years ago on the Parchman family plantation and is entirely self-sustaining. The inmates sew all of their own clothes and bedding, they make all of the tack and saddles for the horse patrol, and they grow all of their own food, including corn, okra, hogs, and, more recently, catfish. Because Parchman is 85% African American and its population has historically fluctuated with the labor needs of the agricultural season, it is often described as a plantation (Oshinsky, 1997).

While at Parchman, we and our students met with inmates and learned lessons firsthand from prisoners doing a stretch of time that is unimaginable. Walter Lott spoke to our class, and in his discussion, he made it clear that his life was ruined from the first day he was sent to Parchman. The lives of his family members were also ruined.

Walter has been imprisoned in Parchman since he was 19 years of age. When we met him the first time, he was age 38 and had been incarcerated for nearly 20 years. He began by telling the class that he was convicted of strong armed robbery, which he admitted he committed while strung out on crack. Walter, who is African American, had also been convicted of raping a white woman, although as with other cases we have discussed in this chapter, he and several staff at Parchman contend that this conviction was based on a "confession" that was beaten out of Walter by the local police. We include this detail in order to reinforce the argument made earlier that myths and beliefs about African American men influence in significant ways their experiences with the criminal justice system and incarceration.

After telling the class why he was there, he told of the inhuman treatment and conditions inside Parchman. Walter, a male, was turned into a "female bitch" by stronger males in the prison population, was even "sold" for bounty such as cigarettes—Parchman has a policy whereby prisoners cannot have money—and made to perform oral and anal sex with whomever made the purchase, regardless of whether Walter consented or not.

When we met Walter during the class visit, he was working in the Parchman chapel and thrived on his position of spokesman to groups like our own. When we met Walter for the second time, he had lost his living space as a result of reorganization in the cell blocks. This reorganization resulted in a structural reduction in his privileges.[20] His connections with prison officials, a form of social capital on the inside, are his *only hope* for getting reassigned and having his privileges reinstated. Thus, for inmates, social capital is as important on the inside as it is on the outside.

Social capital is one of the primary factors necessary for successful reentry (Mukamal, 2004). For many inmates like Walter, who have no social support on the outside, reentry to the free world can be as daunting as the thought of entering prison. In the summer of 2005, Linda McIntyre, a Parchman Farm official (Reception Center Administrator and tour guide), told us that Walter had lost his bid for the 11th time to be paroled. She also said that Walter, now an adult male, was afraid of leaving Parchman because he did not know how to live on the outside. This is akin to the fictitious character Brooks in the film *Shawshank Redemption*; Brooks is paroled after a long time in prison, and shortly thereafter he hangs himself in a halfway house because he was very unsure of how to make it outside of the institutional life to which he had become accustomed.[21]

Furthermore, all of Walter's family members (mother, father, sisters, and brothers) either are dead or have disowned him and severed contact with him. He has no social support in the free world and acknowledged during our visit in 2005 that he will probably die at Parchman, and because he has no family on the outside to claim his body, he will be buried inside the prison he entered at age 18.

It should be clear that an extensive social capital network is necessary for survival inside prison; it is also the case that the physical relocation of these men from their own communities to other communities, often far from home, breaks their social networks and renders them alienated and unable to connect with others in their network groups and families on the outside.

Social Capital In and Out: An Illustration From North Carolina

North Carolina provides several interesting examples of social capital, and because we live in North Carolina and are familiar with the geography, we chose it as our illustration.

Maintaining relationships with family and friends on the outside is one of the major predictors of both surviving incarceration and reentering the free world successfully (Fogel, 1993; Fogel & Martin, 1992; Houck & Loper, 2002; Mukamal, 2004). Therefore, in order to better understand some of the barriers and struggles faced by inmates and the families they leave behind, we designed a "thought" exercise in which we analyzed the racial distribution of North Carolina counties, the location of prisons, and the travel distance between them. Like many other southern states, North Carolina is racially diverse as a whole, but the racial composition of individual counties varies from less than 10% African American to more than 65% African American.[22] Similarly, prisons are not equally or randomly distributed across the various counties or regions of the state. Analyzing the race/ethnic distribution by county and comparing it to rates of incarceration by county, we see that the "blackest" counties have the highest rates of incarceration by far, and the "whitest" counties have the lowest rates. Incarceration rates are three to five times higher in the "blackest" counties than they are in the "whitest" counties (see Figure 9.5).

The relationship between incarceration rate and prison construction is, however, far more complex (see Figure 9.6). Each of the counties with a relatively high (25%–65%) black population has prisons. What is more interesting is that several prisons, including some of the larger institutions housing 400–1,174 inmates, are located in the "whitest" counties (2%–10% black) with the lowest rates of incarceration (115–242 per 100,000 residents). This suggests that in North Carolina, as in other states, inmates are required to serve their time outside of their communities of origin.

In North Carolina, this may mean taking an individual from the eastern, coastal region of the state and relocating him or her to the western mountain region for the term of his or her incarceration. For those not familiar with the geography of this region, this may amount to a 6- to 7-hour drive (325 miles) or a bus ride. This is the thought exercise. We decided to determine what it would be like for the family of an inmate who fit this description: The family lived in the eastern part of the state, and we chose New

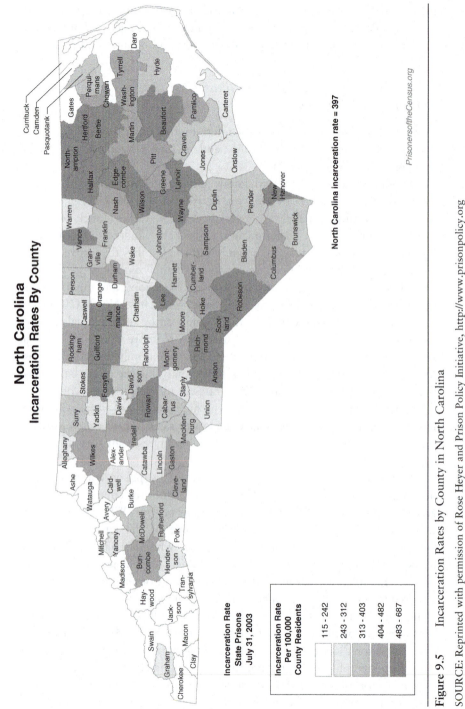

North Carolina
Incarceration Rates By County

North Carolina incarceration rate = 397

Incarceration Rate
State Prisons
July 31, 2003

Incarceration Rate
Per 100,000
County Residents

- 115 - 242
- 243 - 312
- 313 - 403
- 404 - 482
- 483 - 687

PrisonersoftheCensus.org

Figure 9.5   Incarceration Rates by County in North Carolina

SOURCE: Reprinted with permission of Rose Heyer and Prison Policy Initiative, http://www.prisonpolicy.org

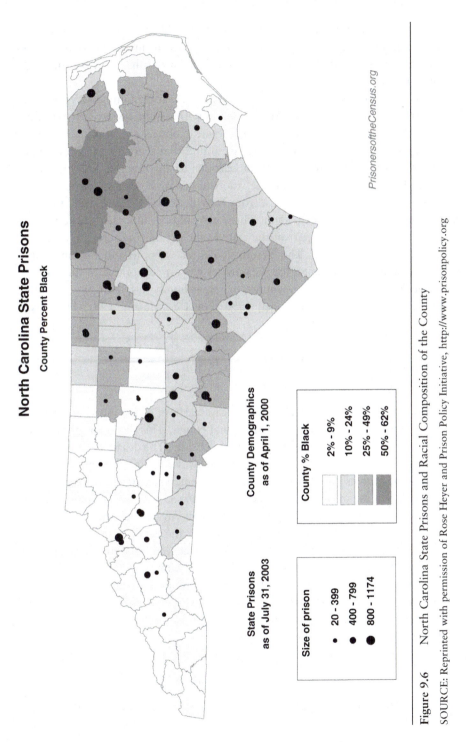

North Carolina State Prisons
County Percent Black

State Prisons
as of July 31, 2003

Size of prison
- • 20 – 399
- ● 400 – 799
- ⬤ 800 – 1174

County Demographics
as of April 1, 2000

County % Black
- 2% – 9%
- 10% – 24%
- 25% – 49%
- 50% – 62%

PrisonersoftheCensus.org

Figure 9.6 North Carolina State Prisons and Racial Composition of the County

SOURCE: Reprinted with permission of Rose Heyer and Prison Policy Initiative, http://www.prisonpolicy.org

Bern, North Carolina, in Beaufort County (a "black" county with a high incarceration rate and no prison). The inmate is incarcerated in Avery County, North Carolina, a mountain county, which has a prison housing 800–1,174 inmates.

As part of our thought exercise, we assumed that the family does not have access to a car (according to many inmates with whom we have spoken, this is fairly typical because so many of the incarcerated are from low-income families). In researching bus routes, we found that there are no Greyhound bus routes from anywhere in North Carolina to any town in Avery County. The closest bus was to Asheville, more than an hour away from Avery County. The travel time, by bus, from New Bern was 17 hours, and the fare was $88 round trip, per person. Thus, it would be difficult for a family to travel from the eastern part of the state to the prisons in the western mountain region of the state. The circumstances, as we note, disrupt family life and decimate social capital for the inmates who are uprooted for their incarceration. And when inmates cannot maintain family ties, their prognosis for successful reentry is slim (Fogel, 1993; Fogel & Martin, 1992; Houck & Loper, 2002; Mukamal, 2004).

Political Capital: Census Recalculation and Felon Disenfranchisement

Incarceration also depletes political capital, both of the individual and of the community from which the individual comes. This depletion of political capital is critical both symbolically and practically. The disenfranchisement of felons has symbolic power because it takes away a right—the right to vote—that is the quintessential symbol of being an American citizen (Kerber, 1997). Second, because of the high rates of incarceration of African Americans, disenfranchisement also takes away the power of African American communities to choose their political representation at the local, state, and national levels. In fact, the outcome of the 2000 presidential election was shaped in part by felony disenfranchisement (Uggen & Manza, 2002).[23] Finally, the relocation of inmates from their home communities to prisons in other counties, in other parts of the states, changes the way that resources are allocated by the state and federal government. We begin by discussing the way that the U.S. census is affected by relocating inmates.

The Impact of Incarceration on the Census

Currently, the U.S. census, which is used every 10 years to redraw congressional districts so that each district has the same number of residents, allows rural communities with prisons to "count" inmates as citizens. Because in most states prisons are in rural regions but the majority of inmates originate from urban communities, the relocation of inmates to rural prisons has significant outcomes for the census and ultimately for both the counties that house the prisons and the counties from which the inmates originate. This practice allows rural counties to grow and thereby get more congressional representation, whereas urban communities dwindle and get fewer representatives and fewer tax-based economic resources. Note that the inmates counted as citizens of rural communities are disenfranchised and thus cannot vote (Mukamal, 2004). Therefore, they are in no way "citizens" of these rural communities.

We choose to illustrate this last point using data from New York. New York City loses 43,740 residents annually to the districts of upstate legislators, where they are incarcerated in rural areas. Inmates have been moving up there for decades, but since 1982, all new state prisons in New York have been built upstate. As a result of census rules, rural upstate communities counting the prisoners as "citizens" are actually *overestimating* their populations beyond the 5% rule established by the U.S. Supreme Court. In fact, the population of some upstate towns consists mostly of inmates. The majority of Dannemora, New York's population is incarcerated in the supermax prison there, and 43% of the town of Coxsackie's population is in prison (Wagner, 2004)!

The data and map provided in Appendix L illustrate the way this process works across the entire United States. As many as 21 counties in the United States have more than 21% of their population incarcerated as recorded by the census. In four counties, that figure is nearly 33%. We note that these counties are both rural and, for the most part, southern; the poorest regions of the country are seeing improvements by further decimating urban ghettos.

And, like so many other things we have discussed in this book, this process is racialized as well. For example, the majority of inmates coming from the boroughs of New York City are African Americans who live in districts that are predominantly African American. They are relocated and counted in counties that are predominantly white. Thus, congressional representation and federal and state resources are rerouted from predominantly African American districts to predominantly white districts.

Felony Disenfranchisement

Most Americans know that there is some relationship between felony status and the political system. For example, ex-felons cannot be elected president.

But many fewer people understood the relationship between felony status and voting until the 2000 presidential election, when the issue rose to the national scene as part of the voting debacle in the state of Florida that resulted in the outcome of the election being determined in the U.S. Supreme Court.

It is not surprising that most Americans do not know much about the relationship between felony records and voting because the disenfranchisement laws actually vary tremendously from state to state. All but two states (Maine and Vermont) have some sort of restrictions on voting for people with felony convictions. The restrictions vary from (a) a restriction on voting while incarcerated (12 states) to (b) restrictions on voting while incarcerated and/or on parole (24 states) to (c) a lifetime ban on voting for all convicted felons (12 states; Mukamal, 2004). This becomes even more complex because some states, including seven of the states that impose a lifetime ban on voting, have a process of restoration that can be invoked at a later point in time. In some states, this process is easy and straightforward, and in others, it is a process that is nearly impossible to navigate. For example, in North Carolina, where felons are banned from voting until they complete their entire sentence (including parole and/or probation), the Department of Corrections supplies felons who are being discharged with the information about reinstating their right to vote. (In North Carolina, all that is required is for the ex-felon to re-register to vote.) In other states, the process is lengthy and involves filing paperwork at the state's Department of Corrections.

Following the 2000 presidential election, which brought the disenfranchisement issue to national attention, the Legal Action Center surveyed local board of election officials and found that in many states, the voting officials did not understand the laws in *their own states* (Mukamal, 2004). This was the problem in Florida. Many of the voters who were denied their right to vote in the 2000 presidential election were ex-felons whose rights had been restored in another state, but whose restoration was not being recognized in Florida despite the fact that this is illegal. Much of the confusion occurred at local polling places, where board of elections officials did not understand the law (Mukamal, 2004).

How important was the disenfranchisement debacle in Florida in 2000? Professor Chris Uggen did an analysis in which he first identified the demographic characteristics of those people *wrongly disenfranchised* and then examined the previous voting patterns for these groups. By extrapolating the voting records on top of the election outcome, his research demonstrates that had African Americans who were wrongly disenfranchised in Florida in the 2000 presidential election had their right to vote restored and recognized, the outcome of the election would have been clearly in favor of Vice President Gore (Uggen & Manza, 2002).[24] Thus, the consequences of felony disenfranchisement are significant and affect the lives of all Americans. Regardless of one's opinion regarding felony disenfranchisement, it is clear what a powerful policy it is.[25]

Other Bans—Social Services

In addition to the disenfranchisement and barriers to employment that ex-felons face, as part of the 1996 TANF reform (which we discussed at length in Chapter 8) and the changing drug laws of the 1980s and 1990s, a series of bans was imposed on ex-felons that prevents them from accessing many of the social programs that provide basic-level support. Proponents of these bans argue that they work as an incentive to keep young people out of the kinds of trouble that will result in a felony, with the primary focus here being involvement with drugs. Opponents of these bans argue that denying ex-felons, particularly individuals with felony drug convictions, access to social welfare programs that provide housing, income support, and educational support amounts to stacking the deck against people who, without these support programs, will not be able to successfully reenter the free world. They argue that this contributes to the revolving door that now characterizes prisons.

Similar to the disenfranchisement rules, the bans on social welfare programs vary from state to state. Our intent here is to paint a broad picture of the bans, and we encourage the interested reader to visit the Web site of the Legal Action Center (http://www.lac.org) and obtain their report for a more detailed understanding of the bans as they are imposed across the various states.

Employment Bans

As we showed earlier, Pager's (2003) work confirms that a felony record creates an enormous barrier to employment. This is especially true for African American men. In addition to the discrimination they face with potential employers, they also face bans on certain types of jobs and employment certificates. Mukamal's (2004) research notes that

> employers in most states can deny jobs to people who were arrested but *never convicted* of any crime. . . . Employers in a growing number of professions are barred by state licensing agencies from hiring people with a wide range of criminal convictions, even convictions which are unrelated to the job or license sought. (p. 10)

To make matters worse, Mukamal notes that some of the licensing bans apply to trades that inmates are taught in prison as part of rehabilitation programs. For example, she notes that many prisons offer the chance to certify in barbering, but most states ban individuals with a felony record from holding a barber's license (Mukamal, 2004)! Thus, the disconnect is between the skills that prisons teach to inmates and the jobs they will be able to obtain once they reenter the free world. And as we have noted, barriers to employment are one of the key factors related to recidivism (Mukamal, 2004).

Driver's License

Another outcome of the reformation of drug laws in the 1980s and 1990s was a law that allowed the federal government to deny highway funds to any state that refused to impose a minimum 6-month revocation of the driver's licenses of individuals convicted of a felony drug offense (Mukamal, 2004). Although 32 states have modified this law to offer restrictive licenses that allow drug felons to travel to work, school, or treatment programs, 18 states do not. Four states require that the revocation of the license last beyond 6 months (Mukamal, 2004). Clearly, driving restrictions have a significant impact on a former inmate's chances of getting and holding a job. In fact, the literature on welfare notes that one of the keys to a successful transition from welfare to work is having reliable transportation (Edin & Lein, 1997).

We assume, then, that the same applies to successful reentry. Thus, this driving restriction is one more barrier facing drug felons who are looking to turn their lives around. Furthermore, we note again that this specific restriction does not apply to felons convicted of violent or heinous crimes such as felony rape, murder, or child molestation. So, as we think about these contradictions, we wonder what the purpose and intent of the restrictions are really about.

Cash Assistance, Food Stamps, and Public Housing

In Chapter 8, we summarized the ban that individuals with a drug felony face with regard to receiving cash assistance and food stamps and living in public housing. The lifetime bans that are imposed in the majority of states pose significant barriers to the successful reentry of drug felons, especially women with minor children.

Student Loans

Recently, the system of higher education assistance that was available for inmates was dismantled by a key funding decision.

The Higher Education Act of 1998 makes students convicted of drug-related offenses ineligible for any grant, loan, or work study assistance. This federal barrier cannot be lifted by states. *No other class of offense, including violent offenses, sex offenses, repeat offenses, or alcohol-related offenses, results in the automatic denial of federal financial aid eligibility.* (Mukamal, 2004, p. 18, emphasis added)

This single act completely dismantled the opportunities for inmates as well as ex-convicts to pursue any postsecondary education. Research on wages, the racial and gender wage gaps (which we discussed at length in Chapter 7), welfare to work (which we discussed in Chapter 8), and recidivism all point to education as a key factor in eliminating inequality (Edin & Lein, 1997; Mukamal, 2004; Padavic & Reskin, 2002). Higher education leads to better jobs and higher wages, it keeps people out of poverty, and it is closely tied to reducing recidivism. This ban, then, stands as yet another barrier to the successful reentry and reintegration of drug felons into their families and communities. Proponents of this law argue that it prevents drug users from using student loan monies to feed their drug habits.

Opponents argue that it affects millions of incarcerated men and women and significantly reduces their possibilities for successful reentry. We wonder how many more times we need to pose the question: What exactly is the desired outcome of this law? And why does it target drug offenders and not violent offenders? Because education is a key component to any rehabilitation program, this law seems to undermine any rehabilitation efforts in which prisons engage.

We conclude this section by asking what chance African American families have of surviving the incarceration of one of their members, mothers and fathers, when they face such serious barriers to reentering the free world and reintegrating into family life? Ex-convicts face barriers to employment, including bans on licensure, bans on the receipt of cash assistance and food stamps, disenfranchisement, driving restrictions, bans on public housing, and bans on obtaining funding for higher education. Although these bans vary from state to state, the one constant theme is that all of the barriers and bans are the *most* severe for drug felons. And because a high percentage of African Americans are incarcerated for drug offenses, the impact on African American families is nothing short of devastating. Thus, we turn to an examination of a disturbing new trend: the incarceration of men and women who leave minor children behind.

Parenting From Behind Bars and the Adverse Effects on Children

Along with the precipitous rise in incarceration in the past 20 years has been a steady rise in the number of female inmates, and with that a dramatic rise in the number of mothers who are incarcerated and who leave minor children at home. We begin with some statistics.

Statistics on Parents

Both male and female inmates can be and are parents. Approximately 75% of women who are incarcerated in jail and in state and federal prisons are mothers of minor children. Incarcerated mothers average 2.11 children under the age of 18 (Greenfeld & Snell, 1999). Males serving time in state prisons reported that they have nearly 11 times as many minor children as women serving time in state prisons, and 40% said they had lived with the children prior to entering prison. Males in federal prison had nearly 15 times the number of minor children as reported by women in federal prison, and more than 80% of men with these young children reported that they had lived with the children prior to entering prison (Greenfeld & Snell, 1999). About two thirds of women in state prisons and half of women in federal prisons who had young children had lived with those children prior to entering prison (Greenfeld & Snell, 1999; Mumola, 2000).

Statistics on Children

An estimated 2.8% of all U.S. children under age 18 have at least one parent in a local jail or a state or federal prison. About 1 in 40 children have an incarcerated father, and 1 in 359 children have an incarcerated mother. These estimates translate into more than *1.3 million* minor children who are the offspring of women under correctional sanction; more than 250,000 of these children have mothers who are currently serving time in prison or jail (Greenfeld & Snell, 1999; Mumola, 2000).

As with so many other aspects of the criminal justice system, racial disparities are profound, and losing a parent to incarceration is a burden disproportionately born by African American children.

> Of the Nation's 72.3 million minor children in 1999, 2.1% had a parent in State or Federal prison. Black children (7.0%) were nearly 9 times more likely to have a parent in prison than white children (0.8%). Hispanic children (2.6%) were 3 times as likely as white children to have an inmate parent. (Mumola, 2000, p. 2)

The increasing number of women going to prison coupled with the fact that 25%–33% of African American men are in jail or prison leaves many African American children without either parent at home (Pettit & Western, 2004).

The vast majority of women in prison are mothers with children under 18 (70 percent). Almost two-thirds (64 percent) of these mothers lived with their children prior to incarceration and one-third was the sole parent living with their children. With just over one-quarter (28 percent) of children of incarcerated mothers being cared for by their fathers, most children of imprisoned mothers are cared for by other people—primarily grandmothers, but also other relatives, too. Still 10 percent of the children end up in foster care or in an agency. (Sokoloff, 2003, p. 35)

These cycles of incarceration result in prison becoming part of the fabric of family life. According to Lyke (2003),

Some children have not only parents, but aunts, uncles, sisters and brothers in the system. The family tree could be built on booking photos. "We occasionally have children, parents and grandparents locked up on different floors, all at the same time," says Karen Pohio, community programs manager for the King County Department of Adult and Juvenile Detention.

Parenting From Behind Bars: The Importance of Visitation

One of the keys to successful reentry, as noted above, is the ability of inmates to keep in contact with their families, typically through visits, during the period of incarceration. One challenge that mothers face arises from the fact that because there are fewer female inmates than male inmates, there are fewer maximum-security prisons available for women. Therefore, women are more likely to be incarcerated far from their families' homes (Chesney-Lind, 1998; Mauer & Chesney-Lind, 2002). More than 60% of mothers in prison are incarcerated more than 100 miles from their children, making visitation difficult, financially prohibitive, and often impossible (Bloom & Steinhart, 1993; Wolf, 2006). Furthermore, female inmates report that being separated from their children is the hardest part of their incarceration.

Previous research indicates that women who have less contact with their children reported higher stress levels during incarceration (Fogel, 1993; Fogel & Martin, 1992; Houck & Loper, 2002). Specifically, mothers given long sentences report more difficulty adjusting to prison life, and one of the key factors, in addition to the length of the term, is the distance between the prison and family members (MacKenzie, Robinson, & Campbell, 1989). This stress can translate into anger.

Because women with longer sentences may anticipate and experience few family visits over time, they may experience more anger than short-term inmates who can look forward to reuniting with their families much sooner.

This anger may be translated into higher instances of rule-breaking behavior and conflict with other inmates and staff members. (Thompson & Loper, 2005, p. 729; see also Islam-Zwart & Vik, 2004)

In contrast, both long- and short-term male inmates experience significantly higher rates of visitation and overall contact with family members (Flanagan, 1980; MacKenzie & Goodstein, 1985; Toch & Adams, 2002; Zamble, 1992). As Thompson and Loper (2005) noted, "These visits may allow long-term male prisoners to feel less isolated from the outside world and therefore experience less anger and conflict than women with longer sentences" (p. 729).

The Effects of Incarceration

The effects of incarceration on parents and their children, especially if they were living together at the time of arrest and incarceration, are devastating. As we noted in the discussion about pregnant inmates often being forced to give birth while shackled, there are no national policies for what to do with children when their custodial parent, usually the mother, is arrested and/or incarcerated. Some counties and states have policies, and others simply have guidelines. So, for example, upon being arrested, a woman may be given an hour to make arrangements for the minor children in her care, or equally likely, she will be handcuffed immediately and transported in one law enforcement vehicle to the local jail while her minor children are transported, also in a law enforcement vehicle, to the local department of social services, where they will be placed in foster care. This lack of a national policy for dealing with mothers and their children has severe consequences for both.

The effects of incarceration on parenting have long-term effects on the children. Children who have a parent who has been in prison are six times more likely to go to prison themselves (Wolf, 2006). Sokoloff (2003) notes that "50 percent of young people in juvenile correctional facilities today have a parent or close relative in prison" (p. 42).

A 1993 study found that when children were placed with caregivers during their mother's incarceration, 40% of the male teenagers had some involvement with the juvenile justice system, 60% of female teenagers were or had been pregnant, and 33% of all children experienced severe school-related problems (Conner, 2003). Thus, it is imperative that we learn more about the process of parenting from prison in order to decrease the negative impact of incarceration on mothers and the life chances of their children.

Finally, we note that in addition to the challenges mothers face in keeping in contact with their children from behind bars, legal policies may force them to lose permanent custody of their children.

Reunification laws became more punitive in 1997 under the Adoption and Safe Families Act (ASFA), which states that if a mother does not have contact with a child for six months, she can be charged with "abandonment" and lose rights to her child. Likewise, if a child has been in foster care for fifteen of the prior twenty-two months, the state may begin proceedings to terminate parental rights. However, women [inmates] are often transferred from one facility to another, thus missing important deadlines and court dates that can result in termination of their parental rights. . . . The threat of losing their children is quite real. (Sokoloff, 2003, p. 35)

Calvin's Story For any parent, parenting in prison is complex. An inmate we met at Parchman, Calvin, is serving two 30-year sentences for drug offenses. (This is his second stint in Parchman; he previously served an 8-year sentence for his first drug offense.) Calvin is attempting to maintain a relationship with his son (his daughter, he told us, will not speak to him). He says that he used to ask his wife (now his ex) to bring the children to visit, but after awhile, he asked that she and the children stop visiting because it was just too painful for all. He described the 2-hour visit. It was awkward at first, then just as it was feeling comfortable, they were told there were only 30 minutes remaining in the visit. Those last 30 minutes, according to Calvin, were excruciating because they were spent anticipating the inevitable good-bye. Calvin, at 6 feet 5 inches and 250 pounds, was an excellent athlete, and his son has followed in his footsteps. Although he hasn't seen his son in many years, they talk on the phone and write letters. His son will be going off to college, to Mississippi State, on a football scholarship. And Calvin beamed as he told us about an event a few months before our visit when he was able to watch his son play football for the first time. His son's team was playing in the Mississippi State High School Championship, and the game was televised. Calvin watched his son play on a tiny black-and-white TV, and he recalled that he had to arrive at the crack of dawn in the TV room in order to be sure he controlled the remote control!

The main point in Calvin's story is that many male and female inmates want more than anything to maintain parental relationships with their children, and yet there are many structural constraints to doing so, including the relocation of prisoners, the cost of phone calls and visits, and the likelihood that mothers in particular will lose custody of their children.

As we have noted, the effects of incarceration are especially profound on African American children, who are disproportionately likely to have a parent in prison. As many as 10% of African American children have a father in jail at any given time, and as many as 25% have a father who has been incarcerated. Clearly, then, incarceration adversely affects family life. When fathers are absent, they are not contributing economically to their children's welfare, and it's difficult to estimate the impact of the weekly or monthly treks that children make to prison to visit their fathers. Many African American children visit a prison before they visit a library or museum. Worse, because many urban inmates are incarcerated in rural prisons far from home, some children of prison inmates may have little to no face-to-face contact with their fathers during their formative years.[26]

Yet no national policy addresses the temporary care of these children upon the arrest of their mothers nor the transfer of custody, either temporary or permanent, during their mothers' incarceration. In addition, there are few programs that facilitate parenting from prison or reestablishing custody and a relationship after release.

The Impact of Bans on Family Life After Release

Because most individuals who are incarcerated will return home and to their communities and neighborhoods, we conclude this section by examining the barriers to reintegrating into family life. Our major focus here is on the role that bans play in this process.

Each individual ban creates a barrier to reintegration, but when considered together, the bans imposed on drug felons make it very difficult for these individuals, many of whom are mothers with minor children, to reintegrate with their families. And because the majority (59%) of all women incarcerated are incarcerated for drug felonies, the impact of these bans is widespread (Sokoloff, 2003). Therefore, let us consider an example that would be typical: an African American mother with minor children who emerges from a stay in prison with a felony drug conviction. When she emerges from serving her time, hoping to get a second chance at life and raising her children, she faces some significant barriers:

- Employment: If Pager's (2003) data are generalizable to women, then the prospects that she will be able to find a job are slim. Only 3% of African American men with a felony were called back for an interview.
- Cash assistance and food stamps: This mother will face a lifetime ban on receiving cash assistance and food stamps. Although she would be able to collect cash assistance and food stamps on behalf of her children, the total benefit to the family would be significantly reduced—by one third if she has two children—because of her ineligibility based on her felony conviction.
- Public housing: If she is moving back into the majority of states, she is likely to face a ban on living in public housing. Not only is she barred from renting a unit in her name, but in many cases, she is barred from living in a unit with anyone else in her family. Therefore, if her children are living with her mother (their grandmother)—which is the situation more than half the time

(60%)—she will be barred from moving back in with her family (Renzetti, 2001). This is despite the fact that housing would provide a realistic transition to reintegration.

- Driver's license: She will have her driver's license revoked for a minimum of 6 months, making it difficult to travel to a job (if she can get one); travel to the welfare office to receive the benefits to which her children are entitled; or take her children to school, child care, and other appointments, such as the doctor.
- Educational funding: This mother will also face a lifetime ban on all funding available for higher education, including Pell grants, student loans, and work study. Despite the fact that it is clear that education is highly correlated with higher earnings (Padavic & Reskin, 2002), she will be barred from the funding necessary to further her education and possibly keep her family off of welfare and out of poverty.
- Disenfranchisement: Should she live in the majority of states, she will either be permanently disenfranchised or have to engage in a lengthy and complex process to reinstate her right to vote. We note that although this may be her lowest priority, it is also the easiest ban to overcome.

What are the odds, then, that this mother will be able to successfully reintegrate with her family and not recidivate and wind up back in prison? In comparison, a serial rapist or child molester, who would face only the ban on public housing, disenfranchisement, and difficulty finding a job, would appear to have better odds at achieving this second chance than a mother convicted of possessing 5 grams of crack cocaine. The new drug laws lead to the incarceration of nearly 60% of all female inmates, and 91% of the women incarcerated for drug felonies are African American (Sokoloff, 2003). Coupled with the bans that are tied directly to felony drug convictions, it is clear that the war on drugs, especially with a lack of available treatment, *is nothing short of a war on African American women and their children.*

Physical Capital

The economic benefits a prison brings to a community, except for the possible increases associated with census discrepancies, are debatable. Although a few jobs are created, prisons are actually very expensive to run. Although the government pays part of the cost of incarceration, the inmates themselves seldom contribute to the cost of their own incarceration.[27] They don't pay rent. They don't pay for food, and they obviously don't contribute toward upkeep and maintenance. This structure is a physical space that provides housing for the convicted but receives little in return directly from the inhabitants.

It is quite expensive to house a single prisoner in a jail or prison. Rough estimates show that it costs most states more to house a prisoner per year than to educate a citizen in college for that same year. With an average cost per year to house a single prisoner at $23,183.69, when multiplied by approximately 2 million prisoners nationally, one arrives at the figure of $46.3 billion per year for incarceration in the United States.

Hence, there has to be another method to pay for, again in the public or private facility, the costs of incarceration. Early on and directly after the Civil War, African American life chances were grim (Oshinsky, 1997). One could even argue that although peonage replaced chattel slavery and, after the turn of the century, newly built prisons replaced peonage, the connection is stronger than that. According to David Oshinsky (1997), the real cost to house prisoners was borne by the prisoners themselves via the "convict lease system." In this section, we explore the ways in which prison labor has evolved to the point of being part of the global economy.

Penal Capital (Prisoner Labor)

The use of prisoners to make products has changed from the days that they made license plates[28] for the state where the prison is located, to being deeply embedded in the production and service economy of the nation. Private commerce that used prisoners as labor has been under way for centuries in Anglo societies, dating back to the 1600s and before (Hallett, 2004). This fits with the findings of Oshinsky (1997), showing that on the backs of prison labor, postbellum capitalism flourished.

During the 20th century, penal capital moved from the raw convict leasing system characterized by Oshinsky (1997) to a service economy that mirrors the larger U.S. economy. From an economic perspective, this penal capital allows a middleman like Signature, in Washington State, which moves products such as Starbucks, to win contracts and outbid other packagers because it uses prison labor. It does not have to pay market wages, it does not pay health insurance or vacation benefits, and it does not have to worry about severance pay or layoffs.

One aspect of the prison industrial complex that has perhaps received less attention is the role that the use of prison labor plays in the postindustrial political economy of the United States in the early 21st century. Various legislation that began in the 1970s and was "beefed up" in the mid-1990s opened up the ways in which prison labor could be used in both public and private industry.

There are at least four different industries in which prison labor may be used. We will briefly summarize them, provide examples of each, and conclude this section with a discussion of the outcomes of this form of economic production for inmates, prisons, and local communities.

Factory Work

In the case of license plates, for example, factories are set up inside the prison and inmates work for low wages, usually 40 or 50 cents an hour. The product is then shipped out to the "client." Although this particular type of prison labor has been around for a long time, it has expanded significantly in the past 5 years. Today, many states and counties have "corrections businesses" that allow them to produce goods and sell them to other state and local government agencies as well as to nonprofit organizations. For example, in Iowa, students attending public schools may very well sit at desks made by felons, and colleges such as Grinnell have purchased all of their dorm furniture from the Iowa Inmate Labor Program. In fact, Grinnell College is such a good client that Iowa Prison Industries produces a special line of furniture called the "Grinnell Group" (see their Web site at http://www.iaprisonind .com/html/prodcat/rfdormres.asp).

These examples make it clear that state prisons have gotten into the for-profit business of factory work. In many states, such as Mississippi, a single prison produces all of the uniforms for inmates, corrections officers, and law enforcement officers, as well as holsters and equipment for the entire state. By using prison labor to produce all of their supplies, the state is able to keep costs low for the entire Department of Corrections.

Manual Labor

The practice of partnering with the state and local Department of Transportation has also been popular for many years. As you drive along interstate highway systems, you may see inmates digging ditches, picking up trash, mowing, and doing other sorts of highway labor. As with factory labor, this form of inmate labor is expanding. Inmates now use heavy construction equipment, such as jackhammers, in various projects, including the construction of tunnels in Pennsylvania. (These same inmates managed to take the jackhammers "home" and use them to tunnel out of their home, the Western Pennsylvania Penitentiary in Pittsburgh!)

This form of inmate labor has been popular for decades because the work is often backbreaking, and it is difficult to find laborers; if the work were unionized, it would be very expensive. It is also reminiscent of, and most likely based on, the chain gangs popular in the 19th and 20th centuries, especially in the South. Many municipalities, counties, and states post significant savings to the taxpayers by relying on inmate labor for these sorts of projects. However, this use of prison labor is not without controversy.

In communities that have recently suffered significant declines in manufacturing jobs, local residents are becoming more vocal in their critique of these practices. In a rural Iowa community, for example, critics of this practice note that inmates have "taken" the jobs of countless citizens. In a community that has seen a decline in agricultural manufacturing (meat packing), this loss of jobs is serious, and local citizens, many of whom are now unemployed or underemployed, resent the fact that jobs they could take are now being filled by prison inmates. "In the case of the state liquor warehouse, 12 workers just lost good-paying jobs to prisoners who are paid 37 cents an hour. Currently, 500 state government jobs and 190 private-sector positions are being filled by prisoners" ("Fallon Requests Info," 2004).

Although prisons may bring some jobs into a community, especially jobs as corrections officers, this gain is offset by the fact that the inmates themselves may be competing with local citizens for jobs in the free market.

Direct Marketing to Local Communities

For much of the past century, some prisons were engaged in industries that provided goods for local markets. For example, prison farms such as Parchman in the Mississippi Delta and Angola in Louisiana have for decades targeted a portion of their prison-grown agricultural produce (mostly vegetables and, more recently, goods like catfish) to local merchants for sale and consumption in local communities.

After the laws were loosened that prohibited the direct competition between prisons and free enterprise, this prison enterprise has now expanded to include goods that are produced in factory settings. At the Eastern Oregon Correctional Institution, a medium-security state prison located in Pendleton, Oregon, that houses about 1,500 inmates, prisoners were engaged in textile factory work making the denim uniforms for all the inmates in the entire Oregon State Prison system.[29] The popularity of their denim grew, and they now market their clothing line, sewn in the Prison Blues Garment Factory, appropriately named "Prison Blues," for purchase over the Internet![30]

At first glance, this form of inmate labor seems nothing but positive. As extolled on the Prison Blues Web site, inmates learn a marketable trade that they can take with them when they reenter the free world. Also, they keep busy during the day, and they earn some money that is used to pay for their expenses in prison as well as for financial obligations, such as child support, that they have with the state.

However, we argue that industries such as this, be they agricultural or manufacturing or service, by definition, as with public works, take job opportunities away from local citizens. For example, the economy is quite depressed in the agricultural regions of the Mississippi Delta, and the fact that the State of Mississippi, through the Department of Corrections, has a stronghold in the farm-raised catfish market means that local farmers have less of an opportunity to make a living with this agricultural commodity (Gillette, 2004).[31]

Service Sector Work

Perhaps the most recent change in inmate labor, and the one that seems to be the most controversial and disturbing, is the use of inmate labor for a variety of service sector work that is subcontracted through middlemen for some of the nation's leading manufacturers. There are estimates that in any given day, the average American uses 30 products that were produced, packaged, or sold out of a prison! Through this type of service sector work, prison industries have truly infiltrated the global market.

"Another source of profit for private companies is prison labor. Companies that use prison labor include IBM, Motorola, Compaq, Texas Industries, Honeywell, Microsoft, Boeing, Starbucks, Victoria's Secret, Revlon, Pierre Cardin" (Evans, 2005, pp. 217–218). Every year, inmates at Twin Rivers Corrections Unit in Monroe, Washington, are busy during the holiday season because inmates there package Starbucks coffee and Nintendo "GameCubes" for sale by retailers all over the nation.

> Twin Rivers, part of a four-unit prison that houses mentally ill inmates, high-security felons, and participants in the state's Sex Offender Treatment Program, is also home to one of three facilities operated by Signature Packaging Solutions, one of 15 private companies that operate within the state prison system and use inmate labor to supplement their outside workforce. (Barnett, 2002, p. A7)

Prisoners are engaged in everything from making electronic cash registers for McDonald's to sewing lingerie for Victoria's Secret to packing Starbucks coffee. As noted previously, one can easily come to the conclusion that this is a positive movement in the evolution of prisons because it provides work, it teaches job skills that are transportable, and it allows inmates to earn some money while they are on the inside. However, critics, including many inmates at the Twin Rivers Corrections Unit, are skeptical of the underlying reasons for this evolution in prison industries. They do not necessarily believe it is indicative of a rehabilitative movement in prisons, but rather is driven entirely by companies seeking another way to maximize their profits.

Others suspect that DOC's motives are more pecuniary than pure-hearted, noting that by shaving nearly 50 percent off the top of an inmate's paycheck, the department slashes its own expenses while subsidizing the companies in the program, which aren't required to pay for inmates' health insurance or retirement. "They figure that if somebody's sitting around, doing their time and doing nothing, they don't make any money off them," Strauss says. . . . Richard Stephens, a Bellevue property-rights attorney, is suing DOC on the grounds that the program is unconstitutional, allows businesses that use prison labor to undercut their competitors' prices, and unfairly subsidizes some private businesses at the expense of others. . . . *Private businesses are "paying prison workers less than they're paying on the outside, but they aren't reducing the markup to the consumer" they're pocketing the profits.* Another key difference, Wright notes, is that prisoners can just be sent back to their cells whenever business goes through a lull; "on the outside, they have to lay off workers. It's much more difficult," Wright says. (Barnett, 2002, p. A7, emphasis added)

The use of inmate labor allows middle-level companies like Signature Packaging to underbid their competitors by cutting their labor costs. And prisons benefit as well because by engaging their inmates in this sort of economic production and then charging inmates for their own incarceration, they are able to keep down the costs of running the prison. Wright, an inmate at Twin Rivers, sums it up:

"They need to know that they are buying these products from a company that is basically getting rich off prisoners." Wright, sent to Twin Rivers for first-degree murder in 1987, *believes parents would be disturbed to know that their child's GameCube was packaged by a murderer, rapist, or pedophile.* "These companies spend a lot of money on their public image," Wright says, "but then they're quick to make money any way they can." (Barnett, 2002, p. A7, emphasis added)

Race, Class, and Gender Paradigm

Virtually every aspect of crime and incarceration is significantly shaped by race, class, and gender. We have examined differences in the types of crimes committed, the types of treatment by law enforcement and the criminal justice system (sentencing), as well as differences in incarceration and postrelease. Only when we are attentive to these three separate and interlocking systems of oppression can we best understand incarceration in the contemporary United States and its impact on individuals, families, and communities.

Specifically, we are arguing that the prison industrial complex and its attendant "prison industries" mimic the slave mode of production. In the end, wealthy whites (primarily men) are profiting by not paying a living wage to African American inmates (also primarily men). Thus, corporations are engaging in an exploitive labor practice, what Marx termed the *extraction of surplus value*. By not paying what the labor is worth when inmates are working farms, building furniture, or assembling products for giant multinational corporations such as Microsoft and McDonald's, corporations make additional profits. When large corporations from Microsoft to McDonald's engage in this practice, they also receive an unfair advantage over their competitors. Finally, we must note here that the whole scene is reminiscent of the plantation economy of 17th-, 18th-, and 19th-century America. The slaves were black chattel. They had no rights, and they were a captive labor force. All of this is the same for today's prisoner.

Everybody knows that the nation's prisons and jails are full of African American men. Everyone knows that 25%–33% of African American men over the life course will spend at least part of their lives in jail or prison. Yet the race, class, and gender perspective illuminates the fact that the rates of incarceration vary significantly by social class and educational attainment. Here, we add to this knowledge by discussing the outcomes for African American individuals, African American families, and African American communities.

Because African Americans are seen (viewed) as a minority group that threatens the existing distribution of economic rewards and political power, as well as public safety, the use of coercive social control (prison) has been and remains a major method of social control used against African Americans. This form of coercive social control began in the rural South after the Civil War and continues today as a significant part of mass incarceration of African American males between the ages of 15 and 35 (Myers, 1990).

We have demonstrated in this chapter that the prison industrial complex strips African American men (and women) of human, social, and political capital (Smith & Hattery, 2006a, 2006b, in press-a). Perhaps more devastating, however, is the evidence that the PIC is a modern form of slavery that has devastating consequences on the African American community as well. Families are separated, social capital ties are broken, and whole communities are left with few human and social capital resources. In fact, not only are individuals disenfranchised, but because of the relocation of inmates and census rules, communities of need see their citizens (and consequent resources) removed and transferred to other, more economically advantaged, primarily white communities.

Perhaps most important for our discussions in this book are the devastating consequences of mass incarceration on African American families. Although there are many explanations for the instability of African American families, including poverty, low educational attainment, high rates of unemployment, and social welfare programs that provide a better standard of living than minimum wage work (recall the discussion in Chapter 8), incarceration plays a major role in shaping and disrupting African American family life. Poor African Americans are more likely to be incarcerated than affluent African Americans (Western, 2006), but because of the extremely high rate of incarceration, most African Americans, of all social classes, have a family member who has been or currently is incarcerated. For example, consider the case of Rhodes scholar and literary award winner John Wideman. Professor Wideman grew up in a low-income neighborhood in Philadelphia at a time when more and more African American men were being incarcerated. Therefore, it is not surprising that his brother, whose experiences provide the basis of Wideman's book *Brothers and Keepers,* was incarcerated. Furthermore, Wideman's own son was sentenced to life in prison at age 15 for stabbing a fellow camper at a summer camp. This example illustrates the pervasiveness of incarceration for African American families: It reaches into all social classes.

African American children are born while their mothers are shackled to the bed and a guard with a pump shotgun stands watch. African American children make the journey each week or month or year to visit their fathers and mothers in prison. African American children suffer when their mothers, who have served their time, emerge from prison with a drug felony that prevents them from accessing social welfare services such as TANF and public housing that would allow them to provide at least some standard of living for their children. And African American boys grow up knowing that, by adulthood, one out of three of them and their peers will have been to prison. African American men are removed from their households, they are unable to support their children financially and emotionally, and this affects their intimate relationships. Marriage and even long-term, committed relationships are threatened by the very real possibility that they will be disrupted by incarceration. As a result, African American men and women are less likely to form committed relationships to begin with (LeBlanc, 2003).

Mass incarceration is not just a matter of racism; it is also shaped by gender and by the intersections of race, class, and gender. For example, the majority of African American women who go to prison (59%) are convicted of drug possession. We detailed the impact that drug laws have had in contributing to the mass rate of incarceration of African Americans, but also to the creation of a series of bans that make successful reentry and reintegration a virtually unachievable goal. Recidivism is all but guaranteed. These bans on welfare, public housing, educational aid, employment, and political agency make it virtually impossible for parents being released from prison to have a second chance at life and at raising their children. Ultimately, it is the children who pay the price.

The coupling of long-term incarceration of African American women for drug possession with the bans on social services amounts to a war on African American women and their children. This war ensures, by its impact on the life chances of these children, along with the cordoning off of so many African American men in prison, that African Americans of each generation are effectively removed from competition in the labor market, political arena, and capitalist economy, thereby ensuring that the goods and rewards in these systems will accumulate only to whites. A race, class, and gender lens allows us to see the powerful connections among these systems of oppression and privilege.

Solutions

> Americans have tended to view the U.S. as the guardian of the highest ideals of justice and fairness. But that is a belief that's getting more and more difficult to sustain. . . . Called into question is the very existence of an ancient liberty of which this country has until now been very proud: freedom from arbitrary arrest and detentions. (Herbert, 2005b)

> While society in the United States gives the example of the most extended liberty, the prisons of the same country offer the spectacle of the most complete despotism. (de Tocqueville, 1833)

Solutions to the problem of mass incarceration come from many sources. First, we must note that we are not advocating the emptying of American prisons. Many people are incarcerated because they have committed crimes that need to be punished and/or because they pose a serious threat to American public safety. However, we note that there are many structural causes of crime that need to be addressed. We find that the primary cause is blocked access to the opportunity structure.

Throughout this chapter, we have used the theoretical framework of University of Wisconsin Professor Erik O. Wright. He argues that one negative but predictable outcome of capitalism is the need to "remove" individuals who have no skills to offer in the free labor market. He refers to these individuals as the unexploitable. They are unexploitable in the sense that labor cannot be extracted from them by employers. Increasingly, young African American men have come to represent the unexploitable. And increasingly, according to Wright (1997), we cordon off these unexploitable into urban ghettos and prisons. The areas of cordoning off are not unrelated. When one fills an urban ghetto with uneducated people with little in the way of employment skills and one removes factories and other low-skilled work from these ghettos, crime is an almost inevitable outcome. Therefore, one of the clearest ways to address the high rate of incarceration is to develop the human capital of all children, preparing them for gainful employment, and then engage them in the kind of economic development that provides workers a way to earn a wage on which they can support their families. Although this may seem like a simple solution, it would require radical social transformation.

Perhaps the clearest way to address the issue of American's addiction to incarceration is to reengineer the way that we address drug use in our society. We are not advocating the decriminalization of drugs; we are, however, advocating alternatives to incarceration for low-level drug offenses. For example, we wonder about the collective gain in handing out 5- to 10-year sentences to individuals for the possession of 5 grams of crack cocaine. The sentences are out of line in comparison to violent crimes that often result in shorter sentences.

We also argue that drug addicts, their families, and the collective whole would benefit more by treating the addictions as health problems rather than simply locking the individuals away. Furthermore, we are highly concerned with the ways in which felony drug offenses are tied to bans on social services, educational resources, and other tools that are necessary for survival in the free world. These bans, along with a virtual dismissal of all rehabilitative services in prison, together present significant barriers to successful reentry and reintegration and virtually guarantee recidivism. Prisons become nothing more than warehouses for inmates whose greatest crime is an untreated addiction (Haney & Zimbardo, 1998). Therefore, in order to seriously address the mass incarceration that characterizes the United States and bring it more in line with other industrialized nations, we must reconfigure drug laws and the bans that follow the convicts back into the free world.

Finally, we reiterate the strong relationship between mass incarceration and race. Not only are African Americans incarcerated at disproportionately high rates, but there are serious and documented racial biases in the criminal justice system. We cited evidence for racial profiling and racial disparities in sentencing. But even more important is the relationship between sentencing guidelines and the type of crime committed. It should be obvious to all that the length of sentence will be positively correlated with the seriousness of the crime and the threat the convict poses to public safety. Although there is bound to be debate about what constitutes the worst crime or the biggest threat to public safety, we are struck by the fact that *convictions for drug offenses carry longer sentences than convictions for child molesting.* We are further struck when we examine the racial profile of the drug offender as compared to the child molester. We posit that drug offenses receive such long minimum sentences because the convicts are disproportionately African American and that child molesters receive relatively short sentences because they are disproportionately white men. We have struggled to understand this apparent disparity when we are certain that most Americans would find child molesting to be a more serious crime that poses a bigger threat to public safety. It is only when we analyze these race and gender disparities through the lens of the race, class, and gender paradigm that these inconsistencies and illogical policies become clear. We agree with Wright (1997) that with the passing of the 20th century, and with it, the belief that genocide was immoral, mass incarceration serves the same function of removing a whole class of people from social, political, and economic life.

Notes

1. We first heard the term "incarceration addiction" in the keynote address delivered by Marsha Weissman at the University of North Carolina Law School annual Conference on Race, Class, Gender, and Ethnicity in February 2006. Therefore, we are indebted to Marsha for this term.

2. State crimes include, among many others, murder, rape, most drug charges, and burglary.

3. Federal crimes typically involve trade, fraud, or crimes that cross state lines. Perhaps the most famous federal prisoner of late is Martha Stewart, who served her sentence in Virginia.

4. We note that our discussion in this chapter will be limited to the types of jails and prisons outlined above. There are, however, at least four other types of incarceration institutions that we will not discuss: (a) immigrant detention prisons—these house immigrants detained for a variety of offenses, including simple violations of immigration; (b) military prisons—these house members of the armed forces who are convicted in the court martial procedure; (c) international prisons/detention centers that are run by the United States—most recognizable would be Guantanamo Bay, Cuba, and Abu Ghraib, Iraq; and (d) CIA secret prisons that are alleged to be run by the United States but on non-U.S. territory. Although these prisons are important, they are not the topic of discussion in this chapter.

There are several reasons why we do not address these four types of prisons. First, because all of these types of prisons are run by the U.S. government and/or the U.S. military, it is very difficult to obtain information about them. Second, because these prisons are not, for the most part, incarcerating high numbers of African Americans, they have a much less significant impact on African American families. We do note, however, that there is a great deal of overlap between the prison administrators and guards in U.S. prisons and those at Guantanamo Bay and Abu Ghraib.

The exportation/internationalization of the prison industrial complex (PIC) is clearly seen at Abu Ghraib. The building and running of the Abu Ghraib military prison was under the direction of Lane McCotter, former director of the Utah State prison system. It was at Utah, under McCotter's watch, that prisoners were inhumanely treated, forced to be shackled to boards for days, and where prisoner Michael Valent died after spending hours nude in a restraint chair in 1977 (Butterfield, 2004). Also, former Army Spec. Charles A. Graner, Jr., plays into this exportation/internationalization of the PIC to Abu Ghraib because he was the ringleader of the torture at Abu Ghraib, having learned his craft at State Correctional Institution–Greene in southwestern Pennsylvania. There, Granger routinely beat prisoners, often laughing while doing so (Zernike, 2005).

5. This work was originally published in three volumes in 1973, and in it, Solzhenitsyn probes the inner core of the Russian prison system, detailing the experiences of not only himself, when he was being held captive, but the experiences of almost 300 other prisoners, including women and children. The chronicle weaves the journey of how the prisoners get to the outpost of Russia by train, describes their meager food rations, and describes the work details and the psycho mind games used by the trustees to "break" them for probable return to society.

6. Goffman presented himself at a mental hospital claiming only that he was "hearing voices." He was admitted and stayed as a patient for 10 days. During that short time, even though he never again reported any psychiatric symptoms, he was diagnosed with schizophrenia, prescribed medicine (which he did not take), and treated in every other way as a patient. During his stay, he was able to observe both the staff and other patients, and based on these observations, he developed the theory of "total institutions."

7. Figures on incarceration vary depending on what types of institutions (jails, prisons, military prisons, etc.) are included in the count.

8. For a good background report on the specifics of women in prison, especially for the last two decades of the 20th century, see Chesney-Lind (2002).

9. Barbara Chasin (2004) makes this point over and over (see especially pp. 235–239).

10. We note that women who have labored and delivered wonder about this practice.

11. There is a wide literature available on racial sentencing disparities (see, for example, Mauer, 2000).

12. Although we did not speak directly to this piece of the racialization of the American prison, we note that the American prison is the most racially charged environment on earth. This is even more true if it is a maximum security prison. Based on this racially charged environment, fueled in large part by the presence of racial/ethnic gangs, many states segregate their prison populations by race. Recently, the U.S. Supreme Court ruled that segregation in the prison system violated the 1954 decision in *Brown v. Board of Education* and required that the California prison system desegregate its prison population (Gumbel, 2005).

13. Some of the worst examples of this are the cases in which white men and women who have committed a crime have blamed it on a "black man" (Glassner,

2000). For example, when Susan Smith drowned her sons in South Carolina, she appeared on TV publicly proclaiming that she had been carjacked by a black man. When Charles Stuart murdered his pregnant wife in Boston, he, too, blamed it on an intruder: a black man. This practice is so widespread that there are research reports on these racial hoaxes, and we encourage the reader to examine this topic.

14. This figure represents approximately 111,000 African American men.

15. "Expanded dramatically by the implementation of policies associated with the 'drug war,' incarceration rates skyrocketed by the 1980s. By the mid-1980s, entrepreneurial profit-making with convicts had reemerged—as a new explosion in the number of African American prisoners occurred as a result of the drug war" (Hallett, 2004, p. 49).

16. Still one of the best sources for these data is the work of the Washington, DC Sentencing Project (see especially Mauer, 2001).

17. We note the experiences of Mr. Darryl Hunt, a North Carolina man who was exonerated after spending nearly 20 years in prison for a rape and murder he did not commit. In both press interviews (http://darrylhunt.journalnow.com) and private conversations, he indicated that despite being completely exonerated, he cannot get any kind of a job. He attributes this to the fact that he has a 20-year gap on his resume, and that members of the Winston-Salem community, especially those in the white community, continue to believe he is guilty despite the exoneration based on conclusive DNA evidence.

18. One sociologist, Orlando Patterson, feels that the reason there is little work on this subject is because of the "devaluing" of African American life. See Chapter 3, "American Dionysus: Images of Afro-American Men at the Dawn of the Twenty-First Century," in Patterson (1999).

19. The full Darryl Hunt case is available at http://darrylhunt.journalnow.com

20. Before Walter's reassignment, his job as chapel assistant allowed him to leave his cell late each morning and return early, and he was housed with other inmates doing inside work. Now he is housed in a cell with inmates doing agriculture work. He is required to leave the cell much earlier each day, and he must return when they return, hot and sweaty from the fields. To those of us in the free world, these changes in his circumstances might seem insignificant. But to an inmate, these changes represent a serious deterioration in the quality of his daily life.

21. We note that this is another outcome to be expected from total institutionalization as described by Goffman.

22. For a full analysis of two of the most southern states, Alabama and Mississippi, see Hattery and Smith (in press).

23. In fact, Uggen's research showed that *illegal* disenfranchisement in Florida changed the outcome of the 2000 presidential election.

24. Thousands of African Americans who were wrongly disfranchised filed a lawsuit, *Johnson v. Bush*, that was finally refused at the U.S. Supreme Court.

25. Although it is difficult to determine exactly why this ban was originally imposed, the Dred Scott decision set off a series of voter disenfranchisement laws, especially in the South, that were designed specifically to deny African Americans the right to vote. It is clear that the Dred Scott opinion helped pave the way for

Florida to intentionally disenfranchise African Americans in 1868, a practice that was then continued in 1968 when Florida rewrote its state constitution. As a result, African Americans today are disproportionately disenfranchised for life in Florida (Shofner, 2001). It is estimated that 16% of the African American voting age population in Florida is currently disenfranchised (Uggen & Manza, 2002).

26. In New York, most prisoners come from New York City, but most of the prisons are hundreds of miles away in upstate New York. In a state such as Wisconsin, for example, almost 3,000 Wisconsin prisoners are housed outside the state, making it much more difficult to keep families in close contact with each other.

27. Some state and private prisons have adopted a requirement that inmates work, typically contracts they fill for private corporations ranging from Microsoft to Victoria's Secret, and the inmates are required to pay a sizeable portion of their paychecks back to the prison, effectively paying for their own incarceration. For example, Oregon enacted legislation that required that all able-bodied prisoners in the Oregon State prison system engage in productive work.

28. We note that in some states, prisoners do make license plates. Colorado, Ohio, New York, and California still have this industry inside their prisons. The point is simply that they are no longer restricted to this type of work.

29. At Parchman, inmates make all of the inmate uniforms as well as a significant portion of the law enforcement uniforms for the entire state of Mississippi DOC (Department of Corrections).

30. A visit to their Web site (http://prisonblues.com/) reveals that they market denim products for sale to consumers not only in the United States but also in Japan! So, Japanese consumers can now buy "Prison Blues" garments, manufactured by inmates in the Eastern Oregon Correctional Institution, over the Internet! We note that the proliferation and popularization of prison life as demonstrated by this garment line is pervasive in the music industry, made popular by hip-hop artists like 50 Cent and Snoop Dogg.

31. Catfish farming was once one of Mississippi's top agricultural commodities, grossing approximately $255 million dollars annually. Now, all of this has changed, and as Hugh Warren, executive vice president of the Catfish Farmers of America, put it, "We're struggling right now." The catfish farmers who used to get 75 cents per pound are now down to approximately 60 cents per pound (see Gillette, 2004).

10

Conclusion: Solutions to a Long-Standing Problem

Race, Class, and Patriarchy in the 21st Century

The problem of the Twentieth Century is the problem of the color line.

—Du Bois (1903), p. 13

Simply put . . . if whites are selfishly motivated to discriminate against blacks to enhance their own material well-being, then when the government forces them to end a particular practice, they will simply look for other means to maintain white privilege. If an older discriminatory mechanism based explicitly on race becomes impossible to sustain, whites will substitute new ones that are more subtly associated with race. The specific mechanisms by which racial stratification is achieved may thus be expected to change over time as practices shift in response to civil rights enforcement. Whenever one discriminatory pathway is shut down another is soon invented.

—Massey (2005), p. 148

I wanted to make money. 'Cause you know, I lived in some of the nicest hotels. My friend, he had a place. I can show you a receipt right now of $31,000 at Crossland and North Point [a local hotel that rents rooms by the week]. It's a hotel studio. I stayed there for four *years. It was a room about this size, but it had everything that you could ever want. You want to see the receipt? This was a good place to be. I never had a real job on my own for four years. And everybody said, well, why don't you get a place of your own? And I'm thinking, this is no money.*

—Evie (North Carolina)

Summary and Review of the Primary Themes

In this book, we have focused on several interlocking indices that we feel tell the story of contemporary African American family life. One of the critiques of this book will no doubt be that we did not talk enough about affluent African Americans. Indeed, Du Bois (1951) suggests the opposite; historically, scholars have focused extensively on the upper classes and have ignored those at the lower ends of the system of stratification.

> We have the records of kings and gentleman *ad nauseam* and in stupid detail; but of the common run of human beings, and particularly of the half or wholly submerged working group, the world has saved all too little of authentic record and tried to forget or ignore even the little saved. (p. vii)

This is a "flaw" of many research reports on African American civil society: the focus on the poor at the exclusion of the middle class and affluent. Certainly, there is a slightly robust African American middle class, and African Americans are also represented among the affluent and even among the super rich. African Americans such as Robert Johnson and Oprah Winfrey own their own corporations.[1] However, we argue here that the health and well-being of any community, including African American civil society, can be measured only by the health and well-being of its weakest or most disadvantaged members. Former U.S. President Jimmy Carter once noted that

> . . . the measure of a society is found in how they treat their weakest and most helpless citizens. As Americans, we are blessed with circumstances that protect our human rights and our religious freedom, but for many people around the world, deprivation and persecution have become a way of life. (Carter, n.d.)

Throughout this book we have, in fact, made the argument that African Americans are in many ways denied access to some of the rights, privileges, and opportunities that characterize the American Dream. Indeed, we would rewrite Carter's quote this way:

> Some Americans are blessed with circumstances that protect our human rights and our religious freedom, but for many Americans, especially African Americans, deprivation and persecution have become a way of life.

In other words, the measure of our own society is the measure of how we treat our weakest and most vulnerable members. Although we are not arguing that poor African Americans are weak, we do recognize that they are vulnerable: economically, politically, and socially. Therefore, our focus on those living on the margins is the best way to assess the standing of African American families and African American civil society.

Taking an example from the classroom, we measure our successes in teaching not by the final papers written by our strongest students, but rather by the papers written by the students who have struggled throughout the semester.

Another measure of prosperity in every society is a measure of how well the next generation will do. Oddly enough, the late senator from New York, Daniel P. Moynihan, the author of one of the most contested studies of the African American family (Moynihan, 1965), wrote that the measure of a society is how well the next generation does or how far the next generation outdistances the previous generation; in other words, how far children outdistance their parents. One of the pieces of data that explains our focus on this particular stratum of African Americans is the state of African American children in America.

Moynihan noted in 1985 that "family disorganization," once a concern mainly of minorities, has become a "general feature of the American population," and he illustrates this claim by pointing to the growing number of impoverished preschool children and illegitimate births (Moynihan, 1985). We note that in 2005, African American children

- are disproportionately likely to be born to an unmarried mother (75%; Dye, 2005).
- are more likely to be in foster care and to spend more time in foster care, and are less likely to ever be adopted (Green, 2002).
- are less likely to graduate high school (in some regions, the high school graduation rate is only 50%; Greene & Winters, 2005).
- are less likely to have health care insurance (8–10 million are uninsured; DeNavas-Walt et al., 2004).
- are the most likely to be poor (50%–75%; Current Population Survey, 2004).

Finally, we chose to focus our attention in this book on poor African American families because this is the nature of the discipline of sociology. Historically, our discipline has been designed to identify and analyze social problems in order to design and offer solutions for the betterment of society (Duneier, 1992; Riesman, 1950; Wilson, 1978, 1987). As academics and as individuals, we have dedicated our lives to the betterment of human society, and therefore, we must focus on those segments of society that require our attention. Finally, we note that structural changes that will improve the life chances of those at the bottom will undoubtedly have a "trickle up" effect. In other words, by proposing structural changes that are designed to eradicate racial bias and discrimination on behalf of poor African Americans, the end result should be a decline of racial bias and discrimination for all African Americans, including those at the top.

We specifically chose as the centerpiece of our book those African Americans who are on the margins of society and most likely (more than anybody else in American society) to be struggling with these interconnected items that we've identified—poverty, family forms, HIV/AIDS, incarceration, education, and intimate partner violence (IPV)—which in our model tells us about the health and well-being of African American families and African American civil society.

The data we have used to tell this story and to build this model have been based on several sources, including data collected by federal agencies such as the U.S. Census Bureau and the Bureau of Justice Statistics, the research of other scholars, and our own face-to-face interviews. We want to emphasize that the strength of this book is the interviews that we conducted ourselves with African American men and women living on the margins, men and women who are struggling with the issues we raised here. It is from listening to them talk about their own lives that we were able to develop a deeper understanding of the myriad ways that this web of social problems is woven together and the ways that the interactions of these forces shape the lives of real people, people who are struggling to raise children, make families work, and live without violence. It is in their voices that we learn the truth about the severe consequences of these forces on the lives of citizens of these United States.

We argue that only when the life chances of all African Americans, when the educational attainment of all African Americans, when the standard of living of all African Americans, when the life expectancy of all African Americans, and when the incarceration rate of all African Americans are in line with the standards for *all Americans* will we have reached a point of equal opportunity such that we no longer need to examine the lives of African Americans living on the margins.

Degrees of Separation

One of the key differences in African American civil society as compared to American culture more generally is the limited degrees of separation African Americans have to those living on the margins. What do we mean? We mean that for African Americans, the probability that any individual has a family member—a parent, partner, child, brother, or sister—who is incarcerated or living with HIV, or living with IPV, or living in poverty is extraordinarily high. In the white community, for example, many of the social problems we have discussed in this book are cordoned off or segregated by social class.

The affluent and even families in the upper middle class are relatively isolated from them. However, for several reasons that we will discuss here, the social problems we have described in this book are not segregated from affluent families or those in the professional classes in the African American community. Thus, the issues that we have discussed throughout the book affect *most* African American families—if not directly, then indirectly.

There are three important factors that prevent these social problems from remaining segregated by class in African American civil society: high rates of social problems, severe housing segregation, and limited and only recent access to the opportunity structure. These three forces work together such that most African Americans are only one degree away from those living on the margins.

High Rates of Social Problems

As we have noted in each chapter of this book, African Americans are disproportionately represented on virtually every negative indicator of well-being we use in our society. African Americans are significantly less likely to be married or in long-term cohabiting relationships (Patterson, 1999). African Americans are more likely to be poor. In fact, at least 50% of all African American children in this country live below the poverty line, and this figure rises to 75% when we include the "near poor," or those living below 200% of the official poverty line (Current Population Survey, 2004; DeNavas-Walt et al., 2004; Orzechowski & Sepielli, 2003). The odds that an African American man will spend some time in prison are nearly 1 in 3 (Bureau of Justice Statistics, n.d.; Harrison & Beck, 2004, 2005; Roberts, 2004). And, according to the Centers for Disease Control and Prevention, at least half a million African Americans (7%–8% of the total population) are infected with HIV/AIDS (CDC, 2004; "HIV Hitting Blacks Harder," 2006). Twenty-five to thirty percent of all African American women experience at least one episode of IPV in their lifetimes (Tjaden & Thoennes, 2000). With rates of these social problems this high, we argue that if you are African American and you are not poor, or have not spent time in jail, or do not have HIV, or haven't been hit by your partner, then you probably know someone who is or has. In fact, you probably have at least one family member who has experienced one or more of these social problems.

In addition to being the most concerned about HIV/AIDS for the nation, African Americans are also most likely to say they personally know someone who currently has HIV/AIDS or has died from HIV/AIDS (64%), compared with about 4 in 10 whites (42%; Kaiser Foundation Family Report, 2004).

Severe Housing Segregation

Studies of housing patterns indicate that 40 years after national-level civil rights legislation and 50 years after the official end of segregation (*Brown v. Board of Education* in 1954), housing in the United States is highly racially segregated (Conley, 1999; Massey, 2005; Massey & Denton, 1993). Patterns of racial segregation that have persisted from the first settlements in the United States through to today have had serious consequences for African Americans.

Housing segregation occurs in the United States along both racial and class lines. However, the intersection of race and class means different things for white Americans than it means for African Americans. Practically speaking, this means that whites live in neighborhoods that are socioeconomically homogeneous, but African Americans are forced to live in racially segregated but socioeconomically diverse neighborhoods. Put simply, whites are able to live wherever they can afford to live. African Americans, however, face racial housing discrimination, which means that they may not be able to live in neighborhoods they can afford if whites are unwilling to sell them homes. What this means for our discussion is that housing segregation contributes to smaller degrees of separation for African Americans than for whites. For example, although we know that some of the social problems we've discussed, such as HIV/AIDS and incarceration, are shaped by social class and are disproportionately part of the lives of the poor as compared to the affluent (because middle- and upper-middle-class African Americans often live in neighborhoods that are socioeconomically diverse), they are far more likely than whites to have neighbors, friends from church or school, and so on who are facing these very social problems. Thus, racial housing segregation collapses the degrees of separation such that poverty, HIV/AIDS, incarceration, and IPV are problems for all African American families and, indeed, for African American civil society.

Limited and Recent Access to the Opportunity Structure

Not only are African American neighborhoods more socioeconomically diverse than white neighborhoods, but the typical African American family is also likely to have more socioeconomic variance than the typical white family. Why? For a variety of reasons—many of which were discussed in Chapter 8—African Americans have been less able to accumulate wealth (Conley, 2001; Oliver & Shapiro, 1995) that can be transmitted intergenerationally, and thus affluent and professional African Americans are far more likely to come from low- and middle-income families than are whites (Wright, 2006). For example, as a result of slavery and Jim Crow segregation in housing, education, and employment, whites have been allowed to accumulate wealth to which African Americans have not had access.

Consider the scenario in which a white family took advantage of the Homestead Act and was given a farm in the Midwest in the early 1800s (African Americans were unable to take advantage of the Homestead Act because they were slaves). Although the family would have struggled on the family farm, with careful management and hard work, the family would be able to increase their landholdings, raise more crops and livestock, and accumulate capital and wealth (even though this was not likely to be liquid—i.e., income or cash). One hundred or 150 years later, as college became a reality for more Americans (read: white Americans), a farm family like this would have been able to send their children to college, even if they had little cash, based on the equity in their land, equipment, crops, and livestock. This access would then launch the next generation into the professional and affluent classes. In addition, the typical family in this scenario would have been able to extend this privilege to all of their children, not just one.[2] Thus, and this is the critical piece, advantage and privilege are accumulated and hoarded in some segments of society and denied in others.

In contrast, African American families have been able to accumulate far less wealth than whites of the same social class. For example, among affluent Americans—those in the top quartile—whites have a median wealth of $208,023, whereas African Americans have a median wealth of only $65,141 (Conley, 2001). In other words, the race-wealth gap among the wealthiest Americans is more than 3 times. (For a lengthier discussion of the wealth gap, we refer the reader back to Chapter 8.) Thus, even when the opportunity structure finally began to open in the post–civil rights era (post-1964), few African American families were positioned to send their children to college, and those who could would only be able to afford to send perhaps one of their children. Thus, the average affluent, professional African American comes from less affluence than his or her white counterparts and is more likely to be the only member of his or her family with this social class status. We remind the reader of Kai Wright, who writes about his father, a prominent African American physician who died at age 57 without a pension and with no real assets. Although his father had gotten to college (and medical school), this had required him to incur significant debt. He worked his whole life to get out of this debt and was able, in turn, to educate his own children. But there was nothing left over.

> But none of us [African Americans] will take part in the historic wealth transfer now under way in America: According to another study Shapiro likes to cite, parents will pass on a total of more than $10 trillion to their adult kids between 1990 and 2040. (Wright, 2006)

The African American professional is often an anomaly in his or her family, a family that will also include working-class and perhaps even poor members. In contrast, white families tend to be more socioeconomically homogeneous. Most white professionals come from families in which most or all of the members fall into this social class. This distinction can be seen in the common phrase uttered by and about African Americans who make it into the middle and professional classes: "Don't forget where you came from!"

So, whereas poor whites and poor African Americans may face similar distressing situations (poverty, unemployment, incarceration, illness), whites of affluence are virtually immune to and disconnected from these social stresses, whereas African Americans of affluence may be only one degree away. In other words, these social problems affect African American families and indeed all of African American civil society, even those who are not living personally with the issue in question.

A Snapshot of the African American Family

African American children are more likely to live in poverty, their parents are more likely to live apart, the wealth of the family is considerably less than all other Americans, their rates of HIV/AIDS are much higher, their rates of incarceration are devastatingly high, their rates of intimate partner violence are higher, unemployment and low wage jobs are becoming the norm, and all of these issues are interconnected with African American families trying to make a go of it in the new millennium.

Although some may counter that this profile describes only a small segment of African Americans, we disagree. Based on just two measures of well-being, we believe that the African American family is in serious trouble. One quarter (25%) of all African Americans are living in poverty, and another

1 million family-age, childbearing-age, working-age African American males are in jail or prison serving sentences that run anywhere from 5 to 10 years in length. We add to this the fact that another half a million African Americans, most of them young (ages 18–40), are HIV positive. The majority of new cases in African American men are from intravenous drug use and abuse, but for African American women, the majority of cases are from unprotected sex with their male partners, many of whom contracted AIDS/HIV while in prison (see Chapter 6).

These interlocking indices all relate to the quality of life in African American families and African American civil society. As the sociologist William J. Wilson, speaking to the issue of joblessness, said,

> For the first time in the twentieth century most adults in many inner-city ghetto neighborhoods are not working in a typical week. The disappearance of work had adversely affected not only individuals, families, and neighborhoods, but the social life of the city at large as well. Inner-city joblessness is a severe problem that is often overlooked or obscured when the focus is placed mainly on poverty and its consequences. (Wilson, 1996, p. xiii)

We take from this exposé that our approach, linking poverty, health, incarceration, and violence, places our book in the position of not just telling the story of African American families and their health and well-being, but because we sat down and talked with so many men and women and even some of their children, we have an understanding of the interconnections and the consequences that shape so many family lives today.

The Struggles

What does all of this mean for African American families? We believe that it means that in post–civil rights America, a place where the opportunity structure is supposed to be open to all, a place where segregation is no longer legal, that the realities paint a grim picture. In post–civil rights America, most African Americans (and most whites) live a very segregated existence. We don't attend the same schools, we don't work in the same jobs, we don't live in the same neighborhoods, we don't worship in the same churches or synagogues, and we don't have access to the same goods in life.

All of the poor—white or African American or any others—face some of the same struggles we have noted here. However, based on our own research and in reviewing the work of others, we know that because African Americans in every social class category have less wealth and less security than similarly situated whites, when a crisis hits, it can be devastating to the poor or near poor, especially those who are African American.

We consider the gas crisis. Although some economists argue that the impact of this is limited, others note that the burden of the impact is borne disproportionately by those least able to afford it: the poor. "For someone who drives 15,000 miles a year and gets 20 miles per gallon, a 60-cent jump means an extra $450 a year at the gas pump" ("High Gas Prices," 2005, p. A12). For a minimum wage worker, this amounts to 3 weeks' take-home pay, an amount that will thrust some individuals and families who cannot seek help from family or friends into crisis. Furthermore, something as "simple" as the gas crisis, which may seem to affect only certain limited parts of life, in fact is part of a larger pattern that not only symbolizes but actually creates the widening gap between the haves and the have-nots. "But the biggest impact of rising costs might be social rather than economic. They will accentuate the growing divisions between those eking out a living and those who find themselves well-off" ("High Gas Prices," 2005, p. A12). For the families we met and interviewed, a health crisis (such as Ronny's recent amputation) for a family with no health insurance can leave them homeless and hungry. These problems are further exacerbated in that they tend to be concentrated.

Undoubtedly the most visible example of this is the devastation in New Orleans in the wake of Hurricane Katrina in the fall of 2005. In many ways, the images that flooded our living rooms through newspapers, television sets, and the Internet provide visual illustrations of what we have described throughout this book. Perhaps the most obvious illustration in these images was the link between race and poverty. Over and over again, the images of people we saw surviving on the rooftops of their homes, waving white flags to catch the attention of rescue helicopters, of people living inside the convention center, of people walking across bridges begging for insulin were images of African Americans.

As social scientists and others began to analyze what had gone wrong in New Orleans, a few key findings emerged.

• Many of the African Americans trapped in New Orleans did not have enough money to be able to effectively evacuate and rent a hotel room or buy food for the several days they anticipated being displaced. The poorest African Americans have only $57 in wealth. (Conley, 2001)

• Many of the African Americans we saw trapped in New Orleans were unable to leave because of health problems that did not allow them to travel. As we saw in Chapter 6, African Americans are more likely than their white counterparts to suffer from chronic diseases such as diabetes and stroke. Furthermore, these individuals were less likely to be taken care of in residential nursing facilities where ambulance evacuation would have been available. Why? Because African Americans are less likely to have the health insurance and wealth necessary to afford this type of care.

- New Orleans is a segregated city (Massey & Denton, 1993). As we noted in Chapter 8, not only did poor African Americans living in the lower Ninth Ward have their homes destroyed when the levies broke, but all of the middle- and upper-middle-class African American neighborhoods were also located in lower-lying parts of the city that were devastated by the levy breaches.

- African American families have faced barriers in their attempts to rebuild their homes and neighborhoods in part because many, even in the middle classes, did not have insurance. Representatives from the Association of Community Organizations for Reform Now explained in our most recent visit to New Orleans that the lack of insurance is a direct outcome of the discrimination African Americans in New Orleans faced from banks and insurance companies, who refused to make mortgages to them and refused to insure their homes regardless of their ability to pay.

- Myths about African Americans stood as barriers to help. For example, former first lady Barbara Bush said of those living in the deplorable conditions in the Houston convention center where hurricane victims were evacuated: "And so many of the people in the arena here, you know, were underprivileged anyway, so this is working very well for them" (September 8, 2005, AP wire).

In other words, what happened in New Orleans and the images coming out of there were not a surprise to those of us studying the state of the African American family. Rather, it was predictable. However, for those Americans who have not been paying attention to the struggles of the African American family, the images were eye-opening. As devastating as the images were and continue to be, they serve as a visual illustration to all we have addressed herein.

The Causes

There are a variety of causes for the types of inequalities and disparities that continue to face African American families. As we noted at the beginning of the book, some of these problems are a result of poor decision making, whereas others are a result of structured and institutionalized racism and oppression. Why are African American families in such poor shape in post–civil rights America? This is a time that should be about celebrating and reaping the benefits of access that were finally granted. The answer in part is that there have been several key shifts in the structures of American society since the early 1970s: the economy, the welfare system, and the growth of the prison industrial complex that have all adversely affected the health and well-being of African Americans.

The Economy

Perhaps the most significant change in American society has been the shift from the industrial economy of the 20th century to the postindustrial economy of the late 20th and early 21st centuries. As the economy has transformed from a manufacturing-based industrial economy to a service economy, jobs have been lost (and not replaced), wages have dropped, and the ability to provide for a growing family has diminished for most and vanished for many. Despite the cruelties of discrimination and Jim Crow segregation of the 20th century, the strong industrial economy meant that when men could find factory and manufacturing work, it was lucrative. In the industrialized North, in particular, African American men (and white men) labored in the steel industry and all of its ancillaries. In cities such as Detroit and Chicago, a man could make a living. The work was difficult and risky, but a man working in the steel mill or the car plant could expect to earn enough money to buy a house and a car and put food on the table and maybe save enough to send a child to a public college.

Although whites had more access and were paid higher wages, this was also a route to the American Dream for African Americans as well. However, the decline in manufacturing, particularly in heavy industry, coupled with the increase in moving factories abroad (outsourcing) has had a devastating effect on employment and wages. Unemployment in areas such as Detroit and Gary, Indiana (the steel capital of the world), soared to 50% and higher. In Gary, for example, over a 20-year period between 1975 and 1995, the decline of the steel industry contributed *significantly* to a loss in manufacturing jobs, jobs paying $50,000 per year.

Since 1975, the U.S. economy has become more hostile to unions and other institutions that fight for fair wages and decent benefits. Today, the majority of Americans work for less money and with fewer benefits. Those who once worked or dreamed of growing up to work in the auto plant now find that with a high school diploma (or not), they are facing a lifetime of low-wage service work: food service, flipping burgers, working in low-skilled health care, and so on (Ehrenreich, 2001). Real wages for men have stagnated and even dropped (Padavic & Reskin, 2002) such that the family life characterized by the male breadwinner being able to buy a house and provide for his wife and children has all but disappeared. And the groups hardest hit by these changes in the economy have been those with the least cushion: the poor and, disproportionately, African Americans.

The changes in the economy come, of course, after a long history of economic inequality that begins with slavery. Although we talked about this in Chapters 1 and 2, it is worth reiterating here: The system of slavery allowed one group (whites) to benefit from and profit off of the "free" labor of another group (African Americans). One need not take a course in Economics 101 to recognize that if a business owner is not paying wages to his or her employees, he or she will increase profits. This is a basic principle of business, and one we see every day: The biggest opponents of minimum wage legislation and employer health benefits are businesses who say they will not be able to turn as large a profit if they have to (a) pay their workers a living wage and (b) pay for their health benefits. Yet for nearly 300 years, whites who owned plantations and ran businesses netted a larger profit because they were not paying their laborers. And just as whites and white-owned companies were growing richer and richer, African Americans were not accumulating wealth or any form of capital. One way to think about this is to realize that it's like running a race, except that whites, as a group, got a 300-year head start. This 300-year head start results in the accumulation of wealth and privilege so that today, whites start out ahead because they inherit more from their parents in the form of financial capital, legacy, and even multinational corporations.

The end of slavery brought increasing economic opportunity to African Americans: They could then work for a wage (or, more commonly, a "share," as in sharecropping), but segregation also impeded their ability to pursue the American Dream. Not only were they denied access to education and job opportunities, but because of housing segregation, even successful African Americans were forced to live in socioeconomically diverse "black" neighborhoods, which meant that the values of their homes increased more slowly. Thus, even with the same effort and attention (buying a nice home, having a manicured lawn, making home improvements, and so on), the mere fact that one lived in a "black" neighborhood meant that the wealth that arises from homeownership was slower to accumulate. "America's racially segregated housing markets boost whites' home equities, while depressing those of African-American families" (Shapiro, 2004, pp. 140–141).

As Columbia University political economist Manning Marable (2005) notes,

Not too far in the distant future lies the social consequences of these policies: an unequal, two-tiered, uncivil society, characterized by a governing hierarchy of middle-to-upper class citizens who own nearly all private property and financial assets, and a vast subaltern of quasi- or subcitizens encumbered beneath the cruel weight of permanent unemployment, discriminatory courts and sentencing procedures, dehumanized prisons, voting disfranchisement, residential segregation, and the elimination of most public services for the poor. (p. 17)

Marable's concerns are pointed directly at African Americans because he sees the walls closing in on public services to poor people, disproportionately African Americans, especially in those households headed by women. According to Professor Marable, these future probabilities worsen as more and more African Americans today become adrift from their collective racial histories.

The Welfare System

The Great Society programs that originated with President Roosevelt in the 1940s and were strengthened by President Johnson in the 1960s have been systematically dismantled beginning with the election of President Ronald Reagan. Perhaps the biggest negative change for families with the 1996 welfare reform passed by President Clinton is the time limit on receiving cash assistance. Renamed Temporary Aid to Needy Families (TANF), the program has a 2-year limit on continuous welfare and a 5-year limit on lifetime benefits. For many single mothers, this is the only mechanism they have for raising their children and providing for their economic needs—food, shelter, health care, and so on—and the time limits are simply too short and the benefits too meager. As Edin and Lein (1997) point out, only one of the several hundred women on welfare whom they interviewed could actually live on the benefits she was receiving, and she faced child neglect charges because her children were malnourished.

This means that in an economy that allows the rich to get richer but has seen a decline in real wages for the working class, welfare is no longer the safety net it once was. Of course, all of this is exacerbated by the fact that Medicaid is a health safety net that no longer reaches the vast number of Americans without health insurance. In fact, the poorest Americans, those who are most likely to have the most serious chronic health issues (diabetes, heart disease, asthma, and even HIV/AIDS), are the very people who are the least likely to have the health insurance provided for the poor through Medicaid.

With so many Americans (40 million) without health insurance—and African Americans are disproportionately represented in this group (20% have no health insurance)—a health crisis such as Ronny's need for quadruple bypass and then a foot amputation can plunge a family into poverty. Similarly, as research on IPV and poverty demonstrates, a poor woman living with violence may not be able to leave if she has already used up her TANF eligibility or is living in public housing (Brush, 2001; Brush et al., 2003; Renzetti, 2001).

Thus, the changing welfare laws, coupled with a less robust economy, make it difficult for many African American families to pursue even the simplest vestiges of the American Dream.

The Growth of the Prison Industrial Complex

We argued in Chapter 9 that people need to "do the time if they commit the crime." However, we also demonstrated, as others have shown (Smith & Hattery, 2006b, in press-a), that the rise in the prison industrial complex has created a requirement to keep people incarcerated. One of the intended or unintended consequences (we argue that it is intended) of the War on Drugs is the growth of prisons and of the population being incarcerated. Once again, this has fallen disproportionately on the African American population. One million African American men, most of them in the prime of their work and reproductive lives (ages 25–40), are in prison. They leave behind 3–5 million children who are being raised without the financial and emotional support of their fathers.

With the rise of African American women being incarcerated, a quarter of a million African American children have a mother who is currently in prison, and 1.3 million have a mother who was in prison or is under correctional supervision. The rabid incarceration of African Americans is not only disruptive to family life, it is devastating to African American families. Of course, we also noted in Chapters 6 and 9 that prisons are one of the primary routes for HIV/AIDS, and thus prison has many other unintended outcomes that are toxic to African American civil society.

Bans

Finally, we note that the combination of changes in the drug laws (the War on Drugs) and the changes in welfare laws (welfare reform) result in the reality that all prison sentences are essentially life sentences (Mukamal, 2004). Although there are variations across states, and in some cases, across types of crimes, individuals—men, women, fathers, and mothers—emerging from prison with a felony record face a series of barriers to successful reentry into the free world and reintegration into family life. These barriers include bans on (a) cash assistance and food stamps; (b) public housing; (c) education funding—Pell Grants, student loans, federal work study; (d) driver's license restrictions; (e) employment restrictions—specifically bans on hiring and on licensure; and (f) political disenfranchisement. Despite variation, all of these bans apply to convicted drug felons. And because African Americans, both men and women, are disproportionately likely to be convicted of a drug felony, and among women, drug felonies account for the majority of prison sentences, some have termed the War on Drugs the "War on African American Women and Their Children." Incarceration has been devastating to African American family life.

Family Form

We argue in this book that family form is not the major issue when discussing the African American family, but neither do we ignore this issue. With major issues such as poverty, incarceration, HIV/AIDS, and the inability for African American men to crack through the barriers that guard well-paying employment, family form takes a far back seat to these larger structural issues.

However, one of the biggest changes in the African American family in the past 50 years has been the prolific growth of the female-headed household. This discussion caused quite a furor when the Moynihan Report (Moynihan, 1965) was published in the 1960s, yet at that time this type of household was relatively small compared to today. For African American families, the percentage of single-parent households went from 30% in 1968 to 56% in the late 1990s (P. Cohen, 1999).

We note that although the African American family may not look very similar in form to all other American families, this feature may not be the worst situation for African American civil society. The question in front of us, then, is how do these contemporary living arrangements that dominate the landscape of African American family life allow for sustenance of family and especially children in these units? Can they adequately prepare young people for futures that have hope instead of hopelessness? Finally, without hope, do despair, poverty, unemployment, and incarceration lead to the type of family violence that affects the families we met in both North Carolina and Minnesota and across the United States?

The Relationship Between Structural Forces and Individual Choices: An Illustration From the Life of a Battered Woman

Throughout our book, we have focused on the interconnecting web of both individual and structural forces that shape all human societies. In our society, these forces have had a deleterious affect on African Americans, to the extent that not only is the turmoil in the African American community caused by the interlocking web of high rates of unemployment, poverty, HIV/AIDS, incarceration, and IPV, but also because some African Americans make bad individual choices that have a negative impact on their respective life chances.

For example, consider our interview with Sheri. She left the state of Georgia with her children and decided to head to a small southern city with a declining positive job rate. When she arrived at the bus station in Winston-Salem in the middle of the night, her only option was to call the local police for a ride to the nearest women's shelter.

There she received the emergency shelter she needed, but not much more. A day or two later, she went to the only mall in town, where she immediately started to talk with a man. This got her an invitation to move in, the next day, with him and his mother. Like Andi, who moved from Chicago to Minnesota, Sheri's decision to move in with a man she barely knew (and his family) put her at increased risk for IPV, and sure enough, that is what happened.

Contextualizing Sheri's "Choices"

According to many scholars we have cited here and our own professional assessment, this type of behavior is not normal under any circumstances. But having conducted the study of health and well-being in African American civil society, we clearly understand and argue that the structural forces present in Sheri's life at the time she left Georgia and ended up in a dangerous situation for herself and her children contributed to the destructive decisions she made that affected not only Sheri but also her children. Sheri was unemployed and homeless (living in a shelter) and turned to a man whom she thought could provide financial support and stability for her life and the lives of her children. Of course, the problem was that Sheri didn't know this man well enough to assess his abilities to support her—financially or emotionally—and the imbalance of power and dependency in their relationship put her at risk for the violence she experienced. Many women, when placed in a desperate situation that forces them to choose between right and wrong, especially if it involves feeding their children, will almost every time choose what looks to them to be the right decision but what looks to outsiders as the wrong decision.

We also noted in the book that scholars who have paid special attention to any number of issues related to the African American family have almost never paid attention to IPV, possibly because IPV is one of the innermost secrets in African American civil society that protects itself from *outside* forces and especially agencies such as the police and family-helping societies.

Intimate partner violence is an *inside* problem that African Americans do not want to air outside the family, let alone outside the community.

When the late blues singer Billie Holiday sings about not calling the cops even when she is being beaten, that seemingly innocent song resonates deep in African American culture as social fact. It is well known, and for good reason, that African Americans are less likely to call the police when there is a disturbance. It is also known that police are less likely to respond to such a call for help, depending on the zip code of the callers (if they are seeking help in poor, nonwhite areas).

Taken together, the post–civil rights landscape in America has brought opportunities and wealth to those African Americans already in the middle or upper classes, but opportunities have never materialized for poor and working-class African Americans. In fact, as we have argued and as data show, schools have resegregated to the point that African Americans today attend schools that are less integrated than those their parents attended (Kozol, 2001). More African American men are in prison or living with HIV than attend college. At schools such as Wake Forest, the percent of minority students each year rises, but simultaneously, the percent of *African American* students admitted and enrolled has declined to the levels of the late 1980s.

The life chances of an African American baby born today are dismal. If he or she is born in rural Mississippi, his or her chances of surviving to the first birthday are lower than those for babies born in Mexico, Brazil, or the Dominican Republic. He or she is more likely to live in a single-parent household than not, to live in poverty than not, to go to prison than to college. He or she can expect to live a shorter life and to die from homicide (if it is a boy) or AIDS.

What Is to Be Done?

In many ways, writing this type of book is discouraging. The problems seem so complex that it can be difficult to imagine solutions. Couple that with the fact that we are not working from a singular theory. Unlike Marxists, who would argue that economic equality will also bring an end to patriarchy and racism, and unlike feminists, who believe that equality in gender relations will result in higher marriage rates and lower rates of IPV, we argue here for a multifaceted approach that addresses the institutionalized oppression in the United States that is based on race, class, and gender with attention to both structural and individual-level forces. And thinking about changing all of these systems requires us to think way outside of the box.

Structural Forces: Race, Class, and Gender

It is clear from our discussion throughout this book that there are at least three systems of oppression that need to be addressed: class inequality, racial superiority, and patriarchy. As we have argued across this book, these systems of domination are interwoven in ways such that each supports the other in creating privilege and opportunity for one group while oppressing and exploiting another. For example, one barrier to economic equality is the dual labor markets that are created by gender and race. Thus, economic equality cannot be achieved without dismantling the systems of patriarchy and racial superiority. Similarly, both of the systems of patriarchy and racial superiority depend on economic inequality. And clearly, one of the major issues facing African American families is the existence of patriarchy within African American civil society (Hill, 2005; Hill-Collins, 2004; hooks, 2000). Thus, at the most abstract level, what we believe is necessary is a dismantling of these three systems of oppression that together create a matrix of domination (Hill-Collins, 2004; Zinn & Dill, 2005).

While we are working on this large-scale project, we offer some important suggestions that could be implemented to address some of the more serious inequalities that we have discussed in this book. One of the most pressing problems facing African American families is poverty. Thus, we start with some economic solutions.

Economic Solutions

Living Wage

There is much work in both research and activism that proposes a living wage. In fact, many cities and states have already implemented living wage laws, and many more such laws were voted in during the 2006 midterm elections.[3] The point behind these laws is to create a real opportunity for Americans who are interested in and willing to work—but who are only skilled enough to find employment in the low-wage economy—to earn enough to stay out of poverty. For example, we note that a family of four, with both members of the couple each working a full-time, minimum wage job, will not make enough money to keep the family above the *official* poverty line, let alone gain access to the American Dream (see Chapter 8). Opponents of living wage legislation argue that paying employees more will cut into their profits. Realistically, this may be a serious problem for small businesses. However, for the corporations in the United States that employ the highest number of Americans, this is clearly not the case. In fact, studies of CEO salaries and employee salaries demonstrate that in 1950, the average CEO earned 15 times the average employee. By 2005, that ratio had grown to 531 times (Anderson, Cavanagh, Hartman, & Leondar-Wright, 2001). Our proposal is not designed to undercut small business, but rather to stabilize the gap between the superrich and the working poor. Finally, we note that most of the states that have instigated living wage legislation are in the Northeast and the Midwest, states that have a relatively low African American population. The states in which most African Americans live, the southern states, have the lowest wages, the least economic development, and no living wage laws. Thus, living wage laws in these states would have an immediate and broad impact on African American families.

Employment

In addition to living wage legislation, we also propose the elimination of employment discrimination that is based on sex and race. A plethora of scientific studies demonstrates clearly that African Americans and women face discrimination in hiring, promotion, and salary (Padavic & Reskin, 2002; Roberts & White, 1999). Both equal opportunity in employment and living wage legislation are especially essential in African American families because the majority of African American children live in female-headed, single-parent households. Both of these measures will help to lift millions of African American children out of poverty.

In addition, one of the central issues tied up in employment discrimination is the employment discrimination faced by individuals with a felony record. As Pager (2003) noted, African American men with a felony record are called back for a job less than 5% of the time (as compared to 15% of the time for white men with a felony record). Because 25%–33% of African American men are incarcerated during their lifetime, and because these men are fathers to millions of children, it is the children who suffer financially because their fathers are unable to find legitimate, stable employment.

Health Insurance

Forty million Americans are uninsured, and African Americans are disproportionately represented in this group. We do not purport to be experts in health care policy, but we do suggest that it is nothing short of embarrassing to know that more than 10% of the citizens of the richest country in the world do not have health insurance, and more than 20% of African Americans, including 8–10 million children, are without health insurance of any type (DeNavas-Walt et al., 2004). As with our suggestions for living wage legislation, we note that if major corporations such as Wal-Mart, the corporation that employs more Americans than any other single employer, extended health care benefits to their employees, this would significantly reduce the number of Americans who are uninsured, and it would come at a cost of only 3% of the gross profits (that run into the hundreds of billions) for Wal-Mart (Greenhouse, 2005). Therefore, we recommend that corporations take responsibility for insuring working Americans and their children. This would leave a small percentage of Americans who could then be insured, at very low cost, by the federal or state government.

Affordable Housing

Anyone who has spent time in a housing project or in low-income housing knows that again, it is nothing short of embarrassing to live in the United States, the richest country in the world, and to know that American citizens live in conditions that are equivalent to those in the worst slums in the poorest countries in the world. This seems an extreme statement until we consider the fact that the poorest African Americans living in urban ghettos or rural poverty live without indoor plumbing or electricity or heat.[4] The lack of affordable housing means that millions of children in the United States grow up in conditions that are unsafe and unhealthy. The lack of affordable housing is one of the major concerns of women who are attempting to leave violent relationships, and poor women who are being battered risk losing their public housing because of the behavior of their husbands and male partners. Furthermore, the ban that felony drug convicts face on public housing creates serious barriers to reentry and reintegration into family life. For many poor families, especially those headed by single mothers who are working minimum wage jobs, rent may take up their entire monthly paycheck. The creation of affordable, decent housing would improve the lives of many African Americans and their children, it would allow many battered women to leave violent homes, and it would facilitate the reintegration of families headed by women with drug felony convictions.

Parental Support for Children

The issue of family formation, as we noted in the extensive discussion in Chapter 3, is highly contested. What we identified in that discussion is that, moral issues aside, millions of American children, and perhaps 50% of African American children, are poor because they are living in single-parent households that are headed by women. Furthermore, in many cases, these children are denied the financial (and emotional) support of their fathers to which they are entitled. Child support and the enforcement of child support is contentious at best. We do not advocate for social engineering policies, such as those tried under Wisconsin Governor Tommy Thompson in the early 1990s that required marriage in order for welfare benefits to remain intact—a policy known as "bridefare." However, we do argue for a child support model that is based on the policies of states like Wisconsin. These policies rest on the assumption that children are *entitled* to the financial support of two parents. Noncustodial parents are court-ordered to pay a percentage of their income through the 18th birthday of the child in question, and all child support monies are handled through a system of wage garnishment. We argue that some portion of child poverty would be eliminated by the enforcement of similar orders nationwide. In the economy of the 21st century, children depend upon the income of two parents in order to stay out of poverty. If these policies were truly enforced, it would make the negative outcomes of nonmarital births and divorce less serious for the nation's children, and for African American children in particular as they are far more likely to live in single-parent households (McLanahan & Sandefur, 1994).

Revamp Welfare

Although welfare was "reformed" only a decade ago (TANF was signed into law by President Clinton in 1996), just as many social policy analysts suggested, children and poor women have paid a hefty price. Certainly, welfare reform policies have resulted in reducing the welfare rolls by millions of Americans; however, this has not guaranteed them a better life by any measure. Of particular importance here are the time limits imposed by welfare coupled with the minimum wage laws. Many of the women we interviewed who were fleeing abusive partners simply needed more time than the 2 years of continuous welfare in order to get on their feet. For many battered women, for example, leaving is a process of false starts. It may take many years for a woman to leave successfully. Coupled with this is the fact that minimum wage, especially in single-parent/single-earner families, is simply not enough money to make ends meet (Edin & Lein, 1997). As we noted in the section on living wages, a minimum wage worker working 40 hours per week will take home only about $800 per month. If he or she has two children to provide for, most or all of that money will go to pay for the child care the parent requires in order to go to work. Thus, the situation becomes a catch-22 of sorts. An ambitious, hard-working mother (father) will find that after working 40 hours each week and paying day care costs, there isn't enough money left over for rent, let alone food. Welfare will become the only feasible option. And with the 2-year continuous, 5-year lifetime cap that is part of TANF, parents will inevitably exhaust their welfare options and be forced to live in dire poverty and/or enter the illegitimate economy.[5] Although whites make up the majority of welfare beneficiaries, African Americans (mainly women and children) are more likely to be on welfare than their white counterparts. Thus, restrictions on welfare hurt African Americans more than they hurt others. Perhaps the best solutions to the question of welfare reform are living wage legislation and affordable housing. We add to that affordable or government-subsidized, high-quality child care.[6] We believe that if people in the lowest income groups could *afford* to work, they would.

Again, we note that the bans on welfare for felony drug convicts are devastating. Coupled with the fact that drug felons have dismal prospects for employment (Pager, 2003), it is difficult to imagine a successful reentry program that does not allow for the receipt of cash assistance, food stamps, and public housing. This creates a situation that not only is ripe for recidivism, but also significantly lowers the probability that a parent coming out of prison will be able to successful reintegrate into family life. The outcomes are devastating to millions of African American families, especially children, who are often then raised by other relatives (grandmothers) or placed in the foster care system.

Welfare also needs to be reformed to reflect a standard of living that is reasonable. Like education, rather than funding welfare with what is available, we advocate funding welfare programs at the level necessary to provide safe, clean housing; nutritious and balanced meals; and above all, the same sort of health care that Americans insured by private health care receive. Thus, we argue that all systems of welfare, including Medicare and Medicaid, need to be revamped to provide not second-class health care or substandard housing (as in the case of HUD), but rather a minimum standard of services that is commensurate with the standard of all Americans. This may seem expensive, but with minimal adjustments to the federal budget and taxes, as well as inputs from employers, this would be achievable and would save money in other areas because crime would be reduced, as would illnesses caused by malnutrition, chronic illness, and so on.

Equal Access to Education

One of the most contested issues in contemporary American society is the issue of affirmative action, especially with regard to access to higher education. Certainly, equal access to higher education is one of the keys to the elimination of many social problems facing African American families. Because education is one of the major mechanisms to building human capital and securing stable, well-paying employment, access to higher education is essential. We do not intend to enter the affirmative action debate, which is so hotly contested that it ended up in the U.S. Supreme Court in the summer of 2003.

We do note, however, that what is seldom talked about is the fact that the primary beneficiaries of affirmative action programs have been white women. What is even more rarely discussed and debated are the forms of affirmative action that have existed for whites of all social classes for the previous 400 years. As we discussed at length in Chapters 7 and 8, as well as earlier in this chapter, whites have benefited from a system of racial superiority that has allowed them to accumulate not just financial capital but also social capital and access to the opportunity structure. The example of farm families illustrates the point. Furthermore, practices such as legacy admission—the preference for the children of alumni in college admissions—is perhaps the most long-standing, powerful form of affirmative action that has ever been in place. We illustrated this with the fact that at schools such as Wake Forest, an institution that began admitting African Americans only in the early 1970s and typically has a student body that is only 5% African American, it is clear that the legacy advantage is racialized: There are very few African American alums to whose children this benefit might accrue.

We also note that affirmative action policies for colleges and universities are, in many ways, too little too late. As Kozol (1992, 2001, 2005) so brilliantly describes in his analysis of public schools in the United States, inequalities in education begin in kindergarten when white and affluent students attend overresourced schools whereas poor students and most African Americans attend inferior, underresourced schools. When we attempt to correct racial discrimination at the point of higher education, we are faced with inequalities in college preparation. For example, an institution such as Wake Forest is likely to argue that in order to increase the percent of African American students on campus, it would have to lower minimum SAT standards. Yet we know that discrepancies in SAT scores are intimately tied to the quality of education students receive in the early years. Thus, many of the issues of inequality that occur in the process of college admission would be solved by creating more balance and equity in the first 12 years of school. *Thus, we propose that the United States invest in all of our futures by investing in all of our children.* Schools need the resources necessary to *educate*, not the resources that are connected to the tax base of a neighborhood—which allows the perpetuation of privilege. Schools must be integrated by social class and race—period. Equality in education would also have a profound impact on alleviating inequalities in employment, wages, and health insurance.

Reduce/Eliminate Discrimination in Health Care

As we discussed at length in Chapter 6, racial disparities in health, health care, illness, treatment, and cause of death persist. A study released in the summer 2005 notes the following:

> In conclusion, we studied racial differences in the receipt of nine major surgical procedures among persons enrolled in Medicare and found that there have been no meaningful, consistent reductions in the gaps in care between black enrollees and white enrollees. Blacks have less access to better doctors, hospitals and health plans, studies indicate. Research also shows that the medical system treats whites and blacks differently, even when they are the same in nearly every way. (Jha et al., 2005, p. 690)

We argued in Chapter 6 that the primary cause of racial disparities in health care is the fact that African Americans are disproportionately likely to be among the uninsured (as noted above) and among those relying on Medicaid rather than private, employer-based insurance. In many communities, Medicaid clinics and clinics that treat insured patients are completely segregated from one another. It is as if two completely separate—and *not equal*—systems of health care exist in the United States. African Americans are disproportionately likely to be receiving second-class, substandard care (Epstein, 2004).

This means that they are offered treatments and procedures less frequently, and when they *are* offered treatments and procedures, the offer comes after they are significantly sicker; as a result, African Americans die more quickly after diagnosis from almost every disease. African Americans have a shorter life expectancy and more potential years of life lost as a result of dying young.

To these issues, we propose both individual and structural solutions. At the individual level, physicians and health care professionals need to end discriminatory practices. All patients need to be treated in the same manner regardless of their race (or gender). However, we argue that the change that will make the most difference in the lives of African Americans is access to the same health care system to which whites have access. As long as African Americans are seen primarily in Medicaid clinics and emergency rooms, they will continue to receive inferior and compromised care that is based on their ability to pay rather than their need, and as a result, they will continue to die earlier and suffer from more illnesses than whites. The primary solution we proposed above, access to employer-based health care insurance, is the first step. Second, we need to eliminate two standards of care and require all physicians and clinics to deliver the best possible care to every patient.

Alternatives to Incarceration for Nonviolent Offenders

As is the case with so many of the issues we have already discussed, one of the major causes of poverty, disease, absent fathers, HIV/AIDS, and IPV is the terribly high rate of incarceration of African American men. There have to be alternatives to long-term incarceration in maximum security prisons for nonviolent offenders.

We know that extended periods of incarceration interrupt family life. Children with a parent in prison have difficulty maintaining a relationship with that parent, and with all of the barriers to reentry and reintegration into family life, these relationships may never be repaired. In African American families, incarceration has a major impact in separating families, leaving many women to rear children as single parents.

When mothers are incarcerated, we know that most often the grandmother is left to rear the children. With 25%–33% of African American men spending time in prison or jail, these facts—unemployability, disenfranchisement, the disruption of family, exposure to HIV—are devastating to African American families and to African American civil society. Just as some have argued that with the high rates of incarceration, we now must look to this as a lifecourse event for African American men (Haney & Zimbardo, 1998), we argue that incarceration needs to be considered a major factor in shaping African American family life.

As we discussed at length in Chapter 9, the majority (more than 60%) of incarcerated African American women are serving sentences for drug possession convictions (Islam-Zwart & Vik, 2004; Zamble, 1992). Because the majority of these women are mothers with minor children for whom they are the primary parent, we underscore the devastating effect that 5- to 10-year sentences have on the children they leave behind. As many researchers in this area note, one result of the new drug laws is that prisons have become warehouses for drug offenders who need treatment—treatment to which they do not have access in prison (Haney & Zimbardo, 1998). Therefore, we propose that alternatives to incarceration be identified and pursued. These might involve supervision (probation), treatment (for alcohol or drugs), and so forth. If alternatives were identified, and fewer African American men and women were incarcerated, the effects could be profound, and positive, on African American families.

Preventing and Interrupting Intimate Partner Violence

As we noted in Chapter 5, intimate partner violence (IPV) is a problem that is ravaging African American families. Part of the tragedy is, of course, that in the face of all of the inequities and discrimination that African American women face in the culture at large, the fact is that 1 in 4 of these women also face violence at home, at the hands of the men who purport to love them.

The thrust of this book was to identify the ways that so many problems facing the African American family are interwoven and connected. In Chapter 5, we discussed some of the ways to prevent IPV, which include reducing other stresses in family life, especially the stresses associated with unemployment and underemployment. Of course, we recognize that most men, of all races and ethnicities, feel a need to work (and they should). Asserting oneself as a man and feeling a sense of self-fulfillment is difficult for many African American men in the current labor market. Therefore, we also advocate for reconstituting ideologies of masculinity such that African American men do not feel that they are masculine unless they are taking care of all of the financial needs of the family.

We also need to identify other sources of masculine identity for men, such as being a supportive partner, being a good parent, and so on. Finally, we note that many of the solutions proposed earlier that would lead to full employment and the ability to earn a living wage should contribute to the reduction in IPV. Similarly, we argue that periods of incarceration and illness are also serious sources of stress on families. If fewer men are incarcerated, and if more men are healthier, as we propose above, we believe that we will also see a reduction in IPV.

When IPV does occur, we fail to deal with it effectively. For example, the criminal justice system and many intervention programs fail to address IPV adequately. In Forsyth County, North Carolina, for example, fewer than half of the men charged with "assault on a female" are ever brought before a judge, and when they are, the majority (75%) are sentenced to attend an intervention program in lieu of jail time or other punishment (Harvey, 2002). Our own research on the efficacy of this intervention program found that less than half of all men sentenced to the program ever attend a single session! When they do attend, there is a marked reduction in recidivism for white men, but the intervention program is significantly less effective for African American men (Hattery et al., 2005).

As a society, when we fail to hold these men accountable, and when we fail to help them learn better ways of relating, we fail them, we fail their female partners, and most importantly, we fail their children. Boys who grow up in a household in which their father beats their mother are significantly more likely to grow up to batter their own wives and girlfriends than are children who grow up in a household without violence (Ehrensaft et al., 2003).

Anyone who has worked with battered women also knows that we fail to provide the support that women need to leave abusive relationships and build better lives for themselves and their children. Although shelters were an initial response to the crisis of IPV as it was identified by feminists in the early 1970s, researchers and practitioners now know that shelters are merely a bandage on a severed artery. All women, whether they have been battered or not, are at risk for IPV when they cannot earn a living wage, when they cannot afford safe housing, and when they cannot afford safe and reliable care for their children. Battered women stay, and women put themselves at risk for battering, because they are forced to depend on men to help them financially, to help them with a place to live, and often to help them watch the children.

Thus, all of the changes we have recommended above should result in a reduction in battering in two ways. First, they would allow women who are being battered to leave successfully, and second, they would allow women the freedom to choose to be with a man (or not), and to be choosy about what kind of man they are with.

As a result of the prevalence of IPV, African American families (and indeed, families of all races and ethnicities) are violent places where people are harmed physically, emotionally, and sexually. We must address this issue in the African American community if we are to create an environment that allows children (and adults) to thrive.

Honesty About HIV

Although we discussed a variety of illnesses and health disparities in Chapter 6, we focus our attention on HIV/AIDS for several reasons: (a) because it is a death sentence, (b) because it is a preventable disease, and (c) because it is now one of the leading causes of death among African American men and women. Just as there has been a refusal to talk about IPV in the African American community, we argue that there has been a similar refusal to talk about HIV/AIDS in the African American community because it pits African American women against African American men.

Much of the reluctance to talk about HIV/AIDS is a reluctance to talk about men having sex with men (MSM).[7] Yet African American men are having sex with men, both consensually (men on the down low) and nonconsensually (prison rape). And the primary way in which African American women are being infected with HIV is by having sex with infected men. So, these men are contracting HIV and then infecting women in their communities. HIV/AIDS prevention must be developed and designed *specifically* to address not only the most common mechanism for transmission among African

American men—IV drug use—but the increasingly common transmission route of MSM. AIDS is killing African Americans at a startling rate, and it is incumbent upon us to force open discussions in the African American community that address this killer.

Individual Solutions

We end our discussion of solutions by returning to the issue of individual choice. We discussed our thinking on this point earlier in the book with a reference to an important article by the Harvard humanities scholar Henry Louis Gates (Gates, 2004). We reiterate below Gates's thinking and our underscoring of these perspectives.

The bulk of the discussions and analysis in this book have focused on the ways in which structures and institutions shape the lives of African American men and women and their families. We have spent considerable space talking about discrimination, blocked access to the opportunity structure that allows for upward mobility, and economic and political exploitation. We have shared the stories of women like Andi, who make poor choices because they feel their choices are severely constrained, and stories from men like Eddie, who, as a professional boxer, took advantage of his pugilist skills to beat his girlfriend into an unrecognizable state. As sociologists, this is where we focused our attention and feel confident that by bringing a new paradigmatic thrust like ours to the study of the African American family—the race, class, and gender perspective—we offer a challenge to scholars to walk away from the "thin blue line" of political correctness and "value neutrality" and return to the kind of engaged scholarship embedded in the work of scholars as diverse as W.E.B. Du Bois, Max Weber, Angela Davis, and Eduardo Bonilla-Silva.

However, we would be remiss in not saying something at the conclusion of this book about the individual choices we make at any given point in time. We all know of people who have persevered despite serious hardship. And one of the threads in these stories is that the individual actor made good choices. For example, Cedric Jennings, whose story is profiled in *A Hope in the Unseen* (Suskind, 1998), made choices that were often unpopular. Raised by a single mother on welfare in southeastern Washington, DC, educated in an underresourced school, surrounded by drug dealers, and growing up with a father in prison, Cedric chose to stay in school. With the help of some key mentors, he pursued his college education at Brown University, an Ivy League college, where he was in the minority both because of his race and because of his social class. Cedric Jennings overcame serious barriers to success in part by making the right choices.[8]

African American men, women, and children have agency. They are not puppets of a system in which they have no control over their individual lives. Despite frequently finding themselves in underresourced schools, for example, they can *choose* to get the best education available to them rather than dropping out of high school, as more than 50% of the young men will do. Despite their perceptions of a tight marriage market and few prospects for a fulfilling job, African American girls can *choose* not to become teenage, single mothers, as far too many of them do. That statistic alone speaks volumes about the problems we discuss in our book. With a rate of 58.8/1,000 births to African American teen girls, a rate that is more than twice as high as that for whites, and with 75% of all African American babies born to single mothers, too many African American children begin their lives in poverty with little hope for a better future. Despite the difficult and unfulfilling job opportunities that await many African Americans in low-income neighborhoods, men and women can choose to work. Perhaps more important than earning a wage, which will not keep them out of poverty, they are role-modeling for their children a world in which adults go to work.

As we close this book, we want to make sure that our thesis herein is clear. We are not advocating that African Americans accept the inequalities they face. We are suggesting that individuals have the agency to choose how to respond to these conditions such that they move beyond them to a place where they are safe and successful in their own lives and can advocate more effectively for social change. That is, we are suggesting that they no longer be voluntary victims to a system, but work from within and without to change it for themselves, their families, and for the next generation of African Americans.

We extend our challenge to white Americans as well. White Americans need to honestly examine the privileges that accrue to them through a system of racial oppression. Although the amount and type of privilege that accrues is also shaped by gender and social class, nevertheless, whites have benefited, both individually and as a class of people, by the system of racial domination that is so deeply embedded in American society. We are not asking that white Americans give back these privileges; it is simply not possible to do so. But once one recognizes this system of privilege, it is incumbent upon the individual to work to dismantle the system that structures the privilege to begin with. Similarly, men need to work to dismantle patriarchy. The wealthy need to work to dismantle the system of class oppression that is so deeply embedded in American capitalism. For example, under the current system, workers making more than $90,000 per year pay no Social Security tax on the money earned in excess of $90,000. Thus, the liability for Social

Security is disproportionately carried by poor, working-class, and middle-class Americans who can least afford this additional burden. All of us who benefit from a system of privilege must acknowledge that and work to level the playing field so that all Americans have equal opportunity to share in the bounties of this great society. We are only as strong as our weakest member. Therefore, we *all* benefit when opportunities are available to everyone.

Final Thoughts

Doing the research for this book has involved extensive reading and research of previous studies, extensive analysis of federal data such as census data and data from the Bureau of Justice Statistics, and most important, listening to the voices of African American men and women who are struggling inside of a system that seems pitted against them.

In his autobiography, Professor John Hope Franklin recounts his experience in trying to enlist for World War II. He reasoned that with his skills in shorthand and typing and a PhD from Harvard (History, 1941), the Navy would be excited about his enlistment. He was turned down on the basis of his race. Below, he tells the story of his visit to the draft board in North Carolina, which told him that if he were traveling (he was giving lectures and commencement speeches), he had to have his blood drawn beforehand in case his number was called. He would have to report immediately, he was told, from wherever he was, for military service:

> When I went to see the draft board's physician, as directed by the clerk, I was not permitted to enter his office and was directed to a bench down the hall near the fire escape. There I was to wait until called. I refused and went back to the draft board's office, requesting a physician who did not think I was vermin. I added that if I was to be drafted, it had to be done with due respect to my humanity. The clerk said there were no other physicians on duty that day and that, with her intervention and assistance, the doctor would see me. When I returned to his office I was immediately ushered into his consultation room. He was all smiles, very cheerful, and ready for a "friendly" conversation. I was not so ready. I rolled up my sleeve, turned my head from his as he drew blood, and returned his cheerful, brainless banter with stony silence.
>
> This last experience forced me to one irrevocable conclusion, that the United States, however much it was devoted to protecting the freedoms and rights of Europeans, had no respect for me, little interest in my well-being, and not even a desire to utilize my professional services. (Franklin, 2005, p. 107)

It was this ordinary experience with segregation that steeled Franklin against Jim Crow practices that he fought against all his life.

One of the things that has become the most clear to us as we have compiled all of this research into the story we tell here, is that in post–civil rights America, we continue to live in apartheid. Virtually every system and institution we have examined, from education to employment to housing to health care to prisons, is segregated into two distinct systems. For years, Jonathan Kozol has been pointing this out in the arena of education. Everything we found confirmed this, and perhaps more stunning is the fact that his description of apartheid in education can be applied to virtually every other major institution operating in the United States. What has changed, as is illustrated in the Massey quote at the beginning of this chapter, is that the category system is no longer designed ostensibly around race, as it was in Jim Crow America. There are no longer schools for whites and schools for blacks or hospitals for whites and hospitals for blacks.

Instead, the system *appears* to be designed around social class. Families who can afford better houses and better schools and better health care receive the best in the world. The poor in America live in homes, attend schools, and receive health care in institutions that could easily be in any developing country in Africa, Asia, South America, or Eastern Europe.

And because a few African Americans who can afford the superior system and institutions are able to access them, Americans feel good about themselves. We believe that we live in a society in which people are simply getting what they deserve, what they worked hard to earn.

Yet because of the ways in which race and social class are inextricably linked, the truth is that this segregated system is still segregated along racial lines. African Americans are educated in segregated schools, they receive health care in clinics staffed only by African Americans, and they work in industries that are "black": cleaning, cooking, and doing the lowest levels of manual labor. And whites live similarly segregated lives. The only contact many whites have with African Americans is in the context of being served: having their homes cleaned, having their children cared for, having their cars washed, and, of course, having their groceries packed.

Fifty years after the famous integration decision of *Brown v. Board of Education,* we live in a land of apartheid with two systems for everything, and these two systems are never equal.[9] These two unequal systems, applied to health care, education, work, banking, and incarceration, have disastrous effects on African American families.

Notes

1. We are mindful that African American companies cater and sell to African Americans almost exclusively. Most African American companies and businesses are marginal.

On November 9 Harlem's Freedom National Bank, the only black-owned commercial bank in New York City, was closed by federal regulators after suffering continued losses on outstanding loans. Usually the Feds place failing banks in conservatorship for up to a year prior to liquidation, during which time they encourage depositors with accounts above the 100,000 level to move their money to safer havens. In Freedom's case, such kindness was not in the cards. ("Redlining a Black Bank," 1991)

2. This scenario is, in fact, the trajectory of one of the authors.
3. A series of living wage laws went into effect in June 2005.
4. For an excellent award-winning documentary, see *Lalee's Kin* by HBO.
5. Again, we recommend *Lalee's Kin* by HBO.
6. Most western European countries provide free or significantly subsidized day care for all children from ages 2 through 5, thus enabling a higher percentage of their female citizens to be gainfully employed.
7. Much of this is rooted in conservative religion that has historically played an important role in African American civil society.
8. The best and most recent account of this is found in historian John Hope Franklin's (2005) *Autobiography,* cited earlier. Franklin endured the harsh segregation that did not allow him to ride public transportation or to use, like white students and scholars, the research facilities of public and private libraries, including state archives in North Carolina. He was asked by a chief archivist if he knew who the "Harvard nigger" was who was there to use the archive, just as the archivist's secretary was making "facials" to her to indicate that it was Franklin to whom she was referring. Franklin also chronicles that he was not about to let these institutional and individual indignities get in the way of his aspirations and forged ahead to an immense amount of success.
9. In closing our book, we acknowledge the intellectual influence of Professor Orlando Patterson (several of his texts have been helpful, but we drew heavily from *Rituals of Blood,* published in 1999). In his work, Patterson does not shy away from the difficult issues. Furthermore, he does not simply offer his opinion on the problems facing the African American community. Rather, he offers empirical evidence, as we have done here, to describe the current state of African American civil society. Finally, as we have tried to do, he offers solutions that address both structural change and individual responsibility. Professor Patterson visited our campus in the spring of 2004 and delivered an outstanding lecture titled "The American Dionysius." Hence, we disagree with the anonymous reviewer that we have "leaned heavily on Patterson" and that we remove Patterson from our references. His work is essential to our own.

Appendix A: Methods and Sample

For a variety of reasons, we felt it was important to collect data in more than one part of the United States. The South has such a particular (and peculiar) sociopolitical economy that we chose the Midwest as a contrast site.[1] The Midwest provides an interesting contrast site in many other ways as well. First, the midwestern states, and Minnesota in particular, have been at the forefront of domestic violence legislation and intervention. The county with which we partnered, Olmsted County, has been awarded several pilot grants from the Department of Justice to create innovate intervention and prevention approaches.[2] Second, states like Minnesota were at the forefront of progressive laws regarding violence against women (rape and battering). For example, in Minnesota, domestic violence is defined in a feminist manner that can include women who batter men and same-sex battering. In North Carolina, however, as previously mentioned, domestic violence is defined in a gendered way: The only conceivable pattern is men beating up women. Thus, the charge retains the vestiges of patriarchy: "assault on a female."

Finally, it is important to note that because the African American population in Minnesota is very small (in this particular county, African Americans make up only 2.5% of the residents), and because most of the African Americans in this county have migrated there over the past generation, we restricted our sample in Minnesota to African Americans who had *not ever* lived in the South. This allowed us to test the southern subculture of violence theory.

In any case, most of the battered women we interviewed in the Minnesota sample are largely still living with their batterers, whereas none of the battered women we interviewed in North Carolina were.[3]

Minnesota Men and Women

We partnered with the Domestic Violence Unit, which is administered within Child Protective Services (CPS). All of the men and women we interviewed were involved with social services, not the court system. Minnesota law requires that if there is a

318

domestic violence incident that involves children "within sight or sound," the responding officer is required to refer the couple to CPS. Among other things, this allowed us to generate a sample that included couples. We conducted 20 interviews in Minnesota with 10 men and 10 women. We conducted interviews with six intact couples (we interviewed both members of the couple, but for confidentiality and safety reasons, the interviews were conducted separately). The remaining interviews were conducted with one member of the couple, with the other member either refusing to be interviewed or being unavailable for interview (several of the partners had moved out of state or were in prison in other counties).

Minnesota Women

Andi—no partner	Mary/Demetrius	Veta/Wells
Candi—no partner	Stella/Will	Wanda/Chris
Kylie/Jon	Tammy/Ronny	
Lara—no partner	Tanya	

Minnesota Men

Chris/Wanda	Hank—no partner	Wells/Veta
Ellis—no partner	Jon/Kylie	Will/Stella
Ethan—no partner	Ronny/Tammy	Demetrius/Mary

North Carolina Men and Women

Men

All of the men interviewed in North Carolina (16) were participants in the Time Out Program, a batterers' intervention program administered by Family Services, Inc., Forsyth County, North Carolina. All of the men who were recruited for interview had been court-ordered to this program as a result of being charged in the criminal justice system with "assault on a female," which is the North Carolina charge applied to any battering behavior that a man commits against a woman. In all cases, the men were charged. They were all offered the opportunity to participate in Time Out (a 26-week program) rather than serve time in jail. Fourteen of the men interviewed were African American and two were white. All of the interviews were conducted by the authors and a former colleague, and all were taped and professionally transcribed.

Women

The women were recruited at a local battered women's shelter in the same mid-sized city in North Carolina. All of the women were living in the shelter at the time of the interview, and all of the interviews were conducted in the shelter by the authors and a former colleague. All of the interviews were taped and professionally transcribed. Of the 24 women interviewed in the shelter, 14 were African American and 10 were white. Many had children living with them in the shelter.

Although the study design had originally called for interviewing partners, in the North Carolina sample, we were able to conduct interviews with only two couples: one white and one African American.

North Carolina Women

C	Connie	Rose
Candy	Evie	Sally
Cheri	Jessica	Sheri
Cindy	Cheri	Valerie

North Carolina Men

Cass	Gus	Manny
Eddie	Jason	Ward
Fred	Jerry	Warren

Analytical Techniques

The quantitative data used in this book all come from secondary data sets. In cases where we conducted unique analyses, standard bivariate statistics were produced using a standard statistical software package, SPSS. The qualitative data we include in this book were analyzed using a thematic coding scheme developed by Strauss and Corbin (1990). Interviews were taped and transcribed, and transcripts were analyzed by looking for themes (Strauss, 1990). Once these themes were identified, bivariate analyses allowed us to compare the ways that themes are correlated with independent variables such as gender, social class, age, region of the country, employment status, educational attainment, marital status, parental status, and so forth.

Notes

1. This allowed us to test the southern subculture of violence theory, which will be discussed throughout the book.

2. For example, Minnesota was among the first states to experiment with mandatory arrest laws.

3. All of these sorts of variation in the sample will be addressed when appropriate. We would argue, however, that rather than making the sample less consistent, these variations contribute to a sample that better represents the experiences of women in the United States who are living with IPV. Thus, we think the sample is one of the strengths of the study.

Appendix B: Marital History for People 15 Years and Over, by Age, Sex, Race, and Hispanic Origin, 2001

White non-Hispanic

MEN

Percent

Characteristic	Total, 15 years and over	15 to 19 years	20 to 24 years	25 to 29 years	30 to 34 years	35 to 39 years	40 to 49 years	50 to 59 years	60 to 69 years	70 years and over
Total (in thousands)	77,085	6,679	5,981	5,811	6,680	7,691	15,781	12,378	7,807	8,277
Never married	27.4	99.4	83.7	48.3	28.1	19.0	12.8	5.7	4.0	3.5
Ever married	72.6	0.6	16.3	51.7	71.9	81.0	87.2	94.3	96.0	96.5
Married once	54.8	0.5	16.2	48.0	61.3	67.1	64.5	60.8	67.3	75.1
Still married[a]	45.1	0.3	14.4	41.0	52.7	53.2	52.8	48.9	58.7	59.2
Married twice	14.0	0.1	0.1	3.6	9.3	12.2	18.9	24.4	21.5	16.5
Still married[a]	11.3	0.1	0.1	3.3	7.9	10.2	15.2	19.2	17.3	12.5
Married 3 or more times	3.8	–	–	0.1	1.3	1.6	3.8	9.1	7.3	4.9
Still married[a]	2.9	–	–	0.1	1.0	1.5	3.1	6.7	5.6	3.7
Ever divorced	23.3	0.1	1.1	8.7	16.8	25.7	32.1	42.8	31.3	18.1
Currently divorced	9.4	–	1.0	5.1	7.8	13.8	13.4	16.6	9.5	5.0
Ever widowed	3.8	–	–	0.1	0.3	0.4	1.2	2.5	7.2	22.3
Currently widowed	2.5	–	–	0.1	0.1	0.1	0.7	1.4	4.0	15.7

Characteristic	Total, 15 years and over	15 to 19 years	20 to 24 years	25 to 29 years	30 to 34 years	35 to 39 years	40 to 49 years	50 to 59 years	60 to 69 years	70 years and over
WOMEN										
Total (in thousands)	82,128	6,310	6,015	5,904	6,696	7,584	15,977	12,880	8,525	12,237
Percent										
Never married	20.7	97.3	70.9	34.1	17.1	12.3	8.1	5.0	2.9	2.9
Ever married	79.3	2.7	29.1	65.9	82.9	87.7	91.9	95.0	97.1	97.1
Married once	60.0	2.7	27.6	59.2	69.6	67.1	64.1	63.8	72.8	78.1
Still married[a]	42.1	2.3	23.4	48.2	58.7	55.0	49.5	48.0	50.2	30.5
Married twice	15.5	–	1.4	6.3	12.0	18.3	22.2	24.1	18.3	15.5
Still married[a]	10.6	–	1.1	5.0	9.5	14.3	16.4	17.0	11.7	6.6
Married 3 or more times	3.7	–	–	0.4	1.4	2.3	5.6	7.1	6.1	3.6
Still married[a]	2.3	–	–	0.3	1.0	2.0	3.9	4.7	3.4	1.2
Ever divorced	25.4	0.1	3.3	14.5	21.9	30.4	38.8	40.4	29.1	17.4
Currently divorced	11.1	0.1	1.9	8.9	10.8	13.5	17.6	17.0	12.1	6.0
Ever widowed	12.9	–	0.2	0.4	0.5	1.2	3.2	8.9	22.2	56.5
Currently widowed	11.3	–	0.2	0.4	0.3	0.7	2.0	6.4	18.4	52.6

a. Includes those currently separated.

Black
MEN

Characteristic	Total, 15 years and over	15 to 19 years	20 to 24 years	25 to 29 years	30 to 34 years	35 to 39 years	40 to 49 years	50 to 59 years	60 to 69 years	70 years and over
Total (in thousands)	11,554	1,507	1,223	1,088	1,149	1,229	2,314	1,505	844	695
Percent										
Never married	43.3	99.2	89.2	60.6	41.5	34.0	25.1	11.6	10.2	3.1
Ever married	56.7	0.8	10.8	39.4	58.5	66.0	74.9	88.4	89.8	96.9
Married once	44.3	0.8	10.8	38.0	51.6	56.3	57.5	62.0	60.8	72.3
Still married[a]	31.4	0.3	9.9	31.2	39.3	42.5	38.2	41.9	43.6	43.8
Married twice	10.0	–	–	1.4	6.7	8.1	13.6	21.9	21.7	20.0
Still married[a]	7.3	–	–	1.4	5.9	7.0	11.0	13.4	16.5	10.8
Married 3 or more times	2.3	–	–	–	0.1	1.6	3.8	4.5	7.2	4.7
Still married[a]	1.5	–	–	–	0.1	1.3	3.2	2.2	3.5	3.1
Ever divorced	18.8	0.2	–	4.2	13.7	18.2	28.1	40.2	35.1	26.9
Currently divorced	9.2	0.2	–	2.8	7.6	9.5	14.0	21.1	12.9	10.3
Ever widowed	3.7	–	0.3	–	0.2	1.0	1.9	4.2	10.9	30.4
Currently widowed	2.9	–	0.3	–	–	0.6	1.0	3.2	8.6	25.2

Characteristic	Total, 15 years and over	15 to 19 years	20 to 24 years	25 to 29 years	30 to 34 years	35 to 39 years	40 to 49 years	50 to 59 years	60 to 69 years	70 years and over
WOMEN										
Total (in thousands)	14,284	1,520	1,465	1,358	1,437	1,526	2,804	1,842	1,215	1,117
Percent										
Never married	41.9	97.9	82.6	59.4	49.5	34.0	27.9	14.4	10.4	6.8
Ever married	58.1	2.1	17.4	40.6	50.5	66.0	72.1	85.6	89.6	93.2
Married once	46.9	1.8	17.4	37.7	44.3	55.5	56.0	66.1	67.5	72.4
Still married[a]	25.1	0.9	14.7	26.7	32.2	35.0	31.1	32.1	27.7	17.3
Married twice	9.8	0.3	–	2.8	6.3	9.2	13.7	16.3	19.3	18.1
Still married[a]	5.0	0.3	–	2.3	5.1	5.4	8.1	9.6	7.5	2.7
Married 3 or more times	1.5	–	–	0.2	–	1.2	2.5	3.2	2.8	2.8
Still married[a]	0.8	–	–	–	–	0.6	1.9	1.6	0.9	0.5
Ever divorced	20.1	0.3	0.6	8.4	12.4	24.6	30.4	38.2	30.3	23.7
Currently divorced	11.9	–	0.6	6.1	6.4	16.3	18.5	24.1	15.7	10.4
Ever widowed	10.5	–	0.3	0.8	1.1	0.9	5.1	13.1	32.0	60.7
Currently widowed	9.7	–	0.3	0.5	0.8	0.9	4.1	11.1	30.2	59.1

SOURCE: U.S. Bureau of the Census (2005).

a. Includes those currently separated.

Appendix C: International Infant Mortality Rates

Rankings Infant mortality rate (all ascending)

Rank	Country	Value /	Unit
1.	Singapore	2.28	deaths/1,000 live births
2.	Sweden	2.77	deaths/1,000 live births
3.	Hong Kong	2.97	deaths/1,000 live births
4.	Japan	3.28	deaths/1,000 live births
5.	Iceland	3.31	deaths/1,000 live births
6.	Finland	3.59	deaths/1,000 live births
7.	Norway	3.73	deaths/1,000 live births
8.	Malta	3.94	deaths/1,000 live births
9.	Czech Republic	3.97	deaths/1,000 live births
10.	Andorra	4.05	deaths/1,000 live births
11.	Germany	4.20	deaths/1,000 live births
12.	France	4.31	deaths/1,000 live births
13.	Macau	4.39	deaths/1,000 live births
14.	Switzerland	4.43	deaths/1,000 live births
15.	Spain	4.48	deaths/1,000 live births
16.	Slovenia	4.50	deaths/1,000 live births
17.	Denmark	4.63	deaths/1,000 live births
18.	Austria	4.68	deaths/1,000 live births
19.	Australia	4.76	deaths/1,000 live births
20.	Belgium	4.76	deaths/1,000 live births

(Continued)

(Continued)

21.	Liechtenstein	4.77	deaths/1,000 live births
22.	Canada	4.82	deaths/1,000 live births
23.	Luxembourg	4.88	deaths/1,000 live births
24.	Netherlands	5.11	deaths/1,000 live births
25.	Portugal	5.13	deaths/1,000 live births
26.	United Kingdom	5.22	deaths/1,000 live births
27.	Ireland	5.50	deaths/1,000 live births
28.	Monaco	5.53	deaths/1,000 live births
29.	Greece	5.63	deaths/1,000 live births
30.	San Marino	5.85	deaths/1,000 live births
31.	New Zealand	5.96	deaths/1,000 live births
32.	Aruba	6.02	deaths/1,000 live births
33.	Italy	6.07	deaths/1,000 live births
34.	Cuba	6.45	deaths/1,000 live births
35.	Taiwan	6.52	deaths/1,000 live births
36.	**United States**	**6.63**	**deaths/1,000 live births**
37.	Croatia	6.96	deaths/1,000 live births
38.	Lithuania	7.13	deaths/1,000 live births
39.	Korea, South	7.18	deaths/1,000 live births
40.	Israel	7.21	deaths/1,000 live births
41.	Cyprus	7.36	deaths/1,000 live births
42.	Slovakia	7.62	deaths/1,000 live births
43.	New Caledonia	7.89	deaths/1,000 live births
44.	Reunion	7.95	deaths/1,000 live births
45.	Estonia	8.08	deaths/1,000 live births
46.	Virgin Islands	8.21	deaths/1,000 live births
47.	Puerto Rico	8.37	deaths/1,000 live births
48.	Cayman Islands	8.41	deaths/1,000 live births
49.	French Polynesia	8.61	deaths/1,000 live births
50.	Hungary	8.68	deaths/1,000 live births
51.	Poland	8.73	deaths/1,000 live births
52.	Bermuda	8.79	deaths/1,000 live births
53.	Chile	9.05	deaths/1,000 live births
54.	American Samoa	9.48	deaths/1,000 live births

55.	Latvia	9.67	deaths/1,000 live births
56.	Nauru	10.14	deaths/1,000 live births
57.	Costa Rica	10.26	deaths/1,000 live births
58.	Kuwait	10.26	deaths/1,000 live births
59.	Netherlands Antilles	10.37	deaths/1,000 live births
60.	Macedonia	11.74	deaths/1,000 live births
61.	Uruguay	12.31	deaths/1,000 live births
62.	French Guiana	12.46	deaths/1,000 live births
63.	Barbados	12.61	deaths/1,000 live births
64.	Jamaica	12.81	deaths/1,000 live births
65.	Fiji	12.99	deaths/1,000 live births
66.	Tonga	12.99	deaths/1,000 live births
67.	Brunei	13.05	deaths/1,000 live births
68.	Serbia and Montenegro	13.43	deaths/1,000 live births
69.	Belarus	13.62	deaths/1,000 live births
70.	Saudi Arabia	13.70	deaths/1,000 live births
71.	Saint Lucia	13.95	deaths/1,000 live births
72.	Grenada	14.62	deaths/1,000 live births
73.	Dominica	14.75	deaths/1,000 live births
74.	Sri Lanka	14.78	deaths/1,000 live births
75.	Saint Kitts and Nevis	14.94	deaths/1,000 live births
76.	United Arab Emirates	15.06	deaths/1,000 live births
77.	Saint Vincent and the Grenadines	15.24	deaths/1,000 live births
78.	Palau	15.30	deaths/1,000 live births
79.	Mauritius	15.57	deaths/1,000 live births
80.	Argentina	15.66	deaths/1,000 live births
81.	Seychelles	15.97	deaths/1,000 live births
82.	Greenland	16.31	deaths/1,000 live births
83.	Russia	16.96	deaths/1,000 live births
84.	Bahrain	17.91	deaths/1,000 live births
85.	British Virgin Islands	18.05	deaths/1,000 live births
86.	Jordan	18.11	deaths/1,000 live births
87.	Malaysia	18.35	deaths/1,000 live births

(Continued)

(Continued)

88.	Qatar	19.32	deaths/1,000 live births
89.	Georgia	19.34	deaths/1,000 live births
90.	Saint Helena	19.85	deaths/1,000 live births
91.	Antigua and Barbuda	20.18	deaths/1,000 live births
92.	Oman	20.26	deaths/1,000 live births
93.	Ukraine	20.61	deaths/1,000 live births
94.	Tuvalu	20.69	deaths/1,000 live births
95.	Panama	20.95	deaths/1,000 live births
96.	Thailand	21.14	deaths/1,000 live births
97.	Bulgaria	21.31	deaths/1,000 live births
98.	Mexico	21.69	deaths/1,000 live births
99.	Colombia	21.72	deaths/1,000 live births
100.	Bosnia and Herzegovina	21.88	deaths/1,000 live births
101.	Anguilla	21.91	deaths/1,000 live births
102.	Solomon Islands	22.09	deaths/1,000 live births
103.	Albania	22.31	deaths/1,000 live births
104.	Venezuela	22.99	deaths/1,000 live births
105.	Suriname	24.15	deaths/1,000 live births
106.	Armenia	24.16	deaths/1,000 live births
107.	Philippines	24.24	deaths/1,000 live births
108.	Ecuador	24.49	deaths/1,000 live births
109.	Trinidad and Tobago	24.64	deaths/1,000 live births
110.	Korea, North	24.84	deaths/1,000 live births
111.	China	25.28	deaths/1,000 live births
112.	Lebanon	25.48	deaths/1,000 live births
113.	Bahamas, The	25.70	deaths/1,000 live births
114.	Libya	25.70	deaths/1,000 live births
115.	Tunisia	25.76	deaths/1,000 live births
116.	El Salvador	25.93	deaths/1,000 live births
117.	Belize	26.37	deaths/1,000 live births
118.	Paraguay	26.67	deaths/1,000 live births
119.	Romania	27.24	deaths/1,000 live births
120.	Samoa	28.72	deaths/1,000 live births

121.	Honduras	29.64	deaths/1,000 live births
122.	Vietnam	29.88	deaths/1,000 live births
123.	Nicaragua	30.15	deaths/1,000 live births
124.	Marshall Islands	30.50	deaths/1,000 live births
125.	Kazakhstan	30.54	deaths/1,000 live births
126.	Syria	30.60	deaths/1,000 live births
127.	Brazil	30.66	deaths/1,000 live births
128.	Algeria	32.16	deaths/1,000 live births
129.	Peru	32.95	deaths/1,000 live births
130.	Dominican Republic	33.28	deaths/1,000 live births
131.	Egypt	33.90	deaths/1,000 live births
132.	Kyrgyzstan	36.81	deaths/1,000 live births
133.	Indonesia	36.82	deaths/1,000 live births
134.	Guatemala	36.91	deaths/1,000 live births
135.	Guyana	37.22	deaths/1,000 live births
136.	Moldova	41.00	deaths/1,000 live births
137.	Turkey	42.62	deaths/1,000 live births
138.	Iran	42.86	deaths/1,000 live births
139.	Morocco	43.25	deaths/1,000 live births
140.	Sao Tome and Principe	44.58	deaths/1,000 live births
141.	East Timor	48.86	deaths/1,000 live births
142.	Cape Verde	49.14	deaths/1,000 live births
143.	Kiribati	49.90	deaths/1,000 live births
144.	Ghana	52.22	deaths/1,000 live births
145.	Iraq	52.71	deaths/1,000 live births
146.	Papua New Guinea	53.15	deaths/1,000 live births
147.	Gabon	54.34	deaths/1,000 live births
148.	Bolivia	54.58	deaths/1,000 live births
149.	Mongolia	55.45	deaths/1,000 live births
150.	Senegal	56.53	deaths/1,000 live births
151.	Vanuatu	56.63	deaths/1,000 live births
152.	India	57.92	deaths/1,000 live births
153.	Maldives	58.32	deaths/1,000 live births

(Continued)

(Continued)

154.	South Africa	62.18	deaths/1,000 live births
155.	Kenya	62.62	deaths/1,000 live births
156.	Yemen	63.26	deaths/1,000 live births
157.	Sudan	64.05	deaths/1,000 live births
158.	Bangladesh	64.32	deaths/1,000 live births
159.	Zimbabwe	67.08	deaths/1,000 live births
160.	Togo	67.66	deaths/1,000 live births
161.	Swaziland	68.35	deaths/1,000 live births
162.	Nepal	68.77	deaths/1,000 live births
163.	Burma	68.78	deaths/1,000 live births
164.	Cameroon	69.18	deaths/1,000 live births
165.	Namibia	69.58	deaths/1,000 live births
166.	Botswana	69.98	deaths/1,000 live births
167.	Burundi	70.40	deaths/1,000 live births
168.	Nigeria	70.49	deaths/1,000 live births
169.	Uzbekistan	71.30	deaths/1,000 live births
170.	Mauritania	72.35	deaths/1,000 live births
171.	Turkmenistan	73.13	deaths/1,000 live births
172.	Gambia, The	73.48	deaths/1,000 live births
173.	Cambodia	73.67	deaths/1,000 live births
174.	Haiti	74.38	deaths/1,000 live births
175.	Pakistan	74.43	deaths/1,000 live births
176.	Eritrea	75.59	deaths/1,000 live births
177.	Comoros	77.22	deaths/1,000 live births
178.	Madagascar	78.52	deaths/1,000 live births
179.	Azerbaijan	82.07	deaths/1,000 live births
180.	Lesotho	85.22	deaths/1,000 live births
181.	Benin	85.88	deaths/1,000 live births
182.	Uganda	86.15	deaths/1,000 live births
183.	Laos	87.06	deaths/1,000 live births
184.	Equatorial Guinea	87.08	deaths/1,000 live births
185.	Guinea	91.82	deaths/1,000 live births
186.	Central African Republic	92.15	deaths/1,000 live births
187.	Congo, Republic of the	93.86	deaths/1,000 live births

188.	Congo, Democratic Republic of the	94.69	deaths/1,000 live births
189.	Chad	94.78	deaths/1,000 live births
190.	Cote d'Ivoire	97.10	deaths/1,000 live births
191.	Zambia	98.40	deaths/1,000 live births
192.	Burkina Faso	98.67	deaths/1,000 live births
193.	Rwanda	101.68	deaths/1,000 live births
194.	Ethiopia	102.12	deaths/1,000 live births
195.	Tanzania	102.13	deaths/1,000 live births
196.	Bhutan	102.56	deaths/1,000 live births
197.	Malawi	104.23	deaths/1,000 live births
198.	Djibouti	105.54	deaths/1,000 live births
199.	Guinea-Bissau	108.72	deaths/1,000 live births
200.	Tajikistan	112.10	deaths/1,000 live births
201.	Mali	117.99	deaths/1,000 live births
202.	Somalia	118.52	deaths/1,000 live births
203.	Niger	122.66	deaths/1,000 live births
204.	Liberia	130.51	deaths/1,000 live births
205.	Mozambique	137.08	deaths/1,000 live births
206.	Sierra Leone	145.24	deaths/1,000 live births
207.	Afghanistan	165.96	deaths/1,000 live births
208.	Angola	192.50	deaths/1,000 live births

SOURCE: http://www.geographyiq.com/ranking/ranking_Infant_Mortality_Rate_aall.htm

Appendix D: Infant Mortality Rates for Mississippi Counties

Infant Mortality/1,000

County	Rate	County	Rate	County	Rate
Webster	0.0	Pontotoc	8.8	Harrison	15.3
Issaquena	0.0	Tate	9.1	Leake	15.6
Perry	0.0	Wayne	9.5	Tunica	15.6
Greene	0.0	Union	10.1	Pike	15.8
Choctaw	0.0	Smith	10.1	Oktibbeha	15.9
Benton	0.0	Lincoln	10.2	Marion	15.9
George	3.9	Covington	10.5	Newton	16.0
Lamar	4.4	Attala	10.9	Copiah	16.0
Jefferson Davis	4.7	Lawrence	11.0	Lee	16.1
Calhoun	4.7	Monroe	11.0	Montgomery	16.6
Madison	4.8	DeSoto	11.7	Coahoma	16.7
Prentiss	5.8	Amite	11.8	Yazoo	17.1
Lafayette	5.8	Adams	11.8	Bolivar	18.3
Lowndes	6.4	Clarke	12.5	Tishomingo	19.0
Forrest	6.4	Jasper	12.6	Yalobusha	19.3
Stone	6.6	Claiborne	12.7	Sharkey	20.1
Kemper	6.7	Lauderdale	12.8	Tallahatchie	20.5
Holmes	6.7	Hinds	13.0	Panola	20.6
Warren	7.0	Walthall	13.2	Franklin	21.6
Washington	7.1	LeFlore	13.3	Neshoba	22.1
Jackson	7.4	Wilkinson	13.4	Chickasaw	22.7
Winston	7.6	Hancock	13.4	Sunflower	23.4
Clay	7.8	Scott	13.8	Carroll	25.9
Rankin	7.8	Pearl River	13.9	Jefferson	26.1
Simpson	7.9	Quitman	14.0	Humphreys	30.1
Alcorn	7.9	Marshall	14.4	Tippah	38.3
Itawamba	8.3	Jones	15.1		
Grenada	8.4	Noxubee	15.3		

SOURCE: All data come from census data compiled by the city-county data book and are available online at http://fisher.lib.virginia.edu/collections/stats/ccdb/

Appendix E: Health Insurance Coverage by Race

	Total People	Total With Insurance	Private Health Insurance			Government Health Insurance				Uninsured
			Total	Employment Based	Direct Purchase	Total	Medicaid	Medicare	Military	
Whites (in thousands)	194,877	173,295 88.9%	149,084 86%	129,261 86.7%	21,865 14.6%	49,743 28%	16,2473 2.6%	31,458 63.2%	7,563 15%	21,582 11%
African Americans (in thousands)	37,651	30,344 80.5%	20,136 66.3%	10,282 51%	1,732 17%	13,195 43.4%	9,292 70%	4,080 30%	1,283 .1%	7,307 19.5%

% People Without Health Insurance

Whites
11.0

African Americans
19.6

SOURCE: http://www.census.gov/prod/2004pubs/p60-226.pdf

Appendix F: Costs for Medical Procedures Without Medical Insurance

Mammogram: $100–$150

Angiogram: $2,500–$3,500

Cardiac bypass: $20,000–$24,000

Cataract removal: $1,800–$2,400

Colonoscopy: $800–$1,100

Hip replacement: $11,000–$18,000

Knee replacement: $10,000–$12,500

Prostate cancer treatment: $20,000–$22,000

Radical mastectomy (breast cancer surgery) without reconstruction: $6,000–$10,000

Appendix G: Educational Attainment by Race and Sex for Americans Age 15 and Over

	None	No HS	HS	Less Than BA	BA	MA	Professional Degree	PhD
WM	348,000 (0.3%)	18.2 million (20%)	26.8 million (29.5%)	22 million (24.5%)	15 million (16.5%)	5.1 million (5%)	1.6 million (1.8%)	1.3 million (1.5%)
WW	337,000 (0.3%)	17.3 million (18.6%)	29.4 million (31%)	25.8 million (27%)	15 million (15.9%)	5.4 million (5.7%)	793,000 (0.8%)	657,000 (0.7%)
AAM	49,000 (0.4%)	3.2 million (26%)	4.2 million (35%)	2.8 million (23%)	1.1 million (9%)	339,000 (2.8%)	93,000 (0.7%)	52,000 (0.4%)
AAW	50,000 (0.3%)	3.7 million (25%)	4.7 million (32%)	3.9 million (26%)	1.6 million (10.8%)	519,000 (3.5%)	75,000 (0.5%)	46,000 (0.3%)

SOURCE: http://www.census.gov/population/www/socdemo/education/cps2004.html

Appendix H: Employed Persons by Occupation, Race, Hispanic or Latino Ethnicity, and Sex

Percent distribution Occupation, race, and Hispanic or Latino ethnicity	Total		Men		Women	
	2003	2004	2003	2004	2003	2004
White						
Total, 16 years and over (thousands)	114,235	115,239	61,866	62,712	52,369	52,527
Percent	100.0	100.0	100.0	100.0	100.0	100.0
Management, professional, and related occupations	35.5	35.6	33.0	33.1	38.4	38.6
Management, business, and financial operations occupations	15.2	15.3	16.6	16.6	13.5	13.6
Professional and related occupations	20.3	20.3	16.4	16.5	24.9	25.0
Service occupations	15.0	15.2	12.0	12.3	18.6	18.8
Sales and office occupations	25.9	25.5	17.4	17.1	35.9	35.6
Sales and related occupations	11.9	11.8	11.5	11.2	12.4	12.4
Office and administrative support occupations	14.0	13.7	5.9	5.8	23.5	23.2
Natural resources, construction, and maintenance occupations	11.0	11.2	19.5	19.7	1.1	1.0
Farming, fishing, and forestry occupations	0.8	0.8	1.2	1.1	0.4	0.3
Construction and extraction occupations	6.3	6.6	11.4	11.9	0.4	0.4
Installation, maintenance, and repair occupations	3.9	3.8	6.9	6.7	0.3	0.3
Production, transportation, and material moving occupations	12.6	12.4	18.1	17.9	6.1	6.0
Production occupations	6.8	6.6	9.0	8.7	4.2	4.1
Transportation and material moving occupations	5.8	5.9	9.1	9.2	1.9	1.9

Percent distribution Occupation, race, and Hispanic or Latino ethnicity	Total		Men		Women	
	2003	2004	2003	2004	2003	2004
Black or African American						
Total, 16 years and over (thousands)	14,739	14,909	6,820	6,912	7,919	7,997
Percent	100.0	100.0	100.0	100.0	100.0	100.0
Management, professional, and related occupations	26.6	26.5	21.6	21.7	30.9	30.6
Management, business, and financial operations occupations	9.3	9.4	8.5	8.9	10.0	9.9
Professional and related occupations	17.3	17.0	13.2	12.8	20.9	20.7
Service occupations	23.1	23.8	19.6	20.0	26.2	27.0
Sales and office occupations	26.3	26.3	18.4	18.2	33.2	33.3
Sales and related occupations	9.6	9.6	8.4	8.4	10.7	10.6
Office and administrative support occupations	16.7	16.7	10.0	9.8	22.5	22.7
Natural resources, construction, and maintenance occupations	6.9	6.8	14.1	13.6	0.8	0.9
Farming, fishing, and forestry occupations	0.3	0.4	0.6	0.6	0.1	0.1
Construction and extraction occupations	3.9	3.8	8.2	7.9	0.2	0.3
Installation, maintenance, and repair occupations	2.7	2.6	5.3	5.1	0.4	0.5
Production, transportation, and material moving occupations	17.0	16.7	26.3	26.5	9.0	8.2
Production occupations	8.2	7.5	10.4	10.0	6.2	5.4
Transportation and material moving occupations	8.8	9.2	15.9	16.5	2.7	2.8

NOTE: Estimates for the above race groups (white, black or African American, and Asian) do not sum to totals because data are not presented for all races. In addition, persons whose ethnicity is identified as Hispanic or Latino may be of any race and therefore are classified by ethnicity as well as by race. Beginning in January 2004, data reflect revised population controls used in the household survey.

SOURCE: Bureau of Labor Statistics: http://www.bls.gov/cps/cpsaat10.pdf

Appendix I: Number of State, Federal, and Privately Operated Correctional Facilities, 2000

Characteristics	Federal	State	Private
Number of Facilities			
Total (1,668)	84 (5%)	1,320 (79%)	264 (16%)
Maximum security	11	317	4
Medium	29	428	65
Minimum	44	575	195
Daily Population			
Under 250	2	469	175
250–749	10	304	46
750–1,449	49	339	33
1,500 or more	23	208	10
Capacity			
Total%	83,113	1,090,225	105,133
Occupied	134	101	89
Staff			
All	32,700	372,976	24,357
Custody	12,376	243,352	14,589
Inmate/Staff Ratio			
All	2.5/1	2.5/1	4/1
Custody	7/1	4/1	7/1

SOURCE: Harrison and Beck (2004).

NOTE: The total figure represents 204 more facilities than a decade ago in 1995.

Appendix J: Probability of Incarceration

Probability of Incarceration for Women

---

11 out of every 1,000 women will be incarcerated in their lifetimes:

5 out of every 1,000 white women

36 out of every 1,000 African American women

Probability of Incarceration for Men

---

90 out of every 1,000 men will be incarcerated in their lifetimes:

44 out of every 1,000 white men

285 out of every 1,000 African American men

SOURCE: Harrison and Beck (2004).

Appendix K: Number of Sentenced Prisoners Under State or Federal Jurisdiction per 100,000 Residents, by Gender, Race, Hispanic Origin, and Age, 2003

| | Males | | | | Females | | | |
	Total	White	Black	Hispanic	Total	White	Black	Hispanic
Total	915	465	3,405	1,231	62	38	185	84
18–19	597	266	2,068	692	28	15	80	39
20–24	1,996	932	7,017	2,267	112	71	286	138
25–29	2,380	1,090	9,262	2,592	147	99	406	152
30–34	2,074	1,042	7,847	2,440	164	109	456	181
35–39	1,895	1,017	6,952	2,226	170	106	491	209
40–44	1,584	873	5,854	1,995	133	82	386	192
45–54	899	501	3,500	1,329	60	36	190	97
55+	208	141	747	397	8	5	22	16

SOURCE: Harrison and Beck (2004).

Appendix L: Counties With 21% or More of Their Population Incarcerated

21 Counties Have 21% or More of their Population Incarcerated

% Population Incarcerated

- 35%, Crowley, CO
- 33%, West Feliciana, LA
- 33%, Concho, TX
- 30%, Union, FL
- 28%, Brown, IL
- 27%, Lake, TN
- 26%, Mitchell, TX
- 26%, Greensville, VA
- 25%, Lassen, CA
- 25%, Anderson, TX
- 24%, Hartley, TX
- 23%, Walker, TX
- 23%, Jones, TX
- 23%, DeKalb, MO
- 22%, Karnes, TX
- 22%, Childress, TX
- 22%, Bee, TX
- 21%, Pershing, NV
- 21%, Madison, TX
- 21%, Lincoln, AR
- 21%, Johnson, IL

PrisonersoftheCensus.org

County	State	Census 2000 Population	Percent Population Incarcerated
Crowley	CO	5,518	35
West Feliciana	LA	15,111	33
Concho	TX	3,966	33
Union	FL	13,442	30
Brown	IL	6,950	28
Lake	TN	7,954	27
Mitchell	TX	9,698	26
Greensville	VA	11,560	26
Lassen	CA	33,828	25
Anderson	TX	55,109	25
Hartley	TX	5,537	24
DeKalb	MO	11,597	23
Jones	TX	20,785	23
Walker	TX	61,758	23
Childress	TX	7,688	22
Karnes	TX	15,446	22
Bee	TX	32,359	22
Lincoln	AR	14,492	21
Johnson	IL	12,878	21
Pershing	NV	6,693	21
Madison	TX	12,940	21

SOURCE: Reprinted with permission of Rose Heyer and Prison Policy Initiative, www .prisonpolicy.org.

References

Adelman, M., & Morgan, P. (2006). Law enforcement versus battered women: The conflict over the Lautenberg Amendment. *Affilia, 21*(1), 28–45.

Adelman, R. (2001). *Beyond the ghetto: The black middle class and neighborhood attainment.* Albany: SUNY Press.

Alan Guttmacher Institute. (1994). *Sex and America's teenagers.* New York: Author.

Alan Guttmacher Institute. (1996). *International comparisons of teen pregnancy rates.* New York: Author.

Alan Guttmacher Institute. (2004). *U.S. teenage pregnancy statistics: Overall trends, trends by race and ethnicity and state-by-state information.* New York: Author.

Altman, L. K. (2004, February 11). New H.I.V. test identifies cases in college students. *New York Times,* p. 18.

American Cancer Society. (2006). *Cancer facts & figures for African Americans, 2005–2006.* Retrieved from: http://www.cancer.org/docroot/stt/stt_0.asp

Amott, T. L., & Matthaei, J. A. (1991). *Race, gender, and work: A multicultural economic history of women in the United States.* Boston: South End Press.

Anderson, E. (1990). *Streetwise: Race, class, and change in an urban community.* Chicago: University of Chicago Press.

Anderson, S., Cavanagh, J., Hartman, C., & Leondar-Wright, B. (2001). *Executive excess 2001: Layoffs, tax rebates and the gender gap.* Washington, DC: Institute for Policy Studies and United for a Fair Economy.

Apel, D. (2004). *Imagery of lynching: Black men, white women, and the mob.* New Brunswick, NJ: Rutgers University Press.

Arias, E. (2002). *United States life tables, 2002* (National Vital Statistics Reports). Atlanta, GA: Centers for Disease Control and Prevention. Retrieved from: http://www.cdc.gov/nchs/data/nvsr/nvsr53/nvsr53_06.pdf

Bach, P. B., Pham, H. H., Schrag, D., Tate, R. C., & Hargraves, J. L. (2004). Primary care physicians who treat blacks and whites. *New England Journal of Medicine, 351*(6), 575–584.

Baldwin, J. (1971). An open letter to my sister Angela Davis. In A. Y. Davis, R. Magee, the Soledad Brothers, & Other Political Prisoners (Ed.), *If they come in the morning: Voices of resistance* (pp. 19–23). New York: Third Press.

Baltzell, E. D. (1964). *The Protestant establishment: Aristocracy & caste in America.* New York: Random House.

Banfield, E. C. (1970). *The unheavenly city: The nature and future of our urban crisis*. Boston: Little, Brown.

Barnett, E. C. (2002). Starbucks admits its contractor uses prison labor. *Michigan Citizen, 24*(14), A7.

Barnshaw, J. (2005, April). *The low down on the down low: Critical intersections in risk among the men who have sex with men (MSM) community*. Paper presented at the annual meeting of the Southern Sociological Society, Charlotte, NC.

Barry, J. M. (1997). *Rising tide: The great Mississippi flood of 1927 and how it changed America*. New York: Simon & Schuster.

Becker, G. S. (1975). *Human capital: A theoretical and empirical analysis, with special reference to education* (2nd ed.). New York: National Bureau of Economic Research.

Begos, K., & Railey, J. (2002, December 9). Sign this or else: A young woman made a hard choice, and life has not been peaceful since. *Winston–Salem Journal*, p. 1.

Bennett, C. L., Horner, R. D., Weinstein, R. A., Dickenson, G. M., Dehovitz, J. A., Cohn, S. E., Kessler, H. A., Jacobson, J., Goetz, M. B., Simberkoff, M., Pitrak, D., George, W. L., Gilman, S. C., & Shapiro, M. F. (1995). Racial differences in care among hospitalized patients with pneymocystis carinii pneumonia in Chicago, New York, Los Angeles, Miami, and Raleigh-Durham. *Archives of Internal Medicine, 158*, 2085–2090.

Bennett, L., Jr. (1987). *Before the Mayflower: A history of black America, 1619–1962* (6th ed.). Chicago: Johnson.

Bertrand, M., & Mullainathan, S. (2003). *Are Emily and Greg more employable than Lakisha and Jamal? A field experiment on labor market discrimination*. MIT Department of Economics Working Paper No. 03–22 and NBER Working Paper #9873.

Blassingame, J. (1979). *The slave community*. New York: Oxford University Press.

Blau, F. (1990). Black-white differences in wealth and asset composition. *Quarterly Journal of Economics, 105*(2), 321–339.

Block, F., Korteweg, A. C., & Woodward, K., with Schiller, Z., & Mazid, I. (2006). The compassion gap in American poverty policy. *Contexts, 5*(2), 14–20.

Bloom, B., & Steinhart, D. (1993). *Why punish the children? A reappraisal of the children of incarcerated mothers in America*. San Francisco: National Council on Crime and Delinquency.

Bocian, D. G., Ernst, K. S., & Wei, L. (2006). *Unfair lending: The effect of race and ethnicity on the price of subprime mortgages* [Report]. Durham, NC: Center for Responsible Lending.

Boger, J. C., & Orfield, G. (2005). *School resegregation: Must the South turn back?* Chapel Hill: University of North Carolina Press.

Bogle, D. (1973). *Toms, coons, mulattoes, mammies, and bucks: An interpretive history of blacks in American films*. New York: Viking Press.

Bonilla-Silva, E. (2001). *White supremacy and racism in the post–civil rights era*. Denver, CO: Lynne Reinner.

Bonilla-Silva, E. (2003). *Racism without racists: Color-blind racism and the persistence of racial inequality in the United States*. Lanham, MD: Rowman & Littlefield.

Bowen, W. G., & Bok, D. (1998). *The shape of the river*. Princeton, NJ: Princeton University Press.

Boyer, D., & Fine, D. (1992). Sexual abuse as a factor in adolescent pregnancy and child maltreatment. *Family Planning Perspectives, 24,* 11–19.

Brady, E. (2006, April 7). Duke lacrosse allegations fit mold. *USA Today*, p. 10-C.

Bragg, R. (1999). Jasper trial defendant says Byrd's throat was cut. *San Antonio Express-News*, p. 1A.

Britton, D. (2004). When sameness is difference: Prisons, gender and justice. *Women, Girls & Criminal Justice, 5*(6), 69–84.

Brooks, D. (2006, January 1). The year of domesticity. *New York Times*, p. A10.

Browne, A. (1987). *When battered women kill*. New York: Free Press.

Brownmiller, S. (1975). *Against our will: Men, women, and rape*. New York: Simon & Schuster.

Brush, L. D. (2001). Poverty, battering, race, and welfare reform: Black-white differences in women's welfare-to-work transitions. *Journal of Poverty, 5,* 67–89.

Brush, L. D., Raphael, J., & Tolman, R. (2003). Effects of work on hitting and hurting. *Violence Against Women, 9*(10), 1213–1230.

Bryant, Z., & Coleman, M. (1988). The black family as portrayed in introductory marriage and family textbooks. *Family Relations, 37*(3), 255–259.

Bullard, R. D. (1990). *Dumping in Dixie: Race, class, and environmental quality*. Boulder, CO: Westview.

Bumpass, L., & Sweet, J. (1989). Children's experience in single-parent families: Implications of cohabitation and marital transitions. *Family Planning Perspectives, 21*(6), 256–260.

Buncombe, A. (2005, September 16). US poultry giant under fire after segregation scandal is revealed. *The Independent* (London), p. 29.

Bureau of Justice Statistics. (1995). *Special report: Violence against women: Estimates from the redesigned survey* (No. NCJ-154348). Washington, DC: Author.

Bureau of Justice Statistics. (2003a). *Intimate partner violence, 1993–2001*. Washington, DC: Author.

Bureau of Justice Statistics. (2003b). *Percent distribution of single-offender victimizations, based on race of victims, by type of crime and perceived race of offender* (Table 42). Washington, DC: Author. Retrieved from: http://www.ojp.usdoj.gov/bjs/pub/sheets/cvsprshts.htm

Bureau of Justice Statistics. (2004). *Census of fatal occupational injuries*. Washington, DC: Author.

Bureau of Justice Statistics. (n.d.). *Criminal offenders statistics*. Retrieved from: http://www.ojp.usdoj.gov/bjs/crimoff.htm

Bureau of Labor Statistics. (2005a). *Employment and unemployment by race and gender*. Washington, DC: Bureau of Labor Statistics.

Bureau of Labor Statistics. (2005b). *Occupational segregation by race*. Washington, DC: Author. Retrieved from: http://www.bls.gov/Table 10

Bureau of Labor Statistics. (2005c). *Occupations by sex*. Washington, DC: Author. Retrieved from: http://www.bls.gov/Table 9

Burton, L. M. (1990). Teenage childbearing as an alternative life-course strategy in multigeneration black families. *Human Nature, 1*(2), 123–143.

Butterfield, F. (2004, May 8). Mistreatment of prisoners is called routine in U.S. *New York Times.* Retrieved from: http://www.nytimes.com/2004/05/08/national/ 08PRIS.html?ex=1399348800&en=bea18d005140f198&ei=5007&partner= USERLAND

Callis, R. R., & Cavanaugh, L. B. (2006). *Census Bureau reports on residential vacancies and homeownership.* Washington, DC: U.S. Census Bureau.

Cameron, S. V., & Heckman, J. (1993). *Determinants of young male schooling and training choices* (NBER Working Paper No. 4327): Cambridge, MA: National Bureau of Economic Research.

Campbell, D. W., Sharps, P. W., Gary, F. A., Campbell, J. C., & Lopez, L. M. (2002). Intimate partner violence in African American women. *Online Journal of Issues in Nursing, 7*(1), 5.

Carlos, E., & Chamberlain, R. (2004). The black–white perception gap and health disparities. *Public Health Nursing, 21,* 372–379.

Carlson, M., Garfinkel, I., McLanahan, S., Mincy, R., & Primus, W. (2004). The effects of welfare and child support policies on union formation. *Population Research and Policy Review, 23,* 513–542.

Carpusor, A., & Loges, W. E. (2006). Rental discrimination and ethnicity in names. *Journal of Applied Social Psychology, 36*(4), 934–952.

Carter, J. (n.d.). Quote retrieved from: http://www.quotationspage.com/quote/ 33341.html

Cass, J. (2006, February 25). Notable Mardi Gras absences reflect loss of black middle class. *Washington Post,* p. A01.

Centers for Disease Control and Prevention. (2000). National and state-specific pregnancy rates among adolescents—United States, 1995–1997. *Morbidity and Mortality Weekly Report, 49*(27), 605–611.

Centers for Disease Control and Prevention. (2003). *National diabetes fact sheet.* Atlanta, GA: Author.

Centers for Disease Control and Prevention. (2004a). Diagnoses of HIV/AIDS—32 states, 2000–2003. *Morbidity and Mortality Weekly Report, 53,* 1106–1110.

Centers for Disease Control and Prevention. (2004b). *2004 surveillance report.* Atlanta, GA: Author.

Centers for Disease Control and Prevention. (2006). *National program of cancer registries fact sheet.* Atlanta, GA: Author.

Changing Face of AIDS, The. (1996). *New York Times,* p. A10.

Chasin, B. (2004). *Inequality & violence in the United States: Casualties of capitalism* (2nd ed.). Amherst, NY: Humanity Books.

Chasnoff, I. J., Landress, H. J., & Barrett, M. E. (1990). The prevalence of illicit-drug or alcohol use during pregnancy and discrepancies in mandatory reporting in Pinellas County, Florida. *New England Journal of Medicine, 322,* 1202–1206.

Chesney-Lind, M. (1998). Women in prison: From partial justice to vengeful equity. *Corrections Today, 60,* 66–73.

Chesney-Lind, M. (2002). Imprisoning women: The unintended victims of mass imprisonment. In M. Mauer & M. Chesney-Lind (Eds.), *Invisible punishment:*

The collateral consequences of mass imprisonment (pp. 78–94). New York: The New Press.

Clark, K. B. (1989). *Dark ghetto: Dilemmas of social power* (2nd ed.). New York: Harper & Row and Wesleyan University Press. (Originally published in 1965)

Clemetson, L. (2004, August 6). Links between prison and AIDS affecting blacks inside and out. *New York Times*. Retrieved from: http://www.nytimes.com/2004/08/06/national/06aids.html?ex=1249444800&en=46c1febaf511c11e&ei=5090&partner=rssuserland

Cohen, C. J. (1999). *The boundaries of blackness : AIDS and the breakdown of black politics*. Chicago: University of Chicago Press.

Cohen, P. N. (1999). *Racial-ethnic and gender differences in returns to cohabitation and marriage: Evidence from the Current Population Survey*. Washington, DC: U.S. Bureau of the Census, Population Division.

Collins, K. S., Hall, A. G., & Neuhaus, C. (1999). *U.S. minority health: A chartbook*. New York: The Commonwealth Fund.

Committee on Ways and Means, Subcommittee on Human Resources. (2006). *A decade since welfare reform: 1996 welfare reforms reduce welfare dependence*. Washington, DC: Author.

Congressional Budget Office. (1990). *Sources of support for adolescent mothers*. Washington, DC: Author.

Conley, D. (1999). *Being black, living in the red: Race, wealth, and social policy in America*. Berkeley: University of California Press.

Conley, D. (2001). The black-white wealth gap. *The Nation, 272*, 20–22.

Conner, D. F. (2003). *Aggression and antisocial behavior in children and adolescents: Research and treatment*. New York: Guilford.

Constantine-Simms, D. (2001). *The greatest taboo: Homosexuality in black communities*. Los Angeles: Alyson Books.

Coontz, S. (1992). *The way we never were: American families and the nostalgia trap*. New York: Basic Books.

Coontz, S. (1997). *The way we really are: Coming to terms with America's changing families*. New York: Basic Books.

Corbie-Smith, G., Thomas, S. B., Williams, M. V., & Moody-Ayers, S. (1999). Attitudes and beliefs of African Americans toward participation in medical research. *Journal of General Internal Medicine, 14*(9), 537–543.

Cosby, B. (2004, July 29). Bill Cosby has more harsh words for black community. *USA Today*. Retrieved from: http://www.usatoday.com/life/people/2004-07-29-cosby_x.htm?POE=LIFISVA

Cose, E. (2000, November 13). The prison paradox. *Newsweek, 136*, 40–49.

Crenshaw, K. (1995). *Critical race theory: The key writings that formed the movement*. New York: New Press.

Crompton, V., & Kessner, E. Z. (2003). *Saving Beauty from the Beast*. New York: Little, Brown.

Current Population Survey. (2004). Welfare receipt by race. Retrieved from: http://pubdb3.census.gov/macro/032004/pov/new26_001.htm

Darity, W., Jr., Dietrich, J., & Guilkey, D. K. (2001). Persistent advantage or disadvantage? Evidence in support of the intergenerational drag hypothesis. *American Journal of Economics and Sociology, 60*(2), 435–470.

Dash, L. (2003). *When children want children: The urban crisis of teenage childbearing.* Urbana: University of Illinois Press.

Daumit, G. L., Hermann, J. A., Coresh, J., & Powe, N. R. (1999). Use of cardiovascular procedures among black persons and white persons: A 7-year nationwide study in patients with renal disease. *Annals of Internal Medicine, 130,* 173–182.

Davis, A. Y. (1983). *Women, race, and class.* New York: Vintage.

Davis, A. Y. (1998, September 1). Masked racism: Reflections on the prison industrial complex. *Colorlines Magazine,* pp. 1–6.

Davis, A. Y. (2003). *Are prisons obsolete?* New York: Seven Stories Press.

Davis, D. B. (1966). *The problem of slavery in Western culture.* Ithaca, NY: Cornell University Press.

de Tocqueville, A. (1833). *On the penitentiary system in the United States.* Philadelphia, PA: Carey, Lee and Blanchard.

Deaver, D., & Ingram, D. (2004, May 5). Minorities have less access to health care, study finds disparities were caused by discrimination, official says. *Winston-Salem Journal.* Retrieved from: http://www.journalnow.com/servlet/Satellite?pagename=WSJ/MGArticle/WSJ_BasicArticle&c=MGArticle&cid=1031775270898&path=!localnews&s=1037645509099

Delgado, R., & Stefancic, J. (2001). *Critical race theory: An introduction.* New York: New York University Press.

DeNavas-Walt, C., Proctor, B. D., & Mills, R. J. (2004). *Income, poverty, and health insurance coverage in the United States: 2003.* Washington, DC: Current Population Survey.

Dickerson, B. (1995). *African American single mothers: Understanding their lives and families.* Thousand Oaks, CA: Sage.

Doherty, W. J., Boss, P. G., LaRossa, R., Schumm, W. R., & Steinmetz, S. K. (1993). Family theories and methods: A contextual approach. In W. J. Doherty, P. G. Boss, R. LaRossa, W. R. Schumm, & S. K. Steinmetz (Eds.), *Sourcebook of family theories and methods: A contextual approach,* pp. 3–31. New York: Plenum.

Douglas, D. M. (1995). *Reading, writing, & race: The desegregation of the Charlotte schools.* Chapel Hill: University of North Carolina Press.

Doyle, L. (1999). *The surrendered wife: A practical guide to finding intimacy, passion, and peace with your man.* New York: Fireside.

Du Bois, W.E.B. (1903). *Souls of black folk.* New York: Kraus Thompson Reprint.

Du Bois, W.E.B. (1908). *The Negro American family.* Proceedings of the Annual Conference on The Negro Problems, Atlanta University.

Du Bois, W.E.B. (1909). *The Negro American family.* Atlanta, GA: Atlanta University Publications.

Du Bois, W.E.B. (1951). Preface. In H. Aptheker (Ed.), *A documentary history of the Negro people in the United States* (Vol. 1). New York: Citadel Press.

Duneier, M. (1992). *Slim's table: Race, respectability and masculinity.* Chicago: University of Chicago Press.

Durose, M. R., Harlow, C. W., Langan, P. A., Motivans, M., Rantala, R. R., & Smith, E. L. (2005). *Family violence statistics including statistics on strangers and acquaintances* (NCJ 207846). Washington, DC: Bureau of Justice Statistics.

Durose, M. R., & Langan, P. A. (2001). *State court sentencing of convicted felons, 1998 statistical tables.* Washington, DC: U.S. Department of Justice.

Dye, J. L. (2005). *Fertility of American women: June 2004* (No. P20–555). Washington DC: U.S. Census Bureau.

Edin, K., & Kefalas, M. (2005). *Promises I can keep: Why poor women put motherhood before marriage.* Berkeley: University of California Press.

Edin, K., & Lein, L. (1997). *Making ends meet: How single mothers survive welfare and low-wage work.* New York: Russell Sage Foundation.

Edney, H. (2006, March 10). *Churches step up AIDS campaign this weekend.* Retrieved from: http://www.nationalbaptist.com/index.cfm?FuseAction=Page& PageID=1000233&ArticleID=492

Ehrenreich, B. (2001). *Nickel and dimed: On (not) getting by in America.* New York: Owl Books.

Ehrensaft, M. K., Cohen, P., Brown, J., Smailes, E., Chen, H., & Johnson, J. G. (2003). Intergenerational transmission of partner violence: A 20-year prospective study. *Journal of Consulting and Clinical Psychology, 71*(4), 741–753.

Ellis, B. J., Bates, J. E., Dodge, K. A., Fergusson, D. M., Horwood, L. J., Pettit, G. S., & Woodward, L. (2003). Does father absence place daughters at special risk for early sexual activity and teenage pregnancy? *Child Development, 74,* 801–821.

Elsner, A. (2006). *Gates of injustice: The crisis in America's prisons.* New York: Prentice Hall.

Engels, F., & Leacock, E. B. (1972). *The origin of the family, private property, and the state.* New York: International Publishers. (Originally published in 1884)

Epstein, A. M. (2004). Health care in America: Still too separate, not yet equal. *New England Journal of Medicine, 351,* 603–605.

Evans, L. (2005). Playing global cop: U.S. militarism and the prison industrial complex. In J. Sudbury (Ed.), *Global lockdown: Race, gender, and the prison-industrial complex* (pp. 215–227). New York: Routledge.

Fallon requests info on jobs lost to prison labor, clarifies "gulag" remark. Entry by Linda Thieman at 10:28AM (CDT) on June 30, 2004; see http://www.blogfori owa.com/blog

Feagin, J. R. (1999). Excluding blacks and others from housing: The foundation of white racism. *Cityscape: A Journal of Policy Development and Research, 4*(3), 70–91.

Fehr, H., Jokisch, S., & Kotlikoff, L. (2003). *The developed world's demographic transition: The roles of capital flows, immigration, and policy.* (NBER Working Paper 10096). Cambridge, MA: National Bureau of Economic Research

Fisher, B. S., Cullen, F. T., & Turner, M. G. (2000). *The sexual victimization of college women.* Washington, DC: Bureau of Justice Statistics.

Flanagan, T. (1980). Time served and institutional misconduct: Patterns of involvement in disciplinary infractions among long-term and short-term inmates. *Journal of Criminal Justice, 8,* 357–367.

Flegal, K. M., Carroll, M. D., Ogden, C. L., & Johnson, C. L. (2002). Prevalence and trends in obesity among US adults, 1999–2000. *Journal of the American Medical Association, 288,* 1723–1727.

Fogel, C. (1993). Hard time: The stressful nature of incarceration for women. *Issues in Mental Health Nursing, 14,* 367–377.

Fogel, C., & Martin, S. (1992). The mental health of incarcerated women. *Western Journal of Nursing Research, 14,* 30–47.

Fogel, R. W., & Engerman, S. L. (1974). *Time on the cross: The economics of American Negro slavery.* Boston: Little, Brown.

Franklin, D. L. (1997). *Ensuring inequality: The structural transformation of the African American family.* Oxford, UK: Oxford University Press.

Franklin, J. H. (2005). *Mirror to America: The autobiography of John Hope Franklin.* New York: Farrar, Straus and Giroux.

Frazier, E. F. (1932). *The Negro family in Chicago.* Chicago: University of Chicago Press.

Frazier, E. F. (1939). *The Negro family in the United States.* Chicago: University of Chicago Press.

Frazier, E. F. (1957). *The Negro middle class and desegregation.* Indianapolis, IN: Bobbs-Merrill.

Friedmann, H. (1980). Plantation societies, race relations, and the South: The regimentation of populations. *Comparative Studies in Society and History, 22*(4), 639–652.

Gates, H. L., Jr. (2004, August 1). Breaking the silence. *New York Times.* Retrieved from: http://www.nytimes.com/2004/08/01/opinion/01gates.html?ex=12490 99200&en=7d01ef033fbbc032&ei=5090&partner=rssuserland

Gelles, R. J. (1974). *The violent home.* Beverly Hills, CA: Sage.

Gelles, R. J. (1997). *Intimate violence in families* (3rd ed.). Thousand Oaks, CA: Sage.

Gelles, R. J., & Straus, M. A. (1988). *Intimate violence.* New York: Simon & Schuster.

Gillette, B. (2004, August 2). Profitability remains elusive for Mississippi catfish farmers. *Mississippi Business Journal.* Retrieved from: http://www.allbusiness.com/north-america/united-states-mississippi/932492-1.html

Glassner, B. (2000). *The culture of fear: Why Americans are afraid of the wrong things.* New York: Basic Books.

Goffman, E. (1961). *Asylums: Essays on the social situation of mental patients and other inmates.* New York: Doubleday Anchor.

Gordon, L. (1988). *Heroes of their own lives: The politics and history of family violence.* New York: Penguin.

Gossett, T. (1963). *Race: The history of an idea in America.* Dallas, TX: Southern Methodist University Press.

Green, M. Y. (2002). *Minorities as majority: Disproportionality in child welfare and juvenile justice.* Washington, DC: Child Welfare League of America.

Greene, J. P., & Winters, M. A. (2005). *Public high school graduation and college-readiness rates: 1991–2002* (Education Working Paper No. 8). New York: Manhattan Institute for Policy Research.

Greene, J. P., Winters, M. A., & Manhattan Institute for Policy Research. (2005). *Public high school graduation and college-readiness rates, 1991–2002.* New York: Manhattan Institute for Policy Research, Center for Civic Innovation.

Greenfeld, L., & Snell, T. L. (1999). *Women offenders.* Washington, DC: Bureau of Justice Statistics.

Greenhouse, S. (2005, May 4). Can't Wal-Mart, a retail behemoth, pay more? *New York Times.* Available: http://www.laborrights.org/press/Wal-Mart/walmart_pay_0505.htm

Greenwood, M., & Peterson, A. (2006, July 2). Let Denton's legacy be an end to wounds from glass ceilings. *San Jose Mercury News,* p. 1B.

Gregory, P. M., Rhoads, G. G., Wilson, A. C., O'Dowd, K. J., & Kostis, J. B. (1999). Impact of availability of hospital-based invasive cardiac services on racial differences in the use of these services. *American Heart Journal, 138,* 507–517.

Gumbel, A. (2005, February 25). California jails end racial segregation. *Independent News.* Retrieved from: http://news.independent.co.uk/world/americas/article12709.ece

Gutman, H. G. (1976). *The black family in slavery and freedom, 1750–1925.* New York: Pantheon.

Haj-Yahia, M. M. (2000). Implications of wife abuse and battering for self-esteem, depression, and anxiety as revealed by the second Palestinian national survey on violence against women. *Journal of Family Issues, 21*(4), 435–463.

Hallett, M. (2004). Commerce with criminals: The new colonialism in criminal justice. *Review of Policy Research, 21*(1), 49–62.

Haney, C., & Zimbardo, P. (1998). The past and future of U.S. prison policy: Twenty-five years after the Stanford prison experiment. *American Psychologist, 53,* 709–727.

Hannan, E. L., van Ryn, M., Burke, J., Stone, D., Kumar, D., Arani, D., Pierce, W., Rafii, S., Sanborn, T. A., Sharma, S., Slater, J., & DeBuono, B. A. (1999). Access to coronary artery bypass surgery by race/ethnicity and gender among patients who are appropriate for surgery. *Medical Care, 37,* 68–77.

Harmon, A. (2005, July 25). Blacks pin hope on DNA to fill slavery's gaps in family trees. *New York Times.* Retrieved from: http://www.nytimes.com/2005/07/25/science/25genes.html?ex=1279944000&en=3c5062dc9612950a&ei=5088&partner=rssnyt&emc=rss

Harrison, P. M., & Beck, A. J. (2004). *Prisoners in 2003* (NCJ 205335). Washington, DC: Bureau of Justice Statistics.

Harrison, P. M., & Beck, A. J. (2005). *Prisoners in 2004.* Washington, DC: Bureau of Justice Statistics.

Harvey, L. K. (2002). *Domestic violence in Winston-Salem/Forsyth County: A study of domestic court cases in 2001.* Winston-Salem, NC: Winston-Salem State University, Center for Community Safety.

Hattery, A. J. (2001a). Tag-team parenting: Costs and benefits of utilizing non-overlapping shift work patterns in families with young children. *Families in Society, 82*(4), 419–427.

Hattery, A. (2001b). *Women, work, and family: Balancing and weaving.* Thousand Oaks, CA: Sage.

Hattery, A. J. (in press-a). *Intimate partner violence.* Durham, NC: Duke University Press.

Hattery, A. J. (in press-b). *Sexual abuse in childhood and adolescence and intimate partner violence in adulthood among African American and white women.*

Hattery, A. J., & Kane, E. W. (1995). Men's and women's perceptions of non-consensual sexual intercourse. *Sex Roles, 33,* 785–802.

Hattery, A. J., & Smith, E. (2004, April). *Cultural contradictions in the Southern mode of segregation: Black tits, white only water fountains, bad blood, and the transmission of semen.* Paper presented at the annual meeting of the Southern Sociological Society, Atlanta.

Hattery, A. J., & Smith, E. (in press). Social stratification in the new/old South: The influences of racial segregation on social class in the Deep South. *Journal of Poverty Research.*

Hattery, A., Smith, E., & Williams, M. (2005). *The efficacy of the Time Out intervention program in Forsyth County.* Winston-Salem, NC: Wake Forest University Press.

Hays, S. (2003). *Flat broke with children.* New York: Oxford University Press.

Herbert, B. (2005a, July 21). Education's collateral damage. *New York Times.* Retrieved from: http://www.nytimes.com/2005/07/21/opinion/21herbert.html?ex=1279598400&en=e18431d44d23fcdd&ei=5090&partner=rssuserland&emc=rss

Herbert, B. (2005b, January 7). Promoting torture's promoter. *New York Times.* Retrieved from: http://www.nytimes.com/2005/01/07/opinion/07herbert.html?ex=1262840400&en=edaebd4efd7de650&ei=5090&partner=rssuserland

Herbert, B. (2006, November 2). Punished for being female. *New York Times,* p. A27.

Heyer, R., & Wagner, P. (2004). *Too big to ignore: How counting people in prisons distorted Census 2000.* Available: http://www.prisonersofthecensus.org/toobig/toobig.html

High gas prices widen divide between rich and poor. (2005, August 15). *USA Today,* p. A12.

Hill, R. (1972). *The strengths of black families.* New York: Emerson Hall.

Hill, R. B. (1999). *The strengths of African American families: Twenty-five years later.* New York: University Press of America.

Hill, S. (2005). *Black intimacies: A gender perspective on families and relationships.* Lanham, MD: AltaMira.

Hill-Collins, P. (1994). Shifting the center: Race, class, and feminist theorizing about motherhood. In E. Glenn, G. Chang, & L. Forcey (Ed.), *Mothering: Ideology, experience, and agency* (pp. 45–66). New York: Routledge.

Hill-Collins, P. (2004). *Black sexual politics: African Americans, gender, and the new racism.* New York: Routledge.

Hirshman, L. R. (2006). *Get to work: A manifesto for women of the world.* New York: Viking.

HIV hitting blacks harder. (2006, February 7). *New York Times*. Retrieved from: http://query.nytimes.com/gst/fullpage.html?res=9407E2D6173EF934A35751C0 A9609C8B63

Hochschild, A. R., with Machung, A. (1989). *The second shift*. New York: Avon.

Hoffman, S., Foster, M., & Furstenberg, F., Jr. (1993). Reevaluating the costs of teenage childbearing. *Demography, 30*(1), 1–13.

hooks, b. (2000). *Feminist theory: From margin to center*. Cambridge, MA: South End Press.

hooks, b. (2004). *We real cool: Black men and masculinity*. New York: Routledge.

Houck, K., & Loper, A. (2002). Incarcerated mothers: Parent stress and its effect on emotional, behavioral, and physical adjustment to prison. *American Journal of Orthopsychiatry, 72*, 548–558.

Huffman, M. L., & Cohen, P. N. (2004). Racial wage inequality: Job segregation and devaluation across U.S. labor markets. *American Journal of Sociology, 109*(4), 902–936.

Hughes, E. C. (1945). Dilemmas and contradictions. *American Journal of Sociology, 50*(3), 353–359.

Insurance settlement could affect 70,000 minority policyholders in N.C. (2005, July 22). *Winston-Salem Journal*. Retrieved from: http://www.journalnow.com/servlet/Satellite?pagename=WSJ/MGArticle/WSJ_BasicArticle&c=MGArticle&cid=1149189057289

Islam-Zwart, K. A., & Vik, P. W. (2004). Female adjustment to incarceration as influenced by sexual assault history. *Criminal Justice and Behavior, 31*(5), 521–541.

Jacobson, J., & Maynard, R. (1995). *Unwed mothers and long-term welfare dependency in addressing illegitimacy: Welfare reform options for Congress*. Washington, DC: American Enterprise Institute.

Jha, A. K., Fisher, E. S., Li, Z. E., Orav, J., & Epstein, A. (2005). Racial trends in the use of major procedures among the elderly. *New England Journal of Medicine, 353*(7), 683–691.

Johnson, M. P., & Ferraro, K. J. (2000). Research on domestic violence in the 1990s: Making distinctions. *Journal of Marriage and the Family, 62*, 948–963.

Jones, J. (1981). *Bad blood: The Tuskegee syphilis experiment*. New York: Free Press.

Kaiser Foundation Family Report. (2004). New survey finds majority of African Americans say U.S. is losing ground on HIV/AIDS. Retrieved from: http://www.kff.org/newsroom/pomr080404anr.cfm

Kalmijn, M. (1993). Trends in black/white intermarriage. *Social Forces, 72*(1), 119–146.

Kane, E. (2006). No way my boys are going to be like that: Parents' responses to children's gender nonconformity. *Gender & Society, 20*, 149–176.

Karabel, J. (2005). *The chosen*. Boston: Houghton Mifflin.

Karger, H. (2005). *Shortchanged: Life and debt in the fringe economy*. San Francisco: Berrett-Koehler.

Kasarda, J. D. (1993). Inner-city concentrated poverty and neighborhood distress: 1970–1990. *Housing Policy Debate, 4*, 253–302.

Katz, J. (2006). *The macho paradox: Why some men hurt women and how all men can help*. Napierville, IL: Sourcebooks.

Kerber, L. K. (1997). The meanings of citizenship. *Journal of American History, 84*(3), 833–854.

Kiecolt, K. J., & Fossett, M. A. (1995). Mate availability and marriage among African Americans: Aggregate and individual level analyses. In C. Mitchell-Kernan (Ed.), *The decline in marriage among African Americans: Causes, consequences, and policy implications* (pp. 121–135). New York: Russell Sage Foundation.

Kimmel, M. (1995). *Manhood in America: A cultural history.* New York: Free Press.

Kimmel, M. (2005). *Manhood in America.* New York: Oxford University Press.

King, D. (1988). Multiple jeopardy, multiple consciousness: The context of a black feminist ideology. *Signs, 14*(1), 88–111.

King, J. L. (2004). *On the down low: A journey into the lives of straight black men who sleep with men.* New York: Broadway Books.

King, R. S., & Mauer, M. (2006). *Sentencing with discretion: Crack cocaine sentencing after Booker.* New York: The Sentencing Project.

Kirkwood, C. (1993). *Leaving abusive partners.* London: Sage.

Kleinfield, N. R. (2006, January 10). Bad blood: Living at an epicenter of diabetes, defiance and despair. *New York Times.* Retrieved from: http://www.nytimes .com/2006/01/10/nyregion/nyregionspecial5/10diabetes.html?ex=1294549200& en=cf246432b2690608&ei=5090

Koss, M. P. (1985). The hidden rape victim: Personality, attitudinal, and situational characteristics. *Psychology of Women Quarterly, 9,* 193–212.

Koss, M. P., Goodman, L. A., Browne, A., Fitzgerald, L. F., Keita, G. P., & Russo, N. F. (1994). *No safe haven: Male violence against women at home, at work, and in the community.* Washington, DC: American Psychological Association.

Kozol, J. (1992). *Savage inequalities: Children in America's schools.* New York: Harper Perennial.

Kozol, J. (2001). *Ordinary resurrections: Children in the years of hope.* New York: Harper Perennial.

Kozol, J. (2005). *The shame of the nation: The restoration of apartheid schooling in America.* New York: Crown.

Kristof, N. D. (2004, September 29). Sentenced to be raped. *New York Times.* Retrieved from: http://www.nytimes.com/2004/09/29/opinion/29kris.html?ex= 1254196800&en=6d572065ccbf6045&ei=5088&partner=rssnyt

LaFree, G., & Drass, K.A. (1996). The effect of changes in intraracial income inequality and educational attainment on changes in arrest rates for African Americans and whites 1957–1990. *American Sociological Review, 61,* 614–634.

Lapchick, R. (2006, January 26). *Decisions from the top: Diversity among campus, conference leaders at Division IA institutions.* University of Central Florida, DeVos Sport Business Management Program. Retrieved from: www.bus .ucf.edu/sport/public/downloads/2006_Demograhpic_release.pdf

Lawless, E. J. (2001). *Women escaping violence: Empowerment through narrative.* Columbia: University of Missouri Press.

LeBlanc, A. N. (2003, January 12). Prison is a member of their family. *New York Times Magazine.* Retrieved from: http://select.nytimes.com/search/restricted/ article?res=F30A10F73E5A0C718DDDA80894DB404482

Lenski, G. (1984). *Power and privilege: A theory of social stratification*. Chapel Hill: University of North Carolina Press.

Leone, J. M. (2004). Assessment of family violence: A handbook for researchers and practitioners. *Journal of Marriage and the Family, 66*, 261–262.

Lerner, S., & Bullard, R. L. (2006). *Diamond: A struggle for environmental justice in Louisiana's chemical corridor*. Cambridge: MIT Press.

Lichtblau, E. (2005, August 24). Profiling report leads to a clash and a demotion. *New York Times*, p. A14.

Lieber, J. (2003). Golf's host clubs have open-and-shut policies on discrimination. *USA Today*. Retrieved from: http://www.usatoday.com/sports/golf/2003-04-09-club-policies_x.htm

Liebow, E. (2003). *Tally's corner: A study of Negro streetcorner men*. New York: Rowman & Littlefield. (Originally published in 1967)

Liptak, A. (2004, April 19). Study suspects thousands of false convictions. *New York Times*. Retrieved from: http://select.nytimes.com/search/restricted/article?res=F30F15FE3A5F0C7A8DDDAD0894DC404482

Liptak, A. (2006, March 2). Prisons often shackle pregnant inmates in labor. *New York Times*. Retrieved from: http://www.nytimes.com/2006/03/02/national/02shackles.html?ex=1164430800&en=3e63bb8cfc7d0f0b&ei=5070

Livingston, I. L. (1985). The importance of socio-psychological stress in the interpretation of the race-hypertension association. *Humanity & Society, 9*(2), 168–181.

Lyke, M. L. (2003, March 6). If mom's locked up, kids are more likely to follow. *Seattle Post-Intelligencer*. Retrieved from: http://seattlepi.nwsource.com/local/111236_2kids06.shtml

MacKenzie, D., & Goodstein, L. (1985). Long-term incarceration impacts and characteristics of long-term offenders. *Criminal Justice and Behavior, 12*, 395–414.

MacKenzie, D., Robinson, J., & Campbell, C. (1989). Long-term incarceration of female offenders: Prison adjustment and coping. *Criminal Justice and Behavior, 16*, 223–238.

MacKinnon, C. (1991). *Toward a feminist theory of the state*. Cambridge, MA: Harvard University Press.

Majors, R., & Bilson, J. (1992). *Cool pose: The dilemmas of African American manhood in America*. New York: Lexington Books.

Marable, M. (2005). Beyond brown. *The Black Scholar, 35*(2), 11–21.

Martin, J. A., Hamilton, B. E., Sutton, P. D., Ventura, S. J., Menacker, F., & Munson, M. L. (2002). *Births: Final data for 2002* (National Vital Statistics Report No. 52(10)). Hyattsville, MD: National Center for Health Statistics.

Massey, D. (2005). Racial discrimination in housing: A moving target. *Social Problems, 52*(2), 148–151.

Massey, D. S., & Denton, N. A. (1993). *American apartheid: Segregation and the making of the underclass*. Cambridge, MA: Harvard University Press.

Matteo, S. (1988). The risk of multiple addictions guidelines for assessing a woman's alcohol and drug use. *Western Journal of Medicine, 149*, 741–745.

Mauer, M. (2001). *Race to incarcerate*. New York: New Press.

Mauer, M. (2002). Race, poverty and felon disenfranchisement. *Poverty and Race Research Council, 11*(4), 1–2.

Mauer, M. (2003). *Comparative international rates of incarceration: An examination of causes and trends.* Presentation to the U.S. Commission on Civil Rights. New York: The Sentencing Project.

Mauer, M., & Chesney-Lind, M. (2002). *Invisible punishment.* New York: New Press.

Maume, D. J. (1999). Glass ceilings and glass escalators: Occupational segregation and race and sex differences in managerial promotions. *Work and Occupations, 26*(4), 483–509.

Maynard, R. A. (1996). *Kids having kids: Economic costs and social consequences of teen pregnancy.* Washington, DC: Urban Institute Press.

Maynard, R. (1997). *Teenage childbearing and welfare reform: Lessons from a decade of demonstration and evaluation research.* Washington, DC: U.S. House of Representatives, summarized from a statement for the Committee on Ways and Means, Subcommittee on Human Resources.

Maynard, R., Nicholson, W., & Rangarajan, A. (1993). *Breaking the cycle of poverty: The effectiveness of mandatory services for welfare-dependent teenage parents.* Princeton, NJ: Mathematica Policy Research.

McCorkel, J. A. (1998). Going to the crackhouse: Critical space as a form of resistance in total institutions and everyday life. *Symbolic Interaction, 21*(3), 227–253.

McCurdy, J. (1990, April 25). Claremont to appeal: Cal. jury awards $1-million to teacher denied tenure for race. *Chronicle of Higher Education.* Retrieved from: http://chronicle.com/che-data/articles.dir/articles-36.dir/issue-32.dir/32a 01101.htm

McLanahan, S. (1985). Family structure and the reproduction of poverty. *American Journal of Sociology, 90,* 873–901.

McLanahan, S., & Sandefur, G. D. (1994). *Growing up with a single parent: What hurts, what helps.* Cambridge, MA: Harvard University Press.

Meierhoefer, B. S. (1992). *The general effect of mandatory minimum prison terms: A longitudinal study of federal sentences imposed.* Washington, DC: Federal Judicial Center.

Merton, R. K. (1972). Insiders and outsiders: A chapter in the sociology of knowledge. *American Journal of Sociology, 78*(1), 9–47.

Messner, M. A. (2002). Playing center: The triad of violence in men's sports. In M. A. Messner (Ed.), *Taking the field: Women, men and sports* (pp. 27–62). Minneapolis: University of Minnesota Press.

Moffitt, R. A. (1997). *The effect of welfare on marriage and fertility: What do we know and what do we need to know?* (No. 1153–97). Madison, WI: Institute for Research on Poverty.

Moore, K. A., Myers, D., Morrison, D. R., Nord, C., Brown, B., & Edmonston, B. (1993). Age at first childbirth and later poverty. *Journal of Research on Adolescence, 3*(4), 393–422.

Moore, K., Papillo, A., & Manlove, J. (2003). *Release of facts at a glance 2003: Reporting trends in teen childbearing in the nation, states and large cities.* Washington, DC: Child Trends.

Moore, R. D., Stanton, D., Gopalan, R., & Chaisson, R. E. (1994). Racial differences in the use of drug therapy for HIV disease in an urban community. *New England Journal of Medicine, 330*(11), 763–768.

Moynihan, D. (1965). *The Negro family: The case for national action.* Washington, DC: U.S. Department of Labor, Office of Policy Planning and Research.

Moynihan, D. P. (1985). *Family and nation.* New York: Harcourt Brace Jovanovich.

Mueller, S., & Dudley, S. (2003). *Access to abortion fact sheet.* National Abortion Federation. Retrieved from: http://www.prochoice.org/about_abortion/facts/access_abortion.html

Mukamal, D. (2004). *After prisons: Roadblocks to reentry: A report on state legal barriers facing people with criminal records.* New York: Legal Action Center.

Mumola, C. M. (2000). *Incarcerated parents and their children* (NCJ 182335). Washington, DC: Bureau of Justice Statistics.

Murdock, G. P. (1983). *The outline of world cultures.* New Haven, CT: Human Relations Area Files. (Originally published in 1954)

Murnane, R. J., Willett, J. B., & Boudett, K. P. (1995). Do high school dropouts benefit from obtaining a GED? *Educational Evaluation and Policy Analysis, 17*(2), 133–147.

Myers, M. A. (1990). Black threat and incarceration in postbellum Georgia. *Social Forces, 69*(2), 373393.

National Center for Health Statistics. (2004). *Health, United States, with chartbook on trends in the health of Americans.* Retrieved from: http://www.cdc.gov/nchs/data/hus/hus04trend.pdf#045

Navarro, V. (2003). *On the issue of health care in America.* Address to the 2003 graduating class of the Johns Hopkins Medical School.

Neuspiel, D. R. (1996). Racism and perinatal addiction. *Ethnicity and Disease, 6,* 47–55.

Nickel, M. (2001). A special report: Slavery, the Brown family of Providence and Brown University. *Brown: The Brown News Service.* Retrieved from: http://www.brown.edu/Administration/News_Bureau/Info/Slavery.html

Nord, C., Moore, K., Morrison, D., Brown, B., & Myers, D. (1992). Consequences of teen-age parenting. *Journal of School Health, 62*(7), 310–318.

Oliver, M. L., & Shapiro, T. M. (1995). *Black wealth/white wealth: A new perspective on racial inequality.* New York: Routledge.

Omi, M., & Winant, H. (1986). *Racial formation in the United States: From the 1960s to the 1980s.* New York: Routledge & Kegan Paul.

Orzechowski, S., & Sepielli, P. (2003). *Net worth and asset ownership of households: 1998 and 2000* (Current Population Reports No. P70-88). Washington, DC: U.S. Census Bureau.

Oshinsky, D. M. (1997). *Worse than slavery: Parchman Farm and the ordeal of Jim Crow justice.* New York: Free Press.

Padavic, I., & Reskin, B. F. (2002). *Women and men at work* (2nd ed.). Thousand Oaks, CA: Pine Forge.

Pager, D. (2003). The mark of a criminal record. *American Journal of Sociology, 108,* 937–975.

Parkin, F. (1979). *Marxism and class theory.* New York: Columbia University Press.

Parsons, T., & Bales, R. (1955). *Family, socialization, and the interaction process.* Glencoe, IL: Free Press.

Patterson, O. (1995). For whom the bell curves. In S. Fraser (Ed.), *The bell curve wars.* New York: Basic Books.

Patterson, O. (1999). *Rituals of blood: Consequences of slavery in two American centuries.* New York: Civitas.

Pattillo-McCoy, M. (1999). *Black picket fences: Privilege and peril among the black middle class.* Chicago: University of Chicago Press.

Peterson, J. L. (1998). Introduction to the special issue: HIV/AIDS prevention through community psychology. *American Journal of Community Psychology, 26*(1), 1–5.

Pettit, B., & Western, B. (2004). Mass imprisonment and the life course: Race and class inequality in U.S. incarceration. *American Sociological Review, 69*(2), 151–169.

Pi, E. H., & Simpson, G. M. (2005). Cross-cultural psychopharmacology: A current clinical perspective. *Psychopharmacology, 56*(1), 31–33.

Pipher, M. B. (1994). *Reviving Ophelia: Saving the selves of adolescent girls.* New York: Putnam.

Platt, A. M. (1991). *E. Franklin Frazier reconsidered.* New Brunswick, NJ: Rutgers University Press.

Plessy v. Ferguson, 163 U.S. 537; 16 S. Ct. 1138; 41 L. Ed. 256; 1896 U.S. LEXIS 3390, argued April 13, 1896, May 18, 1896.

Putnam, R. (1995). Bowling alone. *Journal of Democracy, 6*(1), 65–78.

Qian, Z. (2005). Breaking the last taboo: Interracial marriage in America. *Contexts, 4*(4), 33–37.

Rainwater, L., & Yancey, W. L. (1967). *The Moynihan Report and the politics of controversy* (A Trans-action Social Science and Public Policy Report). Cambridge: MIT Press.

Rangaragan, A., Myers, D., Maynard, R., & Beebout, H. (1994, April). *Life prospects for teenage parents.* Paper presented at the Seminar Series on Persistent Poverty session on the Causes and Costs of Teen Motherhood, Washington, DC.

Reagan, R. (1985). Speech to the National Conservative Political Action Conference.

Redlining a black bank: Freedom National Bank of Harlem closed [Editorial]. (1991, January 7). *The Nation.* Retrieved from: http://www.thenation.com/archive/detail/13886356

Rennison, C. M. (2003). *Intimate partner violence, 1993–2001* (NCJ 197838). Washington, DC: Bureau of Justice Statistics.

Renzetti, C. M. (2001). "One strike and you're out": Implications of a federal crime control policy for battered women. *Violence Against Women, 7*(6), 685–698.

Rich, A. (1980). Compulsory heterosexuality and lesbian existence. *Signs, 5,* 631–660.

Rich, A. (1995). *Of woman born: Motherhood as experience and institution.* New York: Norton.

Richardson, N., Williams, K., & Harris, H. (2006, May). The business of faith: Black megachurches are turning pastors into CEOs of multimillion-dollar enterprises. *Black Enterprise, 36,* 102–114.

Riesman, D. (1950). *The lonely crowd: A study of the changing American character.* New Haven, CT: Yale University Press.

Roberts, B. E., & White, J. E. (1999). *Roberts vs. Texaco: A true story of race and corporate America.* New York: Avon.

Roberts, D. E. (2004). The social and moral cost of mass incarceration in African American communities. *Stanford Law Review, 56,* 1271–1306.

Rodman, H. (1968). Family and social pathology in the ghetto. *Science, 161*(3843), 756–761.

Rogers, D. (Director), & Petzall, J. E. (Writer/Producer). (2000). *When the bough breaks* [Video]. San Francisco: ITVS.

Rollins, J. (1985). *Between women: Domestics and their employers.* Philadelphia: Temple University Press.

Romero, M. (1992). *Maid in the U.S.A.* New York: Routledge.

Roper, P., & Weeks, G. (1993). *Child abuse, teenage pregnancy, and welfare dependency: Is there a link?* Olympia: Washington State Institute for Public Policy.

Royster, D. A. (2003). *Race and the invisible hand: How white networks exclude black men from blue-collar jobs.* Berkeley: University of California Press.

Rubin, R. (2002). *Confederacy of silence: A true tale of the new old South.* New York: Atria.

Russell, D. E. H. (1990). *Rape in marriage.* Bloomington: University of Indiana Press.

Sanday, P. R. (1981). The socio-cultural context of rape. *Journal of Social Issues, 37,* 5–27.

Sanday, P. R. (1990). *Fraternity gang rape.* New York: New York University Press.

Satcher, D. (2004). *Youth violence: A report from the Surgeon General.* Washington, DC: Office of the Surgeon General.

Schlosser, E. (2002). *Fast food nation: The dark side of the all-American meal.* New York: Perennial.

Schnittker, J., Pescosolido, B. A., & Croghan, T. W. (2005). Are African Americans really less willing to use health care? *Social Problems, 52*(2), 255–271.

Schoen, J. (2001). Between choice and coercion: Women and the politics of sterilization in North Carolina, 1929–1975. *Journal of Women's History, 13*(1), 132–156.

Schorling, J. B., & Saunders, J. T. (2000). Is "sugar" the same as diabetes? A community-based study among rural African-Americans. *Diabetes Care, 23*(3), 330–334.

Seccombe, K. (1998). *So you think I drive a Cadillac? Welfare recipients' perspectives on the system and its reform.* New York: Allyn & Bacon.

Segura, D. A. (1994). Working at motherhood: Chicana and Mexican immigrant mothers and employment. In E. N. Glenn, G. Chang, & L. R. Forcey (Eds.), *Mothering: Ideology, experience, and agency* (pp. 211–234). New York: Routledge.

Shapiro, M. F., Morton, S. C., McCaffrey, D. F., Senterfitt, J. W., Fleishman, J. A., Perlman, J. F., Athey, L. A., Keesey, J. W., Goldman, D. P., Berry, S. H., & Bozette, S. A. (1999). Variations in the care of HIV-infected adults in the United States: Results from the HIV cost and services utilization study. *Journal of the American Medical Association, 281*, 2305–2375.

Shapiro, T. M. (2004). *The hidden cost of being African American: How wealth perpetuates inequality.* New York: Oxford University Press.

Shaw-Taylor, Y., & Benokraitis, N. V. (1995). The presentation of minorities in marriage and family textbooks. *Teaching Sociology, 23*(2), 122–135.

Shipp, E. R. (2004, July 30). When meds target blacks. *New York Daily News*, p. 45.

Shofner, R. (2001). Expert report on *Johnson v. Bush*, 00-CV-3542. U.S. District Court, Southern District of Florida.

Smedley, B. D., Stith, A. Y., & Nelson, A. R. (Eds.). (2003). *Unequal treatment: Confronting racial and ethnic disparities in health care.* Washington, DC: National Academies Press.

Smith, E. (2007). *Race, sport and the American dream.* Chapel Hill, NC: Carolina Academic Press.

Smith, E., & Hattery, A. (2006a). Hey stud: Race, sex, and sports. *Journal of Sexuality and Culture, 10*(2), 3–32.

Smith, E., & Hattery, A. (2006b). The prison industrial complex. *Sociation Today, 4*(2).

Smith, E., & Hattery, A. (in press-a). If we build it they will come: The relationship between private prisons, incarceration rates, and prison industries in the US. *Societies Without Borders.*

Smith, E., & Hattery, A. (in press-b). The modern world system: Academics and athletics in the new millenium. *Journal of Sport and Social Issues.*

Smith, S. S. (2005). "Don't put my name on it": Social capital activation and job-finding assistance among the black urban poor. *American Journal of Sociology, 111*(1), 1–57.

Sokoloff, N. (2003). The impact of the prison industrial complex on African American women. *Souls, 5*, 31–46.

Solursh, L. P., Solursh, D. S., & Meyer, C. A., Jr. (1993). Is there sex after the prison door slams shut? *Medicine and Law, 12*, 439–443.

Solzhenitsyn, A. (2002). *The gulag archipelago: 1918–1956.* New York: Harper Perennial. (Originally published in 1973)

Spohn, C. C. (2000). *Thirty years of sentencing reform: The quest for a racially neutral sentencing process.* Washington, DC: National Institute of Justice.

Stampp, K. M. (1956). *The peculiar institution: Slavery in the ante-bellum South.* New York: Knopf.

Staples, B. (2004, September 7). Fighting the AIDS epidemic by issuing condoms in the prisons. *New York Times*, p. A22.

Staples, R. (1991). Changes in black family structure: The conflict between family ideology and structural conditions. In R. Staples (Ed.), *The black family: Essays and studies* (pp. 28–36). Belmont, CA: Wadsworth.

Stein, R. (2005, June 24). FDA approves controversial heart medication for blacks. *Washington Post*, p. 15.

Stewart, J. A., Dundas, R., Howard, R. S., Rudd, A. G., & Wolfe, C. D. A. (1999). Ethnic differences in incidence of stroke: Prospective study with stroke register. *British Medical Journal, 318*(7189), 967–971.

Strain, M., & Kisker, E. E. (1989). *Literacy and the disadvantaged: Analysis of data from the National Assessment of Educational Progress.* Princeton, NJ: Mathematical Policy Research.

Straus, M. A. (1979). Measuring intrafamily conflict and violence: The Conflict Tactics (CT) Scales. *Journal of Marriage and the Family, 41*(1), 75–88.

Straus, M. A., & Gelles, R. J. (1995). *Physical violence in American families.* Piscataway, NJ: Transaction Books.

Strauss, A., & Corbin, J. (1990). *Basics of qualitative research: Grounded theory procedures and techniques.* Newbury Park, CA: Sage.

Stuart, G. L., Moore, T. M., Gordon, K. C., Hellmuth, J. C., Ramsey, S. E., & Kahler, C. W. (2006). Reasons for intimate partner violence perpetration among arrested women. *Violence Against Women, 12*(7), 609–621.

Suskind, R. (1998). *A hope in the unseen.* New York: Broadway Books.

Tanner, M., Moore, S., & Hartman, D. (1995). *The work versus welfare trade-off: An analysis of the total level of welfare benefits by state* (Cato Policy Analysis No. 240). Washington, DC: Cato Policy Institute.

Taylor-Gibbs, J. (1988a). Health and mental health of young black males. In J. T. Gibbs (Ed.), *Young, black, and male in America: An endangered species* (pp. 219–257). Dover, MA: Auburn House.

Taylor-Gibbs, J. (1988b). Young, black males in America: Endangered, embittered, and embattled. In J. T. Gibbs (Ed.), *Young, black, and male in America: An endangered species* (pp. 1–36). Dover, MA: Auburn House.

Taylor, Q. (n.d.). *The Moynihan report.* Retrieved July 15, 2006 from: http://faculty.washington.edu/qtaylor/documents/moynihan_report.htm

Taylor, T. S. (2004, August 1). Blacks find progress slow in joining trade unions. *Chicago Tribune*, p. 1.

Therborn, G. (1980). *The ideology of power and the power of ideology.* London: Verso.

Thompson, C., & Loper, A. (2005). Adjustment patterns in incarcerated women: An analysis of differences based on sentence length. *Criminal Justice and Behavior, 32*(6), 714–732.

Tilove, J. (2005, May 5). Where have all the black men gone? Black gender gap is widening. *Seattle Times*, p. A3.

Tjaden, P., & Thoennes, N. (2000). *Full report of the Prevalence, Incidence, and Consequences of Violence Against Women Series: Research report.* Atlanta, GA: Centers for Disease Control and Prevention.

Toch, H., & Adams, K. (2002). *Acting out: Maladaptive behavior in confinement.* Washington, DC: American Psychological Association.

Tomaskovic-Devey, D. (1993). *Gender and racial inequality at work: The sources and consequences of job segregation.* Ithaca, NY: ILR Press.

Uggen, C., & Manza, J. (2002). Democratic contraction? Political consequences of felon disenfranchisement in the United States. *American Sociological Review,* 67(6), 777–803.

Urbina, I. (2006, January 11). In the treatment of diabetes, success often does not pay. *New York Times.* Retrieved from: http://www.nytimes.com/2006/01/11/nyregion/nyregionspecial5/11diabetes.html?ex=1294635600&en=fde99fd51209 9c16&ei=5088&partner=rssnyt&emc=rss

U.S. Bureau of the Census. (1972). *U.S. census of population: 1970* (Vol. 1). Washington, DC: Government Printing Office.

U.S. Bureau of the Census. (1999). *Race of wife by race of husband: 1999.* Washington, DC: Author.

U.S. Bureau of the Census. (2003). *America's families and living arrangements: 2003, Table A2.* Washington, DC: Author.

U.S. Bureau of the Census. (2004). *Educational attainment by race/ethnicity and gender.* Washington, DC: Author.

U.S. Bureau of the Census. (2005a). *Marital history for people 15 years and over, by age, sex, race, and Hispanic origin, 2001.* Available: http://72.14.209.104/search?q=cache:-c9vMO4UJoIJ:www.census.gov/population/socdemo/marital-hist/p70-97/tab01-hispanic.xls+%22Marital+History+for+People+15+Years+and+Over%22&hl=en&gl=us&ct=clnk&cd=1

U.S. Bureau of the Census. (2005b). *Statistical abstract of the United States 2004–2005.* Washington, DC: Author.

Valentine, C. A. (1968). *Culture and poverty: Critique and counter-proposals.* Chicago: University of Chicago Press.

Villarosa, L. (2004, August 7). Patients with H.I.V. seen as separated by a racial divide. *New York Times.* Retrieved from: http://query.nytimes.com/gst/fullpage .html?res=9C06E2DD103CF934A3575BC0A9629C8B63&sec=health&page wanted=print

Wagner, P. (2004, April 11). *Diluting democracy: Census quirk fuels prison expansion* [Fact sheet]. Available: http://www.prisonpolicy.org/articles/dilutingdemocracy.pdf

Wallace, M. O. (2002). *Constructing the black masculine.* Raleigh, NC: Duke University Press.

Warshaw, R. (1988). *I never called it rape: The* Ms. *report on recognizing, fighting, and surviving date and acquaintance rape.* New York: Harper & Row.

Washington, B. T. (1963). *Up from slavery: An autobiography.* Garden City, NY: Doubleday.

Waters, M. C. (1999). *Black identities: West Indian immigrant dreams and American realities.* Cambridge, MA: Harvard University Press.

Weber, M. (1996). *The Protestant ethic and the spirit of capitalism* (T. Parsons, Trans.). Los Angeles, CA: Roxbury.

Webster, C., & Weeks, G. (1995). *Teenage pregnancy: A summary of prevention program evaluation results* (Seminar 3162). Olympia: Washington State Institute for Public Policy, The Evergreen State College.

Weitzman, S. (2001). *Not to people like us: Hidden abuse in upscale marriages*. New York: Basic Books.

Wells, T. (1998). *Changes in occupational sex segregation in the 1980s and 1990s* (Working Paper). Madison: University of Wisconsin, Center for Demography and Ecology.

Wertheimer, R., & Moore, K. A. (1998). *Childbearing by teens: Links to welfare reform* (No. A-24). Washington, DC: Urban Institute.

Wessel, D. (2006, June 15). In poverty tactics, an old debate: Who is at fault? *Wall Street Journal*, p. A10.

West, E. (1999). Surviving separation: Cross-plantation marriages and the slave trade in antebellum South Carolina. *Journal of Family History, 24*(2), 213–231.

Western, B. (2006). *Punishment and inequality in America*. New York: Russell Sage Foundation.

"Whites only" retirement fund. (2006, January 25). *New York Times*, p. A20.

Williams, D. (2005, June 2). *Wachovia apologizes for slave history*. Retrieved from: http://www.tolerance.org/news/article_tol.jsp?id=1225

Williams, D. R. (1999). Race, socioeconomic status, and health: The added effects of racism and discrimination. *Annals of the New York Academy of Science, 896*, 173–188.

Williams, H. A. (2006). *Self-taught: African American education in slavery and freedom*. Chapel Hill: University of North Carolina Press.

Wilson, F. D. (1984). Urban ecology: Urbanization and systems of cities. *Annual Review of Sociology, 10*, 283–307.

Wilson, W. J. (1978). The declining significance of race. *Society, 152* (112), 56–62.

Wilson, W. J. (1987). *The truly disadvantaged: The inner city, the underclass, and public policy*. Chicago: University of Chicago Press.

Wilson, W. J. (1991). *Studying inner-city social dislocations: The challenge of public agenda research*. 1990 presidential address, American Sociological Association, Washington, DC.

Wilson, W. J. (1996). *When work disappears: The world of the new urban poor*. New York: Knopf.

Wolf, A. (2006). *Reducing the incarceration of women: Community-based alternatives* [Special report]. Retrieved from: http://www.nccd-crc.org/nccd/pubs/2006_WIP_special_report.pdf

Woodson, C. G. (2000). *The mis-education of the Negro*. Chicago: African-American Images.

Wray, L. R. (2000). A new economic reality: Penal Keynesianism. *Challenge, 43*(5), 31–59.

Wright, E. O. (1997). *Class counts: Comparative studies in class analysis*. New York: Cambridge University Press.

Wright, K. (2006, May 24). Upward mortality. Retrieved from: http://www.mother jones.com/news/feature/2006/05/upward_mortality.html

Zamble, E. (1992). Behavior and adaptation in long-term prison inmates: Descriptive longitudinal results. *Criminal Justice and Behavior, 19,* 409–425.

Zernike, K. (2005, January 16). The conflict in Iraq: Abu Ghraib scandal; Ringleader in Iraqi prisoner abuse is sentenced to 10 years. *New York Times,* p. 12.

Zinn, M. B., & Dill, B. T. (2005). Theorizing differences from multicultural feminism. In M. B. Zinn, P. Hondagneu-Sotelo, & M. A. Messner (Eds.), *Gender through the prism of difference* (3rd ed.). Oxford, UK: Oxford University Press.

Zucchino, D. (1997). *Myth of the welfare queen: A Pulitzer Prize–winning journalist's portrait of women on the line.* New York: Scribner.

Zweigenhaft, R. L., & Domhoff, G. W. (1998). *Diversity in the power elite.* New Haven, CT: Yale University Press.

Zweigenhaft, R. L. & Dumhoff, G. W. (2006). *Diversity in the Power Elite: How It Happened, Why It Matters.* Lanham, MD: Rowman & Littlefield.

Index

About the Authors

Angela J. Hattery, PhD, holds the Zachary T. Smith Reynolds Associate Professorship in Sociology and Women & Gender Studies at Wake Forest University. She completed her BA at Carleton College and her MS and PhD at the University of Wisconsin–Madison before joining the faculty of Wake Forest in 1998. Her research focuses on social stratification, gender, family, and race. She is the author of numerous articles, book chapters, and books, including another Sage book, *Women, Work, and Family: Balancing and Weaving* (2001). Her forthcoming book *Violence in Intimate Partner Relationships* will appear in 2007.

Earl Smith, PhD, is Professor of Sociology and the Rubin Distinguished Professor of American Ethnic Studies at Wake Forest University. He is the Director of the Wake Forest University American Ethnic Studies Program. Dr. Smith was the Chairperson of the Department of Sociology, Wake Forest University, from 1997–2005. Prior to his appointment at Wake Forest University, Professor Smith was the Dean, Division of Social Science at Pacific Lutheran University (PLU) in Tacoma, Washington. He also served as Chairperson of the Department of Sociology at PLU. Professor Smith has numerous publications (books, articles, book chapters, etc.) in the area of professions, social stratification, family, and urban sociology, and he has published extensively in the area of the sociology of sport. His most recent book, *Race, Sport and the American Dream,* will be published by Carolina Academic Press in early 2007.

CPSIA information can be obtained at www.ICGtesting.com
Printed in the USA
LVOW04s0344260115

424249LV00007B/43/P

9 781412 924665